Believe and Be Love

Iris Latin America's Story of Impossible
Dreams and Radical Love

BELIEVE AND BE LOVE

© 2013 Caitlin Ann

Cover photo by T.K. Lindsey

Author photo by Annie Scudder

Unless otherwise noted, Holy Scripture quotations are from the New International Version, © 1985, 1995, 2002, 2008 by Zondervan, Grand Rapids, Michigan.

Holy Scripture quotations designated NLT are from The New Living Translation Bible, © 1996, 2004 by Tyndale House Publishers, Inc., Carol Stream, Illinois.

Some dreams feel like a whisper,
Still others like a roar;
But have faith no matter how you feel,
For belief makes vision soar.

And if you think you're just a fool,
Child, open up your eyes.
For the Lord who fathers every dream
Uses the weak to shame the wise.

Though sometimes our most wild dreams
May seem forever far,
Impossible is possible
When you know who you are.

Oh, child of God, you can believe
The dreams inside your heart.
Water them and let them grow
Into a work of art.

For I'm convinced the Father's heart
Beats with the dreams we dream,
No matter how impossible,
How crazy they may seem.

No matter how impossible,
How crazy they may seem…

Table of Contents

Part One: Mexico/Central America

1. Mexico: The Journey Begins — 29
2. Belize: God's Diamonds — 73
3. Guatemala: Power of the Blood — 85
4. El Salvador: The Need for a Savior — 103
5. Honduras: Setting the Captives Free — 107
6. Nicaragua: Finding Love in Weakness — 115
7. Costa Rica: A Story of Redemption — 123
8. Panama: When the Lame Walk — 135

Part Two: South America

9. Colombia: South America Begins — 151
10. Ecuador: Welcome to the Jungle — 175
11. Peru: Peeling, Puking, and Paramonga — 213
12. Chile and Argentina: To the End of the World — 243
13. Uruguay: Missionary Graveyard No More — 273
14. Paraguay: Finding Freedom — 283
15. Bolivia: Poverty, Power, and Pig Fat — 293
16. Brazil: A Country of Contrast — 305
17. Venezuela: Praying for Seeds to Grow — 333
18. The Guianas: South America Complete! — 341

Part Three: The Caribbean

19. Casting New Vision — 357
20. Puerto Rico: Fresh Flavor, New Favor — 363
21. The Dominican Republic: The Lost Get Found — 383
22. Haiti: A New Paradigm for Missions — 411
23. Cuba: A Beautiful Prison — 429
24. Jamaica: One Love — 453

Dedication

This book is dedicated to those who dare to dream impossible dreams.

Thank you to Jesse and Tanya for birthing the vision of the Iris Latin America journey.

Thank you to my teammates for pioneering this wild journey and for having faith when none of us knew what was around the next corner. Thank you for laughing with me through the good times and loving me through the trying times. I will always count you as brothers, sisters, and dear friends.

Thank you to the Caribbean team who stepped out in faith with me and helped make a lifelong dream come true.

Thank you to my family and friends back home who selflessly supported me from afar.

Thank you to Kristen, Annie, and Jackie for the editing help you poured into this book.

And most importantly, thank you Jesus. Without you, I would have no story to tell.

A Word From Heidi Baker

Jesse and Tanya, team leaders, birthed their deepest desire to spread the love of Christ to distant lands. They were soon joined by a selfless band of believers. One member, Caitlin Ann, documents the dangers, the joys, and the many Holy Spirit led adventures.

Like the Good Samaritan, I believe this simple group of Christians gave their possessions, their time, and their love, without wanting anything in exchange. Carrying the glory of God, they experience firsthand what it means to lay down your life for the sake of the gospel. Embark on this trip with them and discover how thousands of lives are transformed.

Heidi Baker
Co-Founder of Iris Global
Mozambique, Africa

The Iris Latin America team's highlighted route from the United States through Mexico, Central America, South America, and the Caribbean

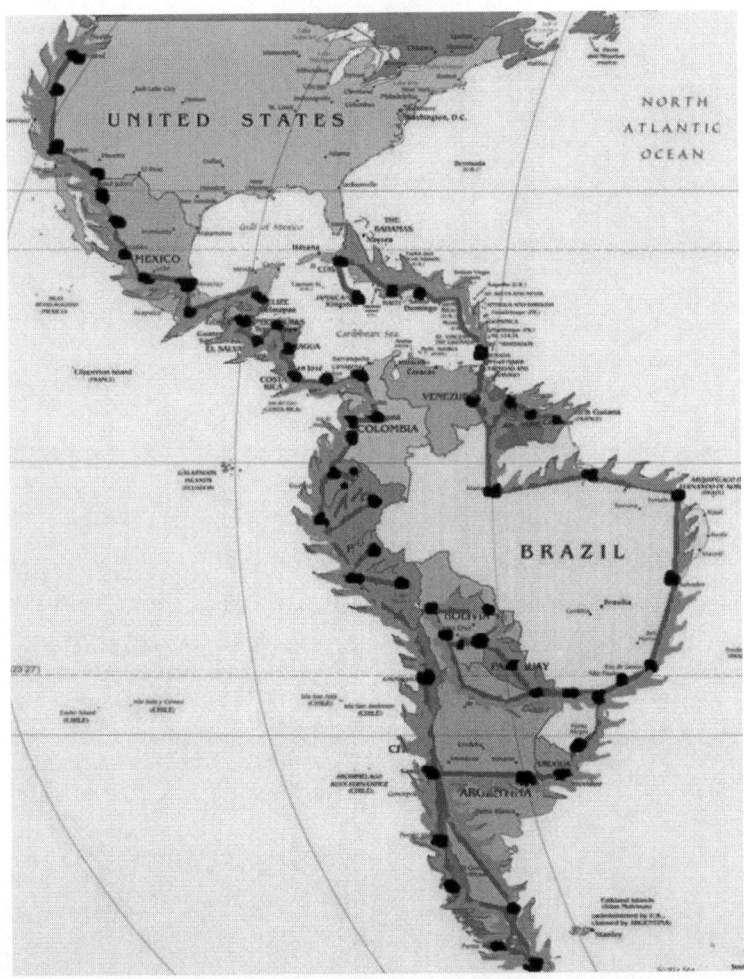

"America Map – Map Pictures." *mappictures.blogspot.com*. <http://mappictures.blogspot.com/2012/06/america-map.html>. November 18, 2012.

Highlighted route with fire graphics added by J.B.G.

*Throughout the following pages, several names have been changed to protect the privacy and identity of certain individuals. However, the names of Caitlin Ann's teammates used in this book are their actual names.

Prologue

Once upon a time, there was a mighty king — the greatest, strongest, most beloved king in all the land. He ruled the most powerful kingdom that existed, and though sometimes his people lost small battles, they never lost a war. In fact, everyone knew it was impossible for this king to ever lose.

There was a little girl who lived in his kingdom but didn't think the king would ever notice her. After all, he was the king, and she was just a little girl. But as she grew up, she found out that the king not only noticed her but knew her by name. In fact, he cared about her deeply. As the king was building his mighty army, he hand-picked the girl to be a part of it. He loved her with all of his heart, and he chose to send her on secret missions throughout the world. And though that little girl got scared sometimes, she always knew she would be alright if she listened to the king's voice.

The king gave the girl his very best. He showered her with gifts she could never have earned on her own and let her in on his greatest secrets. Best of all, the king loved the girl as his very own daughter. The girl had done nothing to deserve such honor, but it was the king's pleasure to give it to her.

One day, the mighty king told the little girl, "It is time for me to die for my kingdom. But do not fear. After I die, my spirit will live inside of *you, and you will do even greater things than I have done." He told the girl to dream impossible dreams, because with his presence, they would become possible.*

Undeservedly, I am this little girl. And Jesus is my loving king. For many years, I did not understand that I had been adopted into God's heavenly family. Nor did I understand the authority and power given me. I had no idea that I could heal the sick or set the oppressed free. But in a tiny village in Mozambique, Africa, God changed my life forever. He uncovered my true identity and invited me into a life that would be impossible without Him showing up.

In 2010, God called me to be part of a team of people crazy enough to believe that His words were actually true. They believed that when Jesus said we would do greater things than He did, He really meant it. They believed that the Bible stories about blind people seeing and crippled people walking and dead people being raised to life were not just stories — they were real events that happened through Jesus' power.

When God invited me to join this team, He told me to write His story down. He would do great things through us, and I needed to tell the world what He was doing. In the process of writing, my laptop was stolen, and much of my text was lost. A month later, I was given a brand new laptop and continued writing. Shortly after, my screen blanked out, and I couldn't type anything. More determined than ever, I got the computer fixed and, once again, continued writing. I know that Satan doesn't want people to find out what God is up to. He doesn't want people to know God's story.

But God's story needs to be told. So here it is. The following pages are the story of the Iris Latin America journey, told through my eyes on behalf of my teammates and on behalf of our great God. This is our story of dreaming impossible dreams and God's story of the radical love that fulfilled them.

*   *   *   *   *

It all began with a young couple, Jesse and Tanya, who had been serving as missionaries in Africa for years, traveling to remote villages where few would choose to go. They did not fear the dark places but instead embraced them as the most promising areas to share God's truth. Jesse and Tanya could feel the heart of God beating for His children who had never heard His name. Their deepest desire was to spread the love of Christ into the most unreached regions of the world.

During the fall of 2010, they traveled to Iris Global's main base in Mozambique, Africa to staff a missionary training school. While at the school base, Jesse and Tanya shared their heart with two students. Jesse and Tanya told them that they dreamt of leaving Africa for a while to travel to the nation of Peru and share the gospel with unreached tribes in the Amazon. As they spoke their dream aloud, the students expanded it, envisioning a journey all the way to the tip of Chile, with the purpose of spreading Christ's love to unreached people groups throughout South America. Soon, the vision grew into a ring of fire encircling the *entire* continent.

Jesse and Tanya later spoke to all of the students attending the missionary school and shared a brief glimpse of their vision. They invited any students interested in South America to join them for a time of prayer for the continent. A few days later, fifty students showed up at their front porch and began to intercede for Latin America. Some students had a specific country in mind; others dreamt for all of South America; still others had visions for Central America and even the islands of the Caribbean. What started as a desire to travel to Peru exploded into a seemingly impossible dream of driving from the

U.S. into Mexico, throughout all of Central and South America, then selling the cars and boating around the Caribbean. All of this would be done in the hopes of both bringing revival to the complacent church and sharing Jesus' love with people who had never heard His name.

Though making such an extensive journey seemed unrealistic and quite dangerous to boot, Jesse and Tanya (and now a growing team of interested people) knew God delighted in transforming the most improbable dreams into beautiful realities. They asked God to confirm their vision, and shortly after, they moved forward confidently believing that this journey was ordained by the Lord.

Throughout this dreaming and vision-birthing process, I just so happened to be one of the students attending the mission school in Mozambique. When I'd arrived in Africa, Latin America was the last place on my mind. I'd lived in Uganda years prior and had dreams of one day starting my own orphanage somewhere in Africa. God had very specifically spoken to me about attending Iris' mission school in Mozambique, and I assumed this was because of Iris' reputation for running exceptional children's homes. I figured I would go to school, learn the secrets behind Iris' success, and move to Africa long-term. I found great comfort in having a plan and in hoping to soon create a home for myself.

Yet, as soon as I arrived in Mozambique, I felt God telling me to lay down my own dreams and to be careful of making a specific place or ministry an idol. God spoke these words into my heart: "Your identity is not Africa. Your identity is not a plan or an orphanage. Your identity is not a missionary. Your identity is *my daughter*. That is who you are. You are *mine*, plain and simple."

Confused as to why God was telling me to put my dreams of Africa and orphanage-building on hold, I prayed for clarity. I knew He had something else for me during this season — but what? Every time I asked the Lord for an answer, He told me to wait.

So I waited.

And waited.

And waited some more.

Well, here's where my story begins to intertwine with Jesse's, Tanya's, and that adventuresome group of dreamers'. The moment I heard Jesse and Tanya talking about their vision for Latin America and the Caribbean, I knew that I needed to run alongside them. It suddenly all became very clear. I needed to run alongside missionaries who weren't afraid to go into dark places. I needed to run alongside people who believed in the impractical. I needed to run alongside people whose love for the Lord had no bounds.

I finished mission school in December 2010 and flew back to the U.S. The Iris Latin America team would depart from the States in September 2011, which allowed nine months for preparation. Jesse and Tanya opened up the trip to anyone who had attended any of the mission schools in Mozambique throughout the last few years as well as those who would attend in the future and join us later on.

During the preparation months, I wavered in my decision to go to Latin America. I began to readjust to my life in California and remembered the wonderful feeling of fitting into a community and developing deep relationships in one place. Being a wandering nomad throughout an entire continent was quite the opposite of planting roots somewhere. I kept teetering back and forth, wondering if I'd made the right decision. I knew my family would not be happy with me traveling to notoriously dangerous terrain and certainly would feel disconcerted that I had no permanent address, phone number, or even country to call home.

One evening in early 2011, I went to a church fellowship meeting, desperately seeking clarity from the Lord. I needed confirmation about Latin America. I wanted to tell my family that I was going but feared they would think I had merely signed up for some hippie jungle tour. How was I going to explain this one? During the meeting, a complete stranger began to prophesy over me. "I see you in a situation where you are asking, 'How am I going to explain this to my family?'" He affirmed, "Don't explain it. Just do it."

Moments later, the fellowship leader asked if anyone needed prayer for physical pain. My back was killing me, and the same man stepped forward to lay hands on me. As he prayed, I could tangibly feel the heat of the Holy Spirit rushing through my body. When the man finished praying for my back, he continued prophesying. "The Lord has called you to travel," he declared. "He's called you out of America. He's called you to go into dark places where others won't go."

If that wasn't validation from the Lord, I'm not sure what is. *Lord, what have you gotten me into this time?* I wondered. *It doesn't make sense, but I guess I'm going.* Shortly after, I emailed Jesse and Tanya to confirm my spot on the team. My fate was sealed.

Meanwhile, Jesse and Tanya were gathering the rest of the team and organizing a fleet to transport us all. They partnered with their dear friend, Christian, another American missionary they'd worked with in Mozambique, to plan the details of the journey. Christian agreed to help serve and lead for the first two months of the trip, while his wife and children stayed behind to attend school in the States. Our three leaders purchased four vehicles for the team — two clunky RVs they affectionately named "Open Heaven" and "New Wine," a large Suburban called "Overflow," and a sleek Durango named "Shekinah" (referring to the manifest presence of the Lord). The SUVs hauled pop-up campers where most of the girls would sleep as we traveled. Others would sleep in the RVs, still others in tents or additional makeshift accommodations. A young guy from Texas, Taylor L., decided to join the team and add his own 1995 Buick station wagon to our convoy, naming our fifth and final vehicle "Counsel and Might."

Our tentative plan was to drive this motley caravan from the U.S. into Mexico, then drive across all of Central America, and eventually ship the vehicles from Panama to Colombia. From Colombia, we would weave our way throughout every country in South America, splitting into smaller groups at points and coming together at others. After circling the continent, we would get rid of our vehicles and travel by boat around the Caribbean.

Jesse, Tanya, and Christian created a rough itinerary for the trip, mapping out locations of different personal contacts and ministries that we planned on visiting during the journey. Much information was up in the air. The trip was scheduled to take eleven months, but the leaders informed us that it may take longer. We would be flexible vagabonds for Jesus, open to the Holy Spirit's leading, traveling with a loose plan but open to change as God led.

When I told people about "the plan," many thought I was out of my mind. They said it would never work. They said this trip was too unplanned, too dangerous — too foolish. I felt like I'd become a joke. However, as I read the word of God, the Bible only confirmed what my team was about to do. Matthew 10:7-10 says, "As you go, proclaim this message: 'The kingdom of heaven has come near.' Heal the sick, raise the dead, cleanse those who have leprosy, drive out demons. Freely you have received, freely give. Do not get any gold or silver or copper to take with you in your belts — no bag for the journey or extra shirt or sandals or a staff, for the worker is worth his keep."

The disciples did pretty well without an intricately-designed plan. Instead, they simply trusted that obeying Jesus' instructions was more important than understanding how every detail would play out. If I were to call myself a true disciple of Christ, I knew I needed to walk in that same trust. Though our journey began with many unknowns and remained full of mysteries throughout, God proved faithful. And our "plan to not have a set plan" yielded fruit that we could never have produced in our own strength. Giving God an open canvas always resulted in a more beautiful picture than anything we could've painted ourselves. Fools in the eyes of the world, my team left America uncertain of what was ahead but believing for something divine.

In September 2011, the first members of our team met Jesse, Tanya, and Christian in Washington State. From there, they drove to Bethel Church (the church to which Iris Global is officially "married") in Redding, California to be commissioned by Heidi Baker, the founder of Iris. The following day, the team drove south to my home territory in Southern California where I joined them. That morning, I hopped in a pickup truck with three old friends, two bags, a bit of cash, and my passport. We drove to a church called Expression 58 in Los Angeles to meet the strangers who would soon become my family.

I sat with my old friends on one side of Expression 58, my new teammates seated on the other. Fidgeting throughout the entire message, I repeatedly glanced across the pews to investigate these mysterious people. After preaching, the leader of the church called the Iris team up front to send us off in prayer. My teammates approached the stage from the right side of the church, and I discreetly slipped in from the left. I looked longingly at my old friends in the congregation as I stood far from them, now among strangers. I was officially a part of the Iris team.

After the service ended, I transferred my luggage from my friend's truck to Overflow, the vehicle that would soon become the closest thing I had to a home. I hugged my old friends goodbye and reluctantly drove off with the team. When I looked out the window at the streets of California, I still saw home; but when I looked at the people sitting next to me, I felt a million miles away.

We drove from Los Angeles to Tucson, Arizona where we met up with a few more team members. By September 14, 2011, we had a team of twenty — Christian, Jesse and Tanya, their beautiful toddler Zoe, and sixteen more of us who had been recruited at different times. People would later join and leave the team throughout various points in the journey, our group's size peaking at thirty-something people but constantly fluctuating. Here's the rundown of the original crew:

Jesse: *The gentle giant.* Jesse stood six foot eight and didn't have an ounce of fat on him. It was impossible to miss his tall, lanky body moving about whenever trying to locate the team leader. He proudly sported a tattoo of all the nations of the world on his right shoulder, an outward display of his heart for every tribe and tongue to know Christ. He had the gifts of limitless faith, spontaneous rap composition, shofar blowing, and coloring outside the lines.

Tanya: *The balancing act.* Tanya was a picture of gentleness coupled with strength. She was easy to laugh with, but despite her loveable demeanor, she was scandalously hardcore. Tanya found a way to balance being a loving mom, supportive wife, daring risk-taker, and a forerunner. Tanya gave birth to her daughter, Zoe, in a cement house in Africa with no painkillers. Women like that don't mess around.

Zoe: *The team favorite.* She was about twenty months old when we started the trip to Latin America and was undoubtedly the most well-traveled little girl you'd ever meet. Zoe's simple faith, fearlessness, and easy trust constantly reminded the team of how we *should* be. Her hobbies included catching bugs, giving kisses to team members, and asking, "Why?"

Christian: *The papa bear.* Christian, Jesse's faithful sidekick, got our team off on the right foot by helping lead as our pastor and friend. Despite his punkish, long hair and tattooed arms, he was a "papa bear" at heart, with a soothing yet protective way about him. But when you least expected it, he'd sneak up behind you and scare the living daylights out of you. Christian had perfected his menacing imitation of a mutant dog and regularly used it to raise my blood pressure. He bragged that his three children had all developed nerves of steel.

Roberta: *The legend.* In her seventy-some-odd years, she'd lived and traveled around the entire world, making her a team legend. Yet, Roberta had been waiting and dreaming of a trip like this for ten years and believed the Iris Latin America team was the answer to a decade-old prayer. Roberta maintained a youthful sense of adventure, curiosity, and adaptability. Her radiant smile, striking, curly hair, and radical dance moves for Jesus helped her stand out in any crowd.

Maria: *The sassy Latina.* Maria had lived in the States for years but grew up in Mexico and had a huge heart to see her home country transformed. Though about thirty years my senior, Maria was always a hit during any moments of girl talk and kept all of us laughing with her sassy comments about dating, life, and love.

Ted: *The spiritual soldier.* Despite our chaotic lifestyle and constant distractions, Ted consistently found a way to sneak off to a quiet place and seek the heart of the Father. He was more concerned with what was happening in the spiritual atmosphere than in the natural and diligently interceded on behalf of the team. Continuously fighting for breakthrough within the spiritual realm, Ted served as one of our prayer warriors.

Melissa: *The "dog whisperer."* No matter what country we were in, she found a stray animal to adopt as the team pet until we crossed the next border. This endearing habit combined with her mischievous laugh, humble nature, and heart of gold made her a person whom everyone adored.

Ben: *The dichotomy.* One minute, he'd be preaching the word of God, praying in tongues, and prophesying with words straight from heaven. The next moment, he'd be making weird faces and lighting his farts on fire. You never quite knew what side of Ben you would get, but either one would make you smile.

Rowan: *The jack of all trades.* If you needed someone to make a meal out of nothing, perform ballet, teach you a Ju-jitsu move, or fashion a balloon animal, Rowan was your man. I'd never met anyone with such a wide range of talents. In addition, he had a brilliant father's heart — always a winning combo.

Gillian: *The small but mighty one.* Like her husband Rowan, Gillian was a Kiwi to the core — sarcastic, witty, and clever. Though tiny in stature, Gillian packed a punch in the spiritual realm. She had an incredible prophetic gifting and boldly spoke the truth as she heard the voice of the Father.

Natalie H.: *The sweet-faced warrior.* Natalie had an uncanny ability to somehow look clean even when the team hadn't showered for days. Yet, this girl was way more than a pretty face. She prayed with authority and shifted the atmosphere when she entered a room. Despite her young age, she carried an unusual confidence and maturity.

Taylor L.: *The protector.* Though younger than many of the girls on the team, Taylor served as a big brother, constantly watching out for us girls and making us feel loved and protected. Like a tender-hearted bodyguard, he made any environment feel safer both physically and spiritually. When he was not busy combating demons, you could find him catching lizards, looking for crocodiles, or talking about how awesome Texas was.

Rose: *The overcomer.* Before joining the team, I prayed for someone to both laugh with and be real with, and God sent me Rose. She was candid, smart, witty, and knew how to plan a good prank. But beyond the fun, Rose was a fighter. As another team member put it, the enemy once tried to knock Rose out, but now she was throwing punches back.

Elizabeth: *The token African.* Being a team birthed in Mozambique, it only seemed right to have an African sister traveling with us. Ironically, South African Elizabeth was the fairest and blondest member of the team. Understanding the true meaning of sacrifice, she willingly exchanged her dresses, high heels, and corporate success for a lifestyle of dirty feet, inconsistent showers, and sleeping on the floor.

Dianne: *The wild mama.* Both a mother and grandmother, Dianne immediately fell in love with Zoe and exuded a true mama's heart. Yet, this grandma didn't spend her time knitting sweaters and playing cards. She rode motorcycles, had tattoos, and loved adventure. Dianne was a wild one.

Breck: *The comic relief.* He spent the first month of our journey quoting the comedy *Nacho Libre* and growing the ugliest mustache he could. Breck loved playing pranks, making cheesy jokes, and telling strangers his name was Simba. Despite his silly and laid-back persona, he was anointed as a powerful leader and preacher and could capture the heart of any crowd.

Katherine: *The secret weapon.* Katherine's charming Southern drawl and feminine exterior beautifully masked a fierce warrior underneath — like an undercover soldier. Always hungry for more of God, she constantly reminded me to never take offense when prayers remained unanswered but to get on my knees and contend for breakthrough. Far stronger than she let on, Katherine was like a little Holy Spirit missile.

Liz: *The servant's heart.* The only Brit to start the trip with us, Liz kept us Americans laughing with her comments about "fit young lads" and her dreams of meeting George Clooney. Liz paid attention to every detail and didn't skip a beat. She was the big sister, mother, and friend that we all needed throughout the journey — a glue holding the team together more times than I could count.

Now add me into the mix, and you've got the original twenty pioneers of this unbelievable journey. Though getting thrown into this group felt a bit intimidating at first, we quickly became family. All it took was one car ride full of laughs and good music to know everything was going to be okay. It didn't take long to learn who had the craziest morning hair, who snored the loudest, who took the longest in the bathroom, or who was the crankiest without coffee. We embarked on a life of traveling together, ministering together, eating together, exercising together, and hanging out together. We discovered the beauty of sharing everything — food, space, tears, money, beds, sickness, and laughter. We quickly learned to love each other through the car breakdowns, the miracles, the adventures, and through the mess.

Part One: Mexico/Central America

Chapter One

MEXICO: The Journey Begins

So here we were — twenty fools in the eyes of the world, ready to cross into Latin America and enter an entirely unknown domain. On September 14, 2011, we drove into Mexico via the Nogales, Arizona border. We arrived at the Mexican border station before noon, thinking we were doing well on time. We needed to get visas for each team member and registration papers for each vehicle. We were hopeful to take care of everything quickly and reach our destination of Pesqueira, Mexico before dark.

Unfortunately, Taylor didn't have his original car registration with him but had chosen to carry a copy instead. The copy was not accepted at the border, and he was instructed to cross back into the U.S. He needed to procure a temporary document that would allow him to drive in Mexico. Unfazed by the dilemma, Taylor patiently got back in his car, asked Maria to accompany him for translation assistance, and drove back to Arizona. The rest of the team waited on the Mexican side of the border, hoping for a quick fix. About five and a half hours later, we were still sitting there, wondering when Taylor and Maria would arrive.

Finally, Taylor's paperwork back in Arizona was settled, and his car reappeared on our side of the border. However, he still needed to complete a bunch of paperwork with the Mexican customs officers, and the delay continued. Although I wasn't particularly thrilled to wait for so many hours, I was quite impressed by the patience and flexibility demonstrated by every member of the team. Not one person complained or got agitated. Right away, I knew this was not an ordinary group of people.

After everything was sorted out, we drove towards our first destination. Maria had tirelessly arranged ministry opportunities for us throughout all of Mexico, and the first stop on our itinerary was the small village of Pesqueira. We were warned by a local pastor that we needed to get there before dark if we wanted to stay safe. Gangsters were known for targeting vehicles along the road to Pesqueira and shooting at them. In addition to gang activity, there was a drug war going on in Mexico that put innocent passersby at risk. It was important to steer clear of certain roads at night. However, by the time Taylor's paperwork was settled, it was already 5:30 p.m. Our destination was several hours away, and there was no way we could avoid driving this road in the dark.

With little choice, we drove towards Pesqueira regardless of the warnings of gang violence. We could either move forward or sleep at the border, which really was no safer. As we drove, it began to pour and hail. Things looked pretty dismal. We had barely crossed our first border, and I felt like we were already under attack. Yet, just as I was tempted to give in to fear, the rain and hailing suddenly stopped, and a rainbow burst across the sky. Fittingly, the name of our ministry, Iris, came from the

Portuguese word for rainbow. And just as a rainbow signified God's promise after the flood, we were reminded of our Lord's promise as we drove through that dark and dangerous road in Mexico.

After several hours of driving, we reached a humble village church in Pesqueira. As we pulled into their dusty parking lot, we were greeted by a cheering crowd — a loving group of Mexicans clapping and yelling with excitement. We situated our vehicles and were almost immediately asked to sit down inside the church to join the enthusiastic crowd for a meal. It was already around 9 p.m., but this church family did not seem even slightly perturbed that we had arrived much later than originally planned. Instead, they told us to sit while they served us freshly grilled beef, tortillas, and a variety of toppings including guacamole, cilantro, pico de gallo, fresh cabbage, and the spiciest salsa in Mexico.

Following our delicious meal, we thanked the church members and set up our pop-up campers and tents. We snuggled into our new "homes," feeling a bit awkward to suddenly be living in such close quarters with people who had been strangers just days ago. Rose and I ended up squished onto a mattress (I use that term loosely) designed for one and a half people, so we got acquainted pretty quickly. You'd be amazed at how fast you can get to know people when you are forced to lie within inches of each other's faces every night. And Pesqueira was just the beginning.

Situated in the church parking lot, we were camped right alongside a busy road where cars constantly drove by and pedestrians wandered throughout the night. I tried to sleep, but the sound of cars and people kept me up. Just when I thought the voices were subsiding, roosters began crowing loudly. As the poultry went mad, a highly intoxicated man walked by and yelled profanities at our campers. Finally, hours into the night, I caught a few moments of sleep. But before I knew it, more roosters were crowing, people were yelling, the sun was rising, and it was time to start the day.

I met with the team for breakfast and a time of worship before we started our first official day of ministry. This was it. We'd met just days ago, but it was time to jump in and figure things out together. Danny, the pastor of the church in Pesqueira, gave our team a brief presentation of what his church was doing and some of their aspirations for the future. He explained that many of the people in his village had come from different areas and spoke indigenous languages in addition to Spanish. He hoped to survey many of the people in the surrounding community to find out what areas of Mexico they had migrated from and what languages they spoke. He showed us a machine that stored mp3 recordings of different Bible messages in three hundred different languages. You could crank a handle on the machine to charge it and then play a message in any of the three hundred dialects.

Danny asked us to split into five different groups and walk throughout the village with the mp3 machines. People from the church community escorted us on our first mission. As we went from house to house, the church members asked people within the village where they originated from and the names of their indigenous languages. We recorded the peoples' names, played a brief message in their respective dialects, and offered to burn discs in their mother tongues to be picked up later at the church. Though many people were able to speak mainstream Spanish, I realized the value of hearing the gospel in one's tribal language. Danny's church wanted to honor the community by providing such an opportunity.

Danny also decided to host a church service that evening for those whom we met throughout the day. It was a Thursday and happened to be Mexican Independence Day, so I doubted many people would show up that night. They would probably be more interested in celebrating the holiday than coming to a little village church service, but we invited everyone we encountered nonetheless. Danny believed it was worth a shot even if only a few people showed up.

As we walked throughout the dusty streets, I was struck by everyone's warmth and friendliness. In lieu of doorbells, all we needed was a loud "Buenos días!" to get peoples' attention. At almost every home, we were warmly received and invited to come and chat. My group offered prayer for those who wanted it and, from the start, began to see God's faithfulness. We prayed for one woman who said she had been having demonic dreams at night. She felt like Satan was attacking her in her sleep and asked why it was happening. We declared that the power of Jesus Christ would reign in her home and renounced all demonic attacks against her.

Another group met a lady who'd had three C-sections. She was in pain all the way down to her feet and asked for healing prayer. When the team prayed for her, her pain left entirely, and she exclaimed, "I didn't expect this to happen!" Those who had prayed laughed with joy, because they *did* expect something to happen. That's precisely why they had prayed in the first place. But despite the woman's doubts, God chose to surprise her and take all pain from His beloved daughter. Still another group encountered a little boy with a bad eye infection. As they prayed for him, he was completely healed, and his eyes became clear and healthy.

After just a couple of hours of house visits, the intense heat caught up with us. Exhausted and dehydrated, we headed back to the church to drink water and rest. We still had a few hours to eat lunch and relax before the evening service began. Jesse, Tanya, and Christian asked for a few volunteers to organize some fun activities and manage the children while their parents were in the service. Danny said we should expect around ten children. Liz and I offered to plan a couple of games but figured we could improvise for the most part. We'd both worked with children before and were confident that we could entertain a handful of children for a few hours.

Despite the expectation for a low turnout, families surprisingly began to pour into the church. As the main service began, Liz and I were left outside with about forty children. They were already bouncing off the walls, eagerly waiting to see what we had up our sleeves. I looked at Liz and laughed nervously, unsure of where to begin. We had limited supplies and only loosely planned activities. We had no translator to help us, and Liz didn't speak Spanish. I spoke some but certainly not enough to be running a large children's program. My previous confidence quickly evaporated. Breck and Taylor appeared and told us that they'd be rotating between helping with the children and assisting inside the church. I was relieved to have a bit of extra help, but the guys didn't speak a word of Spanish either. This meant I was in charge of communicating with the children. *Oh no*, I thought to myself. *I guess I'll be learning Spanish quickly.*

Liz suggested we start by playing with a parachute that Natalie had brought with her. We laid it on the ground and motioned for the children to gather around and grab a piece of the round cloth. Breck threw a ball into the middle, and the children's faces lit up as they realized they could launch the ball into the air using the parachute. Slowly, even the children who had seemed a bit wary of me and Liz began to warm up to us and joined in the fun. However, the joy of waving around the cloth quickly turned into yanking the parachute as hard as possible, and within minutes, it was already ripped apart. One of the children handed me a piece of the parachute as he flashed me a devious smile and continued yanking this new toy up and down as hard as he could.

Okay, time for Plan B. We decided to switch to a game that wouldn't break anything. We got the children into four lines and tried to organize a relay race. I did the best I could to explain the rules to the children, flustered that I had somehow become a translator despite not speaking fluently. The mixture of broken Spanish and kids who didn't listen resulted in a mob of children running to the finish line of the "relay race" simultaneously.

Maybe it was time for a new game *again*. We miraculously arranged the children sitting in a circle and showed them how to play "Duck, Duck, Goose." I didn't know the Spanish word for duck *or* goose, so I changed the name to "Perro, Perro, Gato" (Dog, Dog, Cat). Liz and I demonstrated how to play, and the children caught on quickly and soon were running around, tagging each other and laughing. Breck and Taylor joined in, and the kids burst into fits of laughter as they watched these very big boys running around the circle and playing along.

After a while, the children began to get antsy, so we decided to switch games once more. By the grace of God, Maria came outside for a minute and explained how to play "Simon Dice" (Simon Says). However, she quickly went back into the church and left us to carry out the game without her. After yelling, *"Simon dice toque la boca; Simon dice toque la nariz; toque la cabeza..."* for about ten minutes, my head hurt from concentrating so intensely on Spanish, and I told Liz we needed to do something else. She reached for some stickers to give to the kids in the hopes of distracting them while we racked our brains for another activity. The moment the children caught a glimpse of Liz's bag of goodies, they formed a mob around her, jumping all over her and practically mauling her. Though I should have tried to intervene, I couldn't do anything but laugh. Breck joined in the laughter and whipped out his video camera to document the madness. Eventually, Liz erupted into giggles as well, and the three of us doubled over, surrounded by children going berserk.

Our attempt at a children's program had become a free-for-all, and we were out of ideas. We decided our goal should be nothing more than keeping the children from escaping, hurting each other, or hurting themselves. Finally, after about two hours of chaos, the parents started coming out of the church and taking their children home. Relieved, I bid them *adios* and checked in with the rest of the team.

Those who had been a part of the church service reported an amazing evening. Danny had asked the team what the plan for the night was, but Christian took the lead in breaking free from a rigid program. His idea of planning a church service was planning nothing and expecting God to do things we could never do in our own strength. Danny addressed the congregation, then asked my teammates to come forward and share testimonies. Christian walked up the aisle, asking God for a word of knowledge (a God-given piece of information about someone or something specific) for at least one person in the congregation. *Come on God, give me something*, he prayed. By the time Christian got to the front of the church, he had a word of knowledge to share. "I feel like there are some people here tonight who feel so low that they want to end their lives," he shared. "If you've been feeling that type of depression, don't be ashamed. Please come forward for prayer." A few moments passed, but after a bit of hesitation, two people stood up and came forward. Christian had heard God correctly, and the team prayed for emotional healing and freedom from suicidal thoughts and depression.

Another team member called those forward who had pain in their bodies, and many were healed. One lady was cured of epilepsy, another from abdominal pain. A man who had problems in both his leg and his eye got healed. One woman was suffering from pain on the right side of her body, because her husband often beat her. She came forward for prayer, and her body was restored. Hopefully, her heart found some healing as well. And the craziest testimony belonged to an older gentleman who couldn't walk when he came *into* the church, but he was able to walk *out* of the church at the end of the evening. The Holy Spirit was touching people with His healing power. Yet more importantly, around fifty people came forward to receive Christ. Outer healing is great, but it can only get you so far. The Healer is the one who changes your heart and makes a lasting difference.

Seeing such incredible fruit after only one day in Latin America was an incredible blessing. I'd had no idea what our trip would look like when we started and had secretly feared being ineffective if we stayed in each village for only a short amount of time. But right away, God assuaged my doubt. He showed me that even in one day His presence was powerful enough to shake a village.

Our second day in Pesqueira was quite similar to the first. We visited families in the village and invited them to another service at Danny's church. At one particular house, we stopped for quite some time, playing with the children and practicing our Spanish. Little Zoe was part of my group this time, and she was an instant hit with the village children. The young girls let her play with their baby doll, and when we finally headed back to the church, Zoe began to cry. Though she protested returning the doll, Tanya took it away and tried to give it back to the children. However, they instantly placed the doll back in Zoe's arms, joyfully allowing her to keep it. This act of generosity was remarkable; the children had not hesitated for even a second to give out of their poverty.

In the evening, our team followed the same program as the previous evening — a church service for the community and a children's program outside. Liz and I begged for help from a fluent Spanish speaker as well as more people to help with crowd control. With these simple changes, our program ran much more smoothly. We played some games with a bit more order and acted out skits from the Bible. The kids eagerly watched and then asked for a chance to reenact the skits themselves. We finished the evening without Liz getting mauled or the children breaking anything. We had learned quickly. *Success.*

Meanwhile, the church service inside became another healing session. One of the village women my group had visited the first day attended the service and reminded Jesse that we'd prayed for her to stop having nightmares. She said that she'd finally slept well, in complete peace, without bad dreams. God's freedom was moving.

Before I knew it, it was already time to move on to our next village. With a crack of dawn departure, we left Pesqueira to drive about twelve hours to our next destination, the city of Culiacan. I volunteered to drive a leg of the journey, both excited and a bit nervous about tackling foreign roads for the first time. I started off with relative confidence but became a bit shaken when the calm two-lane highway I was navigating suddenly turned into a bustling city road. I was driving Overflow, our massive SUV, with a very heavy trailer attached to it, and this monster vehicle didn't exactly squeeze through tight city streets. To complicate things even more, I didn't really know or understand the rules of the road in Mexico. There were times when we passed street lights, one red and one green light next to each other, *both* lit up brightly. *What did that mean?* Did it mean *red* or did it mean *green*?

There were also *flashing* green lights, something I'd never seen before, not to mention various street signs that I could only halfway read. I remember passing a sign that said "Peligroso [insert mystery Spanish word here]." I immediately recognized the word signifying "dangerous" but couldn't figure out what the mystery word was. That didn't do much for my confidence.

At one point, I completely missed the fact that there was a street light to my left, not noticing its existence due to its obscure location. This resulted in me literally almost crashing into a semitruck, which would have killed me and three other people on my team. Luckily, the truck driver knew what *he* was doing, and I squeaked by with nothing but an angry honk from the driver. Shortly after, the whole team stopped at a gas station, and the people driving in front of me reported that they had done the exact same thing.

We switched drivers, and as the next person attempted the new roads, it was quickly confirmed that I was not the only driver who was feeling a little confused or disoriented. During the last leg of our day's journey, Maria pulled onto what looked like a small dirt alleyway behind the gas station where we'd just fueled up. It was too awkward to turn around, so she cut through the dirt alley to meet our teammates' vehicles on the other side. Unfortunately, while she maneuvered through the alley, a police officer targeted our car, pulled us over, and began to harass us. He accused Maria of driving the wrong way down a "boulevard." She insisted that there were no signs posted indicating that the road was designed for one-way traffic, and this so-called boulevard really wasn't anything more than a small dirt path anyway. The police officer kept harassing her and asked for her license. Unsure of what to do, Maria handed it over as she and the officer went back and forth in Spanish. Liz, Rose, and I sat in the car watching and waiting quietly. The cop told Maria he was going to give her a ticket for around five hundred pesos (close to fifty dollars). Maria explained that she was not from the area and that it was unfair to charge for a ticket when no signs were posted.

We realized that our vehicle had only women inside and that our other four cars each had at least one guy inside. They had all passed by without any problems. Christian saw that we were having trouble with the police and joined our car. He tried to reason with the cop, but the officer would not relent. After further discussion, the cop said that Maria and Christian needed to get into his vehicle and go to the police station with him. He assumed they would be intimidated and give in to paying the five-hundred-peso fine, putting cash straight into his pocket. Much to the officer's surprise, Christian gladly got right into his police car. Maria followed. The cop looked a bit panicked, because he was bluffing. He had hoped he could fool us and scare us into handing over easy money. Yet, when he realized this was not the case, he let both Maria and Christian go without paying a single peso. He gave Maria's license back and told us to go. Little did we know, this was just a taste of the corruption we would deal with throughout the rest of our time in Mexico.

We continued driving and arrived in our destination city of Culiacan. However, once within the city limits, we lacked directions to a specific location. Some local pastors had invited us to minister at their church and had instructed Maria to call them after we'd reached Culiacan, planning to direct us from there. Unfortunately, a miscommunication I still don't fully understand prompted several hours of driving aimlessly around the city. As we drove in circles of confusion, only one thing was clear — the peaceful atmosphere we'd experienced in quaint Pesqueira was gone.

Instead, Culiacan carried a strong feeling of oppression and violence. The darkness was tangible, and I realized all the rumors I'd heard about the drug wars in Mexico were not rumors at all. As we drove through the dark roads of the city, eight or so vehicles filled with men carrying rifles sped by us on the streets. Some of their faces were covered, and they were wearing dark clothes and camouflage. At one point, we had to screech to a halt and make an abrupt U-turn to avoid driving straight into a confrontation between the men with guns and some men on the street. We assumed the clash and arrest was drug-related and immediately removed ourselves from the vicinity.

Unsure of where to go from here, we headed down a two-lane street, and a car continuously pulled up next to us, trying to get our attention. We wondered why a stranger would be bold enough to try this distracting maneuver, so Christian yelled to the driver, "Are you a pastor?" The driver shook his head, and before he could explain that his passenger *was* the very pastor we were looking for, Christian rolled up his window and assumed the car was being driven by a lunatic trying to follow us around this dark city of violence and drugs. Christian announced via walkie-talkie that we should keep our windows up, lock our doors, and not speak to anyone who drove by us.

We drove a bit longer, still very lost and confused, and finally pulled over to the side of the road. The same car from before appeared another time and parked beside us as a couple of men got out and approached Taylor's station wagon. They attempted to talk to Taylor and Ben, asking them to roll down their windows. However, the guys followed Christian's instructions and pretended they didn't notice the Mexican men banging on their car. Finally, Maria recognized one of the men and realized that this mysterious car likely did, in fact, belong to the pastor who had invited our team to minister in Culiacan. No longer frightened, Maria exited her vehicle and approached the men. Sure enough, the car that we had been trying to lose for miles *was* carrying our pastor. Embarrassed, Maria explained what had happened, and the pastor begrudgingly instructed us to follow him.

We followed his car down isolated dirt roads that quite honestly didn't feel much safer than the major roads with the armed men. We finally pulled into the pastor's yard, where he greeted us formally and told us that he sensed a "spirit of fear" among our whole team. Some looked embarrassed, others genuinely worried, still others amused by the whole situation. Personally, I was just cranky, hungry, tired, and incredibly confused as to where we were. My confusion didn't lessen any when, after five minutes, the pastor instructed us to return to our vehicles and drive right back to where we'd come from. He informed us that we would be staying in the center of the city, not his house. Why he'd made us drive to his house for this five-minute chat remained a mystery. In a daze, I climbed back into Overflow, ready to find wherever we'd be sleeping for the evening.

Exhausted, we arrived at a rundown ghetto where we were directed to a dodgy parking lot across the street from a decrepit "hotel" — our evening accommodation. Only some of our vehicles could fit in the lot, so we were asked to drive the others to another parking lot. The second lot was too small, so the pastor instructed us to get back into the vehicles. We followed him for many miles, wondering if we'd have to walk back to the hotel after parking. Yet, instead of looking for parking, the pastor took us on a detour to grab some dinner. At this point, it was almost midnight, and all I wanted was a bed. Frustrated, I ordered a quesadilla and forced it down as quickly as I could, wishing this long day would end already. By 1:30 a.m., we finally found a place to leave all of our vehicles and reached our hotel. Jesse and Tanya let us know that we were expected to be ready the next morning by 9:15 to attend the pastor's church service. The thought of being awake, dressed up, and showered in less than eight hours made me cringe.

Despite my exhaustion, the moment my head touched the pillow, I became restless and couldn't sleep. I finally drifted off for a couple of hours but then woke up repeatedly throughout the night. I tossed and turned, and just a few short hours later, it was already time to get up and get ready for church. I reluctantly threw on a long skirt and clean shirt and headed to the lobby to meet the team.

We walked down the street to find a crowded sanctuary filled with people. I took a seat in the back, trying to look inconspicuous. As the service began, I could only understand bits and pieces of what the pastor was trying to explain. Suddenly, the congregation began to chuckle at the pastor's words, and I noticed that he kept looking at people from our team. After a few minutes of this, I realized that he was retelling the story of the previous evening. He was teasing our team for deeming him a madman chasing us down in his car. It hit me how ridiculous the past twenty-four hours had been, and I couldn't help but to laugh myself. Intense laughter erupted from behind me. The pastor had a huge smile on his face, and I knew he'd forgiven us for the confusion. The miscommunication had become his new favorite story.

Grinning with amusement, he asked some people from our team to come forward and share a word with the church. A few of my teammates gave words of encouragement and personal testimonies. Jesse, Tanya, and Christian showed the congregation a video from their time living in Africa. Afterwards, the pastor called those forward who needed specific prayer. Many rushed forward, giving our team an opportunity to pray for lots of people. The cry of my heart was to see breakthrough in healing during the trip, and I eagerly laid hands on the sick congregants.

My favorite interaction was with a little girl who was healed of pain in her throat. Though a sore throat may have seemed small to some, my team always celebrated the little breakthroughs, preparing our hearts to receive the big stuff. We knew greater things were to come.

After the service, the congregation kindly treated us to a delicious meal and sent us on our way. It seemed strange to be in Culiacan for just one church service, but I was learning to not ask questions and just roll with the punches. I heard through the grapevine that our next destination was about an hour's drive but had no idea where we were going. We loaded into the cars, and over two hours later, we were still driving. All of a sudden, we pulled over at a little beach oasis called Santuario Naturista. It was a beautiful hotel right on the Pacific Ocean where Maria told us to rest for the evening and the following morning. The next night, we'd get back to work.

Landing at a coastal sanctuary seemed an unexpected blessing, but our high hopes were quickly dashed when we realized we were actually trapped at a vegan mecca. We were forbidden to bring any outside "contaminants" into the hotel, including coffee and peanut butter. Hotel meals that resembled real food played tricks on our eyes but repeatedly disappointed us. Our first breakfast looked like a steaming plate of eggs and a cup of sweet hot chocolate. As I touched my first forkful to my tongue, I realized the "eggs" were actually chunks of tofu in disguise. I tried to wash down the taste with my enticing, thick, brown drink but almost choked as I swallowed what tasted like blended twigs. Lunch and dinner were no better — just a cruel mix of faux hamburger patties and other dishes that masqueraded as meat but tasted like tree bark.

On our second day, we ventured outside the vegan facility and visited one of the work camps in the area. These camps were comprised of people from many different indigenous tribes who hoped to make money and create better lives. They erected small communities, similar to squatter towns, where they could work and live cheaply. Unfortunately, the reality was that many people never achieved their dreams of leaving the camps. The atmosphere was dismal, unhealthy, and violent; and it was not uncommon for people to kill each other within the camps.

A local pastor named Hector, who had a good relationship with a few of the camps, took a group of us to one nearby. There was a small church already established within the camp, and we joined the congregation for their evening service. As we entered the camp, it seemed like we were intruding on other peoples' private lives, traipsing around their secretive slum. I could feel the darkness and oppression, and I felt like we should leave. However, as we walked further into the camp, we saw a tiny church building and its congregation waiting for a church service to begin. We sat among the small crowd and sang along as best we could as a local man led worship. Three members of our team shared testimonies and were received with "amens" and "hallelujahs." Afterwards, we prayed for those who needed healing or prayer. Many of the women complained of abusive home lives and cried as we prayed for them, even though they couldn't understand the words we were speaking. I suppose a warm smile and a hug is pretty universal; sometimes words aren't needed.

The next day, we drove to the region of Cofradia to meet up with an American missionary named Jay who had been living in Mexico for sixteen years. He had spent a lot of time working with an indigenous group called the Cora who mainly lived in a mountainous area outside of the city. We stayed at his mission base in Cofradia for one night and headed into the mountains the following morning. Jay shared a brief history of the Cora people with our group, explaining that they purposely isolated themselves from mainstream society and were suspicious of outsiders. They tended to resolve their conflicts with machetes or gunshots and didn't want people trying to push outside ideas on them. Though this information seemed a little unnerving, Jay reminded us that he had been working with the Cora for years and had gradually and respectfully established relationships with the people. However, the tribe was still a bit wary of foreigners' motivations for visiting their villages. We needed to be mindful of their qualms but confident in Jay's guidance. Jay told us to get a good night's rest, so we could leave early in the morning to drive up to the mountains during daylight hours.

We were told to sleep on cots under shelters called *palapas*. The palapas had thatched roofs but no walls, so we were pretty much sleeping outside. One of the girls asked Jay if there were any animals we should be aware of, and he said that scorpions and tarantulas roamed the compound. *Great*, I thought, *I finally get my own bed and then find out I have to share it with killer insects*. With no other choice, I snuggled into my cot and passed out, mosquitoes eating me alive as I slept underneath the palapa.

In the morning, a group of Mexican men joined us for the drive to the Cora mountains. They had come from various churches to learn more about Jay's ministry. This motley crew of men constantly teased each other and playfully joked with our team. Some spoke English, but even those who didn't communicated effortlessly through hand gestures and laughter. It was clear that every man in the group could joke around but also had a serious relationship with the Lord.

We left our pop-up campers and both RVs behind and traveled in a caravan comprised of Overflow, Shekinah, and a bunch of pickup trucks driven by the locals. We drove for almost seven hours, winding up intense mountain roads to an area called El Cangrejo, which translates to "The Crab." The last three hours of our journey were so bumpy that we had to put our hands over our heads at times to avoid smashing them into the top of the car.

After being thoroughly jostled, we arrived at an emerald plateau, seated between lush mountain peaks. We parked our cars, dropped off our belongings in a tiny cement room where we'd sleep, and walked to the house of Magdeleno, one of the Cora locals. Despite the cultural barriers Jay had warned us about, he had built a good relationship with Magdeleno over time and was now warmly welcomed whenever visiting his home. Magdeleno kindly greeted our team as well and let us know that we were welcome in El Cangrejo. Unlike many of the locals, he was able to speak Spanish in addition to his indigenous language. Some of the women in his household were not able to communicate in Spanish, but Magdeleno assured us that they were pleased with our visit. The family cooked us some tortillas, and we sat around their compound eating and asking Magdeleno questions about the Cora culture. Magdeleno gladly provided answers and insisted that even though some of the Cora people did not show much emotion or act excited by our visit, they were happy with our presence in their village.

A couple of hours later, we walked back to the rundown cement building where we'd left our belongings. We spread out on the cool cement floor and tried to sleep as we listened to an odd medley of animal noises in the background — roosters crowing throughout the night and donkeys braying in the distance.

In the morning, Jay escorted us to a tranquil, grassy area atop majestic cliffs and waterfalls where he asked us to participate in a group devotion. Jay challenged the whole team with the passage from Daniel about Meshach, Shadrach, and Abednego's words before facing the fiery furnace. They promised they would never bow down to a false god and declared that their God would save them from the flaming fire. However, they also noted that even if God *didn't* save them, they would still bow to no other god; they would still proclaim that God was good. (See Daniel 3:16-18.) Jay asked us if our hearts were in a place to produce the same response. If someone got killed on our trip, if tragedy struck, or if things didn't end the way we hoped — would we still declare that our God was good? Though the question seemed just a hypothetical challenge in that moment, I had no understanding of the very real and tough situations headed our way throughout the coming months.

Once we'd seriously reflected for a bit, we returned to Magdeleno's home for breakfast and then divided into two teams. One stayed in El Cangrejo and walked to different homes in the area, inviting the Cora people to a gathering we would host in the evening. The other group headed down to a nearby canyon to enjoy God's creation for a few hours. We were warned that the hike was extremely intense, steep, and tiring but would absolutely blow us away. I was a little scared to sign up for such a hike, but I couldn't pass up the opportunity. This was one of the most breathtaking places I'd ever seen, and I needed to explore more. I heard reports of waterfalls and swimming holes at the bottom of the canyon and knew I would regret never visiting them.

The hiking group walked for about forty-five minutes just to get to the start of the canyon's trail. Once we started trekking down into the canyon, the descent was quite severe. Certain parts of the path were covered in rocks that moved and slid when you stepped on them, and other parts were so steep that I had to slide down on my backside to prevent myself from taking a straight vertical dive. I was so focused on getting *down* that I forgot about the fact that I would soon have to somehow get myself back *up* this canyon.

After about an hour of carefully treading, slipping, and sliding down the rockier part of the trail, we wound up at a formation of large, flatter rocks. We followed these rocks until we hit a small waterfall and muddy swimming hole. The Mexican guys that had come with us immediately stripped down to shorts and jumped off one of the bigger rocks into the water. Wearing long pants and a T-shirt, I envied the freedom men had and wished I could throw off my clothes and jump in too. As I watched the men having fun in the water while I baked in the sun, I couldn't bear the injustice a moment longer. I decided to jump in, clothes and all, and later deal with hiking back up the canyon sopping wet.

I climbed over to a large rock overlooking the swimming hole. When I glanced down, I momentarily panicked, as standing at this angle suddenly made the water look a lot further away. But as the Mexicans cheered me on from the bottom, I had to do it. I jumped and screamed in fear on the way down yet felt nothing but pure refreshment the second I hit the water. This was glorious. As I splashed around, I took in the radiant beauty of everything surrounding me. God had hidden this little swimming hole in a secret canyon in Mexico and given it to us today for nothing more than our simple pleasure. I'd heard a lot about drug wars before entering this country, but I hadn't heard anything about tucked-away coves and hidden natural treasures. Perhaps the world was actually more beautiful than people realized.

Eventually, we had to leave our little oasis and begin the dreaded, steep hike home. As we walked, most of us realized we would run out of drinking water pretty soon. We were all huffing and puffing as we climbed the steep terrain. My waterlogged clothing didn't make the trek any easier. We pulled ourselves up on rocks and swung our bodies in awkward positions to get up the canyon. The need for water grew increasingly dire, and it seemed that several people wouldn't make it unless they rehydrated very soon. Just when I was becoming legitimately concerned, we heard the sound of a waterfall in the distance. I desperately hiked towards it and squished myself between a couple of rocks in order to balance and catch the water dripping off the falls. Thankfully, I loaded up a few bottles and ravenously sucked down the fresh water. Our team pushed on, and about six hours after beginning the hike, we returned to our cement homestead. We were exhausted and sore but had just a few hours to rest before running an evening program in the village.

Meanwhile, some teammates had visited various homes throughout the Cora village, praying for families and delivering bags of food and clothing. They also organized a children's program where they performed songs, acted out skits, and led games. Christian reported that many children and some adults had received Christ that afternoon. Thanks to those who had done house visits during the hike, several Cora people congregated in the village center that evening. We had planned to show *The Jesus Film* in the Cora language, but unfortunately the DVD kept skipping. We finally gave up and decided to improvise. Aurelio, one of the Mexican men traveling with us, stepped up and led the crowd in some songs. Afterwards, we offered to pray for those who were sick. A group of us prayed for a man who'd had an eye problem for a year that caused pain and blurry vision. He announced that the pain left after prayer, and he could now see clearly! The healing power of the Holy Spirit was a new and shocking experience among the Cora. As intercession invited the power of God's love, a tribe of once closed hearts seemed to be slowly opening.

Jay had tirelessly been visiting this community and had been waiting for breakthrough for a long time. He finally saw a glimpse of the fruit of his labor and was moved to tears at what happened during our time in the village. When I saw this normally stoic man shed tears of gratitude, I realized that God had not brought our team to El Cangrejo solely for the Cora people. We had traveled there to encourage Jay. Our time together marked the beginning of a move of the Holy Spirit in healing power among the Cora. Though our time in El Cangrejo was brief, Jay will continue to serve and minister in that village. I am honored to have served alongside a man of such perseverance and blessed to know that his dedication will continue to transform El Cangrejo.

Our team's next destination was the bustling city of Guadalajara, a stark contrast from remote village life. We stayed at the home of a missionary family who worked with an organization called Fire Ministries. While figuring out sleeping arrangements, some people decided to sleep outside in the campers. However, others squished onto the floor of an open room upstairs, which we quickly divided into the testosterone-filled "Man Cave" and the female half of the room, "Pony Island." As we argued about the dividing line's exact location and how unfair it was for the guys to traipse through Pony Island as they pleased, it was clear that we were no longer teammates. We had become brothers and sisters.

"Don't come into the Man Cave!" one of our brothers would yell.

"We can hear you snoring all the way from Pony Island!" a sister would retort.

"Stop crossing over the line!"

"Stop farting! You smell!"

The playful banter went back and forth, and without a doubt, I knew that we were family now.

After a few days in our new home, the "Man Cave" received a new occupant, nineteen-year-old Brent. Better known as Moose, this Canadian addition to the team was immediately adopted as a little brother. Our charming Moose was a mix of playful, profound, goofy, passionate, and just plain cool. He never had a bad thing to say about anyone and managed to maintain a simple, pure joy no matter what.

During our time in Guadalajara, we participated in church services, a Bible school meeting, and inner-city ministry. One particular evening, we drove to a slum inhabited by people from an indigenous tribe in Oaxaca who had immigrated to Guadalajara. Many of them spoke the Mixteco language, but most could speak Spanish as well. We walked down the street, greeting people and playing with the children. A bunch of us congregated in one area and asked if there were any sick people who needed healing. A woman came forward whose face had become paralyzed. She had trouble speaking because of the paralysis. Several of us laid hands on her, and she began to speak, explaining that her face felt hot. In fact, it was no longer paralyzed! Grateful, she invited a few of us to go back to her home and pray some more with her.

Jesse, Christian, a bilingual woman from the local church, and I went to her house and continued to pray. I felt the Lord reminding me of the story of the woman who had been bleeding for twelve years and believed that if she even touched the cloak of Jesus that she would be healed. As she reached for him in a large crowd, Jesus called her out in front of everyone and said, "Daughter, your faith has healed you" (Mark 5:34). I shared the story with the woman and told her that I believed her faith in the Lord had made her well. The four of us prayed for a bit more, and the woman began to cry with joy. She said she felt like something was being cleansed inside her mouth, and she had a sensation she couldn't explain. Her heart was overwhelmed with happiness. As I watched this beautiful, elderly Mixteco woman rejoicing in her healing, my heart was filled with joy as well.

After being in Guadalajara for a few days, we drove about three hours outside the city with our host family. They had friends in a village within San Pedro who had planted a church and wanted us to run an outdoor street service for them. As usual, the team planned only to wait on the Holy Spirit to see what God wanted to do. We started with worship and then called those who were sick forward. This was becoming a simple yet powerful practice for us. I thought about the church where I'd grown up and started to question the typical Western church's effort to design the "perfect church service." So many churches in America have rigid rules about how long each worship song can last, how much time the perfectly-planned sermon should be, how the offering must be presented, etc. But if we structure a service with no freedom for God to show up, all of our planning is in vain. Without His presence, what's the point?

Meticulous planning and rigid structure didn't seem to be Jesus' style. His ministry simply entailed praying for the sick, preaching the good news, and driving out demons. My teammates and I wanted to walk like Jesus did, so we figured we'd do the same. We told people the good news of Jesus, we prayed for the sick, and we prayed for people to be delivered. We told people that Jesus was good. We told people how He'd healed us. We told people He could heal them too. And then we prayed for Jesus to do just that — plain and simple. I never felt the need to convince people to follow Jesus when He did the work himself. During these "church services," God touched people in ways we never could have in our own strength. We didn't sell Jesus. People ran to the front to accept Him.

As we gave testimonies and prayed for the sick in this particular village, people were healed and immediately came forward to share their healings with the congregation. One lady had a hard lump on her back near her shoulder blade which prevented her from moving her arm properly. As the team prayed, the bump softened so that she was able to move her arm. Rose and I started to pray for another woman who complained of pain in her chest and stomach. We prayed for release from physical pain, but nothing happened. Maria came over to translate and found out more information. The woman had gone to the doctor, and he said there was a problem with her appendix. We continued to pray for physical healing, but still nothing happened.

I got a weird feeling that there was some emotional pain that was binding the woman. I hadn't received many prophetic words or words of knowledge before, so I wasn't sure if this strange feeling was from God or from myself. But as I kept praying, the feeling persisted. I finally decided to speak up about what I felt God was showing me. "Maria, I don't know how to say this in a way that isn't rude or accusatory," I explained. "But I really feel like there is some emotional pain this woman needs healing from. I think it's manifesting in the physical, and that physical pain won't go away until we deal with whatever the emotional pain is."

Maria immediately nodded and responded, "I was feeling the same exact thing, but I wasn't sure if I should speak up. I think what we are feeling is right."

"Yeah, something weird is definitely going on here," Rose chimed in. "As we prayed for her, I started to feel a bad pain in my stomach."

We agreed that we needed to take the risk of offending the woman by asking what was going on in her emotional life. When Maria spoke to her, the woman began to break down in tears. As she cried, Maria translated for us and explained that the woman had a bad relationship with her husband. She got no pleasure out of having sex with him, and she only slept with him out of obligation. She was unhappy in her marriage and wrestled with depression. As Maria continued to minister to the woman, more of her story was revealed. The woman admitted that she'd also been abused by her father and had been emotionally scarred by his actions.

Maria explained that forgiving the woman's father and husband was the key to emotional freedom. We prayed for her to be liberated from the sins of her father and husband, to be released from the chains of depression, and to enter full emotional, spiritual, and physical healing. As we prayed, the woman said that the pain started to leave her body. Rose said that the strange pain she'd felt in her stomach also disappeared.

After we prayed a bit more, Jesse spoke in front of the whole congregation about receiving the gift of the Holy Spirit. He told everyone that they could receive the gift of tongues, healing, and words of prophecy. The woman said she wanted to receive the baptism of the Holy Spirit. Maria, Rose, and I continued to pray, this time asking the Holy Spirit to indwell this woman. I prayed she would feel and know the power of God's divine peace, love, and joy. As we prayed, the woman began to speak in tongues and sway back and forth.

Suddenly, the power of the Holy Spirit overcame her, and she fell backwards — hard. I awkwardly helped catch the woman and positioned her in a chair. She just lay there slumped on the chair for a while, and we let her be. I looked around to see what was going on with everyone else, since I'd been so focused on this one woman for quite some time. Several other people had begun to speak in tongues, some also knocked down by the mighty wind of the Holy Spirit. In the past, I'd been quite skeptical about getting "slain in the Spirit," but as I watched these people virtually get knocked down without anyone touching them, I knew the falling was involuntarily and genuine. The Holy Spirit was tangibly touching people, and some strange, supernatural freedom was taking over.

Later on that evening, Maria went back to check on the woman, and she looked completely different. What once had been a face of stress and depression was now a countenance of joy. The woman came up to me and Rose and gave us each a big hug, thanking us. She said all pain was completely gone, she felt joyful, and she was ready to go home and make love to her husband! Amen!

The next morning, we continued our journey towards Mexico City. Maria had a friend named Angela who volunteered to host us in the city for a few days. We planned to park our vehicles in an RV park just outside of the city and then take a bus into the urban center. There were a lot of restrictions about driving in the city, so we figured taking a bus would be a wiser decision than taking the risk of getting pulled over. Upon arriving at Angela's house, she kindly welcomed us and prepared a delicious meal. Angela explained her involvement in local ministry and shared her heart to minister to people living in garbage dumps in Mexico City. There were a couple of dumps that she really wanted to visit with our team, both to share the gospel and to provide food and clothing for the people living there. She told us that we would be out for most of the following day. We needed to get a good night's rest and fill up on breakfast in the morning.

When we woke up and walked to the breakfast table, we found several massive plates of jiggling jello chunks covered in yogurt. Most of us could do nothing but stare at the food that frighteningly moved on its own. I hesitantly sat down, trying both to be thankful for the meal and to not gag at the gelatin, a substance supposedly comprised of animal skin and bones. I could choke down a little bit, but tackling such a large mountain of jello made me queasy. Angela had left the food for us and disappeared, so I wondered if there was a way I could avoid causing offense by sneakily making the jello disappear without actually eating it. However, Breck loudly advocated getting over our disgust and choking it down — all of it.

"Come on team!" he exclaimed. "We are traveling through Latin America and will have to eat bugs and all kinds of weird stuff this year. Seriously, we're falling apart at jello?"

I started to consider what he was saying until I realized that he was on the brink of dry heaving. As I watched him sweat and gag the chunks down, I decided it was better to dispose of the jello without putting any of it in my mouth. I gradually transferred chunk after chunk of gelatin from the plate into some plastic cups, covered them with napkins and threw them in the trash before Angela saw a thing. Victory!

Unfortunately, even those who had conquered the breakfast really had nothing to eat but sugar, and we had a long day of involuntary fasting ahead of us. Our day at the dumps would be a long and intense one. Angela gathered us and directed us to a local bus stop so we could take public transportation to the first dump. It was about a two-hour process to wait for our first bus, switch buses, and then walk to the dump's location. We planned on walking around, gathering people, and then giving away bread and clothes while sharing some testimonies and scripture. In terms of going out of my comfort zone, I didn't think our visit would be that big of a deal. We'd already visited villages and slums, and most places had been pretty dirty. Prior to the trip, I'd worked in some extremely dismal conditions and expected the Mexican dumps to be similar.

I was confident that whatever I encountered in Mexico City would not take me aback.

I could not have been more wrong. Nothing could have prepared me for the absolute filth I was about to enter. The dumps made the slums of Guadalajara look like palaces in comparison. The smell was unspeakable. At the first dump, the innermost part was closed off, so we didn't even go into the depths of the dump. But even the odor lingering on the outskirts was overwhelming. Obviously, there was a stench of trash, but there were putrid streams of sewage as well. At one point, I noticed a river of sewage with a dead dog lying in the middle, his body crushed and mangled. Children played around the area, running about the trash comprised of wasted food, pieces of cardboard, old dolls missing heads, and human and animal feces. I couldn't imagine the worldview of a child growing up in such a place. Inside the dump, any sight of the outside world was completely blocked by mountains of trash. As we walked around, some members of the team invited the people we passed to assemble at the dump's entrance for our planned gathering. I mostly just observed, unsure of what to say or think. The fact that people lived here was frankly more than I could wrap my head around.

After a while, we congregated at the dump's entrance, as did many of the people whom we'd invited. A few of us shared testimonies or words from the Bible. I worked up the nerve to share a word of encouragement, but to be completely honest, I felt I had nothing to offer these people. My life was nothing like theirs. Who was I, a young professional from the States, to tell these people living in a dump that they could find great joy and freedom? It was easy for me to talk about God's provision and love, but these Mexicans would spend the rest of their lives living in piles of trash. How could I even pretend to relate to the severity of their situation?

Yet, something one of us said did strike a chord with a man in the crowd. His name was Carlos, and he approached us for prayer. He had two little boys with him, and he was raising them on his own. I believe one of his sons had HIV, and Carlos felt hopeless and scared. He needed some encouragement, and as we spoke to him and prayed, he broke down in tears. As he embraced the members of our team, there was no longer a barrier between us and the people who lived in the garbage dump. There was no longer a boundary between the hungry, filthy ones and the clean, well-fed ones. As I watched Carlos in the arms of my teammates, I knew that God's love had made us one.

When the gathering was over, Angela escorted us to the next dump. The travel required another hour by bus, and by this time most of us were feeling pretty tired. It was already mid-afternoon, and we were hungry. But regardless, the team agreed to skip eating, trek on, and visit one more dump before calling it a day. I figured the second stop would be pretty much the same as the first but was again shocked by my new surroundings. Upon arrival at dump number two, I immediately choked on an aroma so foul that I genuinely could not bear it. Never in my life had I smelled something that revolting. My nose was so offended by the pungent odor that I had to repeatedly tell myself not to vomit. Amidst the mountains of trash stood large, white pipes that pumped out methane gas, a dangerous pollutant.

In addition to the trash and gas smells, there were vast quantities of animal and human feces. The combination of the gas, garbage, and excrement was absolutely repulsive. I'd been able to speak at the first dump, but this time I was afraid that if I opened my mouth, vomit would spew out. My teammates and I were doing everything in our power to take in breaths without gagging. I hoped our visit would only be a few minutes, but we stayed for almost two hours. By the second hour I didn't think I could stand it anymore. I was using every ounce of my strength to concentrate on not being sick. I had nothing to say, nothing to pour out, nothing to offer.

Maria valiantly preached for a bit, but most of the people seemed relatively unaffected. Hope was dead here. We gave out some clothing and bread, and that seemed to lift peoples' spirits a bit. We offered to pray for the sick, and a little girl came forward. She had an unrelenting cough. As I laid hands on her and prayed, her coughing fits continued. I kept praying, and she kept coughing. *Why even bother praying?* I thought. Even if God did choose to heal this little girl, she would still spend the rest of her life in a garbage dump. It was just a matter of time before she got sick again. She didn't need healing from just a cold; she needed healing from a life of hopelessness. She needed to be broken out of a cycle of poverty and despair. After praying for a while and listening to the cough continue, I couldn't take it anymore. I walked away feeling hopeless and defeated. I was done here. There was nothing I could do to fix this. I walked back towards the bus stop, quietly reflecting on the mess I'd just encountered. My mind felt numb.

We caught another bus back to Angela's house and returned about two hours later. My teammates and I removed our filthy dump clothes, took hot showers, and got into clean, warm pajamas. It was easy for us to wash off the filth of the day, but what about the people who lived in the filth? It just didn't seem fair.

Visiting the dumps was one of those sobering moments where I was reminded of how very human I was — how easily I felt disgusted, how easily I became discouraged, how easily I lost hope. I had no answers for Mexico City, no simple solution for eradicating the poverty in such a dismal situation. But that's when I remembered — God saw. God knew. God cared. I couldn't really fix anything, but God held the world in His hands.

There was so much I didn't understand, yet it wasn't really my job to understand. I knew enough; God lived in the dumps with those people, and He was enough. He had to be.

We slept one last night at Angela's and took a bus back to the RV park outside the city. A new team member was already there waiting for us. Serena, a sweet Aussie with a constant smile on her face, would be with us until Nicaragua. Constantly giving hugs and warmly offering words of encouragement, she became our newest sister. Now twenty-two people, we left for our next stop — Actopan, Vera Cruz.

Or, I should say, we *attempted* to leave. After about six hours of being in the car yet going nowhere, we gave up. We had previously been warned that only certain vehicles were allowed to enter Mexico City each day according to their license plate numbers. For example, if it was Monday and your license plate contained a "6," you were out of luck. If it was a Tuesday and your license plate had a "9," you were in trouble. We'd planned to drive to Vera Cruz via the outskirts of the city, thinking we would cleverly avoid all problems by busing into the city center and now driving around it. However, we quickly learned that the entire state through which we were traveling enforced the odd license plate rule.

Within minutes of leaving the RV park, we were pulled over by police and instructed to follow them to another area. Our caravan of vehicles struggled to stay together in the midst of chaotic traffic. Mass confusion quickly ensued, and my car got separated from the group. While apart, *another* police officer pulled us over, and we explained that we had already been stopped and were trying to find the first police officer who had reprimanded us. Finally, we met up with the rest of the team and parked on the side of the road. Each driver spoke to the policemen while the rest of us sat in the cars, waiting to see what was going on. Through Overflow's windows, I saw a crazy, demonized woman pacing up and down alongside us, yelling curses at our cars. She had two large rocks in her hands and looked like she was about to stone our vehicles. As I sat inside waiting for the interaction with the police to end, I prayed that she wouldn't throw the rocks through our windows and peg any of us in the head. *Ahh,* just another day in Mexico.

Finally, our drivers walked back to the cars and explained that the police had threatened to impound all of our vehicles and slam us with a fine of thirty-five hundred pesos per vehicle, assuming we would retrieve the vehicles two days later. If we paid on the spot, the fine would be lowered to one thousand pesos per car. The reduced fee still totaled about four hundred U.S. dollars, but we felt we had no choice but to fork over the money and carry on.

Relieved to be able to continue driving, we moved forward but were soon stopped again. Traffic suddenly came to a standstill due to severe riots. Everyone turned off their cars and began walking through the streets. Several police cars zipped by, loaded with men ready to throw grenades at rioting crowds in order to break them up. The pandemonium forced us to wait on the street for about an hour. We finally were let through and resumed driving, trying to find our way to the nearest freeway. However, the entrance ramp was blocked off and diverted us for hours. Our detour included driving through meandering dirt roads, fields of flowers, and frustrating loops that brought us right back to where we'd started.

After three hours or so, we finally found a freeway entrance; but moments later, we were pulled over by the police once more. We explained that we'd already paid previous cops and were trying to get out of the state and needed to do so in order to avoid breaking the ludicrous rules about license plate numbers. These police officers explained that Open Heaven's license plate was the only one offending the current day's rule. It was a Monday, and the RV had a "6" on its license plate. No "6's" were allowed on Mondays. The officers asserted that we had been unfairly charged previously, unjustly paying for all five vehicles. Yet, despite their honesty, these cops still charged us a penalty for Open Heaven's plate before letting us go forward.

In six hours or so, we'd been pulled over three or four times, paid hundreds of dollars' worth of fines, and driven almost nowhere. Though we'd been in the car for half the day, I doubt we'd traveled more than sixty miles. We pulled over to get gas and food and collectively decided to call it quits for the day. It was no longer feasible to reach our destination that evening. We just needed a place to set up camp. There was a large grass field behind the gas station, and the employees offered permission to sleep there.

I'd never slept behind a gas station before, but this was just the start of many bizarre camping locations to come. We set up the pop-ups and decided to take some time to pray and talk as a team. As we worshipped together, the tension and frustration from being lost, bribed, and delayed began to evaporate. We chose to make the most of the evening's remainder and to try to get a good rest before starting another long day in the car.

The next day, we made a successful journey and arrived in a small community called Actopan where we were greeted by several friendly faces. Some members of a local family, along with their church family, welcomed us into their gorgeous village oasis and hosted us for the next few nights. We began our time together by sharing a delicious meal and worshipping as one. Despite language barriers, everyone understood the movement of the same Holy Spirit, and we immediately felt unified with the hearts of the people in Actopan.

During our first morning, the team split into small groups, each led by one or two locals. We went door to door throughout a nearby village, offering prayers and an invitation to an afternoon service at a church member's home. I found it amusing that all we had to say was, "Meeting at Paco's house at one!" and everyone nodded, no further directions required. Clearly, this was a tight-knit community, and it was no rare thing to have church services right in peoples' backyards.

About an hour after the service was *supposed* to begin, people started showing up at Paco's. Thirty minutes after they began trickling in, we actually started the service. We were running on Mexican time. Taylor, Ben, Breck, and Christian performed a skit for the congregation wearing "luchador" masks that they'd found in Mexico City (the type of wrestling masks worn by characters in their favorite movie, *Nacho Libre*). Christian starred as an average joe being attacked by demonic spirits. Ben, Breck, and Taylor wore their beloved masks while a narrator announced that each one represented a different demonic spirit — the spirit of sickness, the spirit of sin, and the spirit of religion. One by one, the guys attacked Christian, using their best wrestling maneuvers and causing the congregation to erupt into laughter. Breck even jumped off a wall in Paco's backyard, which crumbled down into pieces, surprising us all and adding to the dramatic effect. In the final scene of the skit, Ted came forward, representing Jesus, and beat up each one of the wrestlers — showing that when Jesus fights for you, you always win. The crowd went wild as our guys jumped on each other, wrestled crazily, and threw fake punches until finally defeated by Ted/Jesus.

Now that we had everyone's attention, a few people from the team got up to preach and share testimonies. Afterwards, we invited people forward for prayer. One man needed healing in his eyes — one eye completely blind and the other on its way.

My teammates prayed, and after claiming healing three times, the blind eye began to open. The man could follow Christian's hand as he moved it and see perfectly out of the other eye! Between this miraculous testimony and the luchador skit, we declared the afternoon a success.

The next morning, we went door to door again, inviting people to another service, this time at a church in Actopan. As we visited home after home, the monotony started to wear me out. However, just as I was tempted to disengage, my heart connected with people we visited, the flatness faded, and I came back alive. That morning, we encountered a sweet, elderly gentleman who invited us into his home. His wife came to greet us and explained that her family was among the first Christians in the town. She said she didn't need any personal prayer or healing but asked that we pray for her young granddaughter.

A coy child smiled at our team as we approached her and asked her name and age. She shyly whispered the answers with a warm smile, and we asked if we could pray for her. Her grandmother explained that the young girl had been vomiting for three weeks. She'd already been to the doctor, but he was not able to offer any assistance. The grandmother had been praying for help, and our team arrived at her door. We laid hands on the granddaughter and prayed for miraculous healing in her body. We couldn't tell if anything had changed but left in faith.

Later that evening, I saw the grandparents at the church service. The grandmother was crying and said that her granddaughter had been healed. I gave her a big hug, praising God and sharing a joy that didn't require any real language skills. Meanwhile, one of the local women had asked our burly, young Taylor to accompany her to a neighborhood home to bring a teenager she knew to church. The woman said this teen desperately needed to attend the service but would not come by his own will. She hoped Taylor would assist her in physically forcing him into the church building. Not sure quite what to do, Taylor escorted the woman to the teen's home. Fortunately, with just one look at Taylor's sturdy build, the boy panicked and quickly agreed to come to church without anyone touching him.

After we preached that evening, we prayed for many people in the congregation, and Taylor approached the teenage boy. Taylor found out that he had been dealing with drug and alcohol addiction and declared freedom over his life. The teen dropped to the floor, crying and coughing. As Taylor continued praying, the boy started puking up slime. This was the first time I'd seen someone delivered from demons that physically manifested in such a graphic way — but this would certainly not be the last. Though it was a little messy on the outside, the deliverance was actually a wonderful thing. At a little church service in Actopan, Mexico, that local teenage boy found freedom.

The next morning, we drove to Chachalacas, a fun beach town near the city of Vera Cruz. We'd been ministering and traveling for about a month with minimal rest, and our leaders decided it would be wise to take a break for a few days. We pulled up to an oceanside campsite and parked just feet from the water. We set up the pop-ups and tents so close to the waves that we fell asleep to their soothing rhythms. For the next few days, I took morning runs on the sand, played in the surf, and ate delicious Mexican cuisine.

One afternoon, Jesse rented three quads (all-terrain vehicles) for the team to use. Just north of our campsite stood huge sand dunes perfect for quading. I'd never ridden a quad before and was scared to drive, so Breck offered me a ride as his passenger. I found myself simultaneously laughing, gasping, and screaming right into Breck's poor ear as he drove recklessly around the dunes. As we finished the ride, I looked at the emerging sunset creating a perfect backdrop against the waves. I was filled with appreciation, joy, laughter, and awe. I had always believed it was important to work hard and pour myself into ministry. But in that moment, I remembered it was equally important to play, to laugh, to smile, and to simply rest in the beauty of God's creation.

A few days of rest fueled us for our next adventure, and we headed to the city of Teposcolula ready to work. From there, the team temporarily split, one group driving onward to minister in Oaxaca, the rest of us staying behind in Teposcolula to work with a local pastor. The pastor had a peculiar list of odds and ends for us, not one related to another. The first task entailed cleaning up a nearby church "building," which was really nothing more than four cement walls. The walls contained openings for windows but no glass to fill them. Open sky took the place of a sturdy roof. The meager structure was surrounded by tall grass and aggressive weeds. The pastor laid down three machetes and told us to clear out the entire area around the church. We took turns hacking at the weeds. I'd never used a machete before and found it quite satisfying to swing the large knife into the plants with all my strength. I was just getting the hang of it when the pastor abruptly told us it was time to move on.

He now drove us to yet another church and asked only Jesse to get out of the car. The pastor needed to change a light bulb in this second church, and since Jesse was almost seven feet tall, he was the perfect size to reach it. The rest of us waited, all agreeing that our day was unfolding into a very random one but deciding to just roll with it and not ask questions.

Next, we drove to a woman's farm in a more isolated area of town. She greeted us with smiles, delicious rice, and warm soup. We had been told we would be helping harvest crops, but on the contrary, the woman instructed us to simply sit in her living room and pray with her. The woman's fourteen-year-old granddaughter emerged from another area of the house, and we quickly realized that she had several health limitations. The girl had some debilitating mental disabilities and was deaf as well. We began to pray as a team and asked God to heal this young teenager.

As we prayed, I saw a picture of the Holy Spirit trying to break through a barrier and enter the room. *However, something was blocking Him.* I hesitated to share this vision with the team, but the more I tried to push the feeling aside, the more I felt I needed to share. I finally told the others, and they began to ask the grandmother questions in an attempt to figure out more. After some discussion, the grandmother admitted that the family had gone to a witchdoctor in the past to try to cure the young girl.

"Well, there's your barrier," Tanya declared.

We spoke to the woman more about witchcraft and explained that soliciting Satan to cure your family invites demons into your life. We told her that if she wanted the Holy Spirit to heal her granddaughter, she needed to break all ties with the devil. The woman agreed and willingly fetched the medicine the witchdoctor had given her. It looked like a mixture of mulch and bird food. The grandmother said she had boiled it and made her granddaughter drink it. She realized that if she chose to accept the truth of Christ, she needed to get rid of the witchdoctor's medicine. She decided to burn it and gathered the supplies she needed to do so.

We went outside while she laid down the "medicine" and the bowl and burned both of them right before our eyes. The woman prayed a prayer of repentance without being persuaded, confessing that she had looked to demonic power to heal her granddaughter and claiming that from now on she would only call on the name of Jesus to heal. Afterwards, we prayed for her and the girl again and unfortunately saw no physical evidence of healing. However, I had a strong sense in my spirit that something powerful transpired. When I prayed for people and didn't see healing, I was often tempted to become discouraged or believe nothing was happening. Yet, despite what my eyes showed me (or didn't show me) that day, I just believed. I knew that something happened. I'm still not sure what, but God did something at that house.

That evening, the team went to a church service in a village about forty-five minutes outside Teposcolula. The church was comprised of only a handful of people, but their hearts were so big that the building felt full. Before the service started, a little girl named Diana approached me and started asking me questions. Taking the opportunity to practice my Spanish and be with children, I asked her some questions as well, and before I knew it, we were *amigas*. As the service went on, several people in the congregation broke out into childish dancing. They were prancing around, giving shouts of praise. I felt sleepily relaxed and content, but I was definitely not in the mood to dance. What I really wanted was to simply sit and soak in God's presence. But little Diana left me with no choice when she approached me and grabbed my hand. She dragged me to the front of the church and started spinning me in circles. At first, I felt a bit embarrassed, but quickly I shed my adult pride. I could only think about the sweet little girl dancing with me as I laughed and decided to act like a fool and enjoy God's bliss. A few others joined me and Diana, and pretty soon I was prancing around with a handful of Mexican children, laughing and praising God.

After the service, a few people from the church invited us over for sweet bread and coffee. Diana hopped on my back, and I ran down the street to their house while she hung on and giggled uncontrollably. I know I'll never see Diana again, but I'm so thankful for the short time we had together. In a moment of fatigue, she gave me the burst of childlike joy that I needed. She reminded me that the Lord loves people who approach Him as children.

Before long, we drove to the village where the other half of our team was ministering. Even though we'd only spent a few days apart, it was great to be reunited. Since we'd become family, we genuinely missed each other when separated. The other group reported that they'd had an amazing time ministering in villages and sharing God's healing. One day, they'd gone into a village with a local pastor who had only been saved for three years. He made up for lack of experience with an incredibly genuine and humble heart. The team ministered in his village for hours, and every time they were about to leave, the sweet pastor found someone else to pray for. Finally, the team prayed for the pastor himself. He suffered from partial deafness and desired to regain his hearing. As my teammates prayed, the pastor was completely healed. He exclaimed, "It's amazing!" as he started crying and hugging everyone on the team, blown away by God's love and power.

Finalmente, our time in Mexico was coming to an end. We were already way behind schedule due to spending a few extra weeks in Mexico than originally planned. Therefore, Jesse, Tanya, and Christian discussed the possibility of cutting Belize out of our itinerary. We could save some time and head directly to Guatemala rather than taking the circuitous route from Mexico to Belize and then Guatemala. In addition, our contact in Belize had fallen through, so we had no solid plans or place to stay. However, a few people from the team felt strongly that we needed to go to Belize. As they expressed their opinion, everyone else quickly agreed that it wasn't right to pass the small nation by.

United in our decision, we began the journey to Belize, knowing lots of extra driving was ahead of us. We planned on driving for two full days, stopping at a border town for a night, then entering Belize the next morning. Unfortunately, our plans quickly changed when the transmission seal on New Wine, the smaller RV, blew after driving for less than a hundred miles. Though we were disappointed by the roadblock, we also realized that God had protected us. Previous to the seal breaking, we had been winding around treacherous mountain roads, and the transmission stayed intact that whole time. If the transmission had had problems in the mountains, we would have been in serious trouble. Yet, the very moment that we pulled over by a mechanic and gas station, all the transmission fluid leaked, and New Wine stopped working. It wouldn't even turn on. We praised God for getting us to a safe place with a mechanic.

Unfortunately, the mechanic in this remote mountain village didn't happen to have the auto part we needed and had to drive back to Oaxaca, where we'd just come from, to get it. We were stranded for the next two nights in this village — a cold, rainy, and dismal place with absolutely nothing to do but hide from the weather. We anxiously waited for the vehicle to be fixed, eager to get back on the road to Belize.

When we resumed our travels, we were warned of dangerous, flooded roads and severe storms. We prepared ourselves for the worst; yet as we drove, we remained under a cover of sunshine. The girls driving in Overflow (myself included) prayed and prayed for dry roads and clear skies. At two points, we saw a couple of rain clouds creeping over us. Instead of worrying that the storm was approaching, we took authority over the weather and prayed that we would have safe skies. Both times, as soon as we prayed, the clouds went away, and sun appeared.

After a smooth journey, we arrived around midnight at a border town in Mexico. We got rooms at a little hotel, finding it strange that this was really our last night in Mexico. Finishing our first country together seemed a significant milestone, though there was much land to traverse ahead of us. It was hard to believe we were just miles away from an entirely different culture and a very different region to pioneer. I saw God moving in remarkable power and love in Mexico, but that was only the beginning.

Chapter Two

BELIZE: God's Diamonds

The next morning, we drove to the border and walked to the departure line, eager to get stamped out of Mexico and explore a new country. The corrupt border officials forced us each to pay a fee of twenty dollars that went straight into their pockets. They refused our request for receipts and didn't even bother trying to hide the fact that they were stealing from us. Unfortunately, we were left with no choice but to hand over the cash if we wanted to be released from the country. After paying and completing the inspection of our vehicles, we crossed into Belize, irritated with the Mexican government but relieved to not be dealing with it any longer.

Immediately, it felt like we were in a totally different world. We were greeted by Rastafarian-looking men who cheerfully announced, "Smile. You're not in Mexico anymore." The locals spoke fluent English in addition to Spanish and crooned with thick Caribbean accents. It felt like we had been teleported out of Latin America and dropped off on an island.

We were so surprised that we forgot we had no plan or place to stay.

We asked around and were directed to an RV park in a small town called Corozal, just miles from the border. We drove there and set up camp for the night. Unfortunately, maintenance was being done at the park, so there were no bathrooms or showers available. Jesse told us we needed to get used to this kind of thing and didn't hesitate to park us there. Though normally not terribly bothered by grim living circumstances, this campsite's lack of bathrooms resulted in a personal test of humility that I will never forget.

One morning, I woke up early and needed a toilet — badly. Jesse and Tanya told the team we could use Open Heaven's dinky toilet if need be; but they were still sleeping inside, and it was way too early to wake them up. I had no problem going to the bathroom outside, but we were located in a wide-open field. The only way to hide myself was to go deep into a woodsy area full of snakes. *Ugh,* I thought to myself. *Why do I always end up in these kinds of situations?*

I tucked a roll of toilet paper under my arm, stumbled around in my pajamas, and wandered away from the tents and campers in an attempt to find a place to hide and go to the bathroom in peace. My choices were the open field or the middle of snake territory. I tried to step towards the snake bushes and immediately started getting eaten alive by aggressive bugs. *Forget it,* I told myself. *I'm just going right here in the field. I don't know what else to do.* Just as I squatted down, a pickup truck full of Belizean men drove by and started honking and screaming at me. PLAN ABORTED. *Dang it,* I thought. *I really have no choice but to go into the snake bushes, or else I'm going to put my modest missionary status in serious jeopardy.* I headed into the bushes and was again interrupted. A man who worked at a restaurant across the street saw me and began to wave frantically and motion me towards him.

Seriously? I wondered. *How has this become my life? What does a girl have to do to go to the bathroom in peace around here?*

"Don't go in there! Nooo!" the man yelled, as he continued to wave me in his direction.

Frustrated, I walked towards the man across the street to listen to what he was saying. "There are snakes in those bushes," he warned me. "Never go inside there! Come and use the bathroom in the restaurant."

I thanked him for his concern and crossed the street to get to the restaurant, gratefully accepting his toilet offer. Afterwards, I humbly walked down the road back to our campsite, still in my pajamas, hair a mess, toilet paper roll tucked under my arm.

A few weeks prior, I'd been a California girl with a nice apartment, good job, and laid-back lifestyle. But that girl was long gone. My definition of luxury had become using a toilet without men watching or snakes biting me. My definition of home had become the current location of my sleeping bag. My definition of family had become people I'd only known for a few weeks.

Fortunately, that family kept me smiling in the midst of humbling circumstances and reminded me to be thankful for whatever was thrown at me. Shortly after arriving in Belize, we were blessed with a new family member, the perpetually inebriated Victor. He had served as staff at my mission school in Mozambique, and I have fond memories of him singing Jake Hamilton songs while getting clobbered by the presence of the Holy Spirit. Victor was so in love with Jesus and felt God's tangible presence so intensely that he looked like he was in a drunken stupor about ninety-five percent of the time. I'd never seen anyone in such a constant state of elation. It was fascinating. I was excited to have Victor join us, though his time with the team would be short. He was engaged to a beautiful girl back home and would only stay with us for a couple of months before returning to the States to be with her.

We gladly welcomed Victor and met as a group to pray together about our plan (a very loose term) for our time in Belize. We hoped to go into the town square and connect with some locals who would be willing to take us into nearby villages to minister. Since we had no agenda, we were all completely open to what God would arrange. Rowan said he'd been praying that God would give us diamonds. We'd heard stories of literal gems falling from heaven, but as Gillian prayed into that, she felt that the "diamonds" he was praying about were people — God's treasures. She felt our mission in Belize was to go and seek these "diamonds."

After our meeting, Breck, Moose, and Taylor went off to find a place to eat in town. As they walked around, a local guy approached them and offered them weed. They declined his offer, and yet another man approached them. "Do you smoke ganja?" he inquired.

The guys said they didn't.

"Do you eat it?" he pried.

They said "no" and kept walking. They finally found a place to eat and sat down at a table. A different group of missionaries, decked out in expensive suits, approached them and struck up a conversation. The Belizean who had asked about eating weed reappeared and sat down with them as well. "I don't know why, but I felt like I was supposed to follow you," he explained, as the well-dressed missionaries disappeared.

The guys began to chat with the Belizean. As they talked about life, they discovered that this man, Godfrey, had recently turned his back on a life of drug abuse and was searching for people to help him. He had struggled with crack, alcohol, and other drugs and had been sober for only a couple of days. "I'm tired of this life. This isn't me," he went on. "I want to stop."

Knowing that the Holy Spirit was the best deliverer, the guys told Godfrey about the necessity of God's guidance. They also gave Godfrey some food and prayed for him, breaking off the chains of addiction and oppression. Afterwards, the boys told Godfrey that they would meet him at the town square in the evening and bring him some clothes. Godfrey walked away feeling encouraged, declaring that his load had been lightened.

Later that evening, a group of us headed to the town square to "seek God's diamonds." Quickly, a group of people gathered around us foreigners and initiated conversations with us. Rose laughed to herself as she noticed the design on one of the Belizean's hats. "Look at his cap," she whispered to me. As I glanced over, I saw a large picture of a diamond on his hat. Surely, we had found the first of God's treasures in Belize.

Godfrey arrived and approached the group as well, recognizing Moose from earlier in the day. He talked about how much the guys had encouraged him and how he truly wanted to be better and do better. "I feel lighter, like something was lifted off of me," he smiled. "I was going down a real bumpy road. But that's not me. That's not Godfrey. I can do better. I can be better." He offered to take us around Corozal, the local connection we had been praying about earlier. Godfrey said he had been praying for an angel to change his life and that we were the answer to his prayers. And we had been praying for God's diamonds in Belize, so Godfrey was also the answer to our prayers.

The following day, we went to a nearby village with Godfrey as well as the Corozal hospital. There was a woman who had drunk bad water that had basically caused the same effect as poison. She was so sick and weak that she could do nothing but lie in bed. One of the girls from our team told the ill woman and Godfrey that Jesus had the power to heal, and they prayed for the woman together. Immediately, she sat right up in bed and exclaimed that she had been healed! She had gone from death to life in a matter of seconds. Godfrey had never seen God heal someone before and was blown away to witness it firsthand.

After a few days in Corozal, we felt ready to move on to another town. However, we didn't want to leave Godfrey behind. We decided to invite him to join our team for the remainder of our time in Belize. Relieved to have the support of other believers, he gladly agreed to accompany us. He said he wanted a fresh start, and if he could find work or housing away from Corozal, it would make his transformation easier. We adopted Godfrey into our family, encouraged him to stay clean, and said we'd do whatever we could to get him back on his feet.

We opted to drive to Dangriga, an area right on the coast, full of Caribbean flavor and home to the native Garifuna people. When we arrived, Godfrey said he wanted to be baptized in the Caribbean Sea. We excitedly walked down to the ocean, and five people from the team waded into the water with Godfrey and baptized him. As he was getting baptized, a local man named Kareem struck up a conversation with Ben on shore and expressed interest in being baptized as well. Ben explained more about the purpose and free gift of baptism and offered to go into the water with Kareem. Without hesitation, Kareem stripped down to his boxers, jumped in the ocean, and was baptized in the name of the Father, Son, and Holy Spirit.

The rest of our time in Belize was pretty slow-paced. Since we didn't have any organized ministry, we mostly hung out with Godfrey and other locals who crossed paths with us. We met a Dangriga local named Charlie who had a list of people in his community who needed prayer. He escorted us from house to house, and we interceded for his friends. The first man we prayed for suffered from diabetes. The disease had stolen his sight and also resulted in a double leg amputation. As we prayed for him and spoke destiny over his life, I saw tears flowing from his blind eyes. Roberta shared a testimony about her own father who had lost his vision and ability to walk in his old age as well. She explained that during this stage of his life, God showed him a creative business idea that brought him prosperity and hope despite his physical condition. Roberta encouraged the Dangriga man that his life had not ended but was just beginning. I could see hope rising in the man and felt tears drip down my own cheeks as I watched this precious man receive a touch from God. Afterwards, we prayed for another diabetic who had lost her legs and some of her ability to hear. Yet, when she spoke to us, she declared, "God is good and has provided for me." Despite all she had suffered, she knew she had everything she could ever need.

Perhaps my favorite house visit was to the home of an ornery old woman named Mrs. Dimple. Though she was elderly and wheelchair bound, she was as sassy as a teenage girl. We asked if we could pray for her, and after she agreed, we prayed silently to ask the Lord what He wanted to say to her. As we laid hands in silence, she barked, "Well, are you going to share with me or what?" We giggled at her abruptness, and Gillian bravely spoke up. "Mrs. Dimple, I really feel like God has given you a prophetic voice. You know the truth, and you just have to speak it. Sometimes people don't like it, because you just can't hold it in. But you have a gift."

"Oh yeah," she agreed. "I speak ma mind and summa dem people don't like it. People, dey come by and tell me rubbish, so I tell dem not to come back. I don't want dem gossipers in ma house."

It was clear she wasn't concerned about what anyone thought except for God. It seemed she didn't even want friends if there was a chance that their conversations would pollute her mind. Mrs. Dimple didn't put up with much, and though taken aback by her blunt demeanor, I appreciated her confidence and conviction. We encouraged her to continue speaking the truth and to use the prophetic voice God had given her. As we prayed for her and others, Godfrey ministered alongside us. He was part of our family now, and we needed his prayers just as much as we needed the prayers of anyone else on the team. I was glad that Mrs. Dimple displayed such bold faith, reminding Godfrey he didn't need to be a foreign missionary to be close to God. He saw a great example of strength and self-assurance in Belizean Mrs. Dimple, and she confirmed that Godfrey could walk in the same conviction.

The following day, we traveled to a village called Punta Gorda. Known as PG by the locals, this area was the quintessence of laid-back Caribbean life. Upon our arrival to PG, we pulled up to a little restaurant on the side of the road in search of some lunch. We struck up a conversation with the owner, John, a fifty-something-year-old Belizean with gray dreadlocks down to his waist. Though a PG native, John had lived in the States for several years and later returned to Belize after missing the slow-paced Caribbean culture. I noticed the teardrop tattoos on his face, recognizing this common gang marking that signified murder. When he alluded to his former days of being "a bad boy" in the U.S., I knew exactly what he was talking about. Each teardrop represented a person he'd killed.

Yet, John had changed his life and was searching to find truth. He had many questions about Christ, so I shared what I believed about Him. John shared his beliefs with me as well, including the theory that when a person dies, he or she is immediately implanted into a woman's womb and reborn. Though I felt I could go in circles all day discussing such ideas, I enjoyed the conversation and prayed that seeds of truth would grow into something later.

While I was conversing with John, Elizabeth and Godfrey bumped into another local guy who began to pour out his heart to them. He wrestled with an alcohol addiction, which you could smell on his breath from ten feet away. The man claimed he wanted freedom and new hope, so Elizabeth shared the gospel with him. She explained that Christ had the power to break chains of addiction, and Godfrey was walking proof. Godfrey shared his testimony of getting clean and gaining freedom through the love of God. The man said he wanted to accept Jesus and be baptized as a symbol of his transformation. Luckily, the ocean was only about thirty feet from the restaurant, so an ocean baptism was easily arranged. Godfrey said he wanted to be the one to baptize the man. He'd been baptized just one day prior and was already baptizing another! It was amazing to see Godfrey share his testimony and impart hope to this man as he believed for the same healing in this stranger's life that he had just received in his.

I loved these divine appointments and was inspired by the transformation in Godfrey's life that was now pouring into other people. However, I still felt like we could be doing more. Our pace was unhurried and relaxed, and it felt odd after such a hectic schedule in Mexico. After running so hard and fast for many weeks, I had trouble slowing down to this leisurely Caribbean tempo. I felt a pressure to *do* more and honestly wondered, "Are we accomplishing enough? Are we spending enough hours doing ministry?"

But then I realized that our ministry was simply hanging out with Godfrey. Whether we were going to different houses to pray for people or just sitting around telling jokes, we were showing this man love. He was hanging out with our team instead of hanging out with his old addict friends who wouldn't be able to support him during his transition off of drugs. God's love is so lavish that it was worth it to Him to send twenty-something people to Belize (a two-day journey out of our way) just to hang out with a guy and give him the encouragement he needed to push through his first few days of sobriety and not have to do it alone. Our God is the God who said he would leave ninety-nine sheep to find the *one* that got left behind. He is not so concerned with *doing*; He's concerned with *loving*.

And our story with Godfrey doesn't end there. Our last day in Belize, we drove to a small town near the border of Guatemala and camped there for the evening. That day happened to be Natalie's twenty-first birthday. Liz had been praying that somehow we'd be able to find a cake in this small town (which seemed somewhat unlikely when we drove in). Personally, I wasn't concerned about a cake. All I could think about was finding a connection for Godfrey before we left. The next day we would drive to Guatemala, and he would stay behind in Belize. He didn't want to go back to the town of Corozal, fearing he would stumble into temptation if he was around his previous bad influences. But how could we just leave Godfrey in this unfamiliar town without a single friend? We could pay for a few nights in a motel or something, but then what would he do?

While I was sitting around worrying, Liz decided to venture into the town to find a birthday cake. At first, I blindly couldn't understand why this was her priority. But Liz felt God's heart for Natalie and insisted that God loved His children and cared about even the little things like a birthday cake for His daughter's twenty-first birthday. As Liz traveled into town praying, she noticed a man riding a bike who happened to be selling pieces of cake from his bike basket. Liz asked him if he could make a big cake for twenty-something people right away. The cake man looked pretty surprised but agreed to do it. Liz returned back to where we were camping, grinning from ear to ear. She said God had answered her prayer and provided a divine appointment. She invited me and a few others to go back into the town later to pick up the cake.

Late that afternoon, Liz, Godfrey, Christian, Rose, and I went to pick up the finished cake. Liz had written down the cake man's phone number, so we went to a pay phone and asked the cake man to come meet us. Moments later, he appeared on his bike and told us to follow him back to his house. We drove down a very bumpy road while he led us on his bike. He allowed us to come inside while his wife finished putting the frosting on the cake. As we spoke to her, we found out that she got up every morning at one o'clock and began working. She baked for hours; then her husband began to deliver the baked goods on his bike once daylight hit. Meanwhile, she was busy raising nine children and running her home. She also mentioned that she was a Christian and liked to do things with the women in her church. I was flabbergasted that she ever had any time to do so. Liz explained that we were Christians as well and that she had been praying for a birthday cake for one of our teammates. As Liz told the woman that she was an answer to her prayers, the woman got teary-eyed. Clearly, making cakes was more than just a business for her. This woman loved serving, loved her family, and loved the Lord.

Meanwhile, Godfrey, Christian, and the cake man were talking outside. Godfrey explained his situation and asked the man about housing options in the area. Turns out, the cake man was a former drug addict who had been clean for seven years. *And* his brother happened to be in the housing market, so he had some connections for Godfrey. Christian decided to pay for one month's rent for Godfrey and got him situated before we crossed into Guatemala.

By the following morning, Godfrey had a free place to stay for the next month as well as a Christian family to connect with. And Natalie, our beautiful birthday girl, had a delicious cake. Liz's prayers were answered, my prayers were answered, Godfrey's prayers were answered, and the cake family was touched by it all. I was amazed at how oddly God weaved everything together — so perfectly, right at the last moment. And while I had been wondering, "Am I *doing* enough?" Liz showed me that we can take time to slow down and care about things like a birthday cake. When we are praying about even the little things, God works them into a plan that is much bigger than what we can construct in our own strength or imagination.

Chapter Three

GUATEMALA: Power of the Blood

Godfrey certainly was one of God's diamonds, our greatest treasure yet. Though we wished he could continue traveling with our team, he had no passport, and it was time for us to cross into Guatemala. Godfrey accompanied the team to the border where we reluctantly said goodbye and wished him the best. We promised to keep in touch and encouraged Godfrey to chase his dreams of getting a stable job, becoming part of a church, and starting a fresh life. We tearfully sent Godfrey on public transportation back to the village he would now call home. (Fortunately, weeks later we found out Godfrey had already acquired a new job and was back on his feet. Several of us kept in touch with him, and he reported positive changes.)

As we departed from Belize, Godfrey warned us to be careful during our time in Guatemala. He said the danger in this country was increasing, and people were regularly shot for simple items like cell phones and cameras. We promised Godfrey we would proceed with caution but also explained that part of our mission was to go to dark places where others were not willing to go. I appreciated Godfrey's concern for our safety, but the thought of leaving him alone in Belize seemed far more frightening. Both sides had to take a leap of faith as we separated. Godfrey trusted that God would protect us in Guatemala, and our team believed in faith that God would provide for Godfrey.

Our team spent hours completing paperwork at the border and planned to only drive about one and a half hours from that point before calling it a day. Our goal destination was an area called Tikal, the location of the largest preserved Mayan city in Latin America with the highest ancient Mayan temples in Central America. Yet, shortly into our drive, Shekinah stopped suddenly in the middle of the road and wouldn't move an inch. We'd had many delays due to vehicles throughout our time in Mexico, but the Durango had never caused a single problem.

After a bit of investigation, we were shocked to find that the car's transmission was completely shot. We towed Shekinah to a mechanic and continued on to Tikal with the remaining four vehicles to camp for the evening. The mechanic said he'd call us with any vital updates. We awaited his phone call, hoping it would be possible to quickly and cheaply replace the transmission. Unfortunately, we instead received the disappointing news that the auto part we needed was not available anywhere in Guatemala. The mechanic said we would either have to ship a new part from the United States or go back into Belize to buy the part ourselves. Christian and Jesse kindly volunteered to travel back to Belize after getting the team settled in Tikal.

We'd heard rumors of an RV park in Tikal, not far from the ancient ruins. Shortly after dropping off the Durango, we found the site and parked our cars in a field of long, itchy grass. The second we stepped out of our vehicles, horrid insects began their attack, feasting on our skin as we unsuccessfully attempted to swat them away. I desperately itched at my skin, feeling slightly panicked at the thought of trying to sleep here. My teammates noticed posted signs that warned of several native animals that could be found slithering through the grass. This did not help my unease. When a local advised us to keep our eye on Zoe because of the jaguars, we'd had enough. We got back in the cars and vowed to find a better, safer place to sleep.

We drove back in the direction from which we'd come. The other RV parks that had been recommended to us apparently no longer existed. We attempted to fit our vehicles in front of a tiny motel's lawn, but after Open Heaven smashed the motel's fence, we decided this was not the wisest idea. We drove aimlessly for a while, unsure of where to go. Finally, we noticed a lake with a large dirt field in front of it that appeared unoccupied. We parked the vehicles and set up camp, hoping for the best. We slept on the field for a couple of nights, creatively finding places to go to the bathroom and adopting the lake as our shower. The daylight revealed the beauty of the lake's crystal clear water, but the evenings felt endless. In the nightly two-minute process of brushing my teeth, I encountered wild horses, stray dogs, mad roosters, tarantulas, and swarms of mosquitoes. The insects attacked so violently that I seriously wished I could rip my skin off. I was fairly certain that the bugs in Central America had bred with dinosaurs at some point to create this horrific mutant bug species. Every time I tried to fall asleep, I dozed off for a few hours, then woke up to the burning itch of bites covering my body. My entire team looked like they'd been suffering from the chicken pox for a month.

After a couple of nights, the police caught wind of our makeshift campsite and asked us to relocate. They said it wasn't safe to stay at this field, and we needed to find a new place to call home. Jesse made arrangements with a hotel just down the street that offered to let us camp in their backyard and use their bathrooms. We could stay as long as we needed to wait for Shekinah to be fixed.

Jesse and Christian left us at the hotel and traveled back to Belize to purchase a new transmission, only to be told the part was not available anywhere in Belize. This left us with only one option — ordering a new transmission from the U.S. Not only would this cost a great deal of money, but it would eat up quite a bit of time. We had people waiting to meet up with the team in Nicaragua, and this delay could push us back several weeks. As we explained our dilemma to the mechanic, he volunteered to venture into Guatemala City, several hours away, and look for the part. Though he'd originally claimed a fitting transmission was not available anywhere in the country, as soon as he realized he might lose our business, he suddenly decided Guatemala might have spare parts after all. We remained in Tikal, waiting for the mechanic's call and hoping for a rapid repair.

We ended up stranded in Tikal for quite some time, waiting for Shekinah with no ministry contacts in the area. Several of us wanted to do *something* but felt a bit lost. Though this was a great opportunity for God's freedom to flow, I wasn't used to such a lack of structure and didn't really know where to begin. Every time I tried to simply relax and rest in God's presence, a swarm of insects began to feast on my legs and distract me. I clawed at my skin, legs bleeding and pulsing with an itchy, burning sensation. I wanted to escape the discomfort but had nowhere to go. The thought of being stuck here until Shekinah was fixed horrified me. I wondered what good God could possibly create from this situation.

Our team met each day to worship, spend time in God's presence, and intentionally wait on God's voice to hear His plan for Guatemala. In Mexico, we had worked tirelessly doing evangelism, whereas Belize was more laid-back and focused on discipleship. As we listened to God, we found He had something entirely different for us during our time in Guatemala. He showed us that the most powerful ministry we could be a part of in this country was intercession.

Our call to intercede for the nation of Guatemala was awakened by the country's nefarious history. The heavy darkness in the atmosphere was almost tangible. Everywhere we traveled, we encountered Mayan idols, statues of false gods, and businesses named after demonic creatures. We found out that the temples in Tikal had been used for performing human sacrifices for hundreds of years to satisfy their gods. Ancient Mayan games were played where the winner became a blood sacrifice. This was considered a great honor in the Mayan culture. It was not uncommon to decapitate people and throw their heads and bodies from the top of the high temples in an attempt to appease the Mayan deities.

Like many cultures and religions, the Mayans believed in an exchange of blood — the blood of their men for the blessing of their gods. In the ritual of trading, blood was the highest sacrifice. As Christians, we also believed in an exchange of blood — the blood of Christ for ours. The Mayans had perverted the gospel of truth, exchanging blood in heinous rituals instead of accepting the blood of Christ for freedom and forgiveness. Our team felt we needed to travel to the ancient Mayan temples and take back what the enemy had stolen. We would go to the holy high places and trade the truly powerful blood — the blood of Christ. We traveled to the ruins in Tikal and climbed up the highest temple we could find. Though deathly afraid of heights, I understood the importance of this blood exchange and forced myself to get to the top. Once we'd all completed the climb, we brought out the elements to take communion. Unable to purchase normal bread and wine, we substituted corn tortillas and some orange Gatorade. It was the closest we could find in our little Guatemalan village, but we figured it wasn't the type of bread or wine that mattered so much as the heart behind what was happening.

As we took the "bread and wine," we made a symbolic blood exchange I hadn't experienced before. In the Old Testament, only the high priests were allowed to go into the "Holy of Holies" in the tabernacle. There was a veil separating the people from God, and common people could not enter into His presence. Yet, when Jesus died for us, the Bible says that the veil was broken. Now anyone can come into the Lord's mighty presence. In addition, Revelation mentions a "sea of glass" that is before the throne of God in heaven. Because Jesus exchanged His blood so that we do not have to die, we are able to go into those heavenly places and exchange His blood for heavenly things. The veil is broken, so we can access God's presence. We can go through the veil or enter the sea of glass before the throne of God and exchange the blood of Jesus for all the things He died for — our salvation, love, healing, freedom, restoration, etc. (See Matthew 27:51, Hebrews 9, 10:19, and Revelation 4:6.)

In addition, we symbolically "stepped onto the sea of glass" or "stepped through the veil" to be in God's presence and to pray for His gifts from heaven. We exchanged the blood of Christ for the salvation of His people. We exchanged the blood of Christ for God's presence in Guatemala. We exchanged the blood of Christ for the freedom of the Guatemalan people. We exchanged the blood of Christ for righteousness. We exchanged the blood of Christ for peace in the nation. We exchanged the blood of Christ for the truth of the gospel to reign over Guatemala and trump the heinous rituals of its history. As we prayed, we cancelled the perverse blood sacrifices made through Mayan rituals, declaring truth over Guatemala. Though very different than the more tangible ministry to which I was accustomed, I realized that this blood exchange had a powerful effect in the spiritual realm.

Praying on the Mayan ruins carried huge significance for our team and marked our time in Guatemala. However, one of my teammates unfortunately experienced a tragedy that tarnished her memories of this country. While in Tikal, Dianne, one of our beautiful team mamas, received devastating news from back home. Her daughter-in-law, Riahnnon, and her grandson were in Costa Rica and had gone for a swim at a beach with bad rip currents. They both began to struggle in the water, and a local surfer was able to rescue only the six-year-old grandson. Devastatingly, Riahnnon's body was nowhere to be found. Dianne's son, who was in the States when this happened, immediately got on a plane to Costa Rica. Dianne booked a flight to Costa Rica as well. Liz volunteered to accompany her on the journey to be an emotional and physical support. The news was so sudden and unexpected that it hardly seemed real.

Days later, we got an email from Liz stating that Riahnnon's body had been found, and her death was sadly confirmed. Dianne decided to take some time to grieve with her family. When Liz flew back to the team in Tikal, Dianne returned to the States with her son and grandson for a while, planning to rejoin the team in South America.

Meanwhile, we finally got a phone call from the mechanic and found out that he had located the transmission we needed in Guatemala City after all. Once he installed the new transmission, we could finally move on. In the meantime, we decided to minister in the village where we were camping. I sat down with a group of the girls on my team and brainstormed different activities for the women and children in the village. While discussing ideas, Melissa joked about making balloon animals and doing a juggling act for the children. We teased her that she would need a clown for her plan, because it sounded like a circus performance. Laughing, we continued brainstorming and listed several alternative ideas.

However, much to our surprise, just a few hours later, a professional Guatemalan clown randomly appeared at the hotel where we'd set up camp. He approached some of the women on the team and said he felt like he was supposed to come to the hotel. I couldn't believe it. It was like God had heard our request for balloon animals, and a clown showed up at our doorstep. This was really weird. The clown informed us that he had been ostracized by his church for choosing this lifestyle to make money. We told him that in our church he was always welcome. We knew his talent could be an asset for ministry, and we invited him to partner with us to help organize a children's program.

Maria and I decided to round up the children from the village and tell them to meet up at a park near our hotel at 2:30 in the afternoon. In America, running a children's event could have taken weeks of advertising, but in a little village, it only took an hour or two. As Maria and I walked around, we greeted any children we saw and told them about the program. As we moved from house to house, children flocked around us and followed us, helping to announce the program and guiding us to the best houses to invite more children. After an hour or so, we had informed half the village about the event.

I headed over to the park with a couple of the girls and saw that many of the children had already gathered. The Guatemalan clown had not yet arrived, so we taught the kids a new game and played as we waited. Mid-game, the clown appeared out of nowhere on a unicycle. The following forty-five minutes were nonstop entertainment and laughter. This guy was good. He loved his job, and the children loved his tricks. After performing, he shared the gospel and asked which children wanted to accept Christ as their Savior. Though this was one of the oddest evangelism methods I'd seen, the clown was no doubt a blessing to these children. It seemed a crime that his church had ostracized him for fitting an untraditional mold. We tried to affirm him and encourage him to continue to use his skills to bless others and advance the kingdom of God.

Every day had its own bizarre ministry opportunity, but when car repairs were done and Christian finally picked up Shekinah, I must admit I was ready to move on. Our next destination was an orphanage in Chimaltenango, a city several hours away. We heard it was cold there at night, which meant a temporary refuge from the bugs. We all hoped the new transmission would get us to Chimaltenango without problems, but as we set off, Christian noticed the Durango was making a funny noise. We continued driving nonetheless, but soon every gear except first stopped working. Consequently, we could either backtrack to the mechanic who clearly didn't know how to repair a car or carry on to Chimaltenango in first gear. We opted to continue driving in first gear, traveling at snail's pace and stopping quite frequently to give Shekinah a break. At around 5 p.m., feeling defeated, we decided to stop for the night at an RV park. We agreed to pray individually about what to do about the Durango and recongregate in the morning. Our first option was to keep driving in first gear with an unpredictable transmission in the hopes of finding a better mechanic in Chimaltenango. Or, we could cut our losses early, ditch the Durango, and carry on in the remaining four vehicles.

We woke up the next morning and met as a group to discuss our plan of action. We unanimously agreed to move on with Shekinah, even if that meant crawling at thirty miles per hour to Chimaltenango. Around 10 a.m., our caravan of now slow and cautious vehicles exited the RV park, praying for a safe journey to the orphanage. We stopped occasionally to let the Durango cool down, but overall it seemed to be holding up fairly well. Around three in the afternoon, those of us riding in Overflow noticed that something had gone awry with the pop-up camper we were hauling. We pulled over to the side of the road to find that one of the tires on the camper had exploded and fallen off completely. When we went to scout out the damage, we found nothing left but the metal rim. Within ten minutes, the guys had put on a spare tire, and we were back on our way.

A couple of hours later, we reached a primitive village where the once-paved roads became a labyrinth of dirt trails. The narrow "streets" were certainly not meant for our large vehicles, and as we drove through, we quickly became the town spectacle. Though we were normally the ones taking pictures of our surroundings, I actually saw a Guatemalan whip out his camera and snap a shot of our convoy. Once we'd reached a quieter section of the village, we pulled over and asked for directions towards Chimaltenango. The locals directed us to a mountain in the distance, claiming the next town wasn't very far. We thanked them for their help and continued down the dusty roads as bystanders continued to gape, smile, and wave.

For a moment, Overflow (where I was riding) got stuck behind a few cows wandering down the street and blocking the road. We got separated from the other vehicles and hit a couple of forks where we were unsure of where to go. Fortunately, everyone from the village was paying attention and knew exactly where the massive procession of white people had gone. At every fork, a curious villager pointed us in the right direction. Slowly, we began to weave our way up the mountain, the roads becoming increasingly primitive. With every turn, we encountered more and more rocks, steeper climbs, and more treacherous turns. Winding our gigantic vehicles through the tiny curves of the mountain road proved progressively more difficult as we ascended.

Each car had its own set of challenges with the terrain. Shekinah putted along in first gear, miraculously making it up the roads while pulling a trailer. Open Heaven, the larger RV, tipped back and forth, its boxy shape inviting disaster. Counsel and Might, Taylor's station wagon, scraped along the roads, its bottom rubbing against protruding rocks. New Wine, the smaller RV, had problems with its brakes operating properly. And finally, at around 6:30 in the evening, just after the sky had turned pitch-black, the tire on Overflow's camper exploded *again*. The spare (and final) tire that had rescued us just three hours previously had now blown. We pulled over to remedy the latest problem, realizing that Shekinah and Open Heaven were already far ahead. Shekinah needed to keep its momentum in order to not die on the mountain, and Open Heaven was following close behind. Luckily, the guys in Counsel and Might pulled over, as did New Wine's driver. A few people looked at the camper's tire and proclaimed it dead. With seemingly no other options, Taylor ran up the mountain towards Shekinah to get a spare tire from the camper it was hauling. Along the way, several ill-tempered dogs tried to attack him, snarling at him as he made his way to the Durango.

Luckily, Taylor returned to us in one piece, but unfortunately his quest for a spare tire was futile. He reported that the remaining spare tire was on a different tread than the tire that had just blown, so the spare would be useless to us. We took another looked at the camper and realized we either needed to leave it behind on the mountain or drag it on a tireless axle, which would quickly destroy the metal. A few locals passed by and said the next town was hours away, very different information than that offered by those at the bottom of the mountain. Some of us discussed the possibility of sleeping in our vehicles and soliciting help in the morning rather than permanently ditching the trailer. That pop-up was currently the closest thing I had to a home, and I had major qualms about leaving it behind. Others decided there had to be something else we could do.

Victor and Taylor quickly accepted this breakdown as a challenge rather than viewing it as a nuisance. The guys got to work, determined to resuscitate the dead tire. The rim was bent, so they hit it with a rock to restore it to proper form. They then tied a rope around the tire, forcing it to squeeze tightly against the rim. Next, they sprayed the tire with sealant and filled it with air. And, by miracles of miracles, after some groaning, grunting, and laughing, the tire was fixed! It was now around eight o'clock, ten hours after we'd left the RV Park. We continued our drive, praying that the fixed tire would remain intact. We had no real idea how far the next village was, and not a hint of civilization was in sight.

Despite the many unknowns, we had little choice but to go forward. We desperately wanted to stop for the night and get some rest. We drove onward along the dark mountain road, praying we would find a place to sleep. Though I didn't think it was possible, the road got worse. It was not only terribly steep and muddy but also plagued by horrific gaps and severe holes. There were several spots where turning at the wrong angle would have resulted in falling off a cliff, creating a heightened sense of danger for the vehicles pulling campers.

I noticed numerous people getting out of Open Heaven and walking behind the RV during certain turns. It wasn't until later that I found out the risk of overturning was so high that Jesse had made his passengers walk these turns so that he would be the only one to fall off the cliff if the RV flipped. When his passengers *were* able to ride in Open Heaven, they experienced an earthquake effect inside. Items stored in the cabinets flew out and injured people. Roberta was bruised terribly from tumbling across the RV, and Natalie got whacked in the eye with a flying shampoo bottle.

Meanwhile, in Overflow, we decided to have a car dance party, blaring our favorite songs and laughing as we flew over bumps. As Breck drove and the girls deejayed, we embraced the situation and just had fun. Yet, things changed when we suddenly started to slide backwards. We'd hit a massive patch of mud on a steep incline and were rolling in reverse. The cliff was directly to my left, and as I looked down from my viewpoint, I realized we were inches from falling off of it. The camper was sliding down the cliff, and Overflow was struggling to not slide down with it. My laughter quickly turned to panic when I realized that if we kept rolling, we were going to plummet down the mountain. I screamed, and all of the passengers quickly exited the vehicle. Breck continued his attempt to steer, and by the grace of God, the Suburban stopped sliding before he rolled off the cliff.

However, Overflow was now stuck — very stuck. The passengers from the other vehicles pulled over and helped us push the Suburban. Despite all our manpower, the vehicle wouldn't budge. We changed strategies and unattached the pop-up trailer, then reattempted to drive Overflow further up the mountain without lugging the extra weight. Fortunately, the Suburban successfully moved forward. However, the heavy trailer still needed to be pushed up the mountain and reattached to the Suburban. Though it required much physical strength, we eventually were able to move the trailer forward and hook it back onto Overflow.

We continued on our way, now with a fuller realization of how dangerous this road was. We prayed we wouldn't slip again or slide down the mountainside. Time ticked away, and still no signs of civilization manifested. We drove onward, occasionally stopping for other mishaps. A couple of times, Counsel and Might overheated and had to cool off before we could continue. In addition, the sewage pipe on Open Heaven fell off. This large piece of metal enabled the toilet inside the camper to drain properly. Because the entire piece fell off, all the pee and poo sitting inside the pipes poured onto the ground and dripped onto a large, muddy hill, creating a waterfall of our own feces. Overflow was stuck behind the waterfall, and Breck said he was going to floor it so we didn't get stuck in the mess. He hit the gas, and our vehicle went flying up the hill of poop — luckily making it over successfully.

This chaotic rhythm of driving, stopping, dealing with messes, and then driving some more continued late into the night. After hours of setbacks, we finally arrived in a small town around 11 p.m. *Yes*, the sweet sight of civilization. Relieved to be off the mountain road, we decided to leave our cars in a parking lot and spend the night in a hotel. We spotted a rundown motel in the distance that looked perfect for us weary travelers. The only catch was getting our cars to the hotel from the main road. Unfortunately, this required turning left onto a road that suddenly dropped about a foot from the main road. Even in the larger vehicles this seemed a risky plunge, but I was convinced Taylor's station wagon didn't stand a prayer. Taylor got out of his car and accessed the situation. I watched from inside Overflow as he grabbed some rocks from the side of the road, trying to create a ramp-like structure. He looked at the rocks, his car, the street, the drop, the rocks, his car, the drop, the rocks. Suddenly, he aborted his plan and threw all the rocks aside. I wrongly assumed he'd very slowly and carefully try to make the drop in his Buick, praying that he wouldn't destroy the bottom of Counsel and Might. Yet, much to my surprise, he slammed his foot against the accelerator and went flying over the drop as his car scraped against the ground with a loud thud. I couldn't believe it. I burst into laughter, astounded by it all. Our day had been craziness upon craziness, and this was the perfect way to go out with a bang — literally.

When we entered our hotel rooms, the dilapidated beds and crusty towels fit the theme of the day perfectly. I was so tired that I didn't mind the fact that my bed seemed to have a chunk missing. I snuggled into bed, my body awkwardly contorting to the strange shape of the mattress. Gunshots sounded in the distance, and I drifted off to sleep.

I woke up the next morning still feeling groggy and unrested. Yet, there was no time to waste. We were still hours from our destination in Chimaltenango. We fueled up on breakfast and pushed ahead. Mid-afternoon, we arrived at the orphanage we'd planned to reach days ago. We were greeted by a team of foreigners who were also traveling around the world doing missions. They had been stationed at the orphanage for a month and were leaving for Honduras the following day. Though our time with this other team was short, we felt an instant connection with their hearts and spent time praying together, encouraging one another, and sharing testimonies from our travels.

Brandon, their team leader, gave us a brief orientation to the orphanage and asked us to pray faithfully for the children there. All of the kids were mentally disabled, and most of them were unable to communicate verbally. Brandon explained that upon his team's arrival to the orphanage, he immediately sensed a strong spirit of infirmity. He found out that two of the children had died very recently, one of them from a freakish flesh-eating disease. As soon as his team arrived at the orphanage, they fell ill right away. The whole team was so sick that Brandon believed there was a spiritual stronghold of infirmity in the area. Though he was ready to move on and leave the orphanage, he felt a burden for the children and asked us to intercede for them and the region as a whole.

We hung out at the orphanage for a few days, praying, helping with odd jobs around the compound, and playing with the children. Shekinah was still not working properly, so we dropped it off at a mechanic for another look and figured we would stay in Chimaltenango as long as it needed to be fixed. In the meantime, we wanted to serve and bless the children.

One morning, just as I was about to see how I could help out at the orphanage, Melissa approached a couple of the girls and said that she thought she saw lice in her hairbrush. Tanya looked through her hair and confirmed her suspicions. Frantically, everyone began to check each other's hair, and we found eggs and lice on seven heads. I recalled Brandon's insight about the spirit of infirmity and knew it was no coincidence that our team had a lice outbreak at this particular orphanage.

I walked with a few of the girls for about a mile in search of lice shampoo and fine combs. I didn't know the Spanish word for lice, but I could say "bugs" and "hair" and figured I could get my point across. I also *thought* I knew the word for comb, which apparently is very similar to the word for male genitalia. As I was trying to explain why I needed a comb for bug removal, I'm pretty sure I was actually telling some people at the pharmacy that my friends had bugs in a very unfortunate location. I wondered why they were looking at me so weirdly and later realized what I'd been saying. However, after many hand gestures and attempts at explaining our lice situation, we finally got the appropriate supplies.

We returned back to the orphanage, and I spent the next seven hours or so picking eggs out of my teammates' hair. I had been declared lice free, but after picking through everyone else's hair for a day, I woke up to find lice eggs in my own hair. The following day was full of more lice removal. The epidemic began to spread, and more people needed treatment. Some had just a handful of eggs, others hundreds, others up to the thousands. It was revolting. We spent hours pulling bugs out of hair, spraying our sleeping mats, and washing our clothes. Some people were horrified by the lice outbreak; others found it amusing. Personally, I found the painstaking process of removing almost microscopic eggs from individual pieces of hair exhausting. After many hours, I decided to take a break from bug removal and was assigned to various other tasks around the orphanage. At this point, I preferred manual labor to lice patrol.

Day after long day passed by at this infirmity-ridden orphanage, and as we checked the status of Shekinah, we discovered it was still far from being fixed. We decided we couldn't waste any more time, and that meant moving on to El Salvador without the Durango. If it ever got fixed, someone from the team would travel back to Guatemala to get the car and then drive it down to meet the rest of the team. If the mechanic gave up, we would make our journey work with only four vehicles.

Between Dianne's tragic news, the heinous bugs, the lice outbreak, and the Durango disaster, Guatemala left a bad taste in my mouth. I was ready to be in the next country and start fresh. However, even trying to exit Guatemala caused problems for our team. Unbeknownst to us, Guatemala, El Salvador, Honduras, and Nicaragua had a special union. As a foreigner, you were allowed ninety days within any of these four countries. When we entered Guatemala, we all received a "90" stamp on our passport that indicated ninety legal days within the union — that is, everyone except Ben.

We realized that one of the border officials in Guatemala had tried to get our team to pay a bribe, and when we refused, he got revenge by purposely stamping Ben's passport incorrectly. Though Ben didn't realize it at the time, as we tried to enter El Salvador, he noticed that his passport was stamped "1" instead of "90." This meant that if Ben wanted to enter El Salvador, he would have to pay a fine for each day he had illegally overstayed his time in Guatemala. We'd been in the country for quite some time, and that would be a hefty fine. As Ben tried to reason with the customs officials, he was escorted into a hidden room and separated from the team. Christian chased after him, so he wouldn't be alone. Hours passed by at the border with no sign of Ben or Christian.

Finally, Ben was released and allowed temporary access to El Salvador under the condition that he visit a government office the following day to sort out more paperwork. We'd been unjustly fined in Mexico, and now Ben had to deal with this nonsense. Third world governments were always full of surprises. And as we crossed into El Salvador, the corruption only got worse.

Chapter Four

EL SALVADOR: The Need for a Savior

Stepping into El Salvador was like walking into a crime scene. The illegal activity in this country was glaringly obvious even at the border. While standing in the passport line, Roberta pointed out a poster full of men's pictures. It was a "Most Wanted" sign — very different than the friendly tourist posters we'd seen at the other borders. Immediately, we could sense that El Salvador was far more dangerous than any of the previous countries we'd visited. This would be interesting.

After getting Ben's passport sorted, we drove to the capital of San Salvador and met up with John, a Youth With A Mission (YWAM) leader who hosted us for the next few days. John was very open about the current situation in El Salvador. He didn't skirt around issues but educated us about what was really happening there. I realized that the name El Salvador meant "The Savior," and if any country needed a savior, it was this one. In 2011, El Salvador was rated the third worst country in the world in terms of homicides, with an average of thirteen murders per day. For a country with a population smaller than

New York City, that was a lot of killings. Instead of billboards displaying "Don't drink and drive," there were signs around San Salvador that read "Don't murder." Unfortunately, the country was pretty much run by gangs, especially the notorious MS13 gang. They were known for being the most brutal and gruesome crew. Instead of killing their victims quickly, they murdered them in heinous and slow ways. They were known to set buses on fire, slaughter women and children, and torture people for their own pleasure. I got to ride with John on the way to one of our outreaches, and he told me that he'd almost been killed by a gang member himself.

Despite the grim stories, I somehow felt at ease in El Salvador. There was just something about the place that won me over. The need there was so great, and the people I met were so open to give and receive love. In this country full of gangs and murder, I oddly felt at home.

On our first day, we ran two church services for beautiful and friendly congregations. The first was at a church of maybe seven adults and ten children. What they lacked in size, they made up for in heart. I spent most of the service with the children, playing games and singing with them. In the afternoon, we headed to a second church, this one much larger. The service lasted for at least four hours. We worshipped, did a drama, preached, prayed for the sick, and then asked the Holy Spirit to touch the church body. Quickly, the church service turned into a massive dance party. People were weeping, laughing, dancing, and rejoicing. An older man I prayed for confided in me that he had lost his home and couldn't provide for his three children. His leg was injured, and this had prevented him from working. I prayed with him as he wept, overcome with compassion and sorrow. Sadly, he was not healed that evening, but I hoped a miracle was on the horizon. The sweet man stole my heart and showed me a gentle humility that starkly contrasted the stereotype of men within a country known for its murder rate. Beneath the hype and the fear, there existed a genuine love in the heart of El Salvador.

The following day, my team visited a government-run orphanage for boys ages ten to seventeen. The place looked more like a prison than an orphanage. And it felt like one. Because the orphanage was run by the government, it was a holding pen, not a ministry. On the boys' eighteenth birthdays, they were kicked out. There was no transition into the "real world." The kids were simply dumped and forced to fend for themselves. With the amount of gangs in El Salvador, I assumed most of them joined gangs to survive. It broke my heart to see such precious young boys headed towards such grim futures. It was clear that the boys didn't get much attention, and they eagerly vied for ours. We played soccer, basketball, frisbee, and football for hours. The kids were going crazy, so excited to have some people to play with. I was glad to visit for the day but sad to know that the kids needed long-term care they would probably never receive.

Later that week, we visited a drug and rehab center for men. I found a softness in the hearts of those men rather than the hardness you would have expected. As a few of my team members shared about their past addictions and the freedom they'd found in Christ, there were many nods and "amens." We prayed for the men, and they openly received. That same afternoon, we assisted the YWAM base with a homeless ministry they ran right at their doorstep. The staff set up an outdoor shower and tables, and homeless people from the community stopped by for showers, fresh sets of clothes, warm meals, and a short devotion. I had the privilege of leading the devotion and simply hanging out with the men who showed up. One of them, Nelson, spoke perfect English and told us outlandish stories from his past. Quite the comedian, he had all of us laughing. This

YWAM ministry reminded me of a homeless ministry I loved back in California. I felt so at home in that moment, just hanging out with these men, talking, and laughing. The more I traveled, the more I believed people were the same everywhere. Everyone liked to talk. Everyone liked to eat. Everyone liked to laugh. People were people.

At the end of our time in El Salvador, we sadly said goodbye to three of our team members. Christian had faithfully finished his commitment to help launch our journey, but after months of traveling with us, it was time to get back to his family. We tearfully hugged him farewell as he assured the team he would try to come visit us in Peru. Rowan and Gillian left as well, flying home to New Zealand, a painfully abrupt but crucial decision. Parting ways from our brothers and sister was traumatic. We truly loved each of the three and would miss them greatly. But we blessed them as they left, knowing the bond of the original twenty could not be broken by circumstance or distance.

Chapter Five

HONDURAS: Setting the Captives Free

After our brief stay in El Salvador, we crossed the next border into Honduras. Odd as it may sound, I felt something change as soon as we hit the border. My heart had felt a real peace in El Salvador that immediately disappeared when I entered Honduras. I didn't feel scared or physically unsafe; I just felt uncomfortable. There was something about the way the men leered at me here that churned my stomach. I had transformed from a woman into an object.

My team passed through the border and drove several hours onward, the tire on one of the pop-up campers exploding twice along the way. Apparently, this was a fun new trend for us. Finally, the axle broke as well, and we were forced to leave the camper on the side of the road. It was dark and far too late to call a mechanic. By the grace of God, we happened to break down in front of a welder's house. The welder offered to watch the pop-up for us to make sure no one broke in during the night. In addition, he agreed to weld the axle back together in the morning. Because we were so accustomed to car problems, we were thankful for such a simple solution. We drove on without the camper, Jesse planning to fetch it the next day.

Exhausted, we arrived in the city of Choluteca late that night. We pulled up to a beautiful hotel and asked if we could pay a few dollars to camp out on their lawn. Though an unthinkable request in the U.S., this seemed to be the way to get by economically in Central America. Some of the girls set up the pop-up that had survived the journey, and the rest of us pitched our tents. We walked through the hotel to use the bathroom and had a quick taste of luxury. Imagining the comfortable beds people were enjoying inside the hotel, we dejectedly returned to our tents and fell asleep on the ground.

The following day, we gained two more teammates — our permanent addition, Natalie M., and her temporarily-visiting friend, Astrid. Though born in Russia, Natalie had lived in several nations including Germany, Australia, and Mozambique. She had most recently worked with children in Africa and had an amazing ability to love those whom others normally overlooked. She spoke English, German, Russian, Portuguese, Spanish, and was working on French — great skills for a traveling team. Natalie M. was fiercely loyal, driven, and bold as a lion; but beneath her confident exterior lay a tender heart full of compassion. Her friend Astrid from Germany would travel with us just until Panama. Though a short-term team member, she quickly became a valued sister. We enjoyed her eager heart to serve and fully pour herself out during her time in Central America.

As we explored the city of Choluteca, we discovered an odd mix of poverty and modern wealth. The city center had a Wendy's and a Pizza Hut, but there were also slums just a few miles away where people lived in garbage dumps. The harsh contradiction was hard to digest. I walked around the town a few times to run errands, and those same uncomfortable leers seemed to follow me. The men in Choluteca treated me and the other females on my team like dogs, hissing at us, whistling, and yelling gross comments. This kind of thing was unfortunately part of life sometimes, but the level of perversion in Honduras was more than I'd expected. Part of me just wanted to hide in my tent for the rest of the week.

Our team was given three choices as to how we could spend our time in Honduras (and hiding in our tents was not an option). Shekinah was finally fixed, and one group needed to go back to Guatemala to retrieve the car and drive it to Honduras. Another team would work with scheduled contacts in an indigenous mountain village several hours away and share the gospel in that community. The last option was to stay in Choluteca and find a place to serve for the next few days. We had no contacts in the city but were simply using it as a base camp on the way to Nicaragua because of its convenient location. Ministering there would provide a wide open canvas.

Despite my disgust for the men in Choluteca, I felt like I needed to stay behind and see what opportunities would arise in this city. I wasn't sure where to begin but knew God would open the right doors for our team. A few people decided to hang out at a local park and see what information they could gather about Choluteca. They happened to meet an American missionary who said she could connect our team with some local ministries.

Roberta went to the woman's church the next day to follow up and met a pastor who was talking about a prison where he sometimes preached. He explained that he had committed to preach at two different prisons on the same day at the same time. He wasn't sure what he was going to do. Roberta gladly jumped in, thankful for the divine appointment, and volunteered our group to run one of the church services. The pastor accepted our offer with gratitude, gave us directions to the Choluteca prison, and told us to arrive there the following day at 1:30 p.m. Two guys and four of us girls ended up going. I was a bit intimidated to walk into a prison full of men, especially after feeling so degraded by the men out on the streets. Yet, ironically, my time visiting the prison is what redeemed my Honduran experience and what broke my heart for the country.

I entered the prison, passing through a large, open area and a bustling soccer field. There were men freely roaming around, not locked into cells. I noticed some of them staring and kept my eyes on the ground as a man led our group to the prison chapel. Once we reached the chapel, I looked up and suddenly didn't feel like I was inside a prison at all. The whole place was more like a small village than a jail. There were guards outside of the prison, but inside the men were free to do what they pleased. Every afternoon, around fifty men gathered together to hold a worship service. They had a sound system, podium, and several chairs filling the room. Though impressed by the chapel, I still felt a bit intimidated and had no intention of getting up to speak in front of all these men.

One of the inmates started us off by leading worship and then invited Moose forward to speak on behalf of our team. Moose shared his testimony and invited any men up who wanted to receive Christ. Five men stepped forward; one was moved to tears as we prayed for him. Afterwards, I was invited forward to share a word. Suddenly, the intimidation disappeared, and I felt like these men were nothing but big brothers sitting in my living room. I forgot my fears, grabbed the microphone, and spoke about freedom. I reminded the men that the Bible said, "Where the Spirit of the Lord is, there is freedom" (2 Corinthians 3:17). I explained that real freedom didn't come from a place, getting out of prison, earning money, or gaining material possessions. True freedom only came from Christ. And because Christ was everywhere, you could be free *anywhere*. Our hope was in something eternal, not the circumstances of today. As I spoke, the inmates encouraged me with "amens," "hallelujahs," and applause. These men were more excited about the love of Christ than most Christians I knew in America — people who had every tangible freedom you could dream of. Despite everything these prisoners had lost, they were still cheering at the word of God.

After I spoke, we invited anyone forward who needed physical healing or prayer in general. Half of the men walked to the front of the chapel. One of the older men just grabbed my heart, and I felt a strong sense that God had called him to be a father and a leader within the prison. I used my best broken Spanish to prophesy over him and tell him that God had a plan for him even inside the prison. I knew he understood what I was trying to say when he exclaimed, "Glory to God!" And, though this didn't happen to me often, I could *tangibly* feel the presence of the Holy Spirit rushing through my body. I knew God was moving in that place and in that man's heart. His face lit up, and I watched as he immediately stepped out into his calling by approaching the younger men, laying hands on them, and praying for them as a spiritual father.

Just before we left, Roberta called up the men who had been falsely accused of committing a crime so that we could pray for justice. She explained to our team that many innocent men in Latin America were thrown into prison, because the judicial system was extremely corrupt. Someone had to pay for every crime committed, but it didn't really matter who paid. Usually, the rich who committed crimes were able to pay their way out and force poor, innocent men to pay the time for their crimes.

When Roberta called the innocent men forward, over half of the church got up from their seats and walked to the front. I was blown away. The man I had just prayed for was part of that group. Despite the fact that they had unfairly been thrown in prison, one of the inmates explained that many of the innocent men had not known Jesus before coming to jail and were thankful that they'd had the opportunity to meet God while in prison. I was so touched by the hearts of these men and completely amazed by their unwavering faith. Sadly, before we knew it, our time was over, and a couple of the men escorted us back to the prison exit to say goodbye.

We thought that afternoon would be our only chance to visit the prison, but two days later, we were given another invitation. We gladly accepted and brought back a few more people from the team. This time, a few people were allowed to enter the second wing of the prison, a higher security area where the worst criminals were located. However, Roberta, Ben, and I returned to the chapel to visit our friends.

The brothers in the chapel welcomed us back with open arms. We worshipped together, and afterwards they invited Roberta forward to impart the word of God. She provided a teaching on our positions as children of God and explained the authority we carried as Christians. Next, Ben came forward and shared a brief word. He spoke about our ability to hear God's voice — that it was our right as children of God to hear the voice of the Father. He took a moment to single out a few of the men and prophesy over them in front of the whole congregation. One of them was a younger man sitting in the middle of the chapel. Ben declared destiny and truth into his life. "Whatever you have done in the past, it is over and finished. You may have made mistakes, but it doesn't matter. God has forgotten your sin and entirely cleansed you. He sees you as righteous." Moments later, that man accepted Christ as his loving Savior.

At the end of the service, a few people came forward for specific prayer requests. The man that I had prophesied over two days earlier approached me and said that I had really encouraged him. He grabbed my hand in utter purity and gave me a smile that made it all worth it. When I'd entered Honduras, I was so frustrated by the gaping men that I felt I had nothing to give. The last person to whom I wanted to show compassion was a male inmate. But this man stole my heart and redeemed all the negative things I'd assumed about Honduras. Though the men on the streets had treated us women like nothing more than a pack of dogs, we miraculously found love and respect in this Honduran prison. Stronger than any culture of chauvinism, the power of Christ and love of God united us in that place. I pray that my Honduran brothers will receive the justice they deserve and that the unfairly accused will one day be freed from the prison. However, I am confident that those who remain incarcerated will allow God to do great things through their lives in prison.

Chapter Six

NICARAGUA: Finding Love in Weakness

The team crossed into Nicaragua after a delayed departure from Honduras, once again due to vehicle problems. As we approached the border, each vehicle was stopped, and the driver in my car, Moose, was asked for his license. He gave the border "official" a fake copy of his license as instructed by our team leaders. We had been warned that corrupt government officials often took foreigners' licenses and refused to return them. Sure enough, the official told Moose that he would not return his license unless Moose paid a ticket for failing to wear a seatbelt. Moose *had* been wearing a seatbelt throughout our entire drive and refused to fall into the trap. He denied the false accusation and drove on, leaving the copy of his license behind, thankful for the warning we had received. We continued on to the Nicaraguan side of the border and got everyone's documents sorted in just three hours — record time for our team. Feeling hopeful that the license snafu would be our only setback of the day, we drove on towards Jinotepe, our destination city.

The drive to Jinotepe went surprisingly smoothly for the first several hours. After so many popped tires, blown transmissions, broken axles, etc., I was shocked at how well we were doing. Shekinah was back with our caravan and running good as new. The other vehicles seemed to be in top form as well. Unfortunately, I got excited a little too soon. When we were about twenty miles from Jinotepe, New Wine started emitting smoke and suddenly died. There was a problem with the transmission, and we were forced to tow the vehicle the rest of the way. Squished into the remaining four vehicles, we carried on and arrived in Jinotepe around 6 p.m.

There, we were greeted by four new teammates as well as Glenn and Lynn, a missionary couple who ran a diverse local ministry called Mateo 5:16. We would work with them for the next few days. Glenn explained that since it was already Friday evening, a mechanic would probably not be able to look at New Wine until Monday morning. This would likely set us back a couple of days, not an atypical experience for our team. I pushed my frustration about the vehicles aside and greeted our four new team members. We welcomed two Aussies, Josiah and Kurt, as well as Susy from England and Rachael from the States. Josiah, a short-term addition, was a dynamic fireball who only needed a couple of days to become the life of the party. Always willing to serve but never taking himself too seriously, everyone appreciated his kind and carefree demeanor. Long-termer Kurt was much more reserved at first glance, very quiet and steadfast; however, he gradually revealed an unexpected wit that cheered me up during many rough moments. Perhaps one of the most genuinely kind, humble, and selfless people we'd met, the entire team quickly elected Kurt as one of our favorites. Susy joined our team for only a few months, departing from us when we reached Peru. She had a kind-hearted and nurturing spirit and seemed to notice those little details everyone else glazed over. In many moments to come, she would offer me hugs, kisses, and words of encouragement that I will never forget. Lastly, Rachael became a permanent addition to our family. She was truly stunning, equally beautiful inside and out, yet daring and fierce to the core. Rachael carried wisdom and spiritual insight beyond her years but also knew how to play around and have a good time.

The next morning, we met with our four new additions and Glenn and Lynn to hear more about Mateo 5:16. Their main mission base was called Nueva Vida (New Life) and was comprised of a large kitchen, a small sewing room for the local women, a little church building, and a few large dormitories (where our team stayed). Glenn and Lynn explained that they also ran a hotel in downtown Jinotepe, oversaw an orphanage, and partnered with several churches. They invited us to join them at any of the Mateo 5:16 church services and to help out at the orphanage during our time in Nicaragua.

I gladly agreed to get involved with the orphanage ministry. Susy and Rachael had flown into Nicaragua weeks prior to meet up with our team and had been living at the orphanage while they waited for our arrival. They had already become accustomed to life there and volunteered to show us the ropes. They taught us how to use public transportation to get from the mission base to the orphanage so that we would have the freedom to come and go as we pleased.

Our first visit began with warm greetings from several friendly faces, a handful of dogs, and a sheep named Princesa. I found that only nine children lived within the small orphanage, all taken care of by a single mama named Juanita. This woman was amazingly gracious and kind and loved each of the children as her own. Susy explained that many of the children had been abused by their families and passed around as sexual objects from person to person. The orphanage had become a safe haven for each of them, and Juanita had become a nurturing mother. When I interacted with these sweet and gentle children, it was hard to believe everything they'd gone through.

During our second full day in Jinotepe, Melissa and I ventured to the orphanage on our own and later joined up with other team members. We enjoyed the adventure of exploring the city and finding the correct minibus downtown, then walking down a dirt road to the children's home — a muddy mess impassable for vehicles. Upon our arrival at the orphanage, Susy explained that if volunteers didn't take initiative to organize activities for the children, the kids often wasted many hours sitting around and watching television. She suggested we create an active game for them with whatever resources we could get our hands on. We decided to design an obstacle course throughout the compound, creatively using the limited supplies available.

We began the course by instructing the children to run through a dirt path lined with roaming chickens and roosters. Next, we had them weave their bodies between the swings on their rickety, worn playground. We then drew a hopscotch course in the dirt that led to the next obstacle. After the last jump, we placed an old table on the ground and told the children to crawl underneath it. Then, we fashioned a soccer goal by balancing a large stick on two chairs. We put a deflated soccer ball a few feet in front of the goal and instructed the kids to kick the ball over the stick before advancing to the next part of the course. Susy gathered some pinecones into a pile and found a bucket that she positioned at a decent throw from the heap. The last challenge was tossing at least one pinecone into the bucket, then running to a specific tree stump and tagging it.

The children eagerly agreed to run the course, and we timed them one by one. After they took their turns, they insisted that I try the obstacle course as well. I did my best, but the little girls put me to shame. Alas, throwing a pinecone into a bucket was harder than I thought.

We returned to the orphanage a third day and ventured into the surrounding communities with some of the older girls from the home. Three of them guided groups of us into a village where we visited peoples' homes and prayed for them. I was blown away by the faith and confidence that these young women possessed. They led us in praying for the sick as well as inviting people from the community to one of Mateo 5:16's churches. The next day, several people attended that church for the first time.

Meanwhile, back at the mission base, New Wine was still not fixed. As we had suspected, the needed repairs would push us behind schedule by a couple of days. Though vehicle repairs had simply become a normal part of life for our team, this particular setback overwhelmed me. We were already weeks behind our original itinerary, and I began to wonder how long this delayed pace would continue. Questions filled my mind:

Will this trip take months longer than expected?

When will I get home?

How much will I miss while I'm away?

Will people be disappointed in me for missing crucial events in their lives while I'm gone?

For some reason, our circumstances in Nicaragua triggered a fear of the unknown deep inside of me. I suddenly hit a point where I realized that I had zero control over this journey. Complete lack of control was my biggest fear.

In addition, our team dynamics were changing so quickly that I could barely keep up. We'd recently lost three teammates;

now four new ones arrived in Nicaragua, and a fifth was soon to join. We met Addison, a young guy interning at Mateo 5:16, and Jesse invited him to travel with us. Addison had spent some time worshipping with our team, amazed by the strong presence of the Lord. He noticed the way we loved each other and wanted to be a part of what we were doing. Addison's testimony was one of the most powerful I'd ever heard. He had been addicted to drugs and was supernaturally delivered from all cravings the second he landed in Nicaragua. God had completely transformed Addison's life and restored him while he interned at Mateo 5:16. Addison prayed about Jesse's invitation to join the team and came across the story of Gideon. (See Judges 6.) In order to confirm God's calling, Gideon had laid out a fleece and asked God to make the fleece wet but the ground dry. Addison decided to do the same thing. He laid out a T-shirt on the ground and asked God to make it wet — but the ground dry — if he was meant to join our team. When Addison checked in the morning, the ground was dry, and his T-shirt was sopping wet. He needed a bit of time to prepare but planned to meet us in Panama.

Though expanding our family was clearly a blessing, it was another reminder that nothing was constant, fixed, or stable. As new people were joining, we were also sadly losing people — a difficult change. Maria, Victor, and Serena all flew home from Nicaragua, each one a permanent departure. Including Christian, Rowan, and Gillian, we had already lost a total of six people. It was hard to grieve our goodbyes and simultaneously get to know new teammates. I wanted them to feel welcomed with joy, but I didn't know how to mourn our goodbyes and be happy at the same time.

Emotionally, I was turning into a wreck. My lifestyle had become turbulent, unpredictable, and unstable. My mind and my heart couldn't keep up with the constant changes. The only thing that I knew wouldn't change was the fact that things would always be changing. Though I was on the trip to serve and minister to others, I realized that I needed someone to take care of *me* for a moment. It is incredibly humbling to admit that you need help when you are the one who is supposed to be offering it. But how beautiful it is to be around people who love you even in weakness. Better yet, how beautiful it is to serve a God who uses the weak things of the world to shame the wise. How wonderful to know a God who uses the least qualified person to win a battle and a God who promises to be close to the brokenhearted. In a moment of complete vulnerability, I decided to just be weak, scared, and brokenhearted before my God and before my team. My teammates gave me the strength I lacked without judgment, expectation, or hidden agenda. Reflecting the heart of God, they simply loved me.

During a particularly tense evening in Nicaragua, a few of us gathered to just talk and hang out. Turns out, I wasn't the only one who had hit a wall of fear and frustration. As we shared our hearts with one another, Taylor said we should pray together for a minute. Somehow a minute of prayer turned into two and a half hours. As a group, we cried out to God in pure desperation, losing all track of time. Even the guys were weeping, genuinely *weeping*, crying out for Jesus' presence. Taylor, Breck, and Ben prayed for me, speaking the truth of God in place of the fears I'd been tackling. A sweet comfort came over me as my brothers reassured me that my Heavenly Father was proud of me and was moved by my heart.

My worry dissipated as I remembered that although life sometimes *felt* particularly out of control, I was never really the one in control in the first place. As these people I'd known for just three months sat with me, encouraged me, prayed for me, and loved me, I saw the Father's love in them. We all hugged each other goodnight and said, "I love you." This was becoming a fairly normal thing — saying "I love you" or giving someone a hug or a kiss before heading to bed. That's just what families do. You know, it's great to minister to other people, but if you can't love yourself or the people right around you, it's useless. I knew my team loved me, valued me, and would always take care of me.

Ironically, I'd thought I was in Nicaragua to serve at an orphanage, but instead I was really the one being served. God's word says that all fruit flows from intimacy with the Father (see John 15); so in order to bear fruit, we need to be intimate with God. While in Nicaragua, I *really* needed to be with Him. God used my desperation to bring me right where He wanted me — close to His heart. Truly, there's no place I'd rather be.

Chapter Seven
COSTA RICA: A Story of Redemption

Border crossing day was generally disgusting, noisy, dusty, and long. I expected nothing less from the Costa Rican border and was pleasantly surprised to find the complete opposite of what I'd imagined. As I left Nicaragua behind, I gladly embraced the luxury of a border station equipped with a coffee shop, flushing toilets, and stores that sold real chocolate. *Pure bliss.* I noticed busloads of tourists passing through, and as I caught a glimpse of a white boy carrying a shortboard, I realized I had just reached Latin America's surfing paradise. My team excitedly drove to a quiet fishing village called Playa de Coco and decided to camp out on the beach for the next few nights. After a long day of travel and border paperwork, I fell asleep to the sound of the waves, thankful for this taste of heaven.

The following day, a group of us went to grab some food at a local restaurant before heading out to do ministry for the afternoon. The restaurant where we ended up was started by two drunk guys who visited Costa Rica and never left, and you could sense that their moral compass wasn't exactly pointing north. It was clear that the owner had way more respect for a bottle of liquor than for any of the women working at his restaurant. The waitress who helped my friends and me was in a terrible mood and was very short with us while taking our order. I was tempted to boycott this restaurant and leave a bad tip to show her how I felt about her attitude. Yet, my kind-hearted teammates, who never ceased to amaze me, approached the situation with the opposite spirit and said we needed to minister to this woman. They reminded me that ministry wasn't a special time set aside to show people we loved them; ministry was living normal life intentionally.

The men on my team sensed the disrespect of women in the restaurant and felt we needed to show our waitress that she was valued. Sweet Liz prayed about what to do and said God told her to give the waitress a bar of chocolate. *Seriously?* I thought. *Not only is that culturally bizarre, but that woman has been rude to us for the past hour.* But Liz stuck to her conviction and boldly ran down the street to a local supermarket and purchased a chocolate bar. When she returned to the restaurant, she approached our waitress and said, "My friends and I thought you looked a bit down, and we just wanted you to know that God loves you so much." She handed the woman the chocolate along with a note that said, "Dios te ama" (God loves you). The waitress' face completely lit up, and she looked like a different woman for the rest of our time in the restaurant. In that moment, I remembered that oftentimes the people who seem like they deserve our love the least are those who actually need it most. Opportunities to show love don't require big mission trips or elaborate plans. It can be as simple as eating lunch in a restaurant with a cranky waitress who looks like she might need a little encouragement.

Later that day, a group of us decided to travel to a nearby beach village to participate in an evangelistic activity called "treasure hunting." I had never done this before but was willing to try. Treasure hunting simply entails searching for the Lord's treasure — His people. You choose a location and ask God for visions or clues to bring you to the people He wants you to bless. As you pray, if God lays anything on your heart, you have to step out in faith and take the risk of following whatever you've received. As we drove to the beach village, the five of us in my car asked the Lord to show us visions of those we would soon encounter. Some of the pictures seemed really random, but God was faithful and ended up weaving them together.

We visited two different beach villages, and I'll never forget the second. This particular beach looked pretty barren, but Natalie M. and I decided to walk along the water and see who we could find. We walked for quite a while, and no one stood out to me. We passed by one man who was just standing alone, looking at the ocean. He said hello, but after saying hello back, we kept walking. I wondered if we should stop and speak to him, but that felt awkward and forced. We continued on a bit more and saw no one, so we decided to turn around.

"There's not really anyone here, but I guess we could go pray for that one guy," I said to Natalie. To be completely honest, I really didn't want to but saw no one else.

As we walked back towards him, Astrid approached us. Earlier, she'd said God had shown her a picture of a pineapple. When we reached Astrid, she explained that as she had been walking along the beach, she saw a top of a pineapple floating in the water, directly in front of the man who Natalie and I were headed towards. I had kind of chosen him by default, but Astrid recognized the pineapple from her vision and felt we needed to approach that man. I still felt pretty hesitant, but Natalie insisted that we go.

"Wait," I pleaded. "We need to think of a question or something so this is not totally awkward."

The girls laughed but agreed that was a good plan.

I swallowed my pride, approached the man, and asked him if he spoke English.

"A little bit," he responded in a thick accent.

"Um, weeeell...we were wondering where a good place to surf is," I asked, trying not to look or sound like a total creep. "The waves here seem pretty small; do you know of a better spot?"

The man didn't know of a good surf break but began to engage in small talk nonetheless. We found out his name was Aynid, and he lived in the area. Natalie noticed the cross necklace he was wearing and asked Aynid why he'd chosen the cross symbol. He said he wasn't a Christian but that he liked crosses. That seemed kind of weird, so we asked him why. He told us that was a good question; he wasn't really sure himself. As we continued talking, Aynid revealed that his family had separated when he was young. It had really affected and hurt him. I could see the pain in his eyes as he opened up his heart to us. We asked him about the tattoos covering his body — gruesome skulls and other angry symbols. He explained that he had been very angry when he got them but didn't feel the tattoos had significance in his life any longer. Aynid declared that he was currently at a point in his life where he needed to make a big decision. He wasn't exactly sure what the decision was, but he recognized that he was facing a turning point.

Aynid went on to explain that he knew something special was about to happen as soon as we walked by him. He could just sense that this moment was going to be a significant one, but he didn't know what to do, so he merely said hello. We told him we also believed this was a divine appointment, that we'd prayed for people to connect with and God had led us to him. We spoke about our faith and let Aynid know that we believed God could set him free from the anger and hurt he'd experienced years ago. He agreed to let us pray for him, breaking off chains from his past and praying truth and love over him. We explained that God's love was so lavish that He would send three girls from Germany, Russia, and the U.S. just to let him know how very loved he was. I could see the wheels turning in his head as he asked himself, *"Is this really true? Is there really a God who loves me this much?"*

Aynid asked each of us our names, and when I said "Caitlin" he looked confused; so I reintroduced myself as Catalina, the Spanish version of my name. He smiled and told me that I had a beautiful name. Aynid then explained that his ex-girlfriend was also named Catalina, and she had been a really significant person in his life. He declared that he now counted us three as significant people in his life. He promised that he would never forget one of our faces. He believed this had been a divine appointment, and we were part of his turning point.

Natalie asked Aynid if he would like to make the decision to accept Jesus. He looked a little hesitant, unsure of what to say. Sensing his fear, I assured Aynid that he was under no pressure and should spend time on his own doing some soul-searching. Though the Lord has blessed me with amazing love that I want to share with everyone I know, I never want to force someone to accept that love unless he or she is ready. Aynid agreed that he needed some time alone, just him and God, to reflect and pray. He knew he was on the brink of a big decision and realized the weight of making the choice to follow Christ. I believe Natalie's bold invitation was the start of a life transformation for Aynid. Though I will probably never see him again, I am confident that something changed inside of him that day on the beach. I could see it. God was undoubtedly doing something in his heart, and I know that he will find the truth he was searching for.

It seemed bizarre that God had used a vision of a pineapple to bring us to Aynid. God is weird like that sometimes. I also felt honored that God had used my name as a piece of this divine encounter. I suppose part of Aynid's hurt had stemmed from breaking up with Catalina, and I knew it was no coincidence that God had sent Aynid a new Catalina to tell Aynid about His love. Inspired by God's bizarre and beautiful redemption, I went back to our little beach camp feeling encouraged and full of faith.

However, my joy was quickly dashed when I found out that Rose had been robbed while I was gone. Thieves had broken into our camp and stolen her phone, iPod, wallet, and bag of valuables from inside the pop-up. Over one thousand dollars' worth of cash and goods had been taken. I was told to check my spot in the pop-up to see if any of my stuff had been stolen, and immediately my heart sank. I'd carried my wallet with me to the beach village, but I'd left my laptop back at the camp. My area in the camper was next to Rose's, and I knew that if her things had been stolen, there was no way my laptop was still there. My head hung low, I went to check and sadly confirmed that my computer, the only thing of real value that I owned, had been robbed. Natalie checked her things and found out that her valuables had also been stolen. I felt like the wind had just been knocked out of me.

The reason why losing my laptop was particularly upsetting is because I was in the middle of writing this very book you are reading. I'd been documenting our journey from the beginning, dreaming of one day publishing it. I'd written quite a lot and couldn't remember the last time I'd saved my manuscript on a flash drive. My first reaction to being robbed was panic that I'd lost my writing. "My book! My book!" I cried, not even thinking about the monetary value of the laptop, all my music, pictures, and other documents I'd lost.

Before leaving for Latin America, I'd known being robbed on the trip was a distinct possibility. It had already happened to me twice in Africa, and I was very scared that my laptop would be stolen while traveling. I couldn't believe that my fear had just been realized. Taylor had been documenting a lot of the trip himself and probably understood more than anyone else how much all my hard work meant to me. He heard what happened and immediately came to the pop-up, where I sat in tears. He wrapped his brotherly arms around me as I cried, mourning the loss of my hours upon hours of hard work. It would take me ages to rewrite everything I'd lost. That thief had no idea what he'd just stolen from me.

After I calmed down a bit, Liz told me I needed to go to the police station and file a report of the robbery. The police officer who wrote the report used old fashioned pen and paper and took hours to record a few simple things. As she documented the theft at snail's pace, other officers came in and out of the office. When they heard where the robbery had taken place, they all responded, "Oh yeah, that's a bad neighborhood. You shouldn't leave your stuff there."

Annoyed I was receiving that advice *now*, I simply glared at the officers and said nothing. I impatiently watched the woman continue to attempt to file the report, writing as if she had learned to use a pen the day before. Everything in me wanted to grab her pen, write the report for her, and run somewhere — anywhere. But instead, I stood there waiting, watching the officers chat amongst themselves, knowing they didn't care at all about what had just happened to me. To them this was just a missing laptop; to me this was a huge roadblock for my dream.

We returned to our camp, and though I tried to sleep, I couldn't. My head was spinning. I finally caught a couple of hours of sleep but soon woke up to the morning heat, feeling groggy and sad. A group of people from my team reminded me that we were heading out to a beach called Playa Avenilla today and asked if I was still coming. I decided to push my frustration with being robbed aside and go with the team, because this was important.

Playa Avenilla was the beach where Dianne's daughter-in-law, Riahnnon, had been killed in a rip current just months before. Though Dianne was currently in the U.S. with her son and grandsons, Liz felt it would be respectful to have a time of prayer at the beach where Riahnnon had died. Playa Avenilla was less than a two-hour drive from our campsite, and a visit would be a good way to honor Dianne and her family from afar.

Liz shared more about the events she'd witnessed in Costa Rica months ago while accompanying Dianne there immediately following the tragedy — providing the team with insight about the trauma she'd seen among Dianne's son, grandson, and the teen surfer who'd saved the grandson but failed to save Riahnnon. As Liz spoke about her experience with Dianne's family and the death of Riahnnon, she realized how much the tragedy had affected her personally. She'd felt little sense of closure when she left Costa Rica months prior, and when she'd rejoined the team in Guatemala, she had buried her angst. Liz continued to push her feelings aside as we traveled throughout El Salvador, Honduras, and Nicaragua. Yet, the moment we hit Costa Rica, old feelings came rushing back. When Liz found out that the beach of Riahnnon's death was relatively close to where we were currently camping, she asked if some people from the team were willing to return to the beach with her. She not only wanted to pray for Dianne's family but also seek some personal closure and attempt to find Johan, the teenager who had rescued Dianne's grandson.

Liz was always an amazing friend to me, so despite my own preoccupations, I knew I needed to go support her and visit Playa Avenilla. I wanted to honor Dianne as well. About ten people total made the trip. When we reached the beach, everyone took some time to walk along the sand alone and pray for Dianne and her family. We recongregated a while later and did a footwashing ceremony for Liz in the ocean, a symbol of service and cleansing. We prayed for closure and healing for her.

Liz felt strongly that she needed to find Johan and see if he'd released himself from the guilt of not being able to save Riahnnon. While Liz prayed about finding Johan, she felt God saying that He would bring Johan to her. Amazingly, after asking just a couple of locals if they knew Johan, he appeared on the beach. *Wow*, the beauty of a small surfer town and "coconut wireless." Liz greeted Johan with a big hug and asked me to translate between Johan and the team. I explained that we were friends of Dianne and wanted to thank him for what he'd done. I told him he was a hero, and our team was so proud of him. I also asked him to share the details of his heroic rescue. He explained how he'd been able to hoist the grandson onto his surfboard but could not find Riahnnon when he looked back into the water. Johan admitted that he wasn't able to sleep for weeks after the incident and took sleeping pills for a while. I asked him how he was doing currently, and he assured us that he was back to normal. We asked if we could pray for him, and he agreed. We prayed for blessing and healing over him as well as release from any guilt. We assured him that both we and God were incredibly proud of him and so very thankful for what he did for our beloved Dianne.

After praying, Liz treated Johan to a cool drink at a restaurant by the beach. While sipping away, he informed us that his mother had died when he was seven years old. Interestingly, Dianne's grandson was around the same age. I found it remarkable that God had chosen Johan to be the one to save Dianne's grandson, someone who understood exactly what it felt like to lose his mom as a little boy. God redeems things in such unexpected ways.

I could see a burden lifted off both Liz and Johan as a result of their reunion and time of prayer. It was such a beautiful moment of redemption. As I walked along the ocean reflecting on what Dianne had lost, suddenly losing my laptop didn't seem so bad. Dianne had lost someone precious to her, someone she could never replace. All I'd lost was a computer. That certainly put things in perspective. And truly, the most important thing in my life was God, and I was so thankful that no matter what, I could not lose Him.

The next day, we made our way towards the Panama border and stopped in a town overnight to cut the journey in half. Before our second long day of driving, Jesse, who normally preferred to leave at the crack of dawn, announced that we would be leaving around 10 a.m. He'd heard a few of us wanted to go surfing, and this would give us time to catch an early morning break before traveling. One of my selfish dreams for this trip was to surf in Costa Rica, but I'd assumed we wouldn't have the time to do it. After feeling like my dream of writing a book had been put on hold, it was amazing to experience a totally different dream come to pass. As I paddled through gorgeous waves, a familiar peace rushed over me. I felt safe and at home. And although I was not a very talented surfer, that day I miraculously caught wave after wave after wave, riding long, perfect sets to shore, watching my board rip through the current. It was like God's gift to me. That morning was the redemptive refreshment

I needed. That perfect surf was my last memory of Costa Rica and is what I carried with me rather than bitterness about being robbed.

Costa Rica was a trying experience, but I'm thankful for it all — the good and the bad. I saw God's power to restore what had been lost in Aynid, Liz and Johan, and myself. Our stories are very different, but they all sing of redemption. Though it's always sad to lose, I am grateful to have experienced the unique restoration that can only appear after loss. I left Costa Rica more determined than ever to push forward, run the race well, chase after my dreams, and watch God continue to give back what had been lost.

Sidenote: *I'd like to express an official thank you to Kevin S., who heard about the robbery and kindly purchased a new laptop for me. Less than two months after my computer was stolen, I received a new one due to his generosity. This was a huge blessing that helped me to continue to write this book. Thank you so much Kevin!*

Chapter Eight

PANAMA: When the Lame Walk

With seven countries already behind us, we headed to our final stop in Central America — Panama. I assumed crossing into Panama would be similar to at least one of the previous seven borders, but the Panamanian crossing was a whole new ballgame. This border was a nightmare of disarray. We were used to waiting several hours at each border, but most of the waiting was due to sorting paperwork for our vehicles. The line to get our passports stamped was usually fairly quick and the entry process relatively simple. However, in Panama, the passport line alone took several hours. When we entered the queue, we were so far back that we couldn't even see the windows where the passports got stamped.

After about two hours or so, we caught a glimpse of the windows but still felt we were making little progress. We eventually noticed that people were standing in one massive lump in front of the windows, and others were making their way into the mess from the side of the line instead of entering from the back. This was making the line longer and pushing us further back, hence why we weren't making any progress. After patiently enduring this unjust system for hours, we finally decided we needed to aggressively make our way to the customs windows or we would never get to Panama. I was warned that if I didn't push ahead, I wouldn't get my passport stamped.

Our whole team bunched together and started shoving our way towards the windows. Even within my group, I somehow ended up in the very back. I was a little scared that I was going to get swept away in the crowd and left behind. I found out that not only did each person need to get his or her passport stamped, everyone also had to get a picture taken with one of the small cameras that pointed out from each of the customs windows. As people continued to butt in front of us, Ben reached his arm ahead of another man, grabbed the camera, and pointed it towards himself. Apparently, this was the appropriate signal for the man behind the window to grant Ben respect. The border official accepted Ben's passport and stamped it. As soon as Ben got his passport back, he slapped down the next passport for Josiah, Josiah did the same for Rose, and Rose the same for me. Four in a row — we mastered the system! An old man next to me tried to push me out of the way, but I hovered over him until I got through. The whole process was insane. I was horrified and amused all at the same time.

Four hours later, our entire team made it through customs and was legally allowed to enter Panama. Now that our people were sorted, our vehicles needed to be searched. The process was slow but smooth, and we were finally granted entry. At long last, we started our drive towards Panama City. Part way through the journey, New Wine died *again*. This vehicle had *just* been fixed in Nicaragua, and now we were back to square one. We were forced to tow the smaller RV and gave up any hopes of making it to Panama City that same day. We decided to stop at a hotel for the evening and find yet another mechanic to look at

New Wine. The hotel owner was a Christian, and when he found out we were missionaries, he graciously allowed us to set up our pop-ups in the hotel parking lot for free as well as use the lobby internet, swimming pool, and bathrooms. He also helped us find a good mechanic to take a look at New Wine in the morning.

The mechanic arrived the following day and fixed New Wine in the blink of an eye. Miraculously, it seemed as though nothing had seriously been wrong to begin with. Thankful and relieved, we set off for Panama City and arrived a few short hours later. We planned to meet a YWAM director named David at a local church where we would spend the next week or so. The YWAM base in Panama City was in the process of buying their own building; but for the time being, they were partnering with the church and using its Sunday School rooms to host teams.

As we drove on a narrow one-way bridge over the Panama Canal, the YWAM church just a half mile away, New Wine (the vehicle I happened to be riding in) began to slide around the bridge and got stuck. There was a curb on the side of the bridge and wooden planks about eight inches from the curb, and the right tires got lodged inside that small gap. Josiah tried his best to floor it and free New Wine from the wicked bridge's grip, but the RV wouldn't budge an inch. The other passengers and I got out and began to push. No success.

Since we were on a one-lane bridge where people took turns going across, we unfortunately were not only blocking people from behind but all of the cars head-on who wanted to cross the bridge in the opposite direction. An angry German man approached us and yelled at us for our stupidity. Onlookers honked and swore at us, enraged that they were unable to pass us and cross the bridge. Fortunately, some others decided to help us instead of curse at us, and we gathered a large force of Panamanian men. As we stood there, stranded on the bridge, we noticed a huge rainbow, a reminder of God's promise. Even in the most frustrating situations, God found ways to remind us that He was still with us and was faithful to fulfill His promises to our team. Standing under the gorgeous rainbow, our team members and the mob of strangers pushed with all our might, and we got New Wine over the bridge.

We pulled over after crossing the bridge to assess the damage and saw that one of the back tires was completely destroyed. David walked over from the church to greet us and explained that we were literally just a few yards from our final destination. Some of the guys stayed with the vehicle and sorted the tire out while the rest of us walked to the YWAM church. We unloaded our things and claimed spaces on the floor that would serve as our beds for the next week.

David cooked a delicious, hot meal for us and gave us a quick orientation to YWAM Panama. As he spoke, it was clear that David's heartbeat matched the heartbeat of Iris. David was radical to the core and expected a mighty move of God during our time in Panama. The locals and the church members had been anticipating our arrival and waiting with great expectancy as well. Their faith level was high, and hearing their great faith built my faith in return. We knew our time partnering with David and YWAM Panama would be something special.

The next morning, we met with Bill, the pastor of the church where we were staying, as well as his wife Ann. They were from the States but had been living in Panama for thirty or so years and led a large congregation comprised of Panamanians, indigenous people, and expatriates. Bill was funny, bold, and straightforward. His boisterous and untamed personality quickly earned him the nickname "Wild Bill" among our team. He showed nothing but excitement for our team's arrival, and his attitude helped me feel appreciated and at home. Ann welcomed us with open arms, encouraging us with gentle hugs and a tender heart. Bill asked us to pray for Ann, who had been suffering from several health problems for years. Praying together opened up good conversation with both her and Bill about the unconditional love of God. Bill and Ann quickly welcomed us into their family and cheered us on throughout our time in Panama.

After our first meeting with Wild Bill, David brought us to a couple of ministry locations in Panama City, including an ill-reputed ghetto where he was connected to the local community. We were warned that if we brought anything of value along, it would be quickly swiped from us. After my experience in Costa Rica, the thought of being robbed again did not sit well. However, I wanted to be a part of this. As we drove into that neighborhood, the graffiti on the streets said it all. There were murals that read, "No more war. Change your neighborhood." It was clear that such taggings were put there for a reason. We parked our car along a little alley, walked into a dilapidated apartment building, wound up a dark, dingy staircase, and entered an open area in the middle of an apartment complex. There was a local pastor preaching, but it was hard to hear a word he said over the chaos. Children were playing loudly, talking over the pastor, and bouncing from seat to seat.

We were instructed to begin talking to people and offer to pray for them. I wasn't quite sure where to start. I noticed a small woman in a wheelchair and approached her with a couple of other girls from my team. We asked if we could pray, and with no show of emotion, she gave a subtle nod. We engaged the woman in a few questions and tried to converse amidst the noise. It was almost impossible to hear her, and trying to understand Spanish in such a loud environment made the challenge even more difficult. Regardless, we figured God understood what was going on and decided to pray to Him for miraculous healing in her legs. We prayed for a few moments, but nothing seemed to happen. After a bit, a woman from the local community grabbed us away and asked us to pray for some others.

Afterwards, Natalie M. felt we should return to the woman in the wheelchair. She looked so incredibly sad and discouraged, and we wanted to at least talk to her a bit more. Healing or no healing, we figured we could at least show her some love. We went back to her wheelchair and knelt down to speak to her. We found out that she'd contracted tuberculosis a while back, and the disease had gone to her spine. It had affected her walking ability, and she'd been unable to walk without assistance for the past year. As we talked to her, children crawled in and out of her lap, then ran off to play. She explained that she had two children, but she was raising them alone as her husband had died nine months ago. This poor woman was only twenty-seven years old. We were the same age, but our stories were so very different. I couldn't imagine already being a widow at our age, raising two children as a single mother. My heart broke for this woman as she shared her sad story.

I told the woman how her Heavenly Father loved her dearly, that He was close to the brokenhearted, and how He longed to heal her. David popped in for translation assistance, and the woman explained that she had once followed Christ but turned away from her faith after marriage. While conversing, she decided to turn back to God for hope. She bowed her head in prayer and rededicated her life to Jesus Christ as David prayed in Spanish with her. After she made this declaration of faith, Natalie and I decided to pray for healing in her legs one more time. The woman had just received healing in her heart (the most important healing), but now it was time for healing in her body.

As we prayed, Natalie sensed that something had happened. I, on the other hand, wasn't convinced. Natalie asked the woman to get out of her wheelchair and try to walk. The woman said she was scared. I was scared too. Though I was hesitant to push her, Natalie insisted. She knew in her heart that the woman had been healed and told her she needed to claim that healing and begin to walk. After a few moments of the woman staring at us in fear, she took the boldest step I'd ever seen. She let Natalie and I help her out of her wheelchair, and she started to move her legs. Slowly, slowly, slowly, she began to walk with our help. She looked like she was in pain. I wasn't so sure we should keep doing this. But as the woman took baby step after baby step, she eventually let go of our arms. And she continued to walk — alone. Completely unassisted, the lame woman was really walking. She was WALKING!

Amazed and overwhelmed, I followed behind her. I felt a tangible presence, almost like a forceful wind, breathing power all around her. It was too intense for words. She made a circle around the apartment complex, and as we headed back towards her wheelchair, I foolishly assumed she would be tired and would want to rest. But the moment we reached her wheelchair, she walked right past it and kept going! Ha! I'd never seen anything like it. Moments before, this woman had been sitting in a wheelchair; this was surreal! She finally paused for a moment, and her eyes welled up with tears. Her once stone-cold face cracked with emotion, and she cried tears of joy for her healing. I began to cry as well, so overwhelmed by the miracle I'd just been a part of.

Days later, our team heard a report from one of the community leaders in that Panama City apartment complex. Apparently, someone had claimed that the woman's miraculous healing couldn't be real. At first, she didn't believe that the woman in the wheelchair had actually been healed. But days later, the woman was still walking on her own. The doubter was blown away, dazed and confused as to how this could be possible. The healing was the talk of the apartment complex. All I know is that when we prayed for healing in Jesus' name, that handicapped woman got out of her wheelchair and started walking. The tears in her eyes told me how very real her healing was.

We also heard a report about a man that some guys on the team had prayed for in the same complex. Apparently, while I was busy talking to the woman in the wheelchair, Melissa was praying for a young man who was part of a local gang. As she prayed, she felt that some of the guys from the team should come pray for him as well. Often, the guys who rode in Counsel and Might prayed and worshipped in their car together, and they created a ritual of *roaring* in unison, symbolizing the power of Jesus, often referred to as the "Lion of Judah." They decided that instead of praying for the young man, they should roar over him. As weird as it may sound, when they released the roar of the Lion of Judah, the young man had a vision of his destiny and saw that he was going to hell if he stayed on the path he was currently on. After the vision, he decided to dedicate his life to Christ. The truth of God's destiny brought him to radical repentance. In addition, he explained that he had been planning a burglary for that very evening, but after his encounter with the Lord, he changed his mind.

The days following these brilliant miracles, my team helped organize a prayer meeting at Wild Bill's church as well as a Sunday morning service. Our faith had been so strengthened by what we'd seen that our expectancy for the meetings was sky-high. The people who attended came with great expectancy as well. They all believed God was going to do amazing things, and He certainly did. Ben received many words of knowledge for peoples' healings, and several people came forward and were healed. We got to pray and prophesy over almost everyone in the church. The tears in peoples' eyes said it all. God was moving.

Later in the week, a few of us traveled to an indigenous village with another YWAM staffer named Chris. We walked a mile or so from the church until we reached a lake with a dilapidated, old dock by the shore. We waited by the dock for one of the men from the village to pick us up in his boat. Chris, Liz, Rachael, Kurt, Zoe, and I hopped into the boat and rode to an island on the lake inhabited by the indigenous man's tribe.

When we arrived on the island, many villagers were waiting for us, ready for prayer. One by one, they came forward, and we interceded for them. We were met with the same great faith we'd encountered on the mainland, and God did many healing miracles on the little island. First, we prayed for a man who had gotten some wood in his eye while working a long time ago, and he'd had blurry vision ever since. While praying for him, Kurt kissed each of his eyes — the strange kind of thing that's right up Jesus' alley. When the man opened his eyes, he said his vision was clear. Another man came forward who had a problem with a disc in his back. After praying, he announced that he was pain-free. Next, we prayed for a woman who'd been told she had a high-risk pregnancy. She was due in just three days and was fearful of giving birth. Rachael declared life over her baby, and the moment she spoke those words, the baby kicked so hard that Rachael practically jumped back. (Days later, we found out that the woman had a successful labor.)

While praying for another lady, Rachael and I both received a word of knowledge about nightmares and wondered if this woman was suffering from demonic dreams. The woman claimed that our word was not for her; however, the villagers said that there was a little girl who constantly battled nightmares. They brought her forward, and as we attempted to pray for her, she screamed and cried relentlessly. I wasn't quite sure what to do, since I'd never heard a child wail so loudly during prayer before. At just the right moment, Zoe toddled forward and laid hands on her. The very second Zoe touched the little girl, she went silent. I loved that God chose to anoint two-year-old Zoe to calm that child. What a wonderfully mysterious God we serve.

The rest of our week included ministering to prison guards and police officers, visiting an American missionary family, and volunteering at a local orphanage for children with AIDS. After days of running alongside YWAM in ministry, we began to prepare for our departure from Panama. Getting into Colombia would be far more complicated than any of our other border crossings. Though Panama and Colombia were connected by land, the roads between them were impassable and overrun by guerrillas and treacherous jungle terrain. The stretch of jungle between Panama and Colombia was called the Darien Gap, better known as "Green Hell." It was virtually impossible to drive a car through. Therefore, we were advised to ship all of our vehicles from Colón, Panama to a port in Colombia called Cartagena and then fly or boat to pick up the vehicles there.

What we hoped would be a quick and painless shipping process turned into a never-ending nightmare. Though our vehicles were shared, Jesse, Tanya, Breck, and Melissa were named the registered owners of the team cars. (And Taylor L. owned Counsel and Might, his Buick station wagon.) These five drove to Colón day after day after day, filling out piles of ridiculous paperwork and jumping through various hoops to get our vehicles on a ship to Colombia.

Each day brought a new set of challenges. The first day, my teammates were turned away, because they were not dressed fancy enough. Most of our clothes were buried in the trailers ready to be shipped, completely inaccessible. Therefore, the five were forced to go to a local mall, buy new clothes, and return to the port. Now looking their finest, they tried to begin processing the paperwork, but each document took an entire day to complete. All of the registered vehicle owners were bombarded with absurd amounts of paperwork and obscure documents. They returned to the port repeatedly throughout the week, each time being handed more documents and hoops they needed to jump through. The rest of the team prayed each day that the nightmare would end; but day after day, our teammates returned to the church, heads hung low, disappointed by the news that they would have to return to the port yet again to wrestle with more documents.

On top of the documentation nightmare, we were told that it would cost just over eleven thousand dollars to ship all five vehicles. Every day, our team prayed for a financial miracle. We didn't even have half that amount of money. Even if we did, the shipping company would only take a certain amount of money per vehicle per day. The payment process alone stretched what we hoped would be a one-day endeavor into a week of dealing with financial nonsense.

After days of wrestling with the shipping company, the paperwork was finally sorted, and we were asked to begin the payment process. Tanya carried three thousand seven hundred dollars cash to the port, stuffed into a tiny wallet, believing for a miracle. We all knew God had called us to South America, and that meant He would provide a way for us to get there, even if it seemed like we were about eight thousand dollars short. Sure enough, at just the right moment, an anonymous donor sent the team twelve thousand dollars, which covered every vehicle expense. To this day, I don't know who gave us this money. If you are reading this, thank you from the bottom of all of our hearts. You are a miracle.

Now that our vehicles were taken care of, we had to make the final decision about how we would get *ourselves* to Colombia. I falsely assumed that if cars were commonly shipped directly from Colón to Cartagena, people must take a common and direct route as well. Unfortunately, this couldn't have been further from the truth. The cheapest route required us to take a plane from Panama City to some little port on Panama's coast, then take a long boat ride, then switch to another boat, then take two four-hour bus rides to Cartagena. After hours of research, this seemed to be the "easiest" way to get to Colombia without spending loads of cash. Though this itinerary would save us money, it was far too complicated and circuitous for my liking.

Sadly, our alternatives were not much better. We could take a 4x4 vehicle to Carti, Panama and wait for a freighter (potentially for days) to let us hitch a ride to Colombia. With the size of our team, hitchhiking on a freighter seemed a bit unrealistic. We could also take a large yacht through some islands off the coast of Colombia and eventually into Cartagena, but this was both expensive and time-consuming. The last option was flying, but we would have to book flights last minute, right before Christmas, which meant limited seats and pricey tickets. We went in circles for days, overwhelmed with the lack of cheap and straightforward options for getting out of Panama.

We finally decided the boating/hitchhiking/busing options to Cartagena were way too complicated, and we needed to give in to buying flights and just deal with the inflated holiday prices. We went online and started booking flights, praying most of us could get on the same plane. The majority of the team was able to get a ticket for that coming Tuesday, but Elizabeth, Rose, Breck, and I couldn't get a flight until Saturday — Christmas Eve. At least we would all be in Cartagena by Christmas and could spend the holiday together as a family. The only ones who would miss our team Christmas were Taylor, who traveled home to Texas for a few weeks, and Josiah, who flew back to Australia for a few months.

Though our split initially felt strange, my time left behind in Panama ended up being a blessing. An American family who owned a missions resort in Panama City had attended one of our team's church services and caught wind that we'd been sleeping on the floor of the church. They generously offered us a free stay at their resort until we left for Colombia. We rested there for several days enjoying real beds, internet, hot showers, and couches that felt like heaven. We watched Christmas movies, made holiday cookies, listened to Christmas carols, and enjoyed spontaneous visits from Wild Bill. Some days we lounged around in our pajamas and never even left the resort. I hadn't realized how badly I'd been craving rest, but my body's reaction to comfort made the need clear. I stayed in bed as long as I wanted each morning, and I slept through an entire night for the first time since Belize.

After thoroughly enjoying our days of luxury, we bid the good life farewell, stuffed our hiking packs, and walked down the street to grab a taxi out of this place. Balancing our lives on our backs, we looked at each other pitifully and remembered that we were still nomads. It had been such a blessing to stay at this comfortable Panamanian resort, but it was time to face reality. Soon, we would be boarding a plane and had no idea what to expect on the other side of the border.

Part Two: South America

Chapter Nine

COLOMBIA: South America Begins

Drugs, violence, coffee plantations, guerrillas, drug cartels...

So many words danced around my head as I prepared to get on the plane to Colombia. I'd heard a lot of negative talk about this country and honestly wasn't sure if the rumors were true or not. One of my friends joked that if I got a white Christmas in Colombia it wasn't because of snow. While I wondered if Colombia was truly just a mess of drugs and violence, I secretly hoped that the country would surprise me.

When the vision for the Iris Latin America team was birthed in 2010, the original plan was to head to South America only. Though the dream eventually expanded to Central America and the Caribbean, there was something special about holding the original vision in our hearts. Our team had gone through some amazing experiences in Central America, but we all felt a shift was coming as we entered South America. There was something significant about reaching the place where the vision for our trip began. Despite negative reports about Colombia, I knew our first destination in South America would bring forth positive change.

On Christmas Eve, Rose, Elizabeth, Breck, and I left Panama and flew to Cartagena, Colombia to meet up with the rest of the team. Jesse met us at the airport and brought us to a YWAM base in the city where we would stay for the next few days. Despite the terrible things I'd heard about the lack of safety in Colombia, I immediately fell in love with this gorgeous country. Cartagena was far more beautiful than I'd imagined — streets filled with glittering Christmas lights, horse-drawn carriages, and street performers. The buildings exhibited European architecture, and I felt more like I was in Spain than South America. Part of Cartagena was known as the "Walled City," where ancient fortresses had been built to keep out invaders. There were still walled areas where you could climb and look at cannons pointing towards the crashing waves of the ocean. Cartagena was lined with the beautiful Caribbean coast and had a bit of island flavor mixed in with the taste of Europe.

Besides lovely scenery, the Colombian people were among the friendliest we'd encountered throughout our journey. Two locals met our team at the YWAM base in Colombia and decided to join us for several months. In addition, we welcomed a short-term sister from Scotland. Liney, born and bred in Cartagena, immediately wowed us with her fiery passion for the Lord, dynamic prayers, and infectious laughter. Full of joy, she overflowed with God's presence and shined light during some of the darkest hours of the trip. Liney served as an amazing translator but also encouraged me to push myself and attempt translating without help, believing in my ability despite my obvious *gringa* accent. Her Colombian sidekick, David, was a charming and encouraging man of God, simply adored by the team from day one. He was the epitome of a "people person," always ready to preach in front of a crowd, speak to a group of kids, hang out with someone in need of love, or simply greet a teammate with a hug and kiss. Lastly, Scottish Lisa joined us for a short but fruitful visit. One of the most pure-hearted people on the face of the planet, I knew I could always depend on Lisa for a warm smile or kind word. Flexible, open, and genuine, Lisa was willing to step in wherever needed and blessed the team with her sweet friendship and heart of worship.

On Christmas Day, our growing family celebrated the holiday together. We started off the day by cooking an extravagant breakfast full with pancakes, eggs, bacon, hot chocolate, and more. Afterwards, we sat together and sang some Christmas carols even though we didn't actually know most of the words. We had already given each other "Secret Santa" gifts back in Panama before Taylor and Josiah left the team, so we didn't have any physical presents to give each other. It was kind of strange to have a Christmas with no gifts, no snow, no tree, and no stockings.

However, we had all written words of affirmation for each person on the team during our time in Panama, and on Christmas Day, we finally got to see what had been written about us. This turned out to be better than any tangible presents we could have purchased. We took turns going around a circle, everyone choosing another teammate and reading his or her words of affirmation aloud. As I listened to what had been written about each person, I realized how well we really knew each other and how much we loved one other. The fact that our team functioned as a loving family was a gift in and of itself.

The rest of our morning was spent praying and worshipping. We prophesied over the remainder of our trip, believing for a new level of breakthrough now that we had entered South America. The weight of the Holy Spirit was thick as we prayed for more. For the first time, it truly hit me that I was part of something much bigger than myself. I realized that dreaming for a few people to be saved or healed was far too small. It was time to dream for a whole nation, even a whole continent. If our team refused to limit God, who knew what He would do?

After dreaming, praying, and laughing together, a bunch of us headed to a nearby mall and got on the internet to contact our families. I'd known there would be no internet access at the YWAM base but had been praying for an opportunity to be able to Skype my family on Christmas Day. God answered my prayer, and I got to see my parents' and sisters' faces via webcam, which was really the only Christmas gift I had been asking for.

In the evening, we shared another family feast and watched a Christmas movie together. I felt extremely blessed and thankful that I could share this day with such a wonderful group of people. Though sunny and sweaty Cartagena didn't feel like my typical American Christmas, it was good enough for me.

Once our holiday celebration was over, we planned to drive to the capital city of Bogotá. We wanted to depart Cartagena as soon as possible; however, we couldn't go anywhere until we picked up our vehicles from the port. We prayed that the vehicles arrived undamaged and that the paperwork at the Colombian port was not as nightmarish as the red tape at the Panamanian port. The registered vehicle owners headed to the harbor and began the battle with the shipping company on the receiving end of things, spending days filling out more ridiculous loads of paperwork to get our vehicles back. Ted possessed documentation that allowed him to pick up Taylor's car since he was currently in Texas, and we feared this would cause confusion. Just as we'd expected, the process was far more complicated than necessary. Because of the paperwork that had to be filled out at the Colombian port, it took two full days to reacquire our vehicles. However, at long last, we were reunited with our trusty fleet; and by miracle of miracles, nothing was stolen or damaged inside the cars.

Finally, we were ready to start our drive to Bogotá. We had been told the roads leading to Bogotá were flooded, and it could take us days to get there. We had a choice among three different routes to the capital and chose ours very carefully. After two very long days of driving, we made it to the outskirts of Bogotá. We heard news that one of the routes we had *not* chosen had been attacked by FARC, the rebel guerrilla group in Colombia. They had attacked and blown up a car on the road. Meanwhile, we'd been driving peacefully for days without any signs of rebels, floods, or roadblocks. The Holy Spirit had led us to the right path.

During our third morning of travel, we drove into a downtown area of Bogotá and met up with a local young woman named Alejandra. She'd attended one of the recent mission schools in Mozambique where she had been a student alongside several of my teammates. She was born and bred in Bogotá and agreed to be our guide around the city for the next few days. Beautiful Alejandra was an amazing host with a genuine heart for her country and people. As she led us around Bogotá, I quickly realized why she loved Colombia so much.

We asked Alejandra for recommendations on where to lodge during our time in Bogotá, and she told us that we were welcome to stay at a local YWAM base. We headed in that direction but quickly discovered that there was nowhere to park our bulky vehicles. We'd heard talk of an RV park nearby and decided to check that out instead. Unfortunately, what we thought would be a short drive turned into a long, painful process of winding through undulating mountain terrain. We drove for so long and got so far away from the city that it felt more like Switzerland than Bogotá. Though the mountains were beautiful, I wondered why we would go this deep into a rural area if our plan was to minister in the city.

We finally reached the "RV park," which actually turned out to be nothing more than a local man's backyard. He pointed us towards an extremely narrow entrance into his yard and instructed us to drive our vehicles through. In the process, we shattered one of the RV windows, got Overflow stuck in the mud, and pretty much destroyed the poor man's lawn. We sheepishly got out of our monster vehicles, and the frigid mountain air stabbed at my face. It was still light outside, but I was already shivering in misery. I looked around. The scenery here was beautiful — but freezing — and miles from the city. I remembered that it was New Year's Eve and wanted to cry. I had envisioned a warm night of salsa dancing or some exotic Colombian celebration, not getting hypothermia on top of a mountain.

Rose reminded Jesse that a couple of people needed to drive back into the city to pick up her friend Kimmie from the airport. She was flying in to join the team for the remainder of the trip and needed someone to get her. Desperate to escape the cold, I volunteered to accompany Rose to the airport, as did a few others. As more and more people requested to join the airport run, it became apparent that no one really wanted to stay here. After winding through the mountains, destroying the man's lawn and the RV window, and wasting hours of time, we headed back *down* the mountain to find a campsite closer to the city. Frustrated by such a counterproductive day, all I wanted to do was bash my head against a wall.

As we worked our way down the mountain, Jesse noticed a simple restaurant that had some grass behind it and asked the manager if we could set up our tents there. The owner said a few dollars per person would grant us access. We were still far from the city and at a high elevation, but it was already 9 p.m., and we needed to sleep somewhere. I was so cold and exhausted that I felt nothing but disgust for this place.

We tried to set up our pop-up campers as usual, but the one where I normally slept snapped and broke as we cranked it up. It was too late and dark to attempt fixing it, so the six of us who'd been planning to use this pop-up were told we needed to either pitch a tent or sleep in one of the cars. As my teeth chattered, I wondered how I would survive the night in a tent without getting frostbite. I'd seen a movie about a guy who got so cold that his toes turned black, and he had to get them amputated. Quite frankly, I wasn't in the mood.

I found temporary relief from the cold as Rose, Alejandra, David, and I headed to the airport to pick up our new teammate, Kimmie. Rose had roomed with Kimmie in Mozambique and had been talking about her arrival for months. Kimmie had spent the last few months finishing up college and was able to join us now that she had graduated. When we received her at the airport, I immediately knew we would get along well. Her friendly attitude, quality sense of humor, and openness made me feel like I'd known her for years. As we drove back to the campsite, we warned Kimmie about the dismal sleeping arrangements. She handled the situation like a champ and gracefully jumped into team life. Before long, she earned the nickname "Kimmie Sunshine," a stunningly radiant person inside and out. Always smiling, encouraging others, and spreading beauty wherever she went, Kimmie quickly became a beloved friend.

We arrived back at the campsite around 11:30 p.m., as the rest of the team was preparing to walk to a nearby viewpoint. They'd been told we could watch fireworks from there at midnight. All of us, Kimmie included, walked to the area that overlooked the city. Despite the glacial temperature, I must admit that Bogotá looked beautiful all lit up. Unfortunately, the fireworks were less than impressive, but our team forced a celebration nonetheless. We counted down to midnight together and all gave each other hugs when the clock hit twelve. Despite feeling massive disappointment in the way 2012 was starting, I knew this new year would be a good one. I was in great company, and even though our lives were strange, they were also richly blessed.

We walked back to our campsite, and I claimed a spot in Overflow, hoping it would be slightly warmer than sleeping in my tent. I awkwardly snuggled into the back seat and wrapped myself in my sleeping bag. Rose crawled into the Suburban as well, and we agreed that the car provided zero extra warmth from the biting air outside. Part of me wanted to cry as I shivered myself to sleep; the other wanted to laugh at how ridiculous my life had become. I was legitimately homeless and found it both terribly miserable and absurdly humorous.

The next morning, we decided it would be wise to search for a warmer place to stay. Jesse walked just a few buildings down and found a set of restaurants with some open land between them. He spoke to the manager of "The Beer Wagon" who explained that he owned an unoccupied building that had once been used as a bar. He offered us lodging on the floor of the bar for five bucks a night. In addition, the manager would provide us with quality food from The Beer Wagon at a discounted price. Jesse gladly took the offer and had the team unload our belongings into the vacant building. It was shaped like a hexagon and had an empty, circular bar counter inside. The girls placed our sleeping mats outside of the counter and left the enclosed space inside the bar for the guys. We'd slept in a lot of weird places, but this one topped the list. Here we were, a group of missionaries, sleeping on the floor around a bar and ordering food from The Beer Wagon.

I had hoped that sleeping inside would provide adequate warmth, but without a heating system, the building provided little relief from the cold. It was impossible to sleep at night, and it didn't take long for exhaustion and sickness to plague our team. We pushed through the next few days, wearily ministering as Alejandra led us. I wanted to give everything I had during my time in Bogotá, but my desire to serve simply did not align with the condition of my body.

One afternoon, Alejandra took us to the red light district of Bogotá to minister to prostitutes. A group of women from a local church accompanied us to the streets. We strolled along sidewalks lined with prostitutes, including a disturbing mix of transvestites, young girls, and middle-aged women. I'd never really seen anything like this before and felt like I was in some sort of warped movie. It was so perverse that it didn't seem real. Alejandra told us to simply share the love of Christ with the women and make sure that, no matter what, we looked them in the eyes and didn't pay attention to their skimpy apparel.

We split into groups of three, and mine approached a middle-aged woman standing on the sidewalk and asked her how she was doing. Though I'd heard women in the sex trade were usually considered "used up" by their mid-twenties, Bogotá was full of prostitutes well into their fifties. I was a bit shocked at the woman's age but tried to hide my feelings and engage her in conversation. As we spoke, I forgot the woman was a prostitute and saw nothing but a hurting person. Her name was Elizabeth, and she was a mother of two. She told us how much she worried about her sons. Their father was out of the picture, and Elizabeth was extremely concerned about the welfare of her family. Though she was dressed in practically nothing, Elizabeth was really no different than most of the middle-aged women I knew back home. She was simply a loving mother who cared deeply about her kids. Unfortunately for her, she had no way of making money other than selling her body.

As we told Elizabeth how loved and precious she was and applauded her caring mother's heart, she welled up with tears. We prayed for her, and I could see that her heart was stirred. Afterwards, Elizabeth asked if it was alright if she gave us each a hug. In a culture where everyone hugged and kissed freely, I was surprised she would ask permission to touch us. Wondering if she feared she was too dirty for us, I smiled and wrapped my arms around her. The pain in her eyes was momentarily replaced by a glimmer of hope. In the midst of perversion and brokenness, I embraced this beautiful moment.

We continued walking down the street and encountered a few other young women who were much more closed off. Two of them were extremely young, and it was clear that they wanted nothing to do with us. We tried to make conversation, but they simply snickered and made eyes at one another. Their walls were thick and high, and they certainly weren't going to let us in. My heart ached to see how prostitution had so cleverly enslaved them. These girls were young and beautiful and had endless potential. It seemed a crime to throw it away, but that was the reality of the sex industry.

After we'd spent an hour or so in the streets talking to various women, our group went to a rehab center for girls who had formerly been prostitutes. We were asked to share a brief message and pray with the women. As we walked into the center, I was taken aback by the sight of these girls. They were youthful and stunning; I could scarcely believe they had just left a life of selling their bodies on the streets.

Liz and Liney shared a few words of encouragement with the women, then explained that our team would like to pray one-on-one with them. We decided to tackle those with physical ailments first. One of my teammates had a word of knowledge that someone needed healing in her eyes. Two sisters in the program came forward and said that they both had blurry vision and wanted to be healed. Susy and Elizabeth (our teammate Elizabeth, not the woman we'd met on the street) prayed for them, and the two sisters were completely healed. They started reading things around the room, realizing they didn't need glasses anymore. The sisters embraced each other and the women on our team, excitedly celebrating their miracle.

Others came forward for prayer, while some remained in their seats waiting to be approached. I quickly realized the spiritual and emotional problems in this place far exceeded the physical. I spoke with a woman who was severely depressed and felt totally alone. She told me that demons choked her at night, and though she wanted to scream, she couldn't speak at all during these attacks. A few of us prayed for her, rebuking the curse of oppression and declaring the freedom of Christ over her life. As we prayed and chatted with her, the heaviness on her seemed to lift, and she began to show a hint of emotion. The icy look on her face began to melt, and she even cracked a smile.

Tanya prayed for a girl who wanted to get out of the rehab center so she could do drugs. Though she knew the rehab center was in her best interest, she felt trapped by the cycle of addiction. After Tanya prayed with her, the girl declared that she had the strength to get through the program.

Susy and Elizabeth prayed for a woman named Paula who had been in the rehab center for twelve days. She struggled with drugs and had been kicked out of other rehabilitation programs. Paula had been told that she was hopeless because she couldn't stay clean, and she started to believe the words that had been spoken over her. Paula gave Susy and Elizabeth permission to pray for her and proclaim liberty from the bondage of addiction. Not only did she accept this new freedom, but she also accepted Christ as her Savior that day.

Liney sat with a small group of girls and shared her testimony about not feeling worthy to have a good husband in the past but learning that God had chosen an amazing man for her. She told the women that the Lord had husbands prepared for them as well. The women asked Liney about having a boyfriend, and she said that she'd never had one. She was waiting for her husband. The girls were flabbergasted; this was completely contrary to the promiscuous ways they'd been taught. Liney explained that they could live in purity and marry husbands who truly loved them. Their pasts were their pasts; Christ died to make them pure. At first, the women were confused by such a foreign concept. It was the first time they'd been encouraged to live in purity and were told God loved them enough to bring them loving husbands. Liney shared in confidence and boldness, challenging all the lies these women had believed for years.

Our team felt a new burst of freedom in that rehab center and left feeling fresh hope for the women living there. As we walked back to our car, one of the Colombians who'd joined us for the day opened up to some of the girls on my team. She had seen the women in the rehab center get healed and explained that she was suffering from breast cancer. She wanted to be healed too. My teammates asked if there was any way she would know if the cancer was cured. She said she had lumps on her breasts, and it would be easy to see and feel if they had gone. My teammates began to pray, and after praying the first time, the lumps began to shrink. Something was definitely happening, but the woman was only partially healed. With increased faith, my teammates prayed again, and this time the lumps disappeared completely! The woman felt her breasts, crying with joy as she realized the lumps were gone. She knew her breast cancer had been healed. Though I believed she was cured, I secretly wanted medical confirmation. Weeks later, Alejandra wrote us to report that the woman had gone to her doctors to verify the healing. Sure enough, they did some medical tests and confirmed that the lumps were wholly gone. The woman was declared cancer-free, and the doctors had no medical explanation for such a miracle.

After spending a few days in Bogotá, we drove to our next Colombian destination, the township of Anolaima. Alejandra had coordinated with a local family who pastored a charismatic church there and wanted a visit from our team. The sweet family welcomed us with open arms and made us feel right at home. They provided free food and housing (with real beds) throughout our time in Anolaima, expecting nothing in return. They had various ministry opportunities for us but were incredibly flexible with when and how we wanted to serve. Their offer of hospitality, freedom, and warmth made all of us want to help this church and family in any way possible.

Though our time in Anolaima was brief, it was full and memorable. One morning, we accompanied the pastor's daughter to visit two senior homes. Most of the people living there couldn't understand a word we said and laughed as we attempted conversation. I was confused whether their senility or our bad Spanish was the problem, but either way I was glad to see them laughing. Mostly, we wanted to encourage the pastor's daughter in her ministry. She was used to ministering without a team, and it was clear that she was thankful to have people run alongside her for a bit.

Our team also took part in a couple of church services — one where we focused on encouraging the youth and filling them with the fire of the Holy Spirit, another where we shared with the church as a whole. Addison shared his powerful testimony of God restoring him after a life of drugs and alcohol. We prayed for many people in the congregation, interceding for physical healing and spiritual freedom.

We also met with the pastor and his family for a more private meeting where the family shared their vision for a project God had laid on their hearts many months ago. They dreamt of purchasing a great plot of land and building a large complex where people could come and seek the Lord. They desired to construct a church, a park, and an area where members of the community could come and relax. We prayed for their plans and asked God's blessing over their vision. My team prophesied over the family and stood in agreement with them for God's miraculous provision in regards to the project.

After just a few days, we'd developed a heart connection with the church, but sadly it was already time to move on to our next destination. Alejandra now led us to a rural area outside the city of Armenia. Here, we met up with Carlos and Maria, two more Colombians who had attended mission school in Mozambique. Both of them had a passion for their home country and longed to see God transform their nation with His love. Full of generosity, hospitality, and passion, they excitedly welcomed our team and took care of us throughout our remaining time in Colombia.

When we arrived outside of Armenia, Carlos and Maria graciously hosted us at Maria's charming family farmhouse where we were greeted with open arms, provided with free lodging, and spoiled with delicious food. We were given fresh milk from the farm's cows each morning and avocados straight from the trees. Carlos and Maria explained that we would stay at the farmhouse for a few days to rest and relax, and then they would bring us to their hometown of Cali to begin ministry. Our time at the farm was intended for simply enjoying the beauty of Colombia and the warm hospitality of Maria's family. Each day, I ran along the dirt roads surrounding the farmhouse, drinking in the beauty of the vibrant scenery. The view from every direction was gorgeous — majestic mountains, lush vegetation, and thriving fields of coffee. This wasn't the violent Colombia I'd been warned about. This was one of the most breathtaking places I'd ever seen.

In between spending time at the farmhouse, we did spurts of ministry in the streets. One afternoon, we met a man hobbling with a crutch who said he hadn't been able to walk properly for a year. After praying for him, he was able to walk without the crutch. That same afternoon, one of my teammates felt God showing her the color blue, and someone else saw a picture of a woman in high heels. While passing through the streets, we noticed an entirely blue building called "Blue Point." We walked inside, discovering a shoe store with a very friendly man at the front counter. As we conversed with him, a woman with red high heels walked into the store. We explained that God had shown us the color blue and high heels, and we believed He was pointing to her. The woman admitted that she had a rough relationship with her son and wanted us to pray for restoration. The store owner observed our interaction with the woman, amazed at how God had brought us together. He wanted prayer as well, so we interceded for the woman and the store owner, blessing her family and his business before heading back home.

In the evening, we drove into a more urban area and continued speaking with people on the streets. Many were homeless and on drugs. Some of my teammates met a homeless man who said that it was his birthday. Sadly, no one had celebrated with him in years. Right there on the street, a few people decided to throw a birthday party for the homeless man. He became a bit shy as they sang to him, astounded that people were actually celebrating his life. Many prayers had been prayed for strangers that day, but they somehow all seemed to pale in comparison to the simple tune of "Happy Birthday." This modest celebration was a landmark moment in the homeless man's life.

We returned to Maria's farmhouse but soon left our taste of Colombian paradise for Cali, our final destination in Colombia. Maria and Carlos had both grown up in the city of Cali, as did David who had joined our team in Cartagena. The three of them attended the same church, Rey de Reyes, an amazing community of believers led by the one and only Pastor Diego. Before driving to our accommodation in Cali, the Colombian crew brought us to Rey de Reyes, where Diego officially welcomed us to his city. He met us with great expectation and shared his excitement to see how the Lord would move during our time in Cali. His passion for Cali was evident, and his desire to see more of God's presence made me excited to be there. It was clear that Diego felt the heartbeat of God and longed for revival among his people.

Carlos and Maria explained that Rey de Reyes was going to supply us with free housing during our time in Cali as well as three meals a day. They had a retreat center about thirty minutes from the church that they wanted us to enjoy — including a private cook, beds, and a breathtaking view of the city. The center was close enough to easily drive downtown but far enough from the city that it had a peaceful, rural feel. It was surrounded by rolling hills, stunning farmland, and rushing waterfalls. I had grown to have meager expectations in regards to lodging, but this place was luxurious in every way. There were probably over one hundred beds for us to choose from, several bathrooms, an outdoor patio, and even a swimming pool. Just when I thought things couldn't get any better, Diego showered us with even more generosity. He offered to pay for much-needed vehicle repairs, taxi fare for airport runs to pick up new teammates, and a general offering to simply bless the team. I had never seen such incredible generosity in my life.

Throughout the next few days, our team grew significantly. We were reunited with Taylor L. after almost a month in the States. Our family had not been the same without him, and it was great to have our brother back. In addition, he brought two new recruits from Texas — his fiercely loyal best friend (also named Taylor) and his sweet and sassy church acquaintance, Angela. Taylor M. became a little brother almost immediately, constantly making me laugh with his goofy faces, funky hairstyles, and incessant questions about the secrets looming inside every girl's mind. Always positive, always fun, always protective, always full of faith, and *always* hungry, Taylor was adopted as my friend, brother, entertainer, and personal food disposal. Angela was open and easy to talk to — a relatable girl and a good listener. I could see there was a fighter inside of her, yet she was beautifully sensitive and delicate. I'd never met anyone with compassion quite like Angela's. Her heart genuinely broke when she saw others in pain, truly allowing her heart to beat with God's heart. Next, Dianne rejoined the team after months of separation due to the sudden death of her daughter-in-law. We'd been praying for her ever since the traumatic news in Guatemala, and it was amazing to have our wild mama back with us. Dianne flew in with a new team member as well, sweet Aleeza from Australia. Aleeza's heart was tender yet adventurous — a winning combination. She was one of the first to serve others but the last to want any credit. Aleeza's humility, soft demeanor, and willingness to try anything made her a perfect fit for our team. Lastly, jungle man Stephen joined us. I'd befriended him in Mozambique and had heard stories of his many years living in the jungles of Peru. He had more missionary experience than most of us and brought wisdom, stability, and integrity to our family. I looked up to him as a big brother and always felt safer when he was around. In addition, Stephen had an uncanny ability to fix everything and anything with nothing. We were all thankful to have MacGyver finally join our team.

For the next couple of weeks, we enjoyed the privilege of running alongside Pastor Diego, Carlos, and Maria. We attended two services at Rey de Reyes where our team was asked to preach, pray, share testimonies of healing, and invite the fire of God to fall on the congregation. The people in this church were hungry, open, and zealous. Our second church service quickly transformed from worship and prayer to a massive dance party. The joy of the Lord reigned in that place.

During the week, Carlos and Maria put us to work. First, we went to a rehab center started by some of Maria's relatives. The center was quite removed from the city, located in an isolated area atop a mountain. Based on the residents' excitement at the arrival of our team, it was a fair guess that the men rarely received visitors. Our group was asked to sit while each man living in the center stood up, one by one, and shared his testimony of how he had wound up there. The men were incredibly open, not at all reluctant to share how long they'd done drugs or how much time they'd spent in rehab.

They shared their hearts with us, and afterwards, we were asked to speak a little bit about ourselves. Before we could open our mouths, all of the men rushed forward and sat at our feet, like children excitedly awaiting a teacher to read them a story. Smiling at their childlike eagerness, we now shared, one by one, explaining where we were from and how we wanted to see God move throughout our journey. The men hung onto our every word, hungry to hear more about what God had already done and what we believed He *would* do. A few people from the team shared testimonies of God's power and provision as well as encouraging verses from the Bible. After sharing, we asked if the men would be open to prayer. They eagerly positioned themselves to receive a blessing, and we walked around to lay hands on each one. At the end of the evening, it felt like we were leaving a family gathering, not a rehab center. The men had become brothers, and they reminded me that the love of God transcended gender, culture, or background. Love made us a family.

The next day, Pastor Diego brought us to a church service in the inner city. We were warned that we were headed to a pretty dicey neighborhood, so I braced myself for the worst. Yet, unexpectedly, the church was one of the most welcoming I'd ever seen. The congregation warmly greeted each of us with a kiss and escorted us to a row of seats reserved for our team. We enjoyed sweet songs of worship and heavenly harmonies flowing from the peoples' tongues. Eventually, our team was invited to come forward to prophesy over the church and share words of edification. Every word was received with enthusiastic applause and "amens." It was a rare blessing to see a congregation *this* desperate for the word of the Lord. It was like they drank in God's word until it overflowed and spilled out as praise.

After speaking to the church as a whole, we ministered to individuals and families in the congregation. One younger girl caught my eye, and I felt an overwhelming need to declare God's love over her. I laid my hand on her shoulder, prayed, and whispered in her ear, "You are beautiful. You are God's daughter. You are precious." Upon hearing these words, she began to weep. Her heart was being stirred, and despite the pain I saw her carrying, I knew she needed to hear the truth. I continued to pray for others, repeatedly met with the same emotion, hunger, and desire for the Lord. At the night's end, it was clear that God had been moving, speaking, and healing in this place. Person after person approached our team and offered countless kisses and hugs before we could exit the building.

The following day, Diego presented our team with an offering from the inner-city church. I was confused. We had been told this was an extremely poor church. It was located in an underprivileged neighborhood, and there was no way they had extra cash to throw around. But small wallets made no difference to huge hearts. This kind church took an offering for our team and blessed us with an incredibly generous amount of money. Blown away once more by the generosity in Colombia, I thanked God for such an amazing example of His love and prayed He would bless this church a hundredfold for the blessings it had given us.

Later in the week, the women on our team were invited to visit a high-security prison in Cali. We waited in line outside of the prison for what felt like hours, then began a long process of paperwork and fingerprinting. We waited so long that we were told our window of opportunity to speak to the inmates would probably be over by the time we got through security. We prayed for divine favor and moments later were told that they'd extended visiting hours so that we could speak to a group of the women. The prison officials released our group in pairs, checking two passports at a time and then sending off each pair to another security check. I was part of one of the last pairs to be released, so I knew I would probably miss most of the time my team had been allotted to share with the prisoners.

Following an eternity of waiting, the jail officials finished doing whatever they were doing with my passport and sent me and Lisa to our next security checkpoint. There, we were fingerprinted and instructed to sit in a chair quietly. A guard brought a dog over to the chair, and he circled around me and Lisa, sniffing for drugs. After we were cleared, we were sent to yet another security checkpoint. Lisa and I were met by an official in front of the women's ward where we were stopped for the third time. The official dug her finger beneath the underwire in my bra, pulled it out hard, then let go, allowing it to snap back against my chest. I jumped in surprise and burst into giggles. Lisa did the same. I don't think the guards were used to people laughing about this. I didn't care. I was just ready to be done with these checkpoints.

At long last, we were granted entry to the room where the rest of our teammates were sharing testimonies with the prisoners. Lisa and I had missed most of the meeting but arrived in time to pray with the women one-on-one. As I asked them what they wanted me to pray for, most requested the same thing. These women had children and were worried about them. None asked to be miraculously acquitted or to receive shorter sentences; they simply wanted their kids to be okay. The women shed tears as we prayed for their families and assured them that God would guard their children. It reminded me of our time with Elizabeth, the prostitute in Bogotá, who cried as we prayed for her children. It didn't matter where we were; a mom was a mom. Reminded of my own mother's love, I enjoyed listening to the women and hearing their hearts for their kids. I suddenly forgot these women had committed crimes and simply engaged in girl talk, laughing and smiling until we were told our time was up. We hugged goodbye and reminded the women to remember how much God loved them. When they lived in the presence of God, even inside prison walls it was possible to experience freedom.

Later that evening, Carlos and Maria organized some street ministry with another local church called Vida Eterna. We met up with a group of twentysomethings from that fellowship who accompanied us to a downtown area of Cali filled with homeless people, transvestites, and prostitutes. We split into small groups, each one given food, sweets, and warm drinks to offer. I was partnered with Natalie M. and a Colombian from Vida Eterna named Camilo. We started our evening by approaching a couple of men sitting on the street. They gladly accepted some food as Camilo told them that God loved them. One man quietly nodded in agreement, looking ashamed yet open to hear good news. The other, blatantly drunk, thought he was beyond repair and began to cry out, "No sé, no sé!" (I don't know! I don't know!) as hot tears poured from his eyes. Camilo tried to reason with him but was quickly interrupted by another drunk man who started to fight with the first. We tried to remove the second man from the situation so we could converse with the original two, but it was no use. After one of the men started grabbing at Natalie, I told Camilo we needed to leave, and we continued down the street, the image of the quiet man's melancholy eyes burned into my mind.

We noticed another homeless man lying on the sidewalk and stopped to offer him some food. He gladly accepted, reaching for the snacks while simultaneously sharing information about his battle with drugs. Because of the mess he'd created in his life, he hadn't seen his family in a long time. We told him God could free him from his addiction and provide restoration in his life. "Do you want Him to give you hope in something better?" we asked.

The man nodded sadly. His own energy and willpower was gone, but if God could heal him, he wanted Him. The man agreed to let us pray for him, somberness surging from his eyes. We continued walking down the street, offering promises of hope and light yet feeling the weight of darkness in this place.

We passed a man who was eating out of the trash and asked him if he wanted any of our food. He refused to accept what we had to offer. We'd been told that some people in Cali had recently attempted a "social cleansing" and killed people on the streets by offering them food filled with poison. I suppose the man questioned our intentions and preferred the safety of eating straight from the garbage. He ignored us and continued to consume mouthfuls of the most grotesque substance I'd ever seen. I gagged as I watched him choke down what looked like rotting worms from a heaping pile of trash.

By around midnight, we met up with the other groups and shared stories of what we'd encountered throughout the evening. I hadn't seen any miracles tonight. Instead I'd witnessed drunk men fighting, a hopeless addict, and a man eating rubbish. I knew I'd never see those men again, and I'd never find out if they quit drinking or stopped using drugs or got off the streets. All I knew was that God told me to go to the dark places where others wouldn't go, and those streets in Cali were dark places. Sometimes my team had the privilege of seeing God operate in the miraculous. But at other times, we simply had to believe in faith that He was there when all we could see was brokenness — among the drunkards, throughout the gloomy streets, and alongside the heaps of garbage.

When the weekend arrived, Carlos and Maria wanted to bless our team by giving us a break from ministry and celebrating Colombian culture with them. Maria invited us to another family farmhouse a few hours outside of Cali. When we got there, a juicy pork barbeque, tasty drinks, and Colombian snacks were awaiting us. Carlos pumped the salsa music, and the Colombians did their best at teaching us how to move our hips the Cali way. Carlos and Maria explained that Cali was the capital of salsa dance, and they wanted to celebrate their culture by hosting a salsa dance competition. Carlos and Maria arranged us in pairs and declared that they would judge our dancing. Though hesitant to perform (due to my severe lack of salsa skills), I ended up having an incredible night of fun and laughter. Undaunted by my inability to learn a single step of salsa, Breck, my superiorly skilled partner, reverted to flipping me over his back to impress the judges. Though this maneuver got us to the semifinals, Aleeza and Kurt, the two Aussies, won favor with the crowd and were named the winning pair.

After hours of attempting salsa, the Americans switched the music to hip hop and showed the Colombians some dance flavor from north of the border. The guys concluded the night by throwing the girls into Maria's pool. We shrieked in surprise, laughed at our sopping clothes, and finally went to bed — wet, tired, but thankful to be in Colombia.

The following evening, we drove back to the retreat center in Cali. We spent the remainder of our time in Colombia dealing with vehicle repairs, fixing the broken pop-up trailer, and taking care of errands while stationed in a large city. Pastor Diego constantly extended his hand of help and generosity. I had never met a man quite like him and wished he could remain with our team until the end of the trip. Carlos, Maria, and Alejandra had become vital members of our team as well, and the thought of soon saying goodbye to them just didn't seem right.

We had come to bless Colombia, but Colombia had blessed us far more. In the midst of a country labeled as a hotbed for drugs and violence, I experienced the complete opposite of what I'd been warned about. I felt incredible love. I watched people get healed and set free. I received unmatched generosity. I enjoyed scenery so gorgeous that only God could have created it. I felt at peace, at home, and in awe.

I don't believe it's a coincidence that a God who uses the weak things of the world to shame the wise started our South American adventure in Colombia. He brought us to a country known for its weaknesses to begin a display of His strength throughout an entire continent. Though my human mind couldn't fathom greater levels of generosity or breakthrough, this was only the beginning.

Chapter Ten

ECUADOR: Welcome to the Jungle

Due to vehicle maintenance in Cali, our team's original date of departure from Colombia was pushed back a bit (shocking, I know). Unfortunately, this caused a visa debacle for Natalie M. Most of us had been given sixty days on our Colombian visas, but Natalie's expired in just forty, which meant that if she didn't leave for Ecuador by the coming Sunday, she would be breaking the law. Natalie could be heavily fined for overstaying her allotted time, so she needed to cross the border ahead of the rest of the team. Meanwhile, Rose had traveled to England for a wedding and afterwards flew to Ecuador's capital, Quito. She had been waiting in Ecuador for days, and I felt uneasy about leaving her stranded in a new country without the team. Liz also felt an urgency to join up with Rose, so she, Natalie, and I began researching ways to get to Quito early.

After going in circles for a bit, it seemed our only viable option was an expensive and long bus ride. I was hesitant to take the bus, since my only other third world bus experiences had been less than pleasant. Yet, we needed to get to Quito, so we started packing for the bus ride nonetheless. Midway through rearranging all of my clothes, Natalie approached me and said Taylor L. might be willing to drive Counsel and Might across the border with us girls and his sidekick, Taylor M. The five of us gathered and discussed whether it was wise to take a single vehicle across the border. We knew it would be risky to drive without our normal convoy, because if there were any car problems, we wouldn't have extra vehicles to fall back on. However, Taylor's car had been one of the most dependable throughout the journey, and the chances of something going wrong seemed unlikely with the car's history. We decided to take the risk and drive to Quito together Sunday morning.

The night before, we reluctantly said goodbye to our Colombian family as well as Lisa, who was flying back to Scotland. We caught a few hours of sleep and left Cali Sunday morning at 4 a.m. A crack of dawn departure was necessary to ensure that Natalie made it across the border by that evening.

Our journey began smoothly — decent roads, no traffic, and an efficiently running vehicle. Liz took the wheel, and both Taylors and I fell asleep in the back of the car. I was woken up by an odd noise coming from the car's engine and Liz's voice trying to awaken Taylor L. "Taylor...Taylor...are you awake? Something doesn't feel right with your car."

The Buick began to jerk and make a horrible noise as Liz pulled over to the side of the road. Taylor woke up and looked under the hood to see what had gone wrong. We tried turning the car off and restarting it, but the engine wouldn't turn back on. After fiddling with the car for a bit, the guys said it would be best to find a mechanic. Taylor M., Liz, and I stayed with the car while Taylor L. and Natalie walked up the street to find help. Moments later, a convoy of police arrived at Counsel and Might.

The men had huge rifles and asked us what was wrong while pointing their guns at our vehicle. Liz offered them Ritz crackers in the hopes that a snack would deter them from shooting us. They noticed the Texas license plate on Taylor L.'s car and asked how long we had been driving. When we explained that we were traveling throughout all of Latin America and had been driving for almost five months, they laughed in surprise. I asked them if they knew anything about cars, and they shook their heads. It seemed the only thing they knew about was carrying guns and staring at white people.

After waiting quite a while, Taylor L. and Natalie appeared in the distance, riding on the back of two men's motorbikes. They had found a few mechanics and hitched a ride with them back to the Buick. Three men examined Taylor's car and explained that the gas pump was broken and needed to be replaced. They had no spares at their shop and insisted the only way we could get one was to hitchhike an hour backwards and hope they had some in the nearest city. The next major city in the direction we wanted to be going was four hours away, and we wouldn't make it. The men advised us to backtrack, spend the night in the city, and wait there while a mechanic fixed the car. We had only been driving for a few hours, and the thought of backtracking for an hour and spending money on a hotel seemed quite a waste. We refused to accept this as our only option and prayed that God would somehow miraculously remedy our situation and make a way where there was no way.

Soon after, the men looking at the car changed their story and said they thought our gas gauge had simply broken; and though we'd thought the car was full of gas, the tank was actually empty. They believed if we filled the car with fuel we'd be fine. One of the men drove back to his home to get us a couple of bottles of gas to dump into the Buick. Just as they'd expected, the car started properly after the tank was filled. The mechanic said he still thought something with the pump was a bit off, but we should be able to make it to Quito without any more problems and get it reexamined after we arrived at our final destination. Relieved that we hadn't agreed to hitchhike backwards, we drove onward.

The rest of our drive went smoothly. We enjoyed the freedom of a smaller team, taking time to stop for photo ops of the gorgeous scenery. We reached the Colombia-Ecuador border around 7:30 p.m. This was the first border we'd crossed in the dark, and though we'd been advised against it, crossing at night turned out to be a blessing. There were virtually no lines, and Natalie got her passport marked with a Colombian exit stamp before getting fined. If we hadn't left so early, we wouldn't have made it on time.

We hit a slight roadblock when Taylor L. attempted to fill out the paperwork for exiting his car from Colombia. Because Ted had picked up Taylor's car for him in Cartagena while he was home with his family, some of the car paperwork was in Ted's name, not Taylor's. The border official told us that Taylor would not be permitted to leave Colombia in his car unless he presented a specific paper that was supposedly in Ted's possession. We explained our situation, but the border official would not budge. It sounded like we would have to wait at the border for the rest of the team. We continued to try to persuade the woman to let us pass through and prayed for favor. After a few moments, the woman softened and told us to drive onward to Ecuador. She wrote down the name of her boss and said that if Ted spoke to her when he crossed the border, they could work out the legal process for the car registration. In the meantime, we were free to pass to the Ecuadorian side of the border to get our passport entry stamps and register Taylor's car for travel in Ecuador. We thanked the woman and excitedly drove out of Colombia.

We met a woman named Marta on the Ecuadorian side, a sweet and enthusiastic border official who handled the car paperwork. When she encountered our group, she eagerly embraced the opportunity to practice her English. Though she was far from fluent, she made a valiant effort; and when we told her that we could understand what she was trying to say, she lit up with excitement. Natalie, Taylor M., and Liz went outside for a moment while Taylor L. and I talked to Marta inside her office. Taylor asked if we could pray for her, and though Marta was not a Christian, she said she'd like to receive prayer. While Taylor prayed, God showed him that He was going to start speaking to Marta in dreams. Taylor told Marta, and she shared that she'd actually already had a very special dream that she believed was from the Lord. However, she didn't know what it meant.

Marta knew it was the end of the world, and she was standing with a few men around her. She felt scared. Marta saw a light coming from heaven with fingers reaching down. Suddenly, a tsunami came from behind her and rushed around her but didn't touch her. When the tsunami missed her, she saw a man and no longer felt scared. He reached out to her and said, "You have been given an opportunity." Then, God began to sing over her.

As she narrated this dream, Marta looked at me and Taylor and asked if we thought it meant anything. My jaw almost dropped to the floor as I nodded "yes." We explained to Marta that God had chosen her and had amazing plans for her life. He was speaking to her in a dramatic and special way. Taylor M., Natalie, and Liz came into the room mid-conversation, and we shared the dream with them. They were amazed at how God was speaking to Marta as well, and each shared words of encouragement with her. Liz said she could see angels on both sides of Marta who traveled with her always. Marta's face lit up as she asked, "With me? Always? *Really?*" She explained that she wanted to know God more but had never really felt His presence. We told Marta that she *did* have the ability to feel God and that the Holy Spirit would encounter her if she wanted Him to. We prayed for her a second time, and she accepted Christ into her heart, tears welling up in her eyes.

After spending an extra thirty minutes or so at the border, we told Marta we needed to continue driving. We explained that our teammates would be crossing the border in a couple of days, and maybe she would meet them soon. We hugged and kissed Marta goodbye as she wept with joy. All five of us realized that if we hadn't broken down for the three hours previously, we would have missed Marta at the border. Even if she had been working earlier, it would have been too busy during the day to take the time to speak to her. Since we arrived in the evening, the border was empty, and we had the freedom to spend time with Marta. I felt so honored and overwhelmed that the Lord had chosen us five to be a part of welcoming this beautiful woman into the kingdom of God.

Though we'd originally planned on making it to Quito in one day's drive, it was too late to make this happen. We decided to look for a cheap hotel to spend the night and continue on to Quito in the morning. We prayed specifically for a hostel that had hot showers, warm beds, wifi, and breakfast available. We also told God that we only wanted to spend ten dollars each. We asked several locals where we could find a cheap hotel and went in circles for quite a while. After we were about ready to give up, we arrived outside a small hostel that looked closed. All the windows were boarded up, but Natalie got out of the car and persistently banged on the door until a small Ecuadorian woman answered. She said there were two rooms available, each with three warm beds for just ten dollars apiece. When we found out there was wifi, hot showers, and breakfast as well, we knew God had answered our prayers. We snuggled into our cozy beds, thankful for a chance to rest, thankful we'd made it across the border in time, and thankful for our divine appointment with Marta.

The next day, we spent a leisurely morning enjoying our hot showers and tasty breakfast. We took off around 11 a.m., thinking we had only three to four hours remaining until Quito. After driving two hours or so, Counsel and Might began to overheat, and smoke poured from the hood. We pulled over to a dirt road, and the Taylors realized that some of the tubing under the hood had broken, allowing most of the coolant to leak out. We were in a very rural area without a mechanic or gas station in sight, so we weren't sure quite where to begin. We decided to wait by the car while it cooled off and hope for a stranger to help us out.

Moments later, a truck full of men pulled over to see what was wrong. One of them, Julio, offered to take me and Natalie to a local store to buy some coolant while the others stayed with the car. Just before we left, the guys said they wanted to push the Buick further from the main street to be safe and asked Liz to steer the car in neutral while they pushed. Natalie and I were already in Julio's car, ready to take off, when we noticed Counsel and Might speeding by with Liz in the driver's seat. I saw a look of panic on Liz's face as she frantically moved the steering wheel, and I watched as Taylor L., Taylor M., and a group of Ecuadorian men chased after the Buick, yelling and flailing their arms. They had thought the car would be too heavy to push away from the main road, but now it was actually speeding out of control, heading straight for a drastic, downhill drop. Liz was pushing on the brakes with no success in decelerating, while the men ran alongside the car as fast as they could in hopes of slowing it down. Unfortunately, their effort was useless, and Liz had no choice but to steer the car into a cement wall to stop it. Natalie and I watched this whole scene from Julio's car in shock until the spectacle ended with a loud

BANG against the cement. Taylor L. jumped back as the front left tire exploded and blew gravel all over him. Liz exited the car, horrified by what had just happened. The Taylors looked stunned. Natalie and I burst into a fit of giggles, unsure of what else to do. Julio gave us a disapproving look and started his car to take us to a mechanic.

Taylor L. told me and Natalie that other than the tire, his car was unscathed by the accident. He had a spare tire and could fix it without a mechanic, but he still desperately needed some coolant. Instead of taking me and Natalie directly to a store to buy the desired items, Julio took us to various stops around the city, finally bringing us back to a store that we had passed miles before. At last, we returned to Taylor's car with two large cans of coolant, but it wasn't enough. Taylor requested three more cans and a new piece of tubing. Julio said he didn't have much time left, so he asked us to quickly hop in the bed of his pickup to take us back to the store. As we drove, it began to rain. A huge rainbow burst across the sky, faithfully reminding our team of God's promises.

Natalie and I bumped along the dirt road in the back of Julio's truck and jumped out in front of the auto store, thankful to be out of the rain for a moment. We asked the salesman for more coolant, but he said we'd just purchased his last cans. We then asked for a small piece of tubing, and the man cut us a chunk from a large hose. We went outside with our tiny purchase, hoping Julio would be waiting in his truck for us, only to find that he'd driven off and left us behind. Without a choice, Natalie and I walked a long, uphill hike back to our friends, huffing and puffing as we arrived. We explained that our mission to buy coolant had failed but that we'd gotten some new tubing. Taylor L. looked at it, smiled, and told us that it was the wrong size. At this point, I couldn't do anything but laugh at our wasted effort.

Both Taylors handled the situation with grace and patiently finagled something together in place of proper tubing. They said if they could fill the coolant tank with water in place of coolant, we'd probably be able to make it to Quito. Between the five of us, we gathered our drinking water from the car, quickly discovering that we didn't have enough to fill the tank. Natalie and I walked down the street and found some sweet local children who offered us a large bucket of water from their home. We thanked the kids, dumped the water into the coolant tank, and went on our way.

By this time, it was late afternoon, and we knew we needed to make up for lost time. We took off with the hopes that the Taylors' innovative creation would be a success. Less than thirty minutes later, the car began to overheat again, and we were forced to pull over to the side of the road. Stranded in a remote spot, we had little choice but to wait for someone to stop and help us. Another stranger offered his assistance and took Natalie and Taylor L. in his car to find a mechanic. Ironically, they ended up back at the same village where Julio had driven us moments before.

Meanwhile, Taylor M., Liz, and I stayed behind with Counsel and Might. In an attempt to avoid the increasingly wet and chilly weather, we sat in the back of the car under blankets and turned on Taylor's laptop to watch a movie while we waited. Indigenous women passed by, staring into the car with a mix of confusion and amusement. It probably wasn't every day that they stumbled upon a Texan car full of white people watching a movie in the back seat. We didn't mind their stares or giggles; we were fully aware of how bizarre our lives had become.

Natalie and Taylor L. eventually returned with a mechanic who made a temporary fix by properly connecting the necessary tubing. It was too late in the evening to find an open mechanic shop and perform a long-lasting repair. The man said we could make it to Quito, but we'd have to get the car permanently fixed after we arrived. We drove on, now just a couple of hours away from Quito, crossing our fingers that we could complete the last stretch successfully. However, a half an hour later, the car began to overheat for the third time, and we abandoned all hopes that Counsel and Might would make it to Quito without a tow truck. It was almost 9 p.m., and nothing was open at this hour.

Despite the frustration, we were thankful that we'd broken down by a large dirt turnout, so we had a safe place to pull over. We were on a windy mountain road, it was pitch-black, and if we'd broken down in any other spot on the road, we would have been at a huge risk for getting hit by another car. The Taylors looked under the hood, realizing the temporary fix had already been ruined. They determined that if we tried to press on any further, we would destroy the engine. We needed to be towed, but we were in the middle of nowhere, with no clue how to reach a towing company or even explain where we'd broken down. Taylor L. said we should call Marco, our contact in Quito (who Rose was staying with), and ask him to pick us girls up while the guys stayed overnight with the Buick. They knew it wasn't safe to leave the car overnight and figured they'd sleep inside and find a mechanic in the morning. We girls insisted that we were family and refused to separate. The guys had always made us feel safe in the worst of situations, and there was no way we would leave them behind on a remote mountain after all the craziness we'd been through together.

We decided to call Marco and explain our situation. He said that if we could give him our location, he would come meet us in his car and bring a mechanic friend with him. Taylor M. randomly pulled out a hiking GPS that used a satellite to provide coordinates of where we were located. I couldn't believe that he just so happened to have such a handy device with him, but boy was I happy that he did. We gave Marco the coordinates, and he entered them into Google Maps to figure out where we'd broken down. He confirmed that we were, indeed, in the middle of nowhere and said he was on his way.

About an hour later, two cars arrived at the dirt turnout. Marco, his wife, Rose, and some friends kindly came to our rescue. We excitedly embraced Rose after weeks of being apart. Marco's mechanic friend looked at the car for a bit and said we definitely needed to be towed. He drove back to the next town and got a tow truck for us. We were told that this was the best road in Ecuador to break down on, because it happened to be the only road in the country where you could get towed for free. We got Counsel and Might onto the tow truck and hopped into the two vehicles that had come to rescue us. The Buick was dropped off near Marco's house where it would be repaired in just a couple of days.

After leaving the car behind, we continued on to Marco's beautiful home. He and his wife, Karina, welcomed us like family, offering us food, drinks, and soft, comfy beds. By the time we arrived at their house, it was already 2 a.m., and we thanked Marco and Karina for being so kind and gracious at such a late hour. Relieved to finally be in Quito, we snuggled into our new beds and passed out with exhaustion.

Soon after, the remainder of our team arrived in Quito. They reported that they had also encountered Marta at the border, who greeted them with great excitement. She shared her dream with the rest of our teammates, giving Stephen a chance to offer further interpretation. I was reminded that God dwelled in even the smallest of details, including what hour a border was crossed in order to intersect with the right person's schedule. He never ceased to amaze me.

We all rested for a couple of days and excitedly began to organize our first jungle adventure. The Amazon basin stretched into several countries, but Ecuador was our introduction to the Amazon. Since our team had grown so much, we decided to divide into two smaller groups while traveling into the jungle. It would be logistically easier to travel into remote areas with less people. We asked the Lord to divinely choose our teams and drew numbers out of a hat, hoping for the best. I was placed on a team led by Jesse and Tanya including Liney, Katherine, Natalie H., Liz, Aleeza, Breck, Taylor L., Ben, David, Moose, Zoe, and myself. The other group was led by Natalie M. and Stephen. Though both teams' leaders had experience managing outreaches to remote villages, none of them had any connections in the Ecuadorian jungle. Our entire trip would be completely dependent on the Holy Spirit and the divine connections the Lord would provide for us. We looked at a map, and each team chose a general area of the country to explore. We would start by hopping on a bus and then play it by ear from there.

We packed our bags with little idea of what we were actually packing for. Since I wasn't sure exactly where we'd end up or what the weather would be like, I tried to pack clothes for any situation. After stuffing my sleeping bag, mat, tent, food, clothes, and toiletries into my hiking pack, my bag was so full that I had trouble balancing when it was strapped to my back. The morning that our jungle adventure commenced, our team began with two local bus rides, awkwardly balancing our bulky hiking packs while standing on the bumpy buses. After about an hour and a half, we arrived at the main bus terminal in Quito. We split into our two smaller teams, bid each other farewell, and bought tickets towards different areas of the Amazon.

Nine hours on a bus brought my group to a little jungle town. We stayed overnight at a small hostel and decided we would boat or bus deeper into the Amazon the following morning. The next day, we met as a team and decided to take taxis to a bustling market area where locals caught boats to remote jungle regions. We prayed for a divine connection, because we needed to find a local who would bring us into his or her village. The majority of the team waited while Jesse, David, and Liney began their search for a key into the jungle. The rest of us explored the market and sampled wood larvae on a stick, juicy grubs that exploded in our mouths when we bit into their bodies. I almost gagged after the tiniest of bites and prayed I wouldn't be forced to eat anything like this once we got into the jungle.

Meanwhile, David and Jesse met a young man named Nongue, a member of the Waoroni tribe. His tribe was notorious for spearing missionaries Jim Elliot and Nate Saint to death in the 1950s. Elliot and Saint became heroes for their martyrdom, and their wives also gained quite a bit of fame throughout the years following their husbands' deaths. The women bravely continued living in the jungle, where they pursued relationships with the Waoroni and eventually led many of them to Christ.

Before I'd left for South America, my greatest fear was traveling to such a dangerous tribe and having a deadly encounter with a spear myself. Yet, things had certainly changed in the last sixty years, and it was obvious that Nongue had been raised in a civilized and more developed environment. He glanced at his cell phone as he volunteered to take us back to his village and allow us to camp out at his property for the next few days.

Despite the obvious developments throughout the years, I immediately felt uneasy and distrustful. Nongue was overly quick to invite us to accompany him without knowing a thing about us. He mentioned that he was studying tourism in Quito, and I feared that when he looked at us, all he saw was dollar signs. Though I was hesitant to go with Nongue, it didn't seem like we had an alternative way to get into the jungle. We couldn't penetrate the Amazon without a native, and Nongue was currently our only option. So I bit my tongue and followed Nongue with the rest of my team.

We hitched a ride across the river on a large canoe and were forced into a gated area coming from the dock. We reached the end of the gate where a jungle official met us and explained that we needed permission to enter any Ecuadorian jungle villages. The oil companies owned and controlled the land and required outsiders to prove some sort of legitimate connection to the local tribes before entering. We explained that we were friends of Nongue and were planning to spend the next couple of nights in his village. The officials looked at us warily and asked us to wait. After much deliberation, they announced that we were not welcome.

I assumed Nongue would continue to his village without us, but instead of ditching us he offered an alternate solution. He said we could boat to the city of Coca and take a bus into the jungle from there. He had an uncle in a remote village a few hours outside of Coca. His uncle was currently living with several other relatives whom Nongue had never met. He said his uncle would welcome us onto his property, and Nongue would have a chance to meet other people from his tribe. After a few days, he would backtrack to his own village.

Still quite skeptical, I wondered why Nongue was so willing to change his plans and felt uneasiness at his offer. I felt even more unsure when he said the canoe ride to Coca would run us about one hundred fifty dollars even though it was only about an hour and a half. I was less than pleased about this option, but it seemed we would be trapped if we didn't take Nongue's offer. We opted for the costly boat ride and docked in Coca a couple of hours later. From there, we walked to the bus station and got tickets to the village of Nongue's uncle.

About two and a half hours later, we were instructed to hop off the bus in the middle of a dirt road — far removed from any signs of civilization. We followed Nongue onto a remote property comprised of dusty terrain, a couple of small, wooden cabins, and a large grass hut. His uncle, Cata, as well as a group of Waoroni women and children, greeted us and escorted us to the grass hut. They told us we could set up our tents inside the hut and sleep there for the next couple of nights. We thanked them for their hospitality and set up our tents before it got dark. My tent ended up directly underneath a spear that was stuck into the rafters of the hut. Taylor saw it and snickered as he sensed the questions building in my mind.

I tried to ignore the fear in my heart and went outside to hang out with the Waoroni women. They seemed nice enough. Most of them stared and laughed as they observed us. One woman kept touching Natalie's hair and speaking to the other women about her. The eldest woman in the tribe asked us if we would like her family to strip down to nothing for a photograph. She explained that they were willing to do so as long as we paid them for the picture. Horrified, we declined their offer as Breck whispered, "Would they like *us* to get naked and take a photograph for them?" The team tried our hardest to suppress our laughter and reminded each other that strange foreigners from the past must have introduced such requests.

The women seemed unfazed by our reaction and returned to staring, laughing, and hair-touching. After a few moments, they announced that they wanted to give each of us a Waoroni name. They had our team line up, and they clumped together in front of us, eyeing us up and down, one by one. They glanced at each of us, then suddenly focused in on one person, stared extra hard, and burst into giggles as they rattled off in Waoroni. Nongue translated for us from Waoroni to Spanish, then Liney from Spanish to English. The women stated a name and then gave an explanation as to where it had come from. This process repeated itself until every person on the team had received a Waoroni name. Most of the women named us after relatives. I was called Gacamo, the name of one of their grandmothers who had been a great warrior. Katherine's name meant "worker bee" in Waoroni. Taylor was named after the sun and moon. Breck was a fruit, Jesse a fish. David was given the name of a maggot. The rest of my teammates were named after family warriors. Ben was actually given the name of the most ruthless warrior who'd slaughtered everyone he encountered. As my teammates received brutal name after name, I noticed a trend. There was a lot of killing around here. The nonchalant mention of descendants who had murdered many people did not help my uneasiness.

    Once we'd received our tribal names, we spent time with the locals, which I found a bit awkward considering the fact that the only word in Waoroni I knew was the name of their murderer grandmother. We walked around the compound a bit and found a local fruit called *guama* growing in the trees. One of the little Waoroni boys gladly scampered up the trees and cut down pieces for us. I'd never seen guama before or tasted anything quite like it. The outside of the fruit looked like a meter-long squash and opened up to reveal large, black seeds covered in a soft, sweet fruit that resembled cotton. We sucked the cotton-like material off the seeds and ate its sweet flavoring without eating the seeds. Before we knew the actual name for the fruit, we noticed the likeness of the cotton wisps to a bunny tail and affectionately referred to the fruit as "bunny farts."

    After snacking on bunny farts for a bit, Nongue took us across the "street" to another home where some other relatives were waiting for us. We were greeted by an elderly woman who chanted for over an hour and asked us to chant along with her. We quickly caught on to the repetitive tune and awkwardly chanted with the Waoroni grandmother. Meanwhile, another relative offered us a soup of plantains and pineapple and insisted that each of us must suck a portion of the soup down, pass it to the next person, and finish it quickly. The soup tasted good but contained such large, stringy chunks of plantain that it was difficult to swallow. We had to suck, chew, and swallow all at the same time. Luckily, team effort resulted in successful disposal of the soup. I was still pretty hungry after my few sips and was pleasantly surprised when we were invited back to Cata's compound for a meal of rice and wild boar. After a long day of travel, it felt amazing to have a good meal and a full belly. Satisfied and grateful, I walked over to our grass hut and tucked myself into my tent.

We woke up the next morning to the sound of Jesse's voice asking us to hurry and wake up, because people from the village had gathered in Cata's compound for prayer. I quickly got dressed and went outside to find several of the Waoroni anxiously awaiting our team to come pray for them. We sat on wooden boards outside, forming a circle that invited intimacy and epic storytelling. David briefly shared the story of Jesus, explaining it in a culturally relevant style, as if he was telling a folktale.

We then asked if we could pray for each person and spent time blessing the family. One of the women explained that she had met some missionaries many years ago who offered to baptize her. At the time, she was not ready to accept Christ and refused the offer. Throughout the following years, she became very ill and suffered from various health problems. She believed God had punished her, but now that He had sent more missionaries, she thought God was giving her a second chance. My heart broke when I saw that this woman had been believing lies and suffering from guilt for years. Liney sat with her for quite some time and explained that God didn't manipulate but operated out of love. He was not a God of condemnation and found no pleasure in causing His children to suffer. Liney explained who God truly was — a loving Father who wanted nothing more than His children to know their inheritance in His kingdom. God *did* give second chances, but that was not dependent on a group of white people. It came only from the love of a Heavenly Father.

After praying and chatting, the Waoronis said that they wanted to divide our team into men and women for a bit. The guys on our team were taken out into the jungle with blow darts and spears to go hunting, and we ladies were left behind with the women. As soon as the men left, the village women presented us with various handicrafts. Instead of showing us how they were made, they tried to sell us their products. I'd been so distracted that I'd almost forgotten my original doubts about this village. But as the women tried to sell us their crafts, I was reminded that we could very possibly be nothing more than a wad of cash to these people.

Frustrated, I waited in the grass hut for our men to return. Everyone was getting really hungry and hoped they would come back with some type of animal. Unfortunately, the hunt was not a success. The guys reported that not only had they not caught anything, they hadn't even *seen* a single animal in the jungle aside from a small bird. They rejoined us girls in the grass hut, where we sat for hours more, all feeling a bit defeated.

Finally, Cata came to join us to tell stories of the past with the translation help of Nongue and Liney. Cata explained that he had once been a great warrior in a brutal tribe that didn't believe in any type of "civilized" living. He spent his youth traveling the jungle. I listened to Cata speak while simultaneously staring at the huge holes in his ears, gauged over an inch in diameter, where tribal piercings had once existed. Cata explained that he fell in love with a woman who wanted to live a more civilized life. She wanted to wear clothes and brush her teeth and use soap — things that were considered enemy to Cata's native tribe. Yet, Cata made a sacrifice and left his tribe to be with the woman he loved. There was sadness in his eyes as he explained how he'd abandoned the life he truly cherished.

Breck asked him to share his happiest moment from the past with us. Nongue stopped in the middle of translating and told us that there was no word for "happy" in Waoroni. We tried to rephrase the question, but Cata simply stared, a distant look in his eyes, empty and sad. He said he used to go to parties in the jungle when he was young, but even this memory was tainted because of the incredible danger of such gatherings. The villages where his tribe went to celebrate were often raided by warriors, so attending these events was always risky and provoked fear in everyone. Cata went on to explain that if he now tried to return to his tribe, the men would immediately murder him. Because he'd started wearing clothes and shampooing his hair, he was considered a traitor. In fact, Cata said the truly barbaric tribesmen could smell scents such as soap and toothpaste from afar, and if they recognized peoples' "civilized scents" they would spear them to death without a second of hesitation.

We asked Cata more about this savage tribe, and he nonchalantly mentioned that we were in great danger of being targeted by men with spears while we stayed at his compound. My teammates and I looked at each other, unsure of how to react to such news. Cata went on to explain that a subgroup of Waoronis, known as the Taguiras, had split into their own tribe many years ago in blatant rebellion against any sign of civilization. Missionaries (like the wives of Jim Elliot and Nate Saint) had come to live among the Waoroni, and when some of the tribe decided to adopt their Western ways, the Taguiras vowed to murder anyone they came across who accepted these behaviors. They hated all outsiders, and if they encountered anyone outside of their tribe, they killed them immediately.

I had been kind of tired from sitting around for hours, but suddenly I felt wide awake. This was serious. If the Taguiras caught wind of our visit to Cata's compound, there was no doubt they would finish our team off in minutes. I could feel my eyes getting bigger and bigger as I hung on to Cata's every word. He told us that while we stayed at his compound, there was a decent chance that the Taguiras would pass through. We found out that seven months ago, some other visitors had stayed with Cata's family, and the Taguiras murdered each of them.

Apparently, when the Taguiras found foreigners sleeping in a Waoroni village, they normally scouted things out the first night and ambushed them the second. We'd made it through the first night successfully, but that meant tonight could be our end. To make matters worse, Cata said the Taguiras made their presence known in Waoroni villages by leaving their footprints in peoples' compounds as a warning. Cata reported that just a week before, they'd found Taguira footprints in their compound, so they were undoubtedly close by.

My heart started to beat faster and faster. I had felt uneasy about Nongue this whole time, but I had no idea we were in such blatant danger. There was no way to get out of the jungle until the following morning, so there was nothing we could do but wait and pray. I had never been so scared in my life.

Cata tried to reassure us that if the Taguiras *did* come and attack us, he would try to defend us. I looked at the spears in the grass hut and felt a glimmer of hope. Yet, all hopes were dashed as he continued, "But if I try to defend you, I will probably also die." I couldn't believe this. A year ago, I'd been living in a nice apartment in Southern California. Now I was sitting in a grass hut waiting to be speared by some savage Amazonian tribesmen. Just when I thought things couldn't get any worse, Cata mentioned that little Zoe would be the greatest prize the Taguiras could capture; she was our biggest risk. If the Taguiras came for us, they would probably kidnap Zoe and raise her in the jungle. Then, they would either spear all the adults *or* spear the men and take us women into the jungle, forcing us to be their wives. As Liney translated this information, she began to laugh uneasily.

"What's happening?" we asked, wondering what the heck was going on.

"It's a nervous laugh," Liney explained, as she continued to listen to Cata's horrific words and translate them for us.

The guys decided to make the most of the situation and embrace their fate. "Stinks to be a girl right now," one of them declared.

"Um, you guys are the ones who are definitely going to get speared," one of the girls retorted.

"Yeah, but we'll go straight to glory," Ben responded. "You'll be stuck in the jungle being a tribal warrior's wife. I'd rather die."

I realized he was right. I would rather get speared to death than be forced to be a Waoroni warrior's sex slave in the jungle for the rest of my life. Either way, I wasn't particularly excited. Violent death or slavery — it seemed a lose-lose situation.

Cata had told us if the Taguiras did attack, it wouldn't happen until dark. We still had a couple of hours before the sun went down. I tried to enjoy my last moments of safety before nightfall but couldn't stop thinking. Nongue cut open a fruit with red dye inside and asked us to let him put war paint all over our faces. I wanted to have fun with it but was too scared that this paint was for an *actual* war. There was no way I could relax.

The sun began to go down, and I watched as my precious minutes of peace disappeared. I wasn't scared of *death*, but unfortunately I was scared of *dying*. I tried to think about anything other than being speared in the middle of the night, but it was impossible. I read Psalm 91 to comfort myself, and it was the first time the words were so literal for me. "You will not fear the terror of night, nor the arrow that flies by day...[N]o harm will overtake you, no disaster will come near your tent" (Psalm 91:5,10).

It was now pitch-black inside our grass hut, and I lay down in my tent but couldn't sleep. I tossed and turned for a long time and finally gave up. Breck had started a fire outside of our tents, and I saw that he was still sitting there. I crept out of my tent and sat on a log by the fire. I read for a bit, then stared at the fire, then read, then stared again. This was going to be a long night.

I didn't need to say anything for Breck to realize I was petrified. He got up and sat beside me. He told me that one day I would be telling my children about all the absurd things I'd done in my life and how they probably wouldn't believe me, but I would tell them only Jesus had given me the strength to do it. Thinking about the children I didn't yet have gave me hope that I would live past tonight. I found an odd comfort in dreaming of the future, and after talking about it for a while, I was calm enough to crawl back into my tent and go to sleep.

By the grace of God, morning came, and I smiled in sweet relief as I realized no one had been speared during the night. Jesse announced that the bus to Coca was already in front of the compound, and we needed to be on board in the next two minutes. I frantically packed up my tent, threw on some clothes, and ran to the bus. I couldn't get on that thing soon enough.

We rode three hours to Coca, suddenly back in civilization and thankful to be there. We decided to rest for a bit, get some food, and arrange a contact for our next jungle village. Jesse had met a woman in a tourist shop during our first time passing through Coca and said we could go back to her shop to arrange a visit to her tribe. She was part of the Shuar tribe, the group who supposedly shrunk peoples' skulls and wore them around their necks. I had learned my lesson in the Waoroni tribe and knew how important it was to find a legitimate contact before entering a new village.

As a few of the girls from the team talked about the woman Jesse had met, I felt that familiar uneasy feeling and knew in my heart we were not meant to go to this woman's village. Liney said she was going to walk to the tourist shop and speak to the woman, so Liz and I volunteered to go with her. We prayed that God would give us discernment and that He would provide us with a divine appointment with a different contact if this woman was not the person we were supposed to travel with. The moment we entered the shop and approached the woman, I was immediately overwhelmed with a feeling of distrust. The woman told Liney our team could come visit her Shuar village if we paid a large lump of cash. She would charge us one hundred dollars to stay at her property and one hundred more to buy the "freedom" to walk around the village and pray for people. It was very clear that this woman was not genuine, and my heart felt no peace.

Fortunately, as we were speaking with the Shuar woman, God honored our prayer and sent a man named Bartolome who overheard our conversation. He politely interjected and asked us where we wanted to go and what we were trying to do. Liney explained that we were simply hoping to go pray for people and be a blessing to one of the local villages. She insisted that we were not tourists looking for some jungle tour and didn't have the money to pay off the woman in the tourist shop.

Bartolome simply responded, "Why would you have to pay to bless people? You can come stay at my village for free. Just bring your own food. I'm a religious leader in my tribe, and it would be great to have you come and pray for people. We need the love of God in our village."

After talking for a few more minutes, we found out that Bartolome was also a Shuar and would bring us to the exact type of village we were hoping for. I could feel warmth in his heart and knew he was the answer to our prayers. His bus was leaving very briefly, so we exchanged contact info and agreed to meet him in his village later. Liney, Liz, and I walked back to find the rest of our team, excited and at peace about where God was taking us.

The next morning, we boarded a bus towards Bartolome's village. We disembarked the bus where he'd instructed Liney and waited for quite some time in the middle of a jungle road. We saw no sign of Bartolome and wondered what we should do if he never appeared. A sweet local woman told us we could sit by her house while we waited. After talking for a while, Bartolome appeared from out of the jungle with another man who looked almost identical to him. He introduced us to his brother, who would be hosting us for the next couple of days. Bartolome gave us the option of traveling to his brother's home via an hour and a half hike through the jungle or a thirty-minute canoe ride. Without a second thought, we opted for the boat ride. However, the canoe was too small to fit our entire team, so we had to ride in shifts.

I rode with the second crew, excited to be canoeing through a river in the Amazon jungle. The scenery was so surreal that I felt like I was paddling through a dream. Our small canoe tipped and rocked as we weaved between logs and tree branches hanging over the murky jungle water. Gorgeous birds flew overhead, and patches of sapphire sky emerged from between the trees. This was exactly how I'd pictured the perfect, untouched Amazon. My team had finally arrived.

We docked our boat by a muddy patch of land and walked up a steep, slick path, desperately trying to avoid slipping in the mud. Once we reached the top of the hill, I noticed a small dirt opening surrounded by three tiny, wooden buildings — a small chicken coop, a tight kitchen, and an open-walled cabin. The rest of our team was waiting for us inside the cabin. We put our hiking packs down on the floor and were immediately instructed to walk over to the kitchen to accept a drink that one of Bartolome's relatives had prepared for us. Our teammates explained that they had just drunk the mysterious potion, and the smirks on their faces said more about the flavor than words could have. The drink was made from ground-up yucca that had been fermented over time. We were told that the locals chewed the yucca to grind it and then spat it into a bowl to let it ferment. Liney said that they'd been warned if we didn't drink every last drop, the cook would throw the liquid into our faces for insulting their culture. My teammates had just drunk three bowls as a group, and our next boatload was expected to consume the same amount.

Despite feeling sick at the thought of drinking a stranger's saliva, I figured it would be worse to insult the family who was so kindly hosting us. I held my breath and began to gulp down as much of the yucca liquid as I could. The fermentation poisoned the flavor, giving the drink a taste of tomato soup laced with nail polish remover. I took a big sip, then passed the bowl to someone else. But as soon as I got rid of a bowl, a new one was passed to me. There were only six of us, and we had three large bowls to finish. After suffering through the soupy mixture and choking down mysterious orange and yellow, we finally finished up our bowls. As soon as we were done, the rest of our teammates burst into laughter and told us they'd made up the rumor about people spitting into the soup. Turns out, chewing and spitting was the traditional way to prepare the soup, but nowadays they ground the yucca with a proper utensil instead of their teeth. Mentally, it would have been a lot easier to drink the soup *not* believing it was full of an indigenous woman's saliva, but we'd completed the task nonetheless. I was proud of my team.

Following our unique appetizer, Bartolome asked us to go pray for one of his relatives, an elderly woman who was suffering from seizures and other health problems. Doctors had pretty much given up on her, but she desperately wanted to be healed. Bartolome warned us that the route to her house entailed some challenging jungle trekking. First, we would need to cross a "treacherous bridge" and should only come if we were able to cross. Second, we were warned to watch below our feet for snakes slithering through the long jungle grass. Finally, Bartolome mentioned that poisonous spiders crawled around the trees; so if we needed to grab branches to prevent slipping on the muddy trails, we were putting our hands in danger.

At this point, in comparison to threats of being speared to death, spiders and a bridge didn't really faze me. I began the trek through the jungle, hoping it wouldn't be too hard. We reached the bridge and saw that it was nothing more than a fallen log over a river. The log was covered in slippery moss, and I thought there was a good chance I'd fall into the river if I walked across. I grabbed someone's hand, finding security in the possibility of falling into the river *together*, and breathed a sigh of relief when we both made it across successfully. We continued onward, trudging through patches of mud, slipping and sliding through the jungle.

After a while, we arrived at a small, wooden house where we were greeted by a local family. There was a beautiful, elderly woman sitting on a stiff bed in a corner. Her family had built a fire by her bed to keep her frail body warm, but she constantly coughed as she inhaled the smoke. I kneeled by her bed and laid my hands on her. The team gathered and prayed for her healing. She was relatively unresponsive, so it was hard to tell if anything was happening in her body. We prayed for some other family members as well and promised to return the following day.

We trekked back through the jungle, this time as the sun was setting. The terrain beneath our feet was getting darker and darker, and I prayed I wouldn't touch any poisonous spiders or encounter any snakes since I couldn't really see what I was walking over or touching. I slid in the mud and grabbed at branches to save me, but most of them snapped as I pulled on them. Somehow, I avoided falling off the path or into the river. One of my teammates shined his flashlight on a huge tarantula he'd discovered, but I kept walking and pretended it wasn't there.

Finally, we made it back to our jungle oasis. We ate dinner, and a woman from the jungle appeared at our homestay after getting word that missionaries were in the village. She had severely injured her leg a while back and had much difficulty walking. She asked us to pray for her. We gathered around her and asked God to heal her leg. After a few minutes, she said it felt a little better but not completely. We prayed a bit more, and she said the same. We continued still, and she reported that she felt a tiny improvement. We carried on with this process for quite a while and finally told her if she wanted to go home to rest, we would come visit her house the next day and continue with the prayers.

The following morning, Bartolome left early for a distant village and said he wouldn't see us anymore. He left us in the care of his brothers and explained that one of them would accompany us to visit peoples' homes in the afternoon to continue to pray. They left the morning free to hunt or explore the jungle. Several of the guys excitedly got their hands on blow darts and spears and headed for the river in the hopes of capturing a crocodile. The Shuar brothers asked us if we could swim as they rattled off a list of animals we might encounter in the river, including anacondas, crocodiles, and piranhas. When we asked what size the piranhas were, they simply replied, "normal," as they placed their hands about a foot apart to demonstrate. Personally, I thought asking if we could swim seemed a bit irrelevant, since there was no way we were getting in that river without a boat. However, I decided exploring on land could be fun and enjoyed a mini trek through the jungle with a few of my teammates. Afterwards, one of Bartolome's brothers led some of us on a hike to the house of the woman with the injured leg as well as back to the elderly woman's house.

We greeted the injured woman with smiles, but all I could see was the sadness in her eyes. Even after praying for her again, she seemed relatively unaffected. I decided to ask her if she had forgiven the person who had injured her, since it was clear there was still pain in her heart. Unsurprisingly, the woman responded that she struggled with anger and hadn't completely offered forgiveness. I explained that though God loved to heal our bodies, He valued healing our hearts even more. We asked if she would consider forgiving the woman who had injured her, and after a moment of hesitation, she agreed. We explained that forgiving the woman wasn't about that other woman at all; it was about finding freedom in her own heart. We prayed one more time, and the woman finally began to show some emotion. Afterwards, Taylor took some pictures of the woman with her husband and children and showed them the photos on his digital screen. The woman's hard countenance cracked as she laughed at the pictures and smiled at the sight of her children. Something was softening. We gave the family a final blessing and continued our hike to the next woman's house.

When we returned to see the elderly woman from the previous day, she seemed surprised that we had kept our promise to visit her. We prayed for her a second time, and as Liz hugged her, tears welled up in her eyes. David explained that most people who lived deep in the jungle only met a handful of people their whole lives. Because they lived so remotely, it was rare to ever meet someone from the outside. The old woman was so moved that we'd come all this way just to pray for her and give her a hug. Though I desired a miracle in this woman's health and was disappointed that I didn't see one, I was convinced that the woman was anything but disappointed. The glistening tears of happiness in her eyes told me she'd received exactly what she wanted — love.

After our visit, we returned to our jungle oasis for the evening. We'd met some Latino hippies on our bus ride from Coca and heard that they were staying just a short stroll from where we'd set up camp. Jesse invited the hippies over for dinner despite reports that they didn't want to spend time with a bunch of missionaries. Jesse walked to their campsite nonetheless, and the hippies reported that they hadn't eaten for days. They were trying to pick roots from the ground while singing, "We are sons and daughters of the earth; I am a daughter of the earth; I am a daughter of the earth…" The offer of an actual meal suddenly made the hippies very open to hanging out with the "God Squad." They stopped attempting to yank roots out of the ground and gladly accepted our invitation to dinner.

We ate a feast of rice and beans, everyone's bellies full and satisfied. After eating, the hippies whipped out a bunch of local instruments and began to perform a medley of songs for us. Thirty minutes or so later, they asked us to sing a song for them.

We weren't quite as musically talented, but we all knew the same worship songs and agreed to sing a few for them. Originally, it had seemed that the hippies were wary of Christians, so I wondered if singing about Jesus would offend them. But as we sang, their faces lit up, and they looked genuinely joyful as they listened. One of the hippies asked David to translate the words of "How He Loves" from English to Spanish. He smiled as he whispered, "He loves us. Oh, how He loves us. And heaven meets earth like a sloppy, wet kiss, and my heart beats violently inside of my chest. I don't have time to maintain these regrets when I think about the way He loves us..."[1] Much to my surprise, the hippie girl got choked up at the sound of these words, and her voice cracked as she squeaked, "It's beautiful."

A few of Bartolome's Shuar relatives joined our mini concert, so we asked them if they would be willing to share some of their tribal songs with us. They were a bit hesitant, but after some serious conferencing, they performed a jumble of offbeat tribal music. It was quite a colorful clash of cultures — hippies from throughout South America, indigenous Shuar people, and a group of foreign missionaries. We sang for hours while laughing, dancing, and sharing the hearts of our cultures with one another.

Finally, I snuck off to my tent to get some sleep. After laying there for a while, reflecting on our time in the jungle, I heard some commotion outside of my tent. I realized one of the boys was unzipping my rainfly and soon saw Taylor's face right outside my door. I immediately knew he was up to mischief and asked him what the heck he was doing. He continued to try to unzip my tent door, laughing but not saying a word. I started yelling, "Whatever you are trying to do...don't!" Moments later, a chicken was thrown into my tent and the door zipped up so quickly that I was trapped inside with the ugly beast before I had a chance to put up a real fight. The chicken began to squawk frenziedly, as did I. My tent was tiny, which allowed little space between the hen and me. I screamed and hid my head under my sleeping bag as the chicken went crazy and I awaited my fate — being pecked to death by poultry. I could hear Taylor, David, and Breck cackling outside my tent as I screamed for help. "There's a chicken in my tent! It's trying to attack me! Somebody…anybody…help me, please!"

I yelled for assistance several times and heard nothing but laughter, so I realized it was up to me to get the chicken outside. Finally, I unzipped the tent door, picked up my sleeping mat, and whacked the chicken with all my might until it jumped outside and ran away. I quickly zipped the door back shut, determined to keep it closed. After my blood pressure returned to normal, I rearranged my mat and sleeping bag. As I nuzzled back into bed, I smelled the putrid scent of chicken excrement. I grimaced at the unpleasant aroma, promising myself to get revenge on the boys later. With thoughts of future retaliation, I fell asleep.

The next morning, I was greeted by impish smiles from Taylor, Breck, and David. Taylor considered himself a genius for dreaming up the prank and David a superstar for catching the chicken. Breck reported that he'd videotaped the whole fiasco and threatened to post it on the internet. It seemed unreal that my life could shift between intensely fearing death by spear one day and laughing about a silly prank days later. I never knew what was headed my way next.

We packed our things and got ready to make our departure from the jungle. Before we left, we prayed for the family that had kindly hosted us for the past couple of days. We asked if there was anything specific we could pray for, and they simply asked that God would send more missionaries to their village. They were eager to learn more about Jesus and hoped the Lord would bring more people to teach His word. It broke my heart to have to leave this beautiful village after only a couple of days when they were so hungry to hear more about the Lord. Unfortunately, we had a commitment to meet the rest of our team and needed to move on. Our team prayed for our sweet Shuar friends and then reluctantly said goodbye.

We took a canoe back through the jungle to the main road that led to the major bus station in Coca. We waited on the street for a while in hopes of catching a bus but were unsuccessful. Finally, a dump truck came by and offered to drive us to Coca if we each paid a dollar. We gladly jumped in the back of the dump truck and spent the next hour getting faces full of dirt and gravel. From Coca, we bought bus tickets to beautiful Baños, a city lined with spectacular rock formations and gorgeous waterfalls. This was our planned meeting point with the team led by Natalie M. and Stephen. From Baños, we returned to Quito and celebrated being one large family again.

Excitedly, the two groups swapped stories of our jungle adventures. When we dramatically recounted the tale of thinking we might be speared to death, some people from my group said they'd secretly wondered if Cata had just been trying to scare us. However, the other group verified that we had been in legitimate danger. They hadn't traveled anywhere near the Waoroni but had been warned of the Taguiras by other missionaries. Several people "in the know" provided matching descriptions of the horrific acts the Taguira tribe was notorious for committing. Cata hadn't just been messing with us; the threat of danger was genuine.

More relieved than ever to be back in Quito, I listened to the other jungle group narrate stories from their time in a different corner of the Amazon. Stephen, Natalie M., Addison, Roberta, Taylor M., Ted, Rachael, Susy, Angela, Elizabeth, Dianne, Melissa, and Kurt blew me away with all that they'd experienced in such a short period of time. This group had begun their time by first traveling to the city of Puyo. After busing there, they found a hostel and decided to wait for a bit, unsure of what to do next. Everyone in that group desired to go deep into the jungle, but they were repeatedly told that this would require flying. Plane tickets could cost up to five hundred dollars, money they simply did not have. The team decided to pray and ask God for direction, and He faithfully gave several people different signs and visions. Susy saw a picture of the end of a road. Natalie saw three heads and an arrow pointing east. Her vision of the eastward-pointing arrow was confirmed when Taylor's brother in the States contacted him to tell him that he had a dream about going to the jungle. He said God had told him if they had an option to go north or east, they needed to go east.

Still without contacts, the team decided to walk around the city and ask passersby about churches, hoping to find someone who could help them get into the jungle. After being directed to Jehovah's Witness churches and other places that weren't even Christian, a couple of people finally stopped and asked God where to go. The Holy Spirit said, "Go left." Obediently, they went left, trekked up a hill, and found a church called Movimiento Misiones Mundial. The pastor was standing at the gate. As the team approached him, he told them that he was holding a leadership meeting and invited them in. Suddenly, they found themselves in the middle of a church service, dancing and singing with the church leaders. The team shared some of their testimonies with the church and told the pastor that they were looking for access to the jungle. He said he had an American missionary friend, Rick, who had his own plane. The pastor contacted Rick, who said he could meet with the team the following morning.

The team met Rick for breakfast, where he interrogated the leaders to find out their motives for going into the jungle.

Rick had been in Ecuador for thirty-five years and had seen the detrimental effects of bad missionary work in the past. He'd flown many people into the famous location where Jim Elliot and Nate Saint had been killed and wondered if the team was just another superficial group who wanted to see a legendary site.

After hearing the group's heart and chatting for a while, Rick decided he could trust them. He told everyone to come to his house in the city of Shell and offered to fly them into the jungle that same day. They could fly in groups of two and three, each ticket just forty dollars. God had just made the impossible possible. Before flying, the group had to go to the end of a road and fly out right where it dropped off — the end of the road that Susy had seen in her vision.

Rick told the group that he could either fly them to the Waoroni tribe in the north or to the Shuar tribe in the east. They decided to follow Natalie's vision and the confirmation from Taylor's brother and go east. Rick knew a couple of Cuban missionaries in the Shuar tribe but failed to warn them that he had agreed to drop off several visitors by plane. In small groups, the team flew into the Shuar tribe, arriving on the very airstrip Nate Saint had once used — grass growing above the plane where they landed, jungle children running around them.

The Cuban couple living among the tribe was the only missionary presence in the area, and no one had visited them throughout the past three years. Suddenly, there were thirteen unexpected people with them. At first, the Cubans were skeptical, because most missionaries flew in, preached, and then left hours later. When they realized the team was going to stay for a while and were open to whatever God instructed them to do, they began to warm up to them and actually became excited to host visitors.

The Cuban man told the team that he would like to divide them in two. One group would organize a leadership summit near his home. The other group would hike six miles into the jungle to a village called San Jose. En route to San Jose, there was a headhunting village called Tres Marias. Tres Marias signified three women, matching the three heads Natalie had seen in her vision. In this village, they had a custom of shrinking heads and were known for having the hardest of hearts. Because white people in the past were fascinated by buying shrunken heads, the locals feared going into Tres Marias with foreigners. Trekking into their village would encourage the people from the Tres Marias community to kill any local guide, shrink his head, and sell it to the white people. None of the locals were willing to risk the danger of entering this area with my teammates.

A local guide agreed to lead Taylor, Natalie, Rachael, and Addison to San Jose if they skirted outside of Tres Marias to avoid danger. As they headed to San Jose, it began to pour, making their six-mile trek a muddy one. For three miles, the mud was up to their knees, but they pushed through and made it to San Jose. Upon arrival, they met the chief — one of the only Christians in his tribe. He knew only three worship songs on his guitar and wanted to learn more. Addison could sing just one song in Spanish and offered to teach the chief how to play it on his guitar. After his music lesson, the team heard the chief playing the song and singing each morning. He was so thankful to learn something new that he gave Addison a spear and a feather crown to take home with him.

The first evening, Taylor, Natalie, Rachael, and Addison were asked to lead a children's program. They followed instructions without hesitation. The next day, they were asked to lead a four-hour service and preach about marriage. This was a slightly more daunting task. Our group of single missionaries wasn't quite sure where to start. They were informed that some people in the tribe believed in polygamy. Even as single people, my teammates at least knew *that* was a bad idea. Taylor and Natalie bravely volunteered to preach and did their best to tackle the subject with wisdom.

Afterwards, they started to visit Shuar homes, where they noticed that from little children to the elderly, many had terrible stomach problems. Several people in the tribe had tumors and horrendous pain in the same area. Someone from the team received a word of knowledge about the issue. She saw spears in the stomachs of the tribal people and felt the Lord saying that these violent roots were causing the pain. The villagers said it was true. People from the same tribe but different communities had speared each other in that very spot around thirty years ago. My teammates prayed for healing from the physical pain but also the deeper spiritual and emotional pain that still lingered within the tribe. They found two people from the two different communities and began the first step of reconciliation and healing — repenting to one another for the war of the past.

In addition, a young village pastor came forward to confess hurt in his family's history. His father had also been a pastor, and one of the father's sons (this young village pastor's brother) had died when he wasn't walking with the Lord. At the same time, two other people from the village died who were believers. A missionary came to the village and declared that those two were with the Lord but the son who had gone astray was in hell. The father felt he had failed his son and carried this shame throughout his life. He quit being a pastor and turned away from his faith. The father's family had a big divide shortly after that incident. His children were hurt. Many people from the village were affected as well. Only three people remained Christians.

It was amazing how a past missionary's declaration had so brutally scarred this tribe. My teammates prayed for forgiveness on behalf of the missionaries who had brought pain. The other family members told them that they wanted to be Christians but thought they weren't good enough. Many of the polygamists within the tribe thought they couldn't become Christians because they had too many wives. My teammates explained that anyone could become a follower of Christ. It had nothing to do with being "good enough" but actually accepting Jesus' sacrifice as the perfect atonement for all sin. His blood could make even the worst sinner clean. A few people decided that this was a pretty favorable offer, including a polygamist with three wives and eight children. He and others gave their lives to Jesus that day.

Next, the chief's wife made a proposition my teammates never expected. She explained that Tres Marias was named after the three founders of the village, and her sister was one of the founders. Because of this connection, the woman was willing to personally take the team into Tres Marias, the dreaded headhunting community. Instead of hiking back to the rest of the team while avoiding Tres Marias as they'd done on their way *to* San Jose, my teammates (far braver than me) took the woman's offer and trekked directly into the infamous village. While in Tres Marias, the team received a word of knowledge about healing for one of the village founders. Moments later, a revered woman with an injured knee accepted prayer and was completely healed. The community known for murdering people and shrinking their heads had just experienced a taste of Jesus' love.

After visiting Tres Marias, my teammates hiked back to where they'd separated from the others. Meanwhile, those left behind were hosting a leadership summit. Stephen felt they were supposed to do a trust fall at this conference, completely unaware that mistrust was the main issue the different village leaders had against each other. After doing the trust fall, two rival village leaders confessed their sins to one another and began to cry and hug in a beautiful moment of reconciliation. The Cuban couple said it was a miracle that these two leaders had now become brothers.

So much had changed in such a short period of time that it was undoubtedly the hand of God moving. Reluctantly, the team said goodbye to the Cubans and the friends they'd made in the jungle in order to meet up with the rest of us. Glad to be together, the whole team spent a few days in Quito catching up and doing ministry in the city. We were eager to share what God had done during our time apart and to celebrate the testimonies of His faithfulness. Personally, I was relieved to be in a big city — far from spears, safe and sound. Yet, little did I know, an entirely different type of battle was right around the corner.

Chapter Eleven

PERU: Peeling, Puking, and Paramonga

Ahh, Peru. Just hearing the name brings up memories of sunburn, vomit, and diarrhea. For such an esteemed country, it sure packed a punch when our team passed through. After crossing the Ecuador-Peru border, our team decided to rest for a few days along the Peruvian coast. We were actually ahead of schedule (for the first time) and had over a week until we needed to meet up with our contact in Lima. Therefore, we thought a few days of relaxation in the sun were in order. There was a cheap campground that offered accommodation for our team right by the water, and we thought this would be a perfect place to rest. Little did I know, I'd be spending more quality time with the communal toilet than with the waves.

Our little "vacation" started off well. I immediately fell in love with our campsite and felt like I was living my dream of being a full-time beach bum. It was perfect. There was a restaurant with wifi for those who wanted a taste of comfort, a grassy area for those who wanted to camp, and hammocks scattered along the beach for those who wanted to fall asleep to the sound of the waves. The water was cool enough to refresh you but warm enough that you could swim for hours. The ebony sky lit up at night with glittering stars, and the rhythm of the ocean hummed me sweet songs of home. This was paradise.

Our first morning at the beach, I went with a few teammates to rent some surfboards and hit the waves. Unlike my surfing bliss in Costa Rica, this time I did nothing but sniff salt and flail around like a drowning rat. The surfboard I rented had a hole in it that absorbed water, and the board got so heavy that I couldn't lift it. I finally gave up and dragged the dang thing from the water to shore, pulling on the leash since I couldn't carry it under my arm. A scrawny local boy stared at me in horror, and I grimaced as I realized he'd probably had a more successful day in the surf than I had.

The following day, I suffered the consequences of spending too long in the sun, my back throbbing with blazing singes. I'd scorched myself so badly that I was convinced I had second degree burns. The large blisters on my skin bubbled in agony, and hundreds of tiny blisters erupted around the bigger ones, creating a landscape of bubbles all over my back and shoulders. My skin looked like a carbonated beverage. Frustrated and in pain, I hid away in the shade for most of the day, disappointed that I had to avoid the sun and sand.

Once the sun went down, I lay on the beach talking with Taylor L. and Rose. The moment I stood up, I felt like death had just smacked me in the face. I began to shiver despite the warmth, my teeth chattering uncontrollably, and I was overcome by waves of nausea. This mystery illness aggressively came out of *nowhere*, and I ran to the bathroom, wondering what was happening to me. I spent the remainder of the night spewing my insides onto the beach, rotating between being too cold and feeling like I was going to sweat to death. The sweet relief of the rising sun woke me around 5 a.m. I left my pop-up and walked over to a hammock in the shade to be able to groan in pain without disturbing the girls who were still sleeping. I hoped I'd vomited out everything inside of me, but my body had a magical way of producing something out of nothing. The bathroom (which was shared by all the campers at this lovely site and had no flusher) became my closest acquaintance for the day. I spent hours running back and forth between the beach and the toilet, praying that I would make it in time and that the bathroom would not be occupied by the singing Frenchman or half-naked hippie who were also staying at the campsite.

I soon discovered that it was possible for food to travel both up *and* down your body and exit from different places simultaneously. The pain that accompanied such a discovery was almost unbearable. To make matters worse, flies surrounded the increasingly dirty toilet, buzzing against parts of my body that should never have come into contact with insects. After hours of enduring such torture, I was completely out of energy and desperately wishing for a bed and a nearby toilet. I hadn't been this sick since living in Uganda six years prior and hoped never to be this sick again. The virus would not relent, and I continued to repeatedly make the run between my sleeping area and the bathroom.

The next morning, I continued to get sick to my stomach, amazed that there was still anything left inside of me. I was dehydrated, exhausted, and in pain. Our team decided to begin our drive towards Lima, and I traveled in Open Heaven, equipped with a toilet, with several other suffering teammates who needed one close by. Driving along bumpy roads was far from a remedy for this stomach virus, but the traveling needed to be done. After a long day, we stopped at another beach city to camp for the night before continuing the drive. Realizing there was no bathroom where we were about to camp, I prayed for an alternative.

Meanwhile, Liz and Natalie M. asked around town for a cheap place to stay. A Peruvian family looking to make a few extra bucks offered sleeping spots on their floor for about two dollars each. Feeling desperate and exhausted, we accepted the offer. Smelly, exhausted, and nauseous, I curled up on the strangers' floor and attempted to fall asleep. A Latino man stood over me, asking questions.

"What's wrong? Are you sick?" he inquired.

"Yes, I'm sick. I have stomach problems. But mostly I am tired," I replied, hoping he would take the hint and leave me to sleep.

"Do you have air in your stomach?" he asked in Spanish, but I wasn't even sure what that meant in English.

I repeated my previous statement, explaining that my stomach felt sick but that I mostly needed sleep.

He continued to stare at me and ask about the air in my stomach, and I wanted to ask *him* about the air in his head.

"I'm very tired," I repeated once more, desperately wanting to go to sleep without this man hovering over me.

He finally snapped out of his trance and disappeared. I closed my eyes, passed out, and slept like a rock until morning.

By the time the sun came up, my stomach felt slightly better, but I was now dehydrated from days of vomit and diarrhea and not being able to eat or drink. This resulted in a more dangerous condition than the first day of the illness. I felt like I was going to faint and could only walk about twenty feet before needing to sit down and take a break. I dizzily walked into

Open Heaven, where I spent the next few hours taking naps and sucking down Gatorade in the desperate hope of healing quickly. The blisters on my back began to puss and pop, so every time I scratched, liquid leaked from my skin onto my clothing. We pulled over for the team to get food, and I tried to sleep in the RV while I waited for them to eat. Evil flies tortured me, savagely buzzing around me as I squirmed in agony. *Lord, help me,* I pleaded. *I can't keep doing this. I am in so much pain and just want to lie still without flies maddening me.* It seemed like the floor was spinning, and I wasn't sure whether it would be better to attempt walking away or to let the flies continue to feast on my blisters. Hours passed by where I flirted with the thought of going home simply to delight in the sweet comfort of a real bed.

The following day, it temporarily seemed like my body was beginning to repair itself; however, my hopes were quickly dashed by the worst waves of nausea yet. During the surges of pain, we drove through a revolting city that reeked of rotting fish. The putrid stench forced me to bury my face in my pillow to avoid gagging. Hours later, we finally arrived at our destination city. We'd been told we were driving to Lima, but this was far from it. The dusty and desolate city they called Paramonga was actually hours from the capital and looked more like a landfill than a city. We pulled up to a small house aside a barren, brown field littered with trash. I couldn't believe people actually lived here but was too tired and sick to really care. I grabbed my bag, set up a sleeping mat on the floor, squished myself in between five other girls, and slept for ten hours. I woke up and wanted nothing but to sleep more. I forced myself to get up and attempted to walk around but continued to be slammed with dizzy spells. *Lord, when will this end?* I pleaded. *Where are you? Please meet me soon. Meet me here. I need you so badly.*

The rest of the day felt agonizingly long and the night even longer. Thoughts of running home taunted me, and I finally gave up trying to sleep. I went outside and bumped into Breck, who joined me on the roof where we sat and reflected on life for the next two hours or so.

I told him how worn out I was and asked if he really thought it was worth it to be on this taxing journey. I felt like I'd turned my back on everyone and everything I loved just to wind up sick and tired in the middle of a garbage dump in Peru.

Breck reminded me that it was always worth it to be obedient to the Lord even when it didn't make sense. He was the one who chose the best path for our lives, and we simply had to trust that He was making the right choice. In the end, we would never lose for being obedient to the Lord. I knew Breck was right but also knew I needed to hear God speak to me. Nothing was making sense at the moment.

The next morning, I woke up to find that all the girls in my room were gone. They'd run off to visit the local church and left me behind to rest. I had space and a few moments alone. This was unbelievable. This never happened. *Thank you, God*, I breathed, overwhelmingly grateful to temporarily escape my normally claustrophobic living environment. Now I just needed Him to meet me in this place and speak to me.

I grabbed my Bible, journal, and a book that one of my dear friends from home had given me. She'd written a personal note inside the book that I decided to reread. I had just read Psalm 32:8 the night before and realized that in her note, she referenced the same psalm. It read, "The Lord says, 'I will guide you along the best pathway for your life. I will advise you and watch over you'" (Psalm 32:8, NLT). Next, I turned to the devotion in the book for the day, February 26th. The whole passage was about trusting in God with my future, and the Bible reference was Psalm 32:8. *Three times* I encountered this same verse. I smiled, knowing God was speaking through His word and confirming exactly what this psalm said — that He had chosen the best pathway for my life. I rested in the comfort that God *had* called me to this stretching journey; and even in the darkest hour, I needed to cling to what God had spoken and remember that I was supposed to be there.

A few nights later, after feeling much stronger both emotionally and physically, I stepped outside for a few moments to worship alone. I gazed at the setting sun, captured by the sky's splendor. I looked down at the dirty field in front of me, aware of the deep contrast between this battered land and the beauty of the sunset. Though a bit saddened by the way the Peruvians had trashed this potentially beautiful terrain, I felt hope as I kept my gaze on the sky. I remembered that no matter what, people cannot ruin the crimson clouds and rays of auburn sunlight that dance through the sky each night at sunset. We can make a million mistakes and try to ignore the presence of God; but in the end, He will not be denied and cannot be destroyed.

Each day I grew healthier, and the strange and barren city of Paramonga actually began to grow on me. My heart for this place softened when a group of teenagers from the church invited us to go play volleyball with them. A few friends and I hit the court and goofed around with the youth for hours. I loved doing something that required no language skills — just a mutual understanding of the rules, an enjoyment of the warm sunshine, and sweet laughter as we whacked the volleyball in every direction we *didn't* want it to go. As the local teens excitedly begged us to keep playing with them, I remembered that no matter where we traveled, *all* people craved fun, friends, and love — even in an ugly town in Peru.

Later in the week, some of the teens joined us at the house for a special Peruvian treat. One of the most desired dishes in Peru was *cuy*, Latin American guinea pig. I generally tried any food offered me, but I did feel a bit squeamish as I looked at the little toes on my plate. I tried to block out all memories of Jellybean and Charlie, my younger sister's pet guinea pigs from our childhood. However, as I ripped off pieces of the cuy's body and struggled to chew on the tough meat, I could hear Jellybean's little voice squeaking in my head. The locals found our team's reaction to cuy quite entertaining and warned us that if we headed to the Peruvian jungle, dog might be the next item on our menu. I shook my head as the locals laughed at me. I had to draw the line somewhere.

Throughout the next three nights, our team was asked to run an evangelistic outreach in Paramonga and one of the nearby towns. I was always a bit reluctant to organize such events, since they normally felt a bit ostentatious and forced. However, I wanted to honor the local church's request, and my team agreed to plan a three-night event. Just before the outreaches began, our dear papa bear, Christian, flew to Peru to rejoin the team for a few weeks. While launching our trip, he'd made a lasting impression on all of our hearts. It was such a blessing to have him back to run alongside us for our remaining time in Peru. Christian brought fresh energy, laughs, and encouragement.

The first night of outreach, Christian joined us as we drove to a nearby town's main square. A few of our guys busted out breakdancing moves, sang a few songs, and performed a skit to draw a crowd. Afterwards, David preached, and we prayed for those who needed healing. A man with a black eye who was bleeding from his face came forward and said that he wanted to accept Christ. As my teammates and I prayed for him, he began to shake uncontrollably as his body flung backwards and he dropped to the floor. I wasn't sure if he was feeling the presence of God or if he was manifesting a demon. To this day, I still don't know what occurred inside that man. All I know is that something of spiritual significance was happening. My teammates and I talked to the young man quite a bit after the shaking stopped, and he seemed a bit disoriented. When we left the man at the end of the evening, I wondered what would become of him. I simply had to trust that God was beginning to work in him, and He was faithful to finish the work He'd started.

On the second night of outreach, we held our meeting in the center of Paramonga. Similar to the previous evening, we drew a crowd with music and dancing. Dianne shared her powerful testimony, and afterwards we offered to pray for anyone who needed healing in their bodies. A man who had been born deaf came forward. Some of my teammates began to pray for healing, and as they prayed, his left ear opened up. He said that he could hear sound in his left ear for the first time in thirty years. Excited, my teammates continued to pray for full healing. Sure enough, after a few moments, his right ear opened up as well. Some bystanders realized that the power of God had just completely restored this man's hearing, and many hungered for their own touch from God.

I met a woman who had pain in her legs and wanted to be healed. As I prayed for her, the tangible presence of the Holy Spirit fell upon us, and I could feel God moving. After praying, the woman said that a lot of the pain had gone, but she wasn't fully healed. I prayed for many others, and it seemed the same thing was happening. People were getting partially healed but not one hundred percent. After quite some time praying, I called it a night and explained that my team would be back in the city square the following evening. If anyone wanted to step out in faith and believe for complete healing, they were welcome to receive more prayer the next night. I had felt God's presence and was confident that He had more to give these people.

The following evening, my team returned to Paramonga's town square, planning on a similar program. However, we found out that the local government had already planned a huge, citywide event for the evening. There were street vendors, musicians, dancers, and crowds of hundreds of people. We quickly realized we had to throw our program out the window and instead embraced an opportunity to simply hang out with some of the Paramonga residents. As I was standing with some friends watching a traditional dance performance, I felt a woman's hand tap me on the shoulder. I turned around and recognized the woman I had prayed for the previous evening. She wasn't satisfied with just a partial healing in her legs, and she had sifted through hundreds of people to find me.

Excitedly, I asked her to walk over to a nearby bench, and I grabbed Taylor L. and Rose to come pray with me. Kurt saw what was happening and joined us as well. We laid hands on the woman, and after a few moments, she smiled and said that the pain in her legs had disappeared. Full of faith, she now asked us to pray for her friend so she could experience healing too. We gladly agreed, and God began to heal her friend as well. Others gathered around the bench, realizing what was happening. After a few moments, this little bench in Paramonga became our own rotating seat of healing. A person would come, get healed, then get up and give the seat to someone else who would sit down, get healed, and then get up for someone else. This went on for forty-five minutes or so, person after person receiving healing and the presence of God. One woman said that after we prayed for her, she felt peace in her heart and a physical air on her. The next man we prayed for said the exact same thing. We explained that the "air" was the Holy Spirit. God was physically manifesting His presence and breathing His air over His children as He healed them.

I found it remarkable that even though our plan to run an outreach event was thwarted by the city's fiesta, God created a way to shower His presence and love upon many of the people in

Paramonga. Though hundreds of people crowded the streets, the determination and faith of that one woman brought us together and eventually attracted many more people. Despite my recent feelings of frustration, illness, and weakness, God chose to use my feeble hands for healing that night. He chose to use the person who felt the weakest to invite His strength to invade Paramonga. As He poured out His strength, people were healed, touched, and loved. I found it quite ironic that in one of the ugliest, dustiest, brownest places I'd seen among the entire journey, I experienced one of the most beautiful evenings thus far.

Our night got even better when the officials running the event invited our team onto their stage. Liney had somehow wormed her way into the hearts of the Paramongan authorities and was granted ten minutes to preach to the massive crowd in the city square. During the previous two nights, we had spent lots of time and effort dancing and playing music to draw a crowd of only thirty or forty people. Yet, this night, without striving at all, we had hundreds of people in front of us, waiting to listen to whatever we had to say. Our team was called up to the stage, and each of us introduced ourselves to the crowd. Liney then grabbed the microphone and explained what our team was doing in Paramonga. She boldly preached the word of God as the crowd applauded in agreement. I loved the irony of how planning and working had gotten us nowhere, but surrendering our own plans provided us the chance to preach to hundreds.

The mayor of Paramonga was moved by Liney's words and asked her to return to the city square the following morning with anyone from the team. There would be another citywide event, and he requested that our team come and pray for him. The next morning, Rose, Roberta, David, Liney, and I returned to the square. Though the event felt a bit scattered and awkward, we endured a long wait to get to pray for the mayor. After quite some time, we were called to the front. Liney thanked the city of Paramonga for so graciously accepting us and encouraged the people to lift up their leaders in prayer. She challenged the crowd by asking who would pray for the mayor and other government officials if the people of Paramonga didn't. Many nodded in agreement. Liney then prayed a passionate blessing over the mayor as the rest of us laid hands on him.

Before I'd left for Latin America, I had received prophecies about getting favor with the government. At the time, I found it hard to fathom how I would be able to gain access to interaction with government officials. But the Lord was always faithful to His word, and I remembered His fidelity as I stood there praying with the mayor of Paramonga.

In just a matter of weeks, I'd gone from being severely ill to laying hands on people who were miraculously healed by God's love. Then, I was handed an opportunity to pray for the leader of the city that had marked such a transformation. God had used me at my very weakest to demonstrate His unfailing strength. And, to make our time in Paramonga even more special, Tanya announced the exciting news that she was pregnant with her second child. In a city that looked like death, new life was coming forth.

I left Paramonga feeling encouraged by God's provision in my most fragile moment. A city that began in misery ended in victory, healing, and new birth. However, despite the boost in my spirit, I couldn't deny that I was still in need of some serious rest. From Paramonga, the team traveled to Lima and temporarily split off into several groups. This was my opportunity to sneak away and get a real break. Liz and I decided to take off on our own adventure and traveled to the beautiful city of Cusco, Peru. One of my closest friends from mission school in Mozambique, Elizabeth, had moved to Cusco just weeks before our team entered Peru. Though Elizabeth and I had first met in Africa, we later found out that we lived in the same area of California. When we'd returned to the States after school, Elizabeth played a vital role in easing the transition from life in Mozambique to life back in California. And now, by the grace of God, my dear African/Californian friend just so happened to be living with a Peruvian family in Cusco where she invited me and Liz to stay for a couple of weeks. The timing of our arrival was a perfect, God-ordained appointment.

But before I gush about my divine getaway, I can't forget about my teammates who embarked on other endeavors. One group opted to stay in Lima, enjoy some time exploring the city, and do ministry with YWAM. Another group comprised of Stephen, Natalie H., Aleeza, our team's Elizabeth, and a visiting friend of Iris named Bridget traveled to the jungle city of Iquitos. Bridget was a British fireball whose laugh was infectiously charming. She served with her small team in the jungle and remained there when the others moved on, promising to join everyone for another visit later on in the journey. A beacon of light, encouragement, and laughter, Bridget was an instant hit. The Iquitos team departed with Shekinah, the Durango, planning to spend a few weeks in the jungle before driving back to wherever the majority of the team was stationed. Unbeknownst to the rest of us, we would never see Shekinah again, and we would reunite with the Iquitos crew much later than originally expected.

The remaining team members headed to a different city in the Amazon, accompanied by our newest long-term addition. Charlotte, just nineteen years old, brought new enthusiasm and colorful flavor to the team. This energetic little Kiwi was like a breath of fresh air. Impressively well-rounded, mature, and steadfast at such a young age, Charlotte was a nice surprise for the team. With a "glass is half full" mentality and a quality sense of humor, we immediately appreciated her presence. Smiling, joking, and radiating bursts of joy, she excitedly embarked on her first adventure with the team.

Charlotte and her group began their quest by heading to Pucallpa, a jungle city accessible by road from Lima. Pucallpa was located on a branch of the Amazon River leading to indigenous villages and unreached tribes. Jesse and Tanya confirmed plans with a missionary in Pucallpa who had arranged for the team to boat into the Amazon from the city. Though pregnant, Tanya didn't hesitate for a moment to venture into the jungle. She'd already survived pregnancy and the delivery of Zoe in Africa; so carrying a child and planning on giving birth wherever we happened to be in nine months didn't faze her for a moment. The most hardcore pregnant woman I'd ever met, she headed to Pucallpa with a smile on her face.

After almost twenty hours of climbing thousands of feet into the Andes, swerving through windy roads, and "tag team puking" in the back of the bus, the team arrived in Pucallpa. Unfortunately, they received disappointing news upon arrival. The river had flooded, and no one could boat into the jungle from Pucallpa until the water receded. While waiting in the city, a local pastor asked the team to minister in his church. Though the team had hoped to go straight into the jungle, the change of events was an answered prayer for the pastor. He said he'd been interceding for his land for years and had prayed for a decade to receive a team like our Iris group in Pucallpa. This pastor was glad the team would be stuck with him for a little while.

Throughout the four days of working alongside this man, the water level went down enough for the team to safely boat into the jungle. The pastor offered to take them, and they began the journey into the Amazon with a seventeen-hour boat ride. Hammocks were slung side by side on the boat while my teammates slept alongside one another as well as Peruvian children who repeatedly kicked them in their heads. The stench of pigs and chickens filled the boat — a promising start for any jungle adventure.

The boat finally docked in the village of Coco, a small indigenous community of fifteen hundred people. Sleeping arrangements there were not much better. The team slept on the floor of an unfinished building, and those without mosquito nets suffered rats biting at their heels all night.

The team spent two nights ministering in Coco before boating even deeper into the jungle. During their first night hosting a Coco church service, some witches from the village came to the service to observe what was going on. They maintained their distance from the front of the church but watched carefully from afar. One man in the congregation who had been deaf for eight years received prayer and was healed. Someone on the team invited the witches to come closer and join in the glory, but they refused. However, the witches saw the miracles happening among the congregants and couldn't deny that many people were being healed and experiencing great joy.

The following evening, the pastor requested another church service. Again, the witches attended. People who had come the previous evening shared their testimonies of healing, confirming what God had done in front of the whole congregation. The witches decided they wanted what these people had and renounced their witchcraft, Liney leading them to repentance.

The team also made some house visits throughout the village for those unable to come to the service. They encountered one lady who had been sick for three years. She had a high fever and was bedridden. The team found some witchcraft fetishes in her room, and the woman repented of her demonic involvement. Some people prayed for her healing, but Kurt decided to simply love her. He hugged and kissed her and just held her hand for around an hour. Kurt and the team departed without realizing the incredible impact of love they'd left behind. Days later, they found out that the lady had gotten up from her bed and was completely healed.

After ministering in Coco, the pastor said he would grant the team's biggest desire — traveling to an unreached people group deep inside the jungle. The team left in a single boat, uncomfortably squished into a vessel comprised of thirteen or so from Iris plus the pastor and his son. They boated for around an hour, envisioning six *more* hours of crammed traveling ahead. The pastor offered that he had a nearby relative with another boat. If they stopped now and helped lead an evening church service in his relative's village, the relative would accompany them in the morning, and they could continue the journey with two boats.

The team did what the pastor suggested, docked for the evening, and assisted with yet another church service. The next morning, they continued on with two boats as promised. The previous night's dinner had been eaten by dogs during the service, and there was no breakfast in the morning. The only items available for purchase in the village were soda and vanilla crackers, which meant a long boat ride on empty stomachs. The pastor's relative said his boat was faster than the pastor's, so it would be best to meet up once they'd reached the tribe rather than travel together.

The pastor's boat (the slower, narrow, wooden boat) traveled four or five hours into the jungle. The passengers, including his son, were growing increasingly hungry with no food except for the crackers. After a while, the pastor admitted that he was lost and didn't know how to find the correct village. It seemed they were caught in a maze of tributaries, and there was no way to tell which way led to the tribe they were aiming for. The pastor's son told his dad he was scared, and the pastor began to panic as well. When people who grew up in the jungle got scared, it was not a good sign. The passengers of this boat started to pray and decided to backtrack a bit. They hoped to find some loggers working along the river and offer some payment to lead them to the right tribe.

Meanwhile, the other boat was having its own debacle with the pastor's relative and his wife who had taken over as the boat guide. They got within fifteen minutes of the village that they were trying to reach and were turned around. Three men from the village, also on a boat, approached my teammates' boat with guns and asked where they were going. The pastor's relative said he was headed to the unreached tribe to start a church. The men asserted that my teammates, the relative, and his wife were not welcome in the village and explained that there was a huge drinking party going on. The chief had left, major drinking had broken out, and if the team arrived in the village, the indigenous people would shoot them.

Liney, realizing the declaration of starting a church was the real reason for such harsh rejection, repeatedly tried to explain that they weren't actually going to the village to start a church. They just wanted to spend time with people and show them love — without an agenda. Yet, Liney was ignored, and the pastor's relative told the tribal men that they would turn around. He was scared and refused to go any further. However, his wife insisted that she had a connection in the unreached village and wanted to continue forward despite the threats. The whole team agreed. Their heart was to go to the unreached and travel to the darkest places. Each person said he or she was prepared to give up his or her life for the sake of the gospel and asked to keep going towards the village.

With fear, the pastor's relative disregarded everyone else's opinion, including his wife's. Liney said that at the very least, they needed to wait for the other boat to catch up with them. They had agreed to wait for the others, and if they turned around now, they risked losing the other half of the team. The relative continued to ignore Liney and turned around as he began to steer the boat back towards Coco. The team yelled and begged him to stop, but he refused.

All my teammates on the boat started praying and taking communion. They hadn't seen the other boat for a long time and realized they were definitely lost. After praying, the wife said she thought she heard the sound of a motor. The narrow stretches of river were surrounded by bushes, so it was impossible to see what was on the other offshoots of the Amazon. Thankfully, the pastor's relative agreed to explore the nearby branches of the river to see if there was another boat. Twenty minutes later, they heard the motor again. They followed the noise and began to yell, "Shika baba!" (Swahili for "Hold onto the Father," a phrase often heard in our mission school in Mozambique). The other boat heard their voices through the bushes and yelled back, "Shabba shika baba! We love you guys!"

When comparing notes later, the two boats realized the first time the relative's group heard a motor wasn't actually the other team's boat. It would have been impossible to hear each other because of how far away they were. Yet, a noise that sounded like a motor mysteriously led the two boats to one another.

The two groups were overjoyed and relieved to be reunited, but they still had a long, dangerous journey back to Coco. They had wasted hours trying to access the unreached village, only to be denied entrance fifteen minutes from the tribe. If things had gone according to plan, the team would have slept in the village and headed back to the city days later during sunlight hours. But because of the situation, they were now faced with no choice but to boat back to Coco as the sun went down. The two boats traveled back in six hours of darkness, weaving through narrow streams of the Amazon, barely able to see where the water stopped and land started. They had just enough light in their dying headlamps to make it back. Jesse stood in front of his boat with a lamp, directing the driver by yelling to the back of the boat which way to turn to avoid crashing into bushes. As the team boated, they prayed they wouldn't crash into the bank or capsize into the river filled with anacondas, piranhas, and crocodiles. Unnervingly, they felt the backs of some crocodiles as they ran them over with their vessels. They finally returned to Coco and Pucallpa, where they made the wise decision to fly back to Lima. From the capital, they would then fly to Cusco and train to Machu Picchu, leaving the cars in Lima a bit longer.

Meanwhile, I'd been in Cusco for over a week, enjoying every second of my luxurious rest. Liz and I arrived in the historic city after a twenty-seven hour bus ride. Though the ride was planned to be "just" twenty-two hours, some rockslides and flooded roads added a few extra hours. Six months prior, such a long ride would have horrified me, yet neither Liz nor I were even slightly fazed at this point.

As we pulled into the Cusco bus station, I saw Elizabeth walking towards our bus, and my heart leapt at the sight of an old friend. I hugged her, grateful to have a tangible piece of home in front of me. Elizabeth felt equally excited to see a familiar face, and our time together in Cusco proved to be the breath of fresh air both of us needed. Elizabeth escorted us to her house where Liz and I were each given our own bed, a real shower, and a consistent place to keep our belongings for a week or two — a much-needed change of pace for us. I even had the chance to store some clothes in my very own drawer, something I hadn't done in six months. I'd never been so excited to use a drawer in my life.

Elizabeth was ready for some refreshment as well. She was studying Spanish in Cusco for a few months before moving to Tacna, Peru where she planned to serve as a full-time missionary. She'd only been in Peru for five weeks when Liz and I arrived and was beginning to feel the weight of the daunting commitment before her. In addition to dealing with severe transition, Elizabeth was the sole Christian in her language school and sometimes felt alone in her faith. Her classes consisted of several hours each day of one-on-one conversations with teachers who were open to speaking about any topics — including sex, marriage, politics, and religion. The teachers enjoyed listening to Elizabeth's beliefs and views on God; however, there was no one else at the school to back up what she was saying. Cusco, like much of Latin America, was a predominately Catholic area. The majority of people would tell you they were Catholic but lacked any evidence of a genuine, intimate relationship with God. In addition, many locals mixed Catholicism with superstitious Incan traditions that perverted the truth of Jesus Christ, making it quite complicated to communicate the pure, untouched gospel. Yet, Elizabeth viewed her class time as a mission field and didn't hesitate to share her beliefs with her teachers, praying that they would be released from religious oppression and embrace the freedom of Jesus' love.

Elizabeth told me and Liz that she had been spending a fair amount of time sharing pieces of her faith with a few women from her language school, including a couple of her teachers. One of them, Patty, had shared several prophetic dreams she'd had with Elizabeth and wanted to know what they meant. She often dreamt things that soon came to pass, and she didn't understand why this was happening. Patty was interested in what Elizabeth had shared with her and wanted to know more.

Elizabeth said Patty was interested in meeting me and Liz and wanted to hang out one evening after class. Elizabeth really wanted us to share some of our testimonies from our trip and build Patty's faith. We didn't want to act overly spiritual or intimidate Patty by preaching at her, so we decided to go to a relaxed restaurant and simply chat about life. We chose a place owned by one of Patty's friends with a laid-back and informal atmosphere. Elin, an Icelandic student from the language school, caught wind of our plans and decided to join us as well. Both Patty and Elin were open and easy to talk to. Patty was especially warm and friendly. The five of us girls sat around a small table and chatted in the best Spanish we could as we laughed and simply enjoyed each other's company.

We weren't talking about anything related to God, so I wasn't sure how I would smoothly transition into a conversation about the power of the Holy Spirit. Elizabeth and I kept making eye contact with one another, speaking through glances, trying to get the other person to slip in something about our faith without sounding completely awkward. Finally, Elizabeth mentioned the fact that Liz and I had seen some pretty intense miracles throughout the last few months, and Patty looked at me with inquisitive eyes. I decided to go for it. I was unsure how I would explain our testimonies clearly in another language, but I opened my mouth, and the words came. At times, I stumbled a bit, but Patty patiently listened. As she smiled in amazement at my stories, I knew she could understand exactly what I was saying. I told her about the woman in Panama who got up out of her wheelchair and began to walk. I told her about the woman in Colombia who got healed of breast cancer. I told her about the man in Paramonga, part of her own country, who had just received the ability to hear after thirty years of deafness. Patty listened intently, eyes growing wider and wider, then turned to Elizabeth to ask, "Is it really true?" Patty looked like a child who wanted to believe but wasn't sure if she was supposed to.

Elizabeth smiled at Patty and nodded. "Yes, it's all true."

Patty desired to understand how these seemingly impossible things could really happen. She assumed Liz and I had some magical powers she did not possess. I explained that miracles had nothing to do with me or Liz or anyone else on the team. It was simply the power of the Holy Spirit and the love of the Father working through us. I told Patty she could do the exact same things we'd done, because the same God could work through *her* hands.

By this point, Patty was fascinated and began to ask several questions. She told me and Liz about some of her prophetic dreams, wondering why she'd dreamt things that had come true shortly after. Elizabeth had previously told me that Patty sometimes consulted psychics, so I wondered which dreams had come from the Lord and which had come from Satan. I explained that prophecy was a gift from the Holy Spirit, but Satan often perverted the gift with tarot cards and psychics. I explained to Patty that God had given her the gift of prophecy and was speaking to her through her dreams. If she chose to use that gift in purity, she could hear more from God and even ask for an increase in gifts.

Patty looked at me as though she were nothing; she seemed confused as to why the Lord would want to speak to her or give her any gifts. I told Patty that she was God's daughter, plain and simple. I explained that in religion, people tried and tried to earn access to God, but it was impossible in our own strength. Even though Patty knew I was a missionary, I told her that I hated religion. I reassured her that I didn't worship a set of rules or try to earn my way to God. My life was all about a *relationship* with God as His daughter. I told Patty her identity was the same — a chosen, beloved daughter of God. She didn't need to do anything other than simply accept His love.

Patty's face lit up, and she said that no one had ever told her that before. She had no idea she was already a daughter of God or that He loved her enough to talk to her and give her gifts without her doing a thing. Her countenance demonstrated her great surprise and deep joy at such a realization. She kept smiling and telling me and Liz that she liked talking to us, that what we had to say was beautiful. Meanwhile, Elin listened to every word, taking it all in but saying very little. I had no idea if she was interested or if she thought we were completely nuts. I think the latter.

I later found out that Patty had been in a relationship for a couple of years and had just discovered that her boyfriend was cheating on her. She'd told Elizabeth she knew she needed to break up with him, but she didn't feel she had the strength to do it. After our conversation about being God's daughter, Patty turned to Elizabeth and said, "I think I can do it now."

After ten days or so in Cusco, the Pucallpa team and most of those who had stayed in Lima flew into Cusco and met me and Liz there. They wanted to visit Machu Picchu, one of the Seven World Wonders, and the only way to get there was to take a train from Cusco. My teammates spent two nights in Cusco before their train left for Machu Picchu, and Elizabeth asked if some of them would come meet with Patty during that time to prophesy over her.

Breck, Kimmie, Liney, and I went with Elizabeth to meet Patty for dinner. Beforehand, I had prayed for Patty and felt the Lord laying a few words on my heart. One of them was a verse from Isaiah that read, "Can a mother forget her nursing child? Can she feel no love for the child she has borne? But even if that were possible, I would not forget you! See, I have written your name on the palms of my hands" (Isaiah 49:15-16, NLT). I shared this passage in Spanish, and Patty's face lit up just as it had a few nights before. Shortly after, Kimmie (who didn't understand any of the Spanish I'd just spoken) asked Liney to translate a similar word, assuring Patty that she was in the palm of God's hand. Patty realized that God had spoken to both of us independently and laughed with joy as He confirmed that she truly was in His hands.

Breck and Liney also prophesied over Patty, and Breck immediately told her that the Lord wanted to heal her depression. Without knowing her for more than a brief moment, God revealed to Breck that there was serious hurt beneath Patty's welcoming smile. She nodded in agreement and began to weep. Liney held her in her arms, speaking comfort and encouragement over her. Breck and Liney spoke to Patty about the Father's ability to heal the broken places in her heart and reminded her how much she was loved. Patty smiled through her tears, repeatedly thanking us, "Gracias, gracias, gracias."

When we parted ways for the evening, it was clear that Patty was pondering all of these words in her heart. She left smiling and laughing, asking when we could meet up to talk again. I knew she'd been touched and prayed that she would seek God more, feel His love more, and be healed by His presence. Months later, while hundreds of miles from Cusco, I received an email from Elizabeth reporting that Patty had accepted Christ and decided to follow Him.

The beauty about our time with Patty is that it didn't feel like "ministry." Sharing the gospel with her wasn't work; it wasn't hard. When I got to Cusco, I made a purposeful decision *not* to do any work. I wanted only to rest, recharge, and take a real break before rejoining the team. However, God used me in moments of rest to bring Him glory. While simply hanging out with Elizabeth and her friends, God used us to share His love. I realized there should be no difference between "ministry time" and "rest time." Ministry is the natural overflow of a heart at rest and in love with Jesus.

The day following our dinner with Patty, my team left to travel to Machu Picchu while I stayed behind in Cusco for a few more days with Elizabeth. Machu Picchu is technically classified as one of the Seven Wonders of the Modern World and considered a place of deep spiritual significance for the Incans. The word *Inca* means "spiritual power," and the Incan culture is full of mystical traditions. There is an eighty-four kilometer trail from Cusco to Machu Picchu where Incans used to trek, winding up at Machu Picchu as the final temple of their spiritual journey. The loftiest people in the Incan Empire once lived in Machu Picchu, including a high priest who used demonic powers to know the past, present, and future.

Just as we'd climbed to the highest ancient Mayan temple in Central America, my teammates wanted to visit the highest holy place in Peru to pray over the country. The Incans had performed various religious rituals and spread demonic superstitions that left people in bondage to false deities. Though their land had been given over to Incan gods, my team decided to reclaim the land for Jesus Christ.

While I remained in Cusco, my teammates explored Machu Picchu, where they spent hours walking around until eventually stopping to pray atop a cliff. They prophesied the destruction of the old world order and declared the newness of the kingdom of Jesus Christ. My team took communion and traded the blood of Christ for His fullness to be released over the earth. Angela felt that the Lord had given her a song to sing over the ancient city as well as a call-and-response war cry. Each person on the team linked arms as a symbol of unification in the spirit realm. They walked to the cliff's edge as one and chanted as loudly as they could:

"Who is approaching the gates?"
"The Lord strong and mighty! The Lord mighty in battle!"
"Who is approaching the gates?"
"The Lord strong and mighty! The Lord mighty in battle!"
(See Psalm 24.)

Their cries attracted the attention of several security guards, who blew whistles in a useless attempt to quiet their chants. My teammates didn't care about looking crazy or sounding crazy. Each person knew that beyond what he or she could see, there was a spiritual battle going on, and the Lord said to fight. As they warred for God's kingdom of light to shine in the darkness, the Lord confirmed that He was moving.

While the group split up for a time of reflection, photo opportunities, and exploration, the Lord gave Angela a powerful vision of Jesus. Sitting atop the ruins and gazing at the ancient city in front of her, Angela saw something beautiful happening in the heavenly realm.

Jesus was present. He was already resurrected, shining in glory. There were nails in His hands and feet and a scar on His side. His splendor started to pour over the ruins, and a new city of glory emerged upon them. Angela could see women dancing in the streets, children playing, and men singing and making music. Women, men, and children alike were wearing white. Everyone was celebrating with great joy.

Though Machu Picchu had once been a land of spiritual darkness, God gave Angela a glimpse of His glory that will one day cover the whole earth.

Meanwhile, Elizabeth and I decided to have our own time of intercession in Cusco. Though I knew visiting Machu Picchu would be incredible, I'd felt I needed to stay behind and pray over Cusco with Elizabeth. From the moment I entered Peru, I could feel a heavy spiritual atmosphere unique to this country. When we stayed at the beach where I'd gotten so sick, I'd seen a dark mass hovering over the water while watching the ocean waves. The darkness and heaviness only got worse as we traveled further into Peru. Some nights in Cusco, I felt like my body was under attack and couldn't sleep.

After one bizarre night, Elizabeth asked me, "Do you remember what you said to me at around 1:45 in the morning?"

I shook my head. I was positive I'd been asleep at that time and had no recollection of saying anything. "What are you talking about?" I asked. "I was sound asleep then."

"You must have been talking in your sleep," she stated. "But you asked me, '¿Sientes esta presencia?'"

My jaw dropped to the floor. Apparently I'd asked her in Spanish, "Do you feel that presence?"

Elizabeth went on to explain, "After you said that, I could feel a male demonic presence in the room. I didn't know what it was. I just knew it was male, but it felt like a demon. I started praying in tongues, and it eventually went away."

Though I was pretty impressed that I had been speaking Spanish in my sleep, I was far more disturbed that I was talking about demons without realizing it. I'd known there was serious spiritual oppression in Cusco; however, when demons were pestering me in my sleep, it was time for spiritual warfare. Elizabeth and I needed to pray.

We took a minibus to the peak of Cristo Blanco, the highest mountain in Cusco. On the crest of the hill stood a huge, white statue of Jesus, arms outstretched and overlooking the city. Three crosses were positioned next to Jesus, adorned with peculiar religious emblems. The Catholic symbols mixed with Incan ones created an odd mix of religion — a perverted representation of the gospel marked by strict traditions and ancient superstitions.

Elizabeth and I prayed over each religious idol on top of Cristo Blanco, declaring the truth of Christ Jesus in place of the cultural perversions. We declared our dreams for Cusco and for Peru — asking God for restored families, passionate churches, radical lovers of Christ, and people who lived out the truth. We took communion with some crackers and water and traded the blood of Christ for the salvation of His people. I anointed Elizabeth with oil and prayed over her, commissioning her as a missionary to the nation of Peru.

As we worshipped, prayed, and proclaimed our dreams aloud, I stood in awe of what the Lord was doing. I thought back on when I'd met Elizabeth in mission school in Mozambique, a huge turning point in my life. I reflected on our return to California and learning how to get back to "normal life" while maintaining a changed heart. Elizabeth had been right by my side as we struggled through the transition together. When I'd left for Latin America, I had no idea when I would see her next. Now here we were, in the Incan city of Cusco, claiming the destiny of Jesus Christ over Peru. God had taken us both so far, and I knew it was no coincidence that we'd ended up in Peru at the same time.

The following day, my team returned to Cusco from Machu Picchu, and it was time to fly back to Lima together. I was sad to say goodbye to Elizabeth but felt refreshed and ready to serve with the team again. Elizabeth was also ready to hit the ground running, empowered to continue ministering within her language school and her city. My time in Cusco was exactly what both of us needed. God had ordained it, and my heart was overflowing with gratitude.

After flying back to Lima, the team reconvened, got our cars, and headed to Tacna, our final stop in Peru. This was the city where Elizabeth would work as a missionary after finishing language school. I was glad to get a chance to visit her future city and ministry. My team visited the Tacna branch of We Will Go Ministries, an organization run by Amy Lancaster, a close friend of Iris Global. Amy was normally based in Jackson, Mississippi but flew to Peru just to spend time with the team. Randy and Kim, the couple who oversaw We Will Go in Tacna, were glad to see Amy, as were we. I'd heard her speak in Mozambique but had never spent any one-on-one time with her. It was great to gain some pearls of wisdom from her life and receive prayer from her. Rubbing shoulders with We Will Go Ministries was a privilege and great source of refreshment before moving on to our next country.

Chapter Twelve

CHILE AND ARGENTINA: To the End of the World

  Upon leaving Peru, our team was bombarded with negative words about Chile from the Peruvian community. Due to a huge clash between these bordering countries, most people in Peru unfortunately had few kind words to say about their southern neighbor. However, despite rumors of terrible food, terrible wine, and downright terrible people, I was excited to see what Chile had in store for my team. So far, every country had yielded a unique blessing, and I was confident that Chile would do the same.

  We had many days of driving ahead of us before reaching our first destination of Santiago, Chile's capital. In such a long country, I realized even several days on the road made only a dent of progress on a map. After two days of travel, we changed plans and decided to stop at a small coastal city for a full day so we could celebrate Easter. We rented a few rooms that were just a stone's throw from the ocean. On Easter morning, a few of my teammates prepared a luxurious brunch for the rest of us. We filled our bellies, then spent the afternoon calling our families back home, hanging out with each other, and taking individual time to reflect on Christ's sacrifice. I walked along the ocean, mesmerized by its mysterious contradiction. The waves were so strong and fierce, yet so calming and steady — a perfect reflection of God's character.

In the evening, our team celebrated with a lamb feast and organized a family church service. A few of us read scripture; others shared what God had recently laid on our hearts. We took communion together, remembering Christ's sacrifice for us and giving thanks for the reason we celebrated. We worshipped, prayed, and gave adoration to our Savior.

The next morning, we continued towards Santiago, where we would minister with a local church for a few days before heading further south. As we drove, we decided to get rid of one of our pop-up campers that we'd been hauling for the past seven months. The pop-up had faithfully served as a makeshift home since September, but after thousands of miles on the road, it had become pretty beat-up. Due to a broken crank, it now took four guys to lift the sides of the camper and set it up (a job I used to be able to do myself). In addition, the next leg of our journey would be too cold to sleep in a pop-up with no heat, so we'd be hauling the camper unnecessarily for miles, guzzling extra gas in vain. Though sad to say goodbye to our closest thing to a home, we knew it had become obsolete. Jesse's family had owned the pop-up before the trip, and he and Tanya bought it off them for one thousand dollars. However, instead of trying to sell the trailer to make the money back, we decided to bless someone with it. We'd been told that there were squatter communities in the area and prayed for the Lord to lead us to the right family.

As we drove towards Santiago, Jesse pulled over within the first hour at a dusty patch of land I assumed was nothing more than a garbage dump. However, this barren terrain was home to several families, and the Holy Spirit undoubtedly had led our team there. A man and a woman immediately approached our vehicles, and we asked them if anyone was interested in using our pop-up as a home. The woman's face lit up with delight. "I've been praying for a portable home for a year," she exclaimed, beaming from ear to ear. "We're Christians, and we have been in need of extra housing for a long time. Every time I see someone drive by with one of those things, I pray that God will give me one. Every time, I pray in faith that He will answer my prayer. Now He has!"

I later found out that the timeframe of when the woman began to pray for the pop-up coincided perfectly with when Jesse and Tanya first started talking to Jesse's family about buying the pop-up from them. I couldn't deny the serendipity of this beautiful timing and was moved by the realization that God had allowed us to be the answer to someone's prayers. After months of pushing that camper up and down, hauling it around, and dealing with its bulky body, it really was a strange blessing to get rid of it. Now this Chilean family was equally blessed to receive it. The sweet woman made each of us a sandwich with gratitude and refused to send us on our way until our bellies were full. We thanked her for the food and continued driving, the sight of the woman's bright, smiling face in the distance.

After many more miles of driving, we arrived in Santiago, where we were warmly received by a small local church and united with yet another new team member. Eclectic Amanda transitioned into our team with remarkable ease, quickly winning people over with her funky style, solid work ethic, and brilliant sense of humor. An amazing musician, she wowed us with her piano, guitar, ukulele, and vocal skills and became a team worship leader right away. She jumped into the chaos of our team in stride, not at all fazed by the fact that she'd just become part of a twenty-two-person sleepover. In Santiago, our entire team slept on the floor of the church's sanctuary together — a dangerous recipe for pillow fights, nighttime pranks, and way too little sleep. The pastor warmly welcomed us like his own family, feeding us three meals a day and coordinating with church members to let us shower in their homes. One woman kindly offered to do laundry for our entire team in her tiny house, a huge blessing for our large group.

Days later, the laundry woman stopped by the church and announced that our clothes were ready if a few people could stop by her house and carry the bags back to the church. She also asked if those who came would be willing to pray for her daughter. She had been badly burned on her leg and wanted to be healed from the pain.

Rose, Amanda, and I went to the woman's house and were greeted by her teenage daughter, her right thigh covered in a large bandage. We laid hands on her and prayed for healing. After a few moments, she smiled and said there was no pain in her leg. A man from the church had also stopped by and asked us to pray for him next. He had diabetes and wanted a miracle in his pancreas. As we prayed for him, the Holy Spirit filled him with overwhelming joy, and he fell to the floor laughing. His whole body shook as he flopped around like a fish, roaring with laughter. I'd never seen anyone react to prayer quite like this before.

We offered to pray for the woman as well before we headed back to the church. I could sense depression and oppression all over her. Rose saw a vision of a snake wrapped around her neck and asked her what was currently happening in her life. Without hesitation, the woman revealed that she was raising four children alone after being left by a verbally abusive husband. We could see such intense sadness in her eyes and were overwhelmed with compassion for her. As we prayed for the woman to be freed from the lies and oppression choking her, she began to cough violently. I remembered the teenage boy delivered from demons in Mexico who coughed up slime as they left his body, and this seemed a similar situation. The man who had been laughing moments before sobered up and ran to get a bucket as the woman continued to expel mucus while we prayed. The coughing finally stopped, and we prophesied over the woman, encouraging her and telling her about her worth and acceptance by God. Her tears of pain transformed into tears of joy, and her countenance completely changed. It was almost as if oppression had been tangibly broken off of her. We embraced the woman, celebrating her newfound freedom.

Another woman heard about our team and came to the church with her husband and children, desperately requesting prayer for repeated demonic attacks. She limped and twitched and made odd noises, eerily staring into the distance as if her mind wasn't quite connected to her body. As we prayed for her, something felt far more unusual than with others I'd met along the journey. I was having trouble discerning what was going on. Often, praying with fierce authority and declaring the truth of Christ resulted in the same type of freedom experienced by the woman who'd done our laundry. However, this time, Jesse said not to be forceful but instead confront the attacks with extreme love. He asked Tanya to simply hug the woman, so Tanya held her in her arms for a very long time. She spoke life over the woman and just kept holding her as she cried, loving her in a unique and radical way.

Our team preached and prayed for the Santiago church's congregation during several gatherings, but we actually seemed to encounter God most often *outside* of the church's tiny walls. Ben, Liney, Kurt, and a few others ventured into the heart of Santiago one day to explore and returned to the team with an amazing testimony of God's healing power. While taking a bus downtown, Ben decided to keep to himself and quietly worship. As he sat on the bus, he felt in his body that someone had leg problems and was having trouble walking. The Lord also gave him a picture of a man with a cane. Ben knew this was a word of knowledge and that God wanted to heal people.

The moment they stepped off the bus to transfer to the metro, Ben turned his head to the left and noticed a guy with a cane also heading to the metro. He grabbed Liney to help him translate and asked Kurt to tell the rest of the group that they were going to go after that man. Ben and Liney ran to find the man but realized they'd lost him. They kept walking and suddenly saw people with crutches everywhere they turned — walking by, sitting down, to the right, and to the left. One particular man stood out to them, and they approached him. The man said he was in a rush but stopped nonetheless, then explained that he had a tumor that had caused a stroke in his brain. In effect, this had paralyzed the left side of his face, and the signal from his brain to his feet was delayed, causing an inability to walk properly. Ben and Liney told him that God wanted to heal him, but the man repeatedly informed them that he was in a hurry, trying to avert their attention. However, they insisted that he had nothing to lose by asking for God's healing.

The man finally agreed to receive a quick prayer, so Ben laid his hand on the left side of his face and prayed. Kurt joined them and prayed as well. Instead of asking for healing, they *commanded* the paralysis to leave by the power of Jesus Christ.

Afterwards, they asked what the man felt. He said that he couldn't describe the presence and heat that was resting all over the paralyzed side of his face. He was so overwhelmed that he couldn't look Ben, Liney, or Kurt in the eyes. The man was shocked that Jesus was tangibly touching him with His fire and walked away stunned by God's presence.

A few moments later, the group noticed a woman with a cane and approached her. She was sweet, tender, and open. She shared her struggle with a degenerative problem in her back that caused intense pain and a need for the cane.

The three laid hands on her back and also asked the woman to put her own hand on her back to symbolize her agreement with God to release healing. As they prayed, Ben started getting prophetic words for the woman and told her who she was in the eyes of Jesus. He declared how accepted and beautiful she was to the Lord. The woman began to weep and said, "No one ever speaks to me like this. I've never heard people speak life over me. I could listen to you all day."

The woman was so touched by God's love that she completely forgot about the pain in her back. Ben reminded her of the original reason they'd prayed and asked her how her back was feeling. The woman bent over to test it out. Ben asked her to walk without the cane in Jesus' name. Immediately, the woman bolted off walking. She went so fast that Ben said she looked like a power walker. The woman returned and told Liney she'd never been able to walk pain-free without her cane. The degenerative condition in her back had just been completely abolished. The woman, Ben, Liney, and Kurt hugged, jumping up and down and rejoicing in her healing together.

The woman said she didn't need the cane anymore and wanted to give it away to someone who did. She bid my teammates farewell and walked away with the cane tucked under her arm, ready to donate it to someone else.

God was moving in the midst of the mundane. He was choosing to show up in places anywhere but special — just a dusty plot of land, a woman's little house, and a metro station. Our time in Santiago gave me fresh revelation about the importance of seeking God's kingdom in every moment. When we looked for God in the ordinary, He began to do extraordinary things.

With renewed excitement for seeing God's kingdom released on earth, my teammates and I continued further south towards the tip of South America. When the vision for the Iris Latin America trip was birthed in 2010, Jesse and Tanya felt led to not only share the gospel in every country in Latin America but specifically to travel all the way to the very bottom of South America. They yearned to ignite revival fire from the tip of the continent and let it fan to flame up the rest of the Latin world.

Our ultimate goal was to reach Argentina's Ushuaia, the southernmost city on the planet, literally deemed "The End of the World." Unfortunately, getting to the tip of South America was not as easy as one might hope. Due to the roads and terrain, it required weaving in and out of Chile and Argentina numerous times through a beautiful but circuitous route. While in Santiago, we decided to leave our vehicles in the capital and take a series of buses and ferries to the tip of South America rather than driving. This would save us time, money, and the hassle of driving through winter weather with our clumsy fleet of vehicles. We threw our warmest clothes into our hiking packs and began a meandrous voyage throughout Chile and Argentina, unsure of when we'd be reunited with our cars and belongings in Santiago.

Our team began our journey to "The End of the World" with an overnight bus ride to the city of Puerto Montt, where we stopped for two nights. Upon our arrival, Liz, Amanda, and I walked around the city to try to find a cheap hostel for the team. As we located our first lodging option, we were greeted by a sweet, older woman who agreed to show us around her hostel. While climbing the narrow steps towards the upstairs bedrooms, she complained of pain in her legs. Amanda said we should pray for her, so we offered to do so before we left. The woman smiled as we laid hands on her legs and asked the Lord to heal her. After a few moments, we stood up and asked her how she felt.

"I feel good," she smiled.

"Do you still feel pain?" we asked.

She began to move her legs and sway back and forth, testing out her knees. A look of genuine surprise overtook her face completely as she declared, "There's no pain! It doesn't hurt anymore!"

We all laughed with joy as she continued to smile in sheer surprise.

"You are angels!" she yelled.

We laughed, knowing we hadn't done a thing through our own power and were far from angels. We had simply depended on God to heal her.

"*God* loves you a lot," we explained. That's precisely why He'd just healed her aching knees.

Two days later, we continued our journey south by first catching a bus and then traveling via ferry for over forty hours. The view of the Chilean sea was supposed to be spectacular, but my excitement for experiencing nature's beauty quickly faded when I realized the inside of the ferry was not much warmer than the icy outside air. The lack of sleeping options didn't inspire much confidence in having a comfortable journey either. The main cabin of the ferry was only one overcrowded room full of cramped seats that made me feel trapped just by looking at them. Knowing we had two nights ahead of us with this arrangement overwhelmed me. In addition, when we boarded, most of our bags had been quickly taken by the boat crew and locked up for the remainder of the ferry trip. My bag had disappeared before I had even a second to grab the essentials, leaving me with no hair brush, no tooth brush, no sleeping bag, and no change of clothes. Though we'd been told the boat ride would last thirty hours, it turned into forty-one, a long ride without any hygienic supplies.

The first night on the boat was one of the longest of my life. Breck, Liz, and I ended up in the same row; then little Zoe joined us, sprawled out over a few seats. While Zoe slept like a rock, we adults awkwardly crammed into our row and desperately tried to sleep ourselves. We squirmed and shifted every thirty minutes or so. I was freezing and gradually stole more and more of Breck's warm, cozy sleeping bag. We rotated between trying to sleep sitting up, lying down (and getting kicked in the head by Zoe), and leaning against each other until finally giving up. We'd repositioned ourselves for hours and failed at every attempt to sleep. Several times, we simply looked at each other and laughed, not knowing what else to do. Our lives were so ridiculous.

After hours of dark, cold, and squirmy sleep deprivation, the sun rose over the ocean, and we welcomed a new day. The boat crew miraculously discovered the beauty of a heating system during day two on the Chilean Sea, and I was elated that the main cabin finally warmed up. I spent the day alternating between getting fresh air outside and returning to my seat inside to defrost.

Despite my hatred for the cold, I must admit that the scenery was breathtaking. The deep, sapphire water splashing against the backdrop of snow-covered mountains was incredible. Before going to sleep the second night, I climbed to the top level of the boat to look at the stars. They shimmered like pure ivory sprinkled atop a black canvas. Several shooting stars danced across the night sky, and I was reminded of how small I was in the grand scheme of things. Yet, within that reminder of my tininess, I ironically hungered to dream for bigger things — remembering that I often limited myself but really should be dreaming beyond the moon. I wanted to look at the stars forever but quickly got cold and headed inside to attempt a second night of "sleeping" on the boat. Fortunately, I actually got a few hours of rest until being woken up by Taylor L. sticking a spoonful of peanut butter in my mouth. I groggily sucked down the protein and sat up to join my teammates for many more hours on the ferry. Finally, by around 6 p.m. on Monday (we'd left on Saturday), we reached land and thankfully docked.

But our southbound traveling was far from over. Chile was so — long. It just kept going. After docking, we took a short bus ride to a nearby city, slept the night, bused to another city for a couple of days, bused yet again, and finished with a short ferry ride to the city of Chile Chico before crossing into Argentina. In Chile Chico, we separated into two hostels, one for the guys and one for the girls. Everyone was exhausted and hoped to catch some sleep before crossing into Argentina the following day. The girls' hostel looked good at first glance, but our high hopes were quickly shattered. The outside temperature was below freezing, and there was no heat in our hostel. The bedrooms were literally the temperature of a meat freezer, and we shivered as we frantically piled on layer after layer of clothing. Rose and I were so cold that we squished into a tiny twin bed together, hoping our body heat would protect us from hypothermia. I put on my gloves and prayed that I wouldn't turn into an icicle overnight. Liney laughed herself to sleep, joking that tomorrow's newspaper would read, "Twelve Foreign Women Dead: Found Frozen in Local Hostel." We heard dogs howling outside and agreed they must be barking an announcement that they were freezing to death.

In the morning, we were woken up abruptly and given ten minutes to pack our things and run to a bus station where we would head to Argentina. As we frantically tried to get ready, Kimmie commented, "I don't know what to wear. We could be on a bus for an hour or on a bus for three days." I laughed in agreement. Our life was full of constant unknowns. Lack of information and miscommunication offered us zero time to plan and nothing to plan for. In our given ten minutes, I managed to pack my bag and brush my teeth but didn't have time to change out of my pajamas. I hustled to the bus station, happy about being on time but displeased with my grubby attire. Unfortunately, our travel time ended up matching Kimmie's remark about spending days on a bus, not the hour we had hoped for.

The Argentine border wasn't far from the bus station, but after crossing the border, we spent several hours busing further south to Rio Gallegos, Argentina. There, we were faced with two options to finally get us to the city of Ushuaia. We could spend the night in this town and bus directly to Ushuaia in the morning. Or, we could board another bus within the hour and take a less direct route to Ushuaia, stopping in the Chilean city of Punta Arenas along the way, then winding back into Argentina.

In my mind, it clearly made sense to wait a day and take the direct bus route to Ushuaia. However, Tanya reminded us that we needed God to order our steps and asked us all to pray for a moment. I closed my eyes to pray and immediately saw the words "Punta Arenas." *Dang it,* I thought to myself. *This doesn't make any sense. We are going out of our way.* However, as I continued to pray, it became increasingly clear. I knew the Lord was telling us to take a detour, and there was a reason for it. After a few moments, Tanya asked the team what we'd heard. Everyone said the same thing. We all felt we needed to cross back into Chile and switch buses in Punta Arenas before going to Ushuaia. Tanya nodded, and we bought tickets for the bus. An hour later, we were on a bus back to Chile.

Upon arrival in Punta Arenas, a few of my teammates went to find a hostel for our group, and we ended up across the street from a small church. I hadn't even noticed that the humble building sprayed with graffiti was a church, but on Sunday morning worship music flooded the air. Taylor L. noticed some familiar songs and was overcome with a desire to worship. He walked over to the church, hoping to sneak in for a few moments, worship in the back, and then return to the hostel.

However, his plan to remain under the radar was quickly interrupted as several people from the church approached him, wanting to know more about him. Nelson, a local teenager who spoke English, asked Taylor some questions and relayed to the pastor that Taylor was a missionary passing through. The church had a deep desire and calling to send out missionaries and asked Taylor if they could pray for him, excited to be receiving a missionary in their church. Taylor went up to the front to receive prayer, and afterwards he shared a few prophetic words for the church. As he spoke, several people began to weep, amazed that this young guy from the States was speaking the very words on their hearts. It was clear that the Lord was moving. Meanwhile, Taylor hadn't mentioned to anyone that his bank account was pretty much empty, and he'd been trusting that God would provide for him. Without Taylor asking for a thing, the pastor took an offering for him, and the congregation provided him with a generous donation.

When the pastor found out there were twenty more of us across the street, he was very excited. He invited us all to worship at the church later that evening. Taylor returned to the hostel and spread the news. Blown away by such an awesome divine appointment, many of us eagerly walked to the church hours later where we were greeted by several youths who warmly hugged and kissed us as well as offered us warm drinks and sweet cakes. For days, Taylor had been talking about his desperate yet unsuccessful quest to find strawberry milk in Chile, and I smiled to myself as I noticed strawberry milk sitting on the church's table. It was good enough to be unexpectedly fed, but God showed that He cared about even the tiniest details and desires of His children.

Many of the youth spoke English, and we hung out and worshipped together for a long time. As I listened to worship songs in English, I found myself overwhelmingly thankful to be singing in my own language. Though we often worshipped together during team gatherings, we hadn't been to an English-speaking church since we'd left the States. I understood most of the Spanish worship throughout Latin America, but I hadn't realized how much it meant to me to sing inside of a church in my heart language. I began to weep as I listened to English praise being released inside a church for the first time in eight months.

After worshipping, we spoke to the youth and realized that we had the same heartbeat for ministry. The weight of the Holy Spirit was heavy among us. The atmosphere couldn't quite be put into words, but it was glaringly obvious that this meeting was something divine. I could feel the power of God's sovereignty, how He'd omnisciently redirected our steps and brought us out of our way to Punta Arenas. This was one of the rare times during the trip where we found a community of believers who shared our deepest heart's cry. The youth in the church desperately longed to be a part of an end-time revival army. The parallels between our vision and theirs were so strong that I was overwhelmed by God's hand in this connection. Turns out, the church began to receive prophetic words in 2010 about lighting revival fire, starting at their church, and letting it blaze throughout the rest of the continent. Jesse and Tanya had birthed almost an identical vision in 2010 while living on the other side of the world in Mozambique, Africa. As we compared timing and vision, we realized it was no accident that we'd been re-routed to Punta Arenas.

The church offered to host us for the next few days and minister with its youth as well as attend some of their nightly meetings. We'd originally planned on getting on the next bus to Ushuaia, but we knew God had plans for us in Punta Arenas and agreed to stay for a few days. The pastor hurriedly arranged for several families to host our teams, splitting us up among six houses.

Melissa and I were put in a house with three little girls — Catalina (age thirteen), Mariana (ten), and Romina (seven). The girls were extremely excited to have two new roommates, playmates, entertainers, and live-in jungle gyms. Coming from a family of three girls myself, I felt instantly connected to the sisters and enjoyed watching them interact with one another. The sisters loved to sing and dance together, invent funny games, and burst into giggling fits. They reminded me so much of the family I'd grown up in. Though I was in some strangers' home in Chile, I felt an odd sense of nostalgia as I played with the little girls.

Immediately after we moved in with our host family, Mariana, the middle daughter, told me that she had a guitar lesson during the afternoon and invited me to accompany her. Though I'd been a part of this family for just minutes, I agreed to tag along. A couple of hours later, her mother dropped us both off on a little sidewalk and instructed us to walk to her office when the lesson was over. From there, she would drive us both back to the house. Mariana nodded, and I foolishly assumed she understood these instructions. The second her mother drove off, Mariana looked at me with confusion.

"I don't know where to go," she admitted.

Less than thrilled that she was announcing this *after* her mother had driven off, I used my less-than-fluent Spanish to gather more information.

"Where do you normally go for your guitar lesson? Do you remember?" I asked as I looked around, not seeing a single sign for a music school or anything of the sort.

Mariana looked at me sheepishly. "This is my first lesson."

Great, I thought. *I'm now responsible for a Chilean child I've known for two hours and have no way of contacting a soul in the city.*

We approached a few people on the street and asked if anyone knew where a music school was. No one had a clue. We decided to enter the only open building on the street. We were reluctantly greeted by a cranky receptionist who insisted there was a green door outside to the right that was part of a music school. We tried the door several times, but it was locked. We paced up and down the sidewalks, looking to see any signs that read "Música" or "Guitarra" or "Escuela" or anything else helpful. We found nothing.

The weather was becoming increasingly cold and windy, and my hands were going numb. I looked at Mariana and suggested we give up and walk to her mom's office. I was hoping she did, in fact, actually know where *that* was.

"No!" she insisted as she worriedly scanned the streets. We stood there speechless for a few moments. Then, out of nowhere, the pastor's daughter, Lis, appeared on a bike.

Lis hopped off the bicycle and greeted both of us, explaining that she was Mariana's guitar instructor and that she would take us a few blocks uphill to an obscure building where she'd teach Mariana. I was relieved to see Lis but confused as well. I still wasn't sure why we'd been dropped off on some distant sidewalk rather than the building, but I just rolled with it. My life rarely made sense these days. I followed Lis to the music school and listened in on the guitar lesson. I tried to learn a few chords, but learning in English was hard enough. I couldn't keep up with the lesson in Spanish. My brain was starting to hurt.

After about an hour, Lis and Mariana wrapped up the lesson, and Lis sent us on our way. Mariana grabbed my hand and escorted me to her mom's office. Fortunately, she knew exactly where it was located. At every street corner, Mariana stopped at least one foot from the curb and instructed me how to cross. She held my hand, looked both directions, and then yelled, "Corre!!!!" (Run!) as she dragged me across street after street.

When we reached her mom's office, she informed us that she still had over an hour's worth of work left. She told Mariana and me that we were free to wander the city as long as we came back to her office by 6:30. I'd just met this kid, and here we were, wandering the streets of Punta Arenas together hand in hand. Mariana brought me to every shoe and clothing store she could find, scampering from floor to floor to show me her favorite vests, sweaters, and boots. She spoke so quickly that I could only understand about ten percent of what she said, but her body language expressed the essentials. This little girl was excited to be free in the city with her new foreign friend.

Later on, her mom dropped us off at the house and told me she was going to get some food with her husband; they'd be back in a little while. I entered the house to find Melissa on babysitting duty with the other two sisters. They were bouncing off the walls, hitting a balloon around, and laughing like little hyenas. Without exchanging a single word, I knew exactly what Melissa was thinking. The look of exhaustion on her face said it all.

We played with the girls until the parents came home. While they were still gone, a mattress delivery man rang the doorbell, and the girls screamed in panic.

"Pretend you are our parents!" they cried. Clearly, they'd been trained not to open the door for strangers unless their parents were home.

"Ummm...." I replied, wondering if a delivery man would believe two white girls in their twenties were the parents of these three.

Finally, Mariana opened the door and declared, "This is my aunt from the United States!"

The delivery man smiled and unloaded the mattress as Melissa and I laughed. The second the door shut, the girls went nuts and started jumping all over the mattress like feral children. I tried to get them to stop, but disciplining a group of girls I'd known for only a few hours (in my second language) was futile.

The parents finally got home, and the girls calmed down a bit. We ate dinner together as I attempted to translate between Melissa, myself, and the family. They kindly tried to learn some English to make me feel less insecure about my Spanish skills. We taught them some tongue-twisters, and they rattled some off in Spanish as we laughed in amusement. The girls' favorite English tongue-twister was, "Fuzzy Wuzzy was a bear. Fuzzy Wuzzy had no hair. Fuzzy Wuzzy wasn't fuzzy, was he?" Catalina determinedly set her mind to learn the whole rhyme and made us laugh with her pronunciation as she tried. Her mom occasionally attempted to throw in random English phrases that sounded ridiculous with her thick accent. Throughout the next few days, Mariana continually gave me both written and oral quizzes on new Spanish vocabulary that she taught me. Despite the language barriers, we quickly developed several inside jokes, and Melissa and I felt like part of the family.

After our first family dinner, the girls escorted us to our sleeping quarters. Mariana and Romina sweetly gave up their shared bedroom for the next few nights so that Melissa and I could have a semiprivate place to sleep. The girls laid out a large mattress in the middle of their playroom and camped out there. Melissa and I gratefully plopped down on our assigned beds, exhausted and ready to sleep. However, the girls were far too excited to let us sleep just yet. First, they unveiled their vast collection of stuffed animals crammed into the abyss of their closet and handpicked those we could snuggle with during our visit. After tucking us in with our new sleeping companions, they repeatedly walked in and out of the room to check what we were doing. Melissa and I told the girls we were sleeping, but they kept coming back and asking why they could hear us talking to each other if we were asleep.

Living with our three Chilean sisters didn't exactly incite the most restful of weeks; however, our time with them was priceless. After passing through place after place, I finally had an opportunity to form a genuine relationship with a few children. My heart was reminded of its simple but deep desire to get to know kids, mentor them, and provoke their lives to change through the love of Jesus Christ. Spending time with Catalina, Mariana, and Romina was a good reminder of what God created me for. In addition, their parents made Melissa and I feel right at home in a foreign culture. Despite all language barriers, it was blatantly clear that this family loved the Lord and shared a hunger for Him that didn't need to be explained. We understood each other's hearts in a way that didn't require language.

Partnering with their church as a whole was also a huge blessing and reminder of God's divine ability and desire to connect His church body. One afternoon, our team gathered with the youth of the church for a worship and prayer time, followed by steaming hot empanadas and coffee. After our bellies and spirits were filled, we divided into small groups and hit the streets. We decided to pray as teams to ask God for clues about who He wanted us to pray for. My group received some weird pictures that seemingly didn't go together — penguins, a scarf vendor, a group of girlfriends, a bicycle, and the name Camilla.

As we walked to the main plaza in Punta Arenas, we noticed a booth where a vendor was selling scarves. As we got closer, we saw that he was also selling penguin stuffed animals. A group of girls approached the booth, one of them on a bike. We greeted the girls and asked their names. One of them said her name was Camilla. I laughed, realizing how all these odd images had suddenly worked together. We asked the girls if we could pray for them, and I pulled one of them aside to prophecy over her. I told her that God had chosen her as a leader, and her peers would follow her example. I explained that this was both a blessing and a great responsibility. I could see the wheels turning in her head. One of the girls from the church asked her about her personal faith. The girl said she wanted to accept Jesus into her heart right then and there. I couldn't believe a vision of a penguin, some scarves, and a bike had gotten us here.

Our week with the church continued to be a great encouragement for all of us. Before we moved on to Ushuaia, the church arranged a Friday night worship service to celebrate our time together. As we worshipped with our Chilean brothers and sisters, a young guy with pain in his knees approached us for prayer. After praying, he wept with the realization that his pain had been healed. We continued to worship, and I saw him jumping up and down, excitedly leaping for the Lord, his knees good as new.

That night, the church blessed us with an incredibly generous offering as well as prayers for our team. Person after person hugged and kissed each one of us, weeping with joy that God had brought us together. I don't think I'd ever felt such love from a group of strangers. We all knew our visions and hearts' desires matched so perfectly and intimately that our unique bond could only have stemmed from God's love. Our connection was so strong that for the first time in eight months, I left a city in tears, overwhelmed by the love I felt in my heart.

To make things even better, one of the men we met in Punta Arenas connected us to a church in Ushuaia and arranged for us to be warmly received and housed for free during our time there as well. After twelve hours on a bus, we were greeted by a smiley, graying man who escorted us to a cozy church in the center of Ushuaia. A huge, hot meal was waiting for us as well as an eager group of youths who wanted to spend time with us throughout the week.

We enjoyed the beauty of this incredible city, thankful that after eight long months of travel, we'd finally reached the end of the world. That statement felt surreal, and the marvel of the earth's southernmost city was stunning. The majestic beauty of the snow-covered mountains in Ushuaia was striking. The reflection of the mountains glittered in the bay, and wispy clouds decorated the sky.

My team spent the week teaching at a YWAM base and partnering with a few local churches. At one service, Ben and I prayed for a little girl who had constant pain in her legs. Her mom said the pain throbbed especially badly in her knees when she played. We prayed for complete healing, and the little girl burst into tears as she explained that she didn't feel pain anymore. Moments later, I noticed her running around with her friends, a smile beaming across her face.

Ben and I also had the opportunity to pray for a young man, probably in his thirties, who had just lost his wife. We tried to speak words of encouragement over him, but our hearts broke at his pain. I hugged this grieving stranger as he cried in my arms, wishing I could magically mend his heart.

Ben got choked up as he reminded the man, "She is in a beautiful place. She's home now. She's home...."

As Ben spoke these words, the man smiled and nodded. "I know it's true," he declared. "I see her in my dreams, and she is happy. She is singing in my dreams."

Sobering moments like these reminded me of why I was on this trip. Sure, I loved traveling and exploring new places. I loved seeing people healed of physical conditions and jumping around pain-free. I loved teaching at YWAM and speaking at churches and sharing stories with congregations. But what I loved the most was seeing peoples' hearts touched by the love of God. I loved that even in the most tragic of situations, I would see these miraculous glimmers of hope that only God could give. Life was short and hard sometimes, but what an amazing gift it was to have faith in something greater. As much as I loved our team's vision of spreading revival fire throughout Latin America, I held in my heart that the most important thing was spreading *love*. Without it, the rest was meaningless.

So here we were. We'd found love at the end of the world, and after eight months of traveling south, we were about to head north for the first time on our journey. Jesse said as we'd traveled south, God was saying, "Lower still." But now He was saying, "Come up here!" It was time.

We discussed how to get back to Santiago where our cars were waiting for us. Busing had cost much more time and money than we'd bargained for, so we thought it would be most simple to fly to Santiago from Ushuaia. However, we found out that we would get slammed with a huge air entry tax if we flew into Chile from another country. Therefore, it would be more economical to catch a cheap bus to Chile and fly to Santiago from a Chilean airport, avoiding international air entry fees. This meant stopping back in Punta Arenas. We planned to simply pass through; but just like our first visit to Punta Arenas, our quick stopover became something more.

As soon as we re-arrived in Punta Arenas, we began our research for onward travel to Santiago. The flights were around three hundred fifty dollars, requiring cash far beyond most of our monthly budgets. Someone from the church caught wind of our return and showed up at our hostel to assist with planning how to get the team back north. He found out that we could take two buses to Santiago for about seventy dollars total — one thirty-hour bus ride and then another shorter overnight bus. The only drawback was that we'd have to wait almost a full week to get these buses. This was much cheaper than any busing or flying options we'd heard of thus far, so we agreed to wait the extra days in Punta Arenas. The church did not want us to have to pay for a hostel, so the families that had housed us previously offered to host us for another week. On Sunday morning, I went to the familiar church, and before even getting into the building, my little Chilean sisters — Catalina, Mariana, and Romina — came running into my arms.

We stayed with our Chilean families until Thursday, when we got on our first bus back north. After two long rides and almost forty hours of driving, we finally arrived back in Santiago. The church that had hosted us before kindly received us for a second visit. During our absence, the congregation had taken care of two new teammates who had flown into Santiago and were awaiting our arrival. Nicole, Colombian and Mexican by blood, was born and raised in Texas and was a gorgeous mix of cultures. A fiery prophetess with Latina flair, Nicole instantly blew me away with her boldness and radical heart for the Lord. Whether approaching strangers with prophetic words or chasing prostitutes down dodgy streets to tell them about Jesus, she really challenged me to get over my fear of man and step out of my comfort zone. But beneath her bold exterior, I also discovered a kind heart and a loyal friend. Carol, a young, fun-loving Brazilian, was a huge blessing in a cute little package. Not only an amazing translator and ministry coordinator throughout our time in Brazil, Carol was simply a sweet, genuine, kind-hearted girl. Whether working with children, adults, prostitutes on the street, or men in rehab centers, she made each person feel valued, loved, and cherished. People were instantly drawn to her, and she was a hit everywhere we went. Incredibly talented, smart, and driven for someone of just nineteen years, I was constantly impressed by Carol.

We joined Nicole and Carol at the church in Santiago and slept on the familiar sanctuary's floor. We arrived exhausted on a Saturday and had a rude awakening early Sunday morning. It was time for church, which meant putting away all of our sleeping mats, pillows, and bags. Though sleepy throughout the Sunday service, I was thankful for the chance to reconnect with some of the women we'd prayed for when we'd first arrived in Santiago. Punta Arenas and Santiago were the first cities we'd revisited throughout the entire trip. After months of passing through place after place, it was strange to travel a loop where we returned to a familiar location. So many times I'd wondered what had happened to certain people after we left them. *Did they maintain their healings? Did they find freedom? Did any moved hearts accept Christ?*

And now, finally, I got to see what happened to a couple of people I'd encountered along the way. Firstly, the woman who'd had demonic attacks (who Tanya had simply hugged and held in her arms) was a different person. She came to the church each day we stayed there, constantly offering to serve us bread, coffee, and other treats. Her face was always smiley, and she seemed more cognizant. Her once distant countenance was now engaged and bright.

The woman who had done our laundry and asked us to pray for her daughter's burned leg also turned up. She came to the service on Sunday and excitedly pulled me and one of the other girls aside. She took us into the bathroom with her daughter so she could show us the part of her leg that had once been so severely burned. The skin had healed perfectly. There was still some discoloration, but all irritation was completely gone. The mother explained that victims of third-degree burns usually suffered from symptoms such as nausea and vomiting, etc. and that her daughter had not suffered from any of this. She was completely healed, skin formed back together beautifully, completely pain-free. The daughter was beaming, touched that God had chosen to give her this testimony. The mother was beaming as well. She was a far cry from the woman who had been sobbing and coughing up demons just weeks before. This was great. Peoples' lives had changed after we passed through, and seeing the effects on just a few peoples' lives gave me the faith to believe that there were many other happy endings we would probably never hear about.

After a few days in Santiago spending time with the church, sorting things with our vehicles, and downsizing personal luggage as much as we could, we embarked on the two-day drive to Buenos Aires, Argentina. This would be our last of at least six or seven Chile-Argentina border crossings, thanks to the meandrous route to and from Ushuaia. While stopping for lunch along the drive, several of the girls noticed that our waitress had a substantial limp. Without hesitation, Nicole asked her what was wrong with her leg. The waitress sat down and showed us that her legs were different lengths, and Nicole asked if we could pray for her legs to be healed. I'd never seen limbs grow out before but had heard many stories of uneven legs becoming even, and I was eager to see this firsthand. Nicole, a few of the girls, and I laid hands on the woman and asked God to fix her legs. Amazingly, just moments later, there was a visible difference. Two legs that had once been different lengths now lined up evenly when the woman put her feet together. God had just physically stretched one of the woman's limbs!

Suddenly, we realized the rest of the team was waiting in the cars, ignitions ready, preparing to drive onward. We quickly said goodbye to the woman and frantically ran to the vehicles to avoid getting left behind. Laughing, yelling "*Waiiiiit!*", and gasping for air, we jumped into the cars just in the nick of time. Excitedly, we told our teammates what had just happened.

Two long driving days later, we finally arrived in Buenos Aires. We stopped at a mall outside of the city to get dinner and contacted the pastor who was planning to host us during our time in the capital. It was already 10 p.m. by the time we got ahold of him, and long story short, by around 11 p.m. we realized that the pastor had bailed on us. We were left to fend for ourselves, and there wasn't a hostel in sight. Jesse caught wind of a few potential campsites where we could park our vehicles and sleep the night; so we began to drive around the city, desperately searching for a place to park and sleep. After driving to site after site only to find each one closed, we stumbled upon an open piece of land around 2 a.m. It seemed we had no other options, and everyone was exhausted. Without realizing we were in the middle of an extremely dangerous neighborhood, we parked our cars in the grassy area and claimed sleeping spots for the evening. We were too exhausted to set up tents, so we slept inside the vehicles, on top of the vehicles, and scattered across a tarp on the ground.

I tried to fall asleep on top of Overflow while Rose, Kimmie, and Angela snoozed inside. Every time I rolled over, the inside of the SUV shook. Likewise, every time the girls inside shifted, I felt like I was experiencing an earthquake up top. After hours of restless sleep, the morning sun woke us all. We groggily got dressed and found a wall to hide behind and use as a bathroom, doing our best to avoid sharp pieces of metal, scattered trash, and used condoms. A couple of police officers pulled over to our "campsite" and began reprimanding us.

"Are you insane? Why are you sleeping here? Don't you know how dangerous this is?" they bellowed.

We explained our situation and said that we were trying to leave. Unfortunately, as we tried to drive away from the field, some of the cars struggled to maneuver through the mud, and Overflow got a flat tire.

After several attempts to get going and one tire fix, we finally left the field and drove to a food court to buy some breakfast and figure out where to go next. We weren't overly surprised that our contact had fallen through, but we still felt a bit lost. Some of my teammates had dreamt of visiting Claudio Freidzon's church, a famous Argentine pastor credited with instigating a revival in the early nineties. Natalie M. had tried to contact his church while in Chile, but she never heard anything back. Several people said there were services happening today and we should simply show up and see what happened. I knew nothing about the church but figured attending a service couldn't hurt.

We drove to Claudio's church hoping for the best and discovered that we didn't need to wait long before the next service. Unfortunately, we also realized that the expected attire was a bit fancier than our current wardrobe. A pastor had once reprimanded us for "looking like hippies," but this place demanded a whole new level of sophistication. Thousands of people attended each service, everyone dressed to the nines in immaculate dresses and tailored suits. They lined the streets before the gatherings, pining to get seats. Once inside the church, everything was very official — recorded sermons, state of the art projectors and speakers, and designated ushers to escort congregants to the appropriate rows.

When we showed up, Natalie M. approached a woman who worked for the church and explained our situation. Natalie reported that she'd been trying to get in touch with the church administration but hadn't heard back. She said we were missionaries and asked if we could do anything to serve the church during our stay in Buenos Aires. The woman kindly took a glance at our team — each of us covered in dirt, smelly from wearing the same clothes through the night and the following day. "Let me talk to a few others," she smiled. And despite our ragged appearance, the woman reserved two rows of seats at the front of the church for us.

A man appeared to escort us to our seats as I became increasingly aware of my own filth. I had never been so afraid of judgment from a pastor, yet Claudio showed us nothing but love. In fact, when he found out that a group of missionaries had stopped by, he called us forward and insisted on praying for us. Though I was unaware of Claudio's prestige, this was apparently a very rare occurrence and an incredible honor. Claudio prayed for us in front of his huge congregation and imparted the anointing he'd received at the beginning of the Argentinian revival years ago. He didn't look at our ratty clothes; he looked at our hearts. He honored us like kings and queens and blessed us with everything the Lord had given him.

Claudio's daughter and son-in-law spoke to us after the service and offered our entire team the very unexpected treat of two nights in a beautiful hotel in downtown Buenos Aires. They'd heard about where we'd slept the night before and were horrified. The son-in-law told us that we were lucky we hadn't gotten robbed or killed. He declared that only the hand of God could have protected a group of foreigners from being victimized in such a rough neighborhood. It was frightening that we'd been so unaware of our surroundings, but fortunately God had protected us and was now providing us with a perfect accommodation. After sleeping on the side of the road, two nights in a hotel felt like quite a luxury. We had beautiful, clean beds with crispy, white sheets, brilliantly hot showers, air conditioning, and a continental breakfast. *Paradise.*

Cleaning ourselves up and sleeping in beds resulted in major rejuvenation and an eagerness to serve. Dressed in a fresh pair of jeans and a clean shirt, I went to the church with my teammates in the morning, offering to serve in any way we could. The church ran a homeless ministry where they needed volunteers to organize things, clean bathrooms, serve food, and hang out with the homeless people that came by. Ironically, when I'd been filthy, I was invited to the front of an extravagant congregation. Now that I was well-dressed and clean, I was assigned to toilet cleaning duty.

After scrubbing the stalls for my homeless brothers and sisters, I went to the dining area to spend time with a group of men from the street. As we conversed, they entertained themselves by asking me about my non-existent love life and scrutinizing my bad Spanish. Though Buenos Aires was famous for tango, good steak, and a thriving nightlife, we experienced a slightly different side of the city.

The capital certainly proved a very different lifestyle than Argentina's cities down south. The issues with homelessness, drugs, and poverty were a stark contrast from the quiet existence we'd experienced in Ushuaia. Unfortunately, we missed countless cities in between, really only getting a glimpse of this massive country. Because of Argentina's extensive geography, we simply didn't have the time to see it all. Before we knew it, it was time to head to our next country, the small coastal nation of Uruguay.

Chapter Thirteen

URUGUAY: Missionary Graveyard No More

Before traveling to Uruguay, I knew close to nothing about this tiny nation. It seemed such an obscure little country in such an obscure little location. I'd almost forgotten that Uruguay even existed, as did many of my teammates. Upon a bit of research, our team found out that Uruguay was often referred to as a "Missionary Graveyard." Very few ministries or churches flourished in Uruguay, and the majority of the population was irreligious. Despite being located in a predominantly Catholic continent, Uruguay was puzzlingly a nation of atheists.

As we drove towards Uruguay, still in Argentina, we were stopped by the police and asked for proof of Argentine insurance — something we'd specifically been told we did *not* need at the Chile-Argentina border. We explained why we lacked such documents, and the officials threatened us with a fine of one thousand dollars. This felt like a flashback to Mexico, where we were constantly being pulled over, bribed, and slammed with fines. We tried to talk our way out of the situation, but the officials simply wouldn't budge. Finally, they dropped the fine to five hundred dollars but said that was their final offer. We either had to pay the five hundred dollars or get our vehicles impounded and potentially spend an evening in jail. Our team had slept in enough weird places; prison was not an option. Begrudgingly, we paid the hefty fee.

However, God wastes nothing, and some good came from the interaction with the officials. While several of my teammates were trying to reason with them, Nicole received a prophetic word for one of the officers. She prophesied over his life, and the man, blown away by God's love for him, received Christ. Unfortunately, he had no authority to drop the fine against our team but recognized the corruption and apologized for what was happening. He wanted to help us, so he offered us free tanks of fuel from a nearby gas station where he had inside connections.

We appreciated his kindness and felt some degree of grace. However, all feelings of favor evaporated as we ran into more trouble the moment we arrived at the border. We were told we couldn't cross into Uruguay without insurance (and we'd just experienced the consequences of not having proper insurance in Argentina). However, we could only purchase insurance miles inside the border of Uruguay, which meant one car had to cross the border illegally to purchase insurance for all four vehicles. Most of us waited on the Argentine side while Liney, Liz, Taylor L., Natalie M., Breck, and Melissa went to a bank in Uruguay to buy it. They saw a noticeably depressed security guard and offered to pray for him. While leaving the bank, Taylor suggested, "Let's pray for all of the employees."

Undaunted by the fact that Uruguay was an atheist country, Liney daringly stood in the middle of the bank and announced, "Can I ask for your attention? We are missionaries, and we want to bless you and your bank!" Amazingly, every single employee left his or her desk and formed a circle in the middle of the bank. My teammates stood beside them and prayed for them.

Blessing the bank was an added bonus to securing insurance for all four vehicles. Those who had gone to the bank rejoined the team at the border and handed over the appropriate documents. Now we were all legally able to drive onward to the village of Colonia. Arriving in this picturesque town reminded me of a quaint European city. During our first evening, I wandered off on my own, walking along the cobblestone streets and admiring the beauty of this cozy seaside town.

I thought about the coastal area where I'd grown up and began to toy with the idea of flying home for a few weeks. Originally, I had no intention of returning to the States until our journey came to an end, but what had started as an eleven-month itinerary was looking more like a year and a half. Several of my teammates were soon flying home out of Uruguay's capital, and Jesse promised to get the team there in time. Often, those who flew in and out had a nightmarish time getting to the right departure city or reuniting with the team upon arrival. A chance to fly at such an opportune time was rare, and I figured I should seize it while it lasted. I prayed about what to do and heard the Lord simply say, "Honor your family." I knew a flight to the U.S. would be a huge financial sacrifice, but this was possibly my only chance to see my family for many more months. I made an uncharacteristically quick decision and called my parents to tell them I'd be home in a couple of days. They were shocked. So was I.

On Wednesday morning, we made our way to Uruguay's capital, Montevideo, with a plan to stay there for the night and then get several of us to the airport without problems on Thursday. On the way to Montevideo, New Wine suddenly disappeared from our rear view mirror. We drove back many miles to find all the passengers waving us down and dancing in the street. Apparently, a wheel had fallen off of the RV; and fortunately, Dianne had pulled over immediately to keep her passengers safe. They could have tipped over if she hadn't used such a skillful maneuver. Because we were in the middle of nowhere, Jesse decided the best option was to leave New Wine on the side of the road and send a tow truck back for it once we reached civilization. We unloaded all the luggage and valuables from inside New Wine and piled them into Open Heaven in addition to several new passengers. In total, thirteen of us were crammed inside Open Heaven, squished into seats and sitting on bags. We didn't mind cramming for a little while. This was nothing new to us. However, the vehicle *did* mind, and the added weight blew a belt within an hour.

By this time, it was dark and freezing cold. Those of us in Open Heaven remained in the RV, parked on the side of the road while Counsel and Might and Overflow went onward. Their drivers found a place to stay and dropped off all of their passengers. About an hour later, they returned to pick up those of us who had remained behind. It was too late to get a tow, so Jesse and Ted slept in Open Heaven to prevent all of our stuff from getting robbed. In the morning, they arranged for both Open Heaven and New Wine to get towed to a service station across the street from our hotel. The cost of Open Heaven and New Wine's repairs totaled a whopping sum of around twenty-five hundred dollars.

Meanwhile, the team spent the night in an extremely questionable sex motel. The only place around, we were forced to sleep in this pay-by-the-hour pit. We packed several girls into four separate rooms and rented one room for all of the guys. The owners thought we were a large group of lesbians and gay men, which was quite an ironic misjudgment. Charlotte,

Elizabeth, and I had one double bed to share between the three of us. Instead of debating who should get stuck on the floor, we laid the wrong way across the bed, which fit all three of us widthwise but left our legs dangling over the edge. Not quickly dismayed, we moved chairs to the side of the bed and added sleeping mats to them to create footrests at just the right height. Laughing at our ingenuity, all three of us tested the contraptions we'd created and marveled at the fact that our creativity had provided the perfect sleeping arrangement for all three of us. This trip had taught us a lot.

Oddly enough, the gas station across the street, which was cleaner than the motel, had wifi and decent food. Charlotte had already emailed several organizations from her nation, New Zealand, to try to get contacts in Uruguay. Through a bizarre chain of connections, she received an email in that little gas station announcing that an Uruguayan named Andreas would help us. However, he was about to fly to Argentina, and if we wanted his assistance, we needed to see him right away.

Just before I flew myself, my teammates and I stopped at Andreas' house where we were received with food, coffee, tea, and open arms. Andreas knew a missionary couple who ran a cheap hacienda just outside of Montevideo and offered to escort us there. En route to the couple's property, my teammates dropped me off at the airport. Though reluctant to be separated from them, I knew I'd made a wise decision.

We said a temporary goodbye, and my teammates drove onward to the missionary couple's estate, which turned out to be the perfect accommodation. Just as we'd been praying for a ministry connection in Uruguay, the couple had been praying desperately for a group of people to come to their hacienda. They were tight on cash and had two unbooked weeks, putting them in a financial crunch. The team's arrival was a relief to the couple, and my teammates were equally relieved to be out of the dodgy sex motel.

During their stay, they learned that the missionaries running the place were part of a German Mennonite church. The congregation regularly held an early morning service in German and a later service in Spanish. Natalie M., fluent in German, attended the first service with a few others. Disappointedly, they encountered a cheerless church full of lifeless hymns sung with dismal voices.

More people from the team showed up to the Spanish service, and the pastor, Reiner, asked each person to come forward and introduce him or herself. Some people shared testimonies with the congregation, including the story of praying for everyone in the bank while attempting to purchase insurance.

The congregation was shocked. "In *our* country?" they asked, bewildered. Uruguay was a missionary graveyard, an "unchurched" nation, a place of stone-cold nonbelievers. The church couldn't believe our team had prayed for an entire secular company in Uruguay. They were shocked that a bank in their country would allow this.

My teammates told Reiner that they wanted to partner with his church during their stay in Uruguay and invited him to visit their hacienda. He accepted, assuming they were just going to ask questions about Uruguay and chat for a while. Much to Reiner's surprise, the Holy Spirit moved powerfully during their time together, and the team began to pray prophetically over him until he was moved to tears. Reiner explained that his father had been a revivalist, but he was warned not to practice the gifts of the Holy Spirit in the German Mennonite church. Reiner felt no freedom to operate in the gifts, but his heart was actually open and hungry for the presence of the Holy Spirit.

After meeting with the team, Reiner decided to throw out the rule book. He'd stifled the movement of the Holy Spirit for years, and he was done putting God in a box. Reiner was ready to live in freedom. He opened the doors to his church to the team, and from that day forward, the team's schedule was filled. They were invited to home groups, business meetings to pray for people, services, and more.

Liz, Natalie M., and Amanda went to a youth meeting where young people from five German Mennonite churches congregated. There were around a hundred youths, and their faith seemed dry. There was no hunger for the presence of God. Undeterred by the stale atmosphere, Liz, Natalie, and Amanda believed for breakthrough. They started prophesying over the youth, and suddenly people wanted to hear more. They'd never heard God speak like this before and became desperate to hear what He was saying. The young people lined up to individually receive the words God had for them. They didn't want to leave the church and ended up staying until around 1 a.m.

Rachael, Charlotte, Liney, Nicole, and Angela went to another service for teenagers. The leader of the group was the son of the American missionaries who ran the hacienda. This young man had never had a prophetic word spoken over him before. The girls prayed for him, and he fell over in the Spirit. They had seen him playing the guitar and prophesied over his ability to write songs. The young man shared his current struggles with debating over whether or not to attend university. Someone had told him if he wanted to serve God he needed to go to university soon, but this was not his desire. Liney shared her testimony about putting university on hold to be a part of this trip. She said it was okay to leave university to serve God. But she also explained that when she was at university, school was her mission field, and she served God there. The concept of being a Christian *at* a university and spreading the gospel to his classmates was entirely new to this young man. He'd never looked at the situation like that before.

Later in the service, he saw God touching the other youths as well. He witnessed kids weeping in the presence of God and falling over from the weight of His glory. The young man returned home to his father (the American missionary) and announced what had happened. "Dad!" he declared. "I never believed God could be like this! I'll never be the same."

The Lord began to move among the adults in the church as well. At one prayer meeting, things started off boring and dry, but people from the team started receiving prophetic words for the church and spiced things up a bit. As they offered to pray for individuals, hungry hearts were revealed. People came forward, and the atmosphere changed. Some of my teammates prayed for a woman with pancreatic cancer who later walked to the front of the church and announced that she believed God had fully healed her. This generated more faith in God's supernatural power. Shortly after, the woman visited her doctor and received medical confirmation of her healing. Excitedly, she relayed the good news to the congregation as well as the team. She was completely cancer-free.

Pastor Reiner was so elated by the movement of the Holy Spirit that he provided the team with a free retreat center on the beach where they could stay and rest before driving to Brazil. In celebration of God's glory, youth from the church came over to the beach house and had a barbeque with the team. Reiner's congregation said the team had forever changed the structure of their church. This was revival at its finest!

The team planned to move forward soon (while I was still in the States), but they were stuck until they got enough money to fix the cars and to pay for fuel to drive to the next country. In a beautiful display of God's provision, people from Reiner's church community started to shower the team with money. The congregation at large, ladies from a women's meeting, and others decided to bless the team in return for their service. At the end of their time in Uruguay, they were given thirty-five hundred dollars, enough to cover all repairs *and* gasoline. God had provided the money that the team desperately needed. More importantly, He'd provided a fresh fire in the German Mennonite church that money could never buy.

During this period in Uruguay, some long-lost team members finally returned to the family, perhaps the greatest miracle of all. Stephen and Aleeza, who had been a part of the Iquitos jungle outreach back in Peru, had been stuck with Shekinah, the dying Durango, for months. Five people had separated from the rest of the team in Northern Peru, using Shekinah to drive to Iquitos. After their time in the jungle, Bridget stayed in Peru to work with an indigenous tribe, Natalie H. flew back to America, and Elizabeth flew home to visit her family (and returned to the team in Argentina). This left Stephen and Aleeza with the burden of fixing a hopeless transmission. Upon hearing their request for reinforcements, Kurt flew up to Peru to help them out. After countless repairs and hitting wall after wall for months, Stephen, Kurt, and Aleeza were still dealing with the Durango nightmare. Because it was illegal to sell a foreign vehicle in Peru, they found themselves trapped. They could not legally leave the car behind in Peru, yet it was impossible to drive forward with a car in its condition.

Eventually, Shekinah endured enough repairs to chug along and make it to Northern Chile, where foreign car sales were legal. However, they barely made it out of Peru on time. Since it had taken so long to fix Shekinah, its legal registration for driving in Peru was about to expire. Stephen, Kurt, and Aleeza crossed over the Peru-Chile border just minutes before midnight on the very last day of Shekinah's legal registration for Peru.

Miraculously, the car was officially stamped out of the country at 11:57 p.m. that night.

From Chile, Aleeza flew home and back for a wedding, only to find Kurt and Stephen still in Chile. They'd dealt with several breakdowns in this new country, but God connected them divinely and provided all they needed while separated from the team. The guys finally found a buyer for Shekinah and were working out the final paperwork to sell it when Aleeza returned.

In the end, Shekinah was sold in Iquique, Chile. From there, Stephen, Aleeza, and Kurt bused back to the team and met everyone in Uruguay after months apart. Though their job certainly wasn't glorious, we counted them heroes for dealing with this mess. They sacrificed months of time away from the rest of the team to carry the burden no one else wanted. This trio reminded me that we often put too much focus on testimonies that resulted in personal glory. However, their selfless service was the reflection of true hearts of honor, endurance, and integrity.

Chapter Fourteen

PARAGUAY: Finding Freedom

Meanwhile, I was back in the States with my family, arranging flights to rejoin the team in South America. I flew into Porto Alegre, Brazil where I was happily reunited with my Iris brothers and sisters who had just arrived from Uruguay. I saw that the team had grown while I was away and found out that more teammates were joining us soon (creating a total of around thirty-five people). With one less car and a growing team, the remaining four vehicles became increasingly cozy. Little did we know, a car meant for five could actually hold up to thirteen or fourteen people. Though traveling was quite crammed and uncomfortable, we somehow always found a way to squeeze everyone into some sort of crevice.

We spent just a few weeks in Brazil's Porto Alegre, Florianópolis, and Curitiba before backtracking to Paraguay and Bolivia. Unfortunately, there was no way to travel to these countries without somehow backtracking or awkwardly weaving quite far out of the way. In addition, these countries were far less developed than some of their neighbors; thus, their roads were poorly constructed, dangerous, and jarring to drive on. Just as we'd left our cars behind and bussed throughout Chile and Argentina, we decided to leave our vehicles in Brazil for a brief period and use public transportation to travel to the two poorest nations in South America.

Days before leaving for Paraguay, we picked up another team member, Scottish-born Kelly. Prior to joining us, this humble yet brilliant chemist had been working on improving a malaria prevention medication. Unlike most scientists, Kelly had a childlike faith that defied all logic and constantly challenged me to believe in what I could not yet see. Her enthusiasm, willingness to serve, and heart for the lost quickly made Kelly a vital part of our traveling family. Bridget, the short-term teammate who had ministered in Iquitos, Peru (with the five-person jungle team), also joined us for another temporary visit throughout Paraguay and Bolivia.

While praying about God's plans for our time in Paraguay, my teammates and I asked Him what He was saying about the country. Many of us felt that Paraguay was a forgotten nation in the eyes of the world, but God had not forgotten His people. These words kept echoing throughout my mind:

"Do not forget the forgotten ones."

We first traveled to Asuncion, the capital of Paraguay, and spent our first night walking the streets searching for the "forgotten ones." Nicole, Kelly, and I explored together, spoke with prostitutes, and prayed for people on the streets and at the local bus station. We met a crippled man at the station who had to drag his whole body by using his arms to slide across the floor. We sat on the floor with the man and talked and prayed. He seemed surprised that anyone had noticed him and joined him on the ground. Some people stared at me, Nicole, and Kelly, wondering what three white girls were doing sitting on the floor of the bus station talking to a crippled man. We wondered why more people *weren't* doing this.

On our way home, we met a Brazilian woman named Ana who said she had no place to stay for the evening. She spoke only Portuguese and barely understood our Spanish, but we tried our best to communicate. We scrounged up a bit of money and handed it to Ana, who declared, "This has to be Jesus. This has to be Jesus!" We invited Ana to a church service we'd be attending the following afternoon, and she said she'd like to go if we could come meet her along the way.

The following afternoon, we found Ana and headed to a local missionary church. The pastor invited us to the front, where a couple of us shared testimonies and words of exhortation. After the service, we connected Ana with the pastor, who turned out to be from Brazil originally, allowing Ana to speak her own language and find some local support in Asuncion. We knew we'd be gone in a few days, so we were thankful for this divine connection. The pastor was really excited to have a chance to minister with our team and kindly invited us to sleep at his church for the next couple of nights.

Meanwhile, Stephen connected with another local pastor from a German Mennonite church. Just as the Mennonites in Uruguay had discovered the freedom of the Holy Spirit, this pastor also believed in the power of the Holy Spirit and did not fit the typical mold of a conservative Mennonite. In fact, his congregation's radical faith had caused a split with the rest of the church. Undeterred by what others thought, they hungered to learn more about God's presence and power. The pastor had a son, Jonathan, who had been seriously injured years prior and believed in the Lord's ability to heal him. He invited any willing teammates to come visit his home and pray for his son.

Twelve-year-old Jonathan had fallen out of a hammock five years ago, hit his neck in just the right spot, and become paralyzed from the neck down. Not only was he unable to move his limbs, the part of his brain that was meant to tell his lungs to breathe ceased to function, and Jonathan was hooked up to a breathing machine that forced his lungs to inhale and exhale. Jonathan often had trouble during the night, and his parents were used to waking up frequently to adjust his breathing apparatus and consequently suffered from sleep deprivation.

Each day in Asuncion, a few of my teammates took taxis to Jonathan's home to visit and pray. The day I met Jonathan was both heartbreaking and inspiring. This sweet, young boy politely greeted me in Spanish yet quickly impressed me with his ability to also speak German fluently and share various phrases from several other dialects. Jonathan connected to David quickly, and the two of them teased and joked like old friends. While David spoke to Jonathan, Jonathan made funny faces at the rest of us, playfully tantalizing David when he wasn't looking. Though Jonathan could move only his head, he used this ability to its fullest to joke around. This kid was both sassy and smart. It was clear that he didn't skip a beat.

We prayed for Jonathan and chatted for quite a long time. Throughout our talks, his ferocious faith was revealed, and I was amazed that such a tragic accident had produced nothing but intimacy with his Heavenly Father. Jonathan knew his Bible unbelievably well and was optimistically awaiting miraculous healing yet utilizing his time of paralysis to commune with God.

I caught a glimpse of pictures of Jonathan and his sisters before the accident — one of the girls hanging off of his back in sisterly affection. I could see that he'd been a playful and strong child. Now he sat before me, propped up in a chair, the sound of heavy breathing interrupted by beeps on his breathing machine.

He would laugh and talk but then suddenly stop for a moment, sobered by the reality of the bodily prison his spirit was living in.

David asked Jonathan what he missed the most about his life before the accident and what he would love to do most if he were healed. Suddenly, Jonathan's precious face lit up as he replied, "Soccer! I want to play soccer!"

As we said farewell to Jonathan that evening, I wondered if and when God would heal this precious child. I felt so much compassion towards him and was in awe of his very real faith that had truly been put to the test. I realized my own faith for his healing was starting to waver, but David reminded me to always hope when he said, "In the future, I'm coming back to Paraguay just for that kid. Really, one day I am going to come back and play soccer with him."

Although Jonathan didn't get healed that day, I remembered the woman from Panama who got out of a wheelchair and the deaf man in Peru who received full healing and the woman with breast cancer in Colombia who was completely cured through prayer. In my moment of weak faith, I prayed that one day David would really come back to Paraguay and play soccer with Jonathan. And I remembered that even though Jonathan was imprisoned by his own body, he had already found freedom.

The following morning, a group of us bused to the most populated prison in Paraguay where we met up with a man named Luis. He had been a gang leader back in the States, turned his life around, become a Christian, and now ministered in one of the most brutal prisons in South America. Kelly had contacted Luis via email and asked if we could partner with his prison ministry while in Asuncion. Kelly wasn't sure if he would respond to a stranger's email, but surprisingly, he invited us to come meet him outside of the prison.

Normally, Luis didn't allow women to minister in the prison. The men inside were almost completely cut off from contact with women, and he knew their reactions to us would be quite offensive. Many of the inmates were lewd, aggressive, and downright dangerous. We'd been in similar situations before and told Luis we were prepared to go inside. Though he'd just met us, something inside him decided to give us a chance. He agreed to let us girls minister in the prison, breaking risky yet exciting new ground for his ministry.

Upon entry, we were split into men and women for a security check. We presented our passports and were pulled one by one into a semiprivate area where we were thoroughly and quite uncomfortably patted down by a prison employee. Afterwards, we reunited with the guys and were led down an outdoor hallway that ended up at the prison chapel. Though the hallway was probably no more than twenty-five yards, it felt like miles. I had thought I was prepared to remain unaffected by the inmates, but even after all the prisons our team had visited, I'd never experienced anything like this. The hallway was lined with men standing behind a barred fence — staring, lusting, hissing, whistling, and violently crying out for our attention. One man gestured at Taylor L., desperately shaking one finger, as if begging Taylor to give him just *one* of us women. I was so revolted that I looked down and ignored every sexual noise and gesture directed at me, refusing to make eye contact with anyone. In seconds, I had somehow transformed from a woman into the lowliest of creatures — an animal being paraded around, on display for nothing more than the pleasure of perverse men. In this moment, I felt far more like property than a person.

Finally, we arrived at the prison chapel, a safe haven from the leering men. I felt secure enough to lift my head and look around. The men there refused to let their environment turn them into beasts; they were searching for something much greater. I immediately felt I could breathe easy here.

Yet, just minutes later, Luis led us back out of the chapel to take a tour of the prison. I took a deep breath, preparing myself to be thrown back to the wolves. The prison building was comprised of three different levels, ranging from extremely dismal to decent living conditions. Luis was aided by inmates in green vests who were "well-behaved" and trusted enough to gain jobs as prison ushers. Groups of the men in green formed walls around my team as we passed from place to place within the prison. We stopped at each of the levels to see how the men lived. Some men in the highest level were provided with bunk beds, but those in the lowest level had to sleep on the ground. The prison was extremely overcrowded, and there simply was not enough space for everyone. We were informed that a good percentage of the men had been falsely accused of crimes, and many of them would serve life terms for crimes they had not committed. Overcrowding and no chance of freedom created an environment of anger and violence. Men didn't hesitate to kill other inmates, because they were already serving the time and had nothing to lose by committing murder within the prison gates.

During our tour, Breck noticed a man at the very end of a hallway and approached him. The inmate invited him into his room to chat for a few moments. Breck spoke words of encouragement into the man's life. "You are a leader. I want you to know you're a son of God." The man became emotional at these words and said he had been asking the Lord for confirmation that he really was a son of God. Now he knew it was true.

After our tour, we returned to the prison chapel where Luis gave us full reign over the service. Kelly introduced the group, and the inmates cheered her on with genuine excitement and "hallelujahs" after just a brief introduction. The inmates led a time of worship before Breck and Nicole were called up to speak. As we worshipped, one of the inmates offered us *maté*, a traditional tea that South Americans loved to share among friends. They typically stuffed the maté leaves into a communal cup, poured water from a large jug into the cup, and used a metal straw to suck out the tea without swallowing the leaves. The drink was always passed around, everyone slurping from the same straw. Praying for protection over my lips, I received the cup with thanks and sipped on the straw the inmates were passing amongst themselves and my teammates. Afterwards, the inmate who owned the maté jug was so moved by Kelly's tenacity in getting our group to the prison that he gave it to her to keep. I imagined that man owned very few personal possessions, so this offering was quite a sacrifice.

After worship, Breck was called up front to preach. Next, Nicole shared her testimony of feeling imprisoned by sin and finding freedom in Christ. Finally, we called anyone forward who wanted personal prayer. We probably prayed for every inmate in the chapel. I was amazed to see so many glimmers of hope amid such a seemingly hopeless place. I met a young man named Richard and could feel the peace and liberty he carried in his heart. I told him that other inmates would sense it also and come to him in search of the same freedom. He smiled and nodded as if to say he already knew. With a coy grin, he walked away, joy radiating from his face.

Nicole and Breck were approached by a man with dark, shadowy eyes and a lost gaze; it seemed as if he wasn't really there. The man confessed that he was involved with witchcraft and drank chicken blood as one of his rituals. Nicole explained that he could receive the same freedom she had and asked if he'd ever received Jesus Christ. The man shook his head, but he said he'd like to. Moments later, he committed his life to following the Lord.

As people prayed, many men were healed of physical pain; but more importantly, hearts were healing and being encouraged. Inside this prison, despite all circumstances, I found men who had been set free.

The following morning, we bused to the city of Filadelfia, where we were hosted by a group of German Mennonites with whom the Mennonites in Uruguay had connected us. They blew us away with their faith, kindness, hospitality, and generosity. The Mennonites provided our team with a free stay at a beautiful resort fully equipped with beds, hot showers, delicious meals, and an outdoor area comprised of a sparkling lake, zip line, docks, and a waterslide.

On Sunday morning, Kimmie, Taylor L., Carol, Aleeza, Kurt, and I helped run the Mennonites' children's church program with a German woman named Hedi. Taylor and Kurt acted out an epic version of the story of David and Goliath, and we shared testimonies of how we'd seen God speak through children and let His power flow out of them. We asked the kids what the Lord was telling them, and I was blown away by some of the things they said. These young children already had visions of preaching in front of crowds, seeing God heal the sick, and becoming worship leaders.

Two days later, Hedi invited our team to her house for lunch. She shared her testimony of living in Somalia and traveling throughout incredibly dangerous areas of Africa to share the gospel. During a visit to London, she met a Bermudan man named Colin, fell in love, and returned to Africa with him. While passing through Northern Uganda, they were ambushed by LRA rebel soldiers. Colin had vowed to protect Hedi at any cost and assured her that he did not fear death. He always told her, "This body is just my house. You can take my house, but you can't kill me! My spirit lives on; this is just my house!" During the LRA ambush, Colin fulfilled his vow to protect his wife, taking several bullets for her and soon after dying in her arms. Hedi was devastated that "his house" had been destroyed, but like Colin, she believed no one had the ability to kill his spirit.

At the time, Hedi was pregnant with her first child and gave birth to a beautiful little girl named Shekinah months later. Years after the ambush, Hedi took Shekinah back to Uganda to visit the exact spot where Colin had been murdered, and Shekinah anointed the land where he had been shot. Instead of living in bitterness and hurt, this family had chosen to travel to a land of murder and declare it as a land of blessing.

Though Hedi had lost the person most precious to her, she managed to live in freedom and love. Though Colin's "house" had been stolen, he declared that no one could steal his soul. Though the inmates in the Paraguayan penitentiary were closed in by walls, many of them had found freedom in the presence of God. And though Jonathan was imprisoned by his own body, he possessed hope that had set him free.

The Bible says, "Where the Spirit of the Lord is, there is freedom" (2 Corinthians 3:17). Paraguay proved this to be true. Despite even the harshest of circumstances, I met people who had found a freedom that could only be attributed to God. Regardless of their physical conditions, these people had faith and hope that brought them beyond their circumstances. Each of their stories challenged me and reminded me that no matter what I faced, I could always live in freedom when I walked in the hope of Christ.

Chapter Fifteen

BOLIVIA: Poverty, Power, and Pig Fat

Witchcraft, demonic superstitions, abysmal roads, and the worst poverty in South America — welcome to Bolivia. My team kicked off our time in our seventeenth country with a shaky border crossing that foreshadowed our Bolivian days to come. Though access to Bolivia required visas for Americans (but not the other nationalities represented on our team), we were not able to acquire them in advance. We decided to risk getting denied entry into the country and bused to the border without them. Upon arrival at the border "station," we saw nothing more than a dry, dusty plot of land, a shack with a Bolivian man inside who stamped passports, and a tiny house that probably belonged to the man. Immediately, the Americans were reprimanded for not previously obtaining our visas and were shoved into a line on the side of the shack.

Kimmie and I went to explore the nearby field to find a place to go to the bathroom. The border official anxiously yelled at us to turn around, afraid we were about to make a run for it. We reluctantly followed orders and waited with the rest of the team for quite a long time. Eventually, the border official said he could only issue three visas for a lucky trio of Americans. The rest of us would have to continue on our bus illegally and work our way towards a migration office hours from the border the following morning. Confused, three team members received the stamps while the rest of us entered as illegal aliens for the following twenty-four hours.

We got back on our bus, and within an hour we were stuck. The warnings about poor infrastructure quickly proved to be true as our bus became wedged in the middle of a sandy road. The men got out to push while the ladies were asked to stand in the back right corner of the bus and jump over the tire when instructed. After quite some time, the bus emerged from the sand, and we continued on our journey. We were off to an interesting start.

We finally arrived in the city of Villa Montes where we spent the night. In the morning, we spent hours getting our paperwork sorted, and one hundred thirty-five dollars later, we were given our visas. I tried not to worry about the overwhelming expenses of the trip and to instead focus on what God had called me to do. Little did I know, finances would be the least of my worries while in Bolivia.

Bolivia possessed a deep beauty; however, much of the country was sadly overrun by witchcraft and demonic practices. As soon as our team entered the nation, we began to feel the effects. It began in Villa Montes with Nicole being physically attacked by a demonic presence. She felt like she was being stabbed by a knife in her chest. The frightening attack lasted for a long time, but when she started aggressively rebuking the spirit, it finally left.

The following morning, our team headed to a village called Caprendita where Tanya's cousin Angela had lived for years. Angela, a tiny and timid blond woman, lived alone in an indigenous community and traveled to surrounding villages to run children's programs and share the gospel. Her Spanish was impeccable, and she had learned how to speak the local tribe's mother tongue as well. Her knowledge and dedication to the culture was remarkable.

Angela let us know that the tribe believed in many demonic traditions and was ruled by fear. They believed in "land owners" — demons that ruled the rivers, the trees, the land, etc. Some of the tribe believed in Jesus as well; however, they thought the land owners were more powerful than Christ and mixed witchcraft with Christianity. Fear dominated the region so heavily that women even believed superstitions such as imminent death if they were to visit the river while on their menstrual cycles.

As soon as we arrived in Caprendita, I could feel the darkness and oppression. Exhausted from not sleeping enough during the journey, I dumped my hiking pack on the ground and immediately took a nap. Chillingly, I encountered a demon while dreaming.

I announced to my teammates, "We don't need to pray. The spiritual oppression isn't that strong here. We don't need to bother." Then I saw a white, mist-like creature at the foot of my bed that looked like a ghost. I tried to scream but couldn't. Somehow, I was able to pray and began to say Jesus' name.

I woke up still praying, my heart beating fast. I knew the demon I'd just seen in my sleep was real and that prayer had driven it away. This was the beginning of my spiritual battle in Caprendita. Throughout my entire time in the village, I truly felt like I was under attack. One night, while desperately trying to get some alone time, I went into my tent to listen to music. Moments later, I began to feel like something was stabbing me in the chest, just as Nicole had experienced days before. Right away, I ran outside to find my teammates, and they prayed for me until the attack stopped. This had never happened to me before, and I was terrified. But then I remembered what my teammates and I preached all the time; we carried the authority of Christ and did not live in fear. These demons or so-called "land owners" only had power if we let them. It was my job to walk in authority and declare that I was a daughter of Jesus. Satan had no power over me.

My teammates preached at a local church to explain this very concept to the tribe in Caprendita. Jesse spoke about God in a culturally relevant way. "My God owns the trees. He owns the rivers. He owns the land and the heavens. My God is Jesus, and He is very powerful. When I pray to my God, all the other land owners must flee, because He is the most powerful land owner. And when you belong to Jesus, you carry the same power."

I noticed that most people in the village were slaves to religious practices but did not seem to have genuine relationships with God. Many chanted, cried, and begged God for things. We told them to simply receive the gifts God had given them as sons and daughters rather than plead like slaves. We explained that they walked in the authority that Jesus Christ had given them through the Holy Spirit. Several people said they'd previously had no concept of these truths and were excited to know that the land owners did not have power over them any longer. One lady at church said that she wanted to preach but kept being physically prevented. Anytime she felt led to share at church, her body went under attack, and she became sick. We taught her about the authority she carried, and she agreed to rebuke the demonic attacks the next time they happened.

The day we left Caprendita, I noticed that the water in the tap shut off. I later found out from Angela that the whole area had been in a terrible drought, and there was normally no water at her base. However, the water tanks had mysteriously filled up as soon as our team arrived, supplying just enough water for our time in the village. When we left, it dried up again. Angela said there was no explanation for such a miracle other than a blessing from God. Water had never appeared and disappeared like that before.

After our time in Caprendita, we bused to Entre Rios, a city about six hours away on terrible, winding roads through mountains and steep cliffs. From Entre Rios, we split into several small groups and traveled to remote villages with local pastors to minister for the next few days. As we boarded our buses and headed to various villages, I was so physically exhausted that I could barely hold back tears. I couldn't remember the last time I'd slept well, the last time I'd been clean, or the last time I'd felt truly rested. I was completely overwhelmed by the thought of heading to a remote village with zero fuel in my tank and didn't think I had enough strength in me to do it. However, I remembered how powerfully God had come through when I was at the end of my rope in Peru and declared out loud that the same thing would happen in this next village.

Hours later, Stephen, Breck, Kelly, Katherine, and I were dumped on the side of a dusty road in the middle of nowhere with a local pastor named Adel. With half my life strapped to my back, I began the trek to Adel's family house in the village of La Cueva. Partway through, we had to stop to remove our shoes and walk through some water; then we continued on the other side with sandy feet and heavy packs.

We finally arrived at the house of Adel's in-laws where we were greeted by Lucilla, the sweetest woman in Bolivia. She offered us some tea and bread, then began to prepare a chicken we'd eat later on. Stephen encouraged me and Katherine to help Lucilla pluck the chicken, and I held back the urge to gag as I ripped feathers out of the rubbery bird. While in her kitchen, Lucilla informed us that she had problems with her stomach and couldn't eat more than one meal a day. She also had terrible headaches. Both conditions had lasted for about two weeks. In addition, Lucilla had felt a tingling sensation in her leg for a long time that made it constantly feel heavy and asleep. We prayed for her, and right away, everything was healed! She began rejoicing and crying, thanking God for touching her.

The next day, we hiked through the village and visited several homes with Adel. We found out that Adel worked in Entre Rios during the week as a carpenter and spent every weekend traveling to La Cueva, often with his wife and son, to visit houses and share the word of God. He also organized church services on Friday evenings and Sunday afternoons. La Cueva still didn't have its own church building, but the community found alternate places to gather each week. We accompanied Adel on his normal travels, amazed by his faith and dedication.

Each household greeted us with open arms, warm hearts, and *tons* of food. In three days, I ate more than I normally consumed in an entire week. In Bolivian village culture, it was considered extremely rude to not finish everything that was put on your plate, which really put my stomach to the test. Every time we arrived at a new home, the family wanted to feed us, even though we'd been fed by the previous household. We prayed for several people within the village, each prayer accompanied by a meal, snack, or drink. Secretly, I was praying I wouldn't throw up any of the food that had been so kindly served to me.

The following day, we continued visiting homes but trekked further into the village. The views as we walked were breathtaking. We hiked through green hills of farmland, occasionally walking next to cows, pigs, sheep, chickens, etc. Vast fields covered the region like a beautiful emerald blanket. After trekking through the fields, we had to cross a river to get to the other half of the community. We took off our shoes, rolled up our pants, and traversed the freezing cold river to get to the other side and continue to visit people.

We spent quite a bit of time with a woman named Feliza. Her husband was an alcoholic, and her family claimed to have seen much demonic activity happening at their house. Feliza's mother-in-law was involved with witchdoctors, and a witchdoctor had cursed the house eighteen years ago. A while back, Feliza and Adel had spent an evening praying for the deliverance of Feliza's husband from addiction. Hours later, in the middle of the night, Feliza's husband screamed as he was delivered from a demonic presence. Eerily, Feliza's daughters, who were away at university, both had an alarming dream that same night. Feeling worried, they called home to check on Feliza and their father.

We decided to pray over the entire house and command the demons to go to Jesus' feet. Katherine saw a hissing demon on Feliza and her husband's bed. I felt a heaviness in my chest as soon as I entered their bedroom. After rebuking the demons, Feliza escorted us to a makeshift hostel in the middle of her village. Though this building's existence seemed quite odd, I happily threw my dirty bag on one of the beds and immediately jumped into the shower.

Clean and excited about having a real bed, I walked into the room where I'd left my bag. Stephen, Breck, Adel, Katherine, and Kelly were all sitting on the beds, a little quieter than normal.

"Okay guys, here's the thing," I announced. "The bathroom is a little weird. The light kind of flickers in and out while the water does the same thing."

"Here's the thing," Katherine responded, repeating my exact words. "We're not staying here tonight."

"What?" I asked, confused as to why we were sitting on the hostel beds and using the shower.

"*They* are sleeping here," Katherine explained while pointing to the guys. "We girls get to stay at the demon house."

I thought she was joking, but the genuine looks of sympathy on Breck and Stephen's faces told me this was real.

"I'm really sorry. I love you girls," Breck mouthed as Kelly, Katherine, and I walked away with Feliza, our heads hung low.

We returned to Feliza's house where she offered us a bedroom filled with sexually inappropriate pictures, two beds harder than rocks, and the fur of some allergen-loaded dog. I immediately reacted to the fur — sneezing incessantly, having trouble breathing, blowing my nose constantly, and itching my increasingly bloodshot eyes. The whole night was horrible. I couldn't sleep at all. I felt like my body was being assaulted and went outside to pray. Kelly noticed that I was awake and prayed for me until I felt at peace. The feeling of oppression left, but I still couldn't sleep.

Finally, the sun came up, and the guys met us at Feliza's house for breakfast. They reported that they'd slept great. Bags under my eyes, I gave them a look that didn't need words to accompany it. I chugged some coffee and hoped for a buzz of energy. Feliza sat at the table with us and shared that she'd dreamt of a serpent during the night. *There was a white snake, and its tail had been cut off. The snake said he was angry, because he could strike no longer.* It seemed Satan's ability to mess with this home had been threatened, and his power there was over. Now all Feliza needed to do was get rid of that dang dog.

Later that day, we visited a few more homes and then went to a large farmhouse for a church service. Because I hadn't slept at all, I didn't know how I would function through an entire service. I started to feel nauseous from lack of sleep, and my stomach felt even queasier when we got to the farmhouse. There, we were greeted with slabs of dead pig piled atop corn and potatoes. The pork was a mixture of meat, skin, huge blobs of fat, and pieces of fur scattered throughout. The amount of carbs alone made me gag as I tried to force it all down, and the hog carcass did not make things any better. Stephen was a hero, choking down so much skin that I dry heaved just watching him. Breck joked about making a sacrificial tumble for the sake of the team and purposefully face-planting with his plate in hand. This would allow him to lose his food and create a distraction while Katherine, Kelly, and I made a run for the trash. We laughed as we fantasized about such a maneuver, but in the end we sucked it up and choked down all of our food.

Our pig feast was followed by a time of worship and sharing words of encouragement with the friends we'd made throughout the last couple of days. I stood up to speak, Stephen beside me translating. Midway through speaking, a chicken jumped off a table and almost struck me in the face. I yelped and grabbed Stephen as both of us, as well as the entire congregation, burst into giggles. "I'm sorry," I laughed, as I watched the chuckling faces of this farming community. "I'm not used to having chickens at church with me!" This was a far cry from my church in California.

After surviving church on the farm, a woman named Gregoria pulled us aside for prayer. We'd met her the day before, and she'd told us how she was struggling with a serious offense against one of the other women in the church. She constantly felt depressed and wanted to leave La Cueva. Living within a community of only thirty people, one broken relationship meant serious trouble. Gregoria also complained of pain in her stomach, and after we prayed for her, she was healed. However, we knew she needed more than physical healing. She needed restoration in her heart. Juliana, a lady we'd met during our first day, came and stood beside Gregoria, and I realized she was the woman with whom Gregoria had an offense. The two women confessed their wrongdoings to us and apologized to each other, hugging and weeping into one another's arms.

In addition, Juliana asked for private prayer and told us that she had lots of hurt in her heart. She felt far from God and wasn't able to receive His love or her husband's love. We talked to her for a long time and took her through a process of emotional healing and affirming her identity. As we spoke and prayed truth over her, Juliana mentioned that she'd had a dream that seemed relevant to our conversation.

God was forming Juliana into a person. He then put a white dress before her, and she said, "What a beautiful dress! I want to wear it." However, she didn't think she was good enough for its splendor.

Then she heard a voice say, "I will put it on you." Juliana realized the dress was for the marriage supper with Christ (a beautiful celebration where Jesus will one day unite with his "bride" [the church], as referenced in Revelation 19:7-10).

Amazed by this dream, we assured Juliana that she was hearing from the Lord. She didn't need to believe she was unloved or to worry about being far from God. Juliana began to realize how powerfully God *was* speaking into her life and decided to receive both His love as well as love from her husband. Her face lit up, and she walked away from the farmhouse, looking and feeling lighter. Joy was genuinely radiating from her.

At the end of the day, we walked back towards the house of Adel's in-laws to pack up, go to bed, and leave early the next morning. The thought of waking up at the crack of dawn sounded like torture. But at just the right time, God blessed us with a gracious man who stopped us on the road and said he was on his way to Entre Rios. He offered to give us a free ride back that night if we could get ready quickly. We excitedly and quickly packed, said our goodbyes to Adel's beautiful family, and jumped into the car.

The next day in Entre Rios, we reunited with the rest of the team and swapped stories from our various villages. Each group had amazing testimonies of God's healing, faithfulness, and goodness. In Entre Rios, some of us walked to the city market and bumped into friends from the La Cueva community who were taking care of errands in the city. The man who lived in the farmhouse where we'd had the pig feast told us that the people of La Cueva had been very discouraged prior to our visit. Yet, he gladly shared that the residents were now extremely encouraged after just a few days together.

I remembered how burned out and exhausted I had felt before busing into La Cueva. I'd had nothing to offer, but God had come through. I knew that such a quick and significant change in the community had nothing to do with anything I (or my teammates) could have accomplished on our own. Again, God had simply shown up in a moment of human weakness and demonstrated His incredible strength and love when I had no strength of my own. In just days, I had seen countless people physically, spiritually, and emotionally healed. This beautiful farming community had shifted from feelings of despair to an attitude of hope and encouragement. As I took part in this community's transformation, I experienced positive changes in my own heart. I no longer felt weary and weak. Instead, I felt rejuvenated by the love of God and full of hope, joy, peace…and pig fat.

Chapter Sixteen

BRAZIL: A Country of Contrast

After an overnight train, seven bus rides, and one overloaded taxi trip, our team finally arrived back in Brazil. We were happily reunited with our vehicles and suitcases we'd left behind. I excitedly rummaged through my bag, rediscovering all the items I'd already forgotten about. I snuggled into clean pajamas and fell asleep, praying for rest good enough to sustain me as we prepared to begin our ministry in Brazil full force.

We started in the illustrious city of Foz do Iguaçu. This well-known region located near the Paraguayan border was home to the grandiose Iguaçu Falls, one of the New Seven World Wonders of Nature. Though impressed by the natural beauty within the city, we took some time to experience the other side of Foz do Iguaçu as well. Several of us ventured to the river dividing Paraguay and Brazil, a scenic waterway surrounded by intense poverty, piles of trash, and dismal slums.

As we walked through the surrounding neighborhoods, I realized that I could no longer carry on a simple conversation with the people around me. I had falsely assumed that my growing Spanish vocabulary was close enough to Portuguese to get by while in Brazil; however, I could not have been more wrong. Though some words were similar, I was completely lost while trying to speak Portuguese. No one could understand my attempts at the language, and when I listened to Portuguese, my untrained ears heard something that sounded more like Chinese than Spanish. Speaking Spanish had been hard enough; Brazilian Portuguese was a whole new ballgame. This would be interesting.

Fortunately, between translators, hand gestures, and simple unspoken understanding, we found ways to get by. Taylor M., who was never fazed by not speaking the language, noticed an old man walking through the slums who could barely see. The man approached a couple of the guys (including fluent-in-Portuguese Jesse) and asked for prayer, explaining that he was blind. Taylor was overwhelmed by a surge of faith and knew the man was going to be healed. In fact, the Lord told him exactly what to pray. Getting a download from heaven, Taylor prayed for the muscles in the man's eyes to be strengthened so that he could focus. Taylor also prayed for the surface of the man's eyes to shift into the right shape. His prayer was very brief, but almost instantly, the man declared an improvement in his vision. Before Taylor could even ask how he felt, the man shouted with excitement. Taylor held up his fingers to test the man's eyesight. The old man could see everything with accuracy. Jesse ran a distance from the man, held up his fingers, and asked if he could see how many fingers he was holding up from afar. Again, the man answered with precision, verifying his renewed eyesight. Thanking Taylor for his prayer, the man left crying with joy.

Foz do Iguaçu was just a tiny taste of Brazil. This country was by far the largest in South America, and we had thousands of miles to traverse. From Foz, we drove through the metropolis of São Paulo before landing in Cabo Frio, a coastal area outside of Rio de Janeiro. Carol's family lived in a beautiful home in Cabo Frio where they generously hosted over thirty of us.

Carol, our team's sole Brazilian, excitedly welcomed us to her city and arranged opportunities for us to bless her church and friends. One afternoon, she brought a group of us to visit a Christian rehabilitation center for men. Each man had a different story, but most had been homeless or addicted to drugs at some point before moving into the center. The residents greeted us with huge smiles and proudly offered us an elaborate meal that included a special type of chicken only served on special occasions. Humbled by their generosity, we enjoyed the delicious lunch before walking to the center's chapel to worship with the residents. Most of the men were voraciously hungry for the presence of God. The rehab center was located in a pretty isolated area, so the men were very excited to have visitors who shared their faith. As we worshipped with them, it felt more like a family seeking God together than a rehab center.

Quite a few people went up front to share words of encouragement, and we offered to pray for each individual afterwards. One older gentleman sitting in front of us had formerly been a gang leader. Before coming to the rehab center, he'd murdered many people. The man had ended up in a wheelchair, which I assume was the result of being shot during his gang days. A couple of people prayed for him, but he was generally unresponsive. Taylor L. disregarded his cold demeanor and boldly went in for a hug. As he embraced this man, something changed. I caught a glimpse of both Taylor and the man, arms wrapped around each other. Several minutes later, I saw that they were still hugging, both now weeping. I didn't know what was happening, but I could clearly see that it was something powerful. The old man's heart was quickly softening, and he began to cry out to God with desperation. After a while, he let go of Taylor and raised his arms towards heaven, cheering and loudly praising Jesus.

We later found out that the night before our visit, this very man had said he wanted to leave the rehab center and declared that he hated God. He had dealt with aggression all his life and only knew how to fight. However, he didn't know how to resist love. Instead of opposing his malevolence with the hostility he was used to, Taylor confronted him with pure love. His warm hug melted away the anger and hurt, and this once bitter man was radically filled with the love of God.

Later that week, a small group of us drove about two hours outside of Cabo Frio to meet up with members of a new church to minister in the red light district of their city. At one or two in the morning, we walked the streets looking for prostitutes and transvestites. I saw a scantily clad woman approach a car and lean in to talk to the driver. After conversing for a moment, she lifted up her miniskirt to prove to the potential customer that she was an authentic woman. The man approved, and she walked around the front of the car, opened the passenger seat, and drove off. As I watched the car disappear, I wondered how that woman must have felt and how scary it would have been to know she was about to sell her body to a stranger.

Moments later, a group from my team approached a transvestite whose street name was "Sabrina." All prostitutes were massively disrespected, but the transvestites in this area were met with particular disdain. They were so hated by some of the public that men would often drive through the red light district and kill the transvestites. While my teammates talked with Sabrina, some men with guns drove by on a motorcycle. The people from the church later explained that the men would probably have shot Sabrina if he had been alone on the street corner. Because my teammates and the church members had surrounded him, the men with guns backed off. My teammates asked to pray for Sabrina, and he requested that they use his real name, Junior, when they prayed. "Sabrina" was just a character he played to make money, but he wanted prayer for his true self — the man Junior that was really inside of him.

After hanging out in the streets for probably an hour and a half, the local church members suddenly hurried us back to our cars. Confused, we asked why we had to leave so abruptly. Much to our oblivion, some people involved in drug trafficking were shooting each other just blocks away. The danger of getting caught in the crossfire put a quick end to our evening. Though disappointed by the circumstances, I knew this was an important wake-up call. Regular gunfire was a reality for the people living and working on these streets.

The following day, we drove back to Cabo Frio, where we retrieved the rest of the team and said a sad goodbye to Carol's parents before driving onward. Adalberto and Luciana had become our team's adopted Brazilian parents, selflessly taking care of our big and rowdy group in their lovely home. They promised that their doors would always be open and that each of us had a house waiting if we ever came back to Brazil.

Leaving beautiful Cabo Frio brought forth a jarring change, as we now headed to the *favelas* (slums) of Rio de Janeiro. Brazil quickly proved to be a land of striking contrast. This diverse country was a fascinating mix of buzzing city life, gang-polluted ghettos, fetid dumps, and stunning stretches of nature. En route to our first favela, we passed through the most touristic parts of Rio, noticing the famous Sugarloaf Mountain and Christ the Redeemer statue. We drove through the legendary Copacabana Beach, where curious onlookers gaped at our American license plates and cheered us on.

The atmosphere changed very suddenly as the wealthy metropolis transformed into a drug-infested favela. Our large cars that had caused entertaining commotion in Copacabana now caused a different kind of commotion inside of the slum. After clumsily struggling to wind our cars up the hilly and narrow streets, we got stuck while trying to turn around and caused a major traffic jam. Wedged in the middle of an awkward corner, we blocked other cars as well as dozens of motorbikes that whizzed by us in a moment of mass chaos.

In the midst of trying to turn our cars around, the pastor who had invited us to the favela miraculously showed up in the middle of the street and helped escort us to a less chaotic parking area. From there, he led us to his church where we would stay for the next few days. The building was located in the heart of the slums — comprised of an indoor sanctuary and a balcony overlooking the streets where worshippers regularly gathered to broadcast worship music throughout the neighborhood. During our first evening, we took part in one of the outdoor services, enjoying the songs raining from the balcony and flooding the streets. David preached from the balcony, more and more passersby gathering in the road to listen. The next day, members of the community came to the indoor sanctuary for more services, where our team shared testimonies, preached, and answered questions about the missionary life. Finally, we brought church to the streets, wandering around the favela to pray for people.

After a very brief stay, we left this favela and were directed to another. Following our vow to visit the darkest places, we traveled to Parada de Lucas, a notoriously dangerous slum in Rio de Janeiro. The entire area was run by drug traffickers and gangsters. Carol got in touch with the director of a YWAM base in the favela and said we were willing to spend three nights at his base. The director explained that this was a bleak place, and no one ever wanted to visit. Carol said our team was called to this type of area and was fully prepared for whatever was thrown at us.

Days before we arrived in the favela, the director contacted Carol to confirm that we were really still coming. He said every group always ended up bailing. They all got afraid and gave up. His voice cracking, he assured Carol, "I don't blame you if you guys back out. Everyone does. I understand if you don't come to visit us; I really do." Standing firm in what she'd agreed to, Carol promised the director that our team would keep our word and visit his base.

When driving into the favela, we had to carefully coordinate times with the YWAM staff. They warned us that since gangbangers ruled the streets, they would shoot strangers who entered their territory unless notified in advance. Because YWAM had a working relationship with the gang members and drug lords, they were able to explain that a group of foreigners were coming to visit and told them not to shoot us when we arrived.

Two YWAM staffers greeted us at a parking lot in the city and escorted us to their barren base that would become home for the next few days. At first glance, I wasn't sure how we would all fit inside. The guys were instructed to sleep in the hallways or on the roof. The girls slept on the floor of a few small bedrooms on the second floor. My room had no electricity and no door. The bottom floor of the building had a tiny kitchen and one toilet that didn't flush. Thirty or so people, days without showering, one non-flushing toilet, and tight sleeping quarters…you do the math.

Any time we left the base, we were escorted by locals who had a relationship with the drug lords in order to keep us safe. The streets were lined with men who had huge machine guns slung around their shoulders and pistols attached to their hips.

The streets were filled with the stench of weed and gang members who carried walkie-talkies to communicate with other gangsters and drug lords — the "protectors" of the favela. Fireworks constantly went off as a signal to warn people of the police's presence. The locals were accustomed to the fireworks and used them to gauge when to get out of the streets. Clashes between police and gangs often erupted, and people were accustomed to getting out of the way of the crossfire.

One day, our team had the opportunity to speak at two different schools within the favela. We acted out a couple of dramas for the kids and spoke at a school assembly for children ages six and up. I talked to them about dreaming big, the constant interruption of fireworks bursting in the distance. Some of the kids laughed when they went off; others didn't react at all. They were completely desensitized to the gang war going on around them. As I looked at the children, I thought about the drug lords and gangsters I'd seen in the favela and how these kids could grow up to become the same. I imagined the gang leaders as innocent children and wondered when their turning points had been.

Despite living among such intense circumstances, these schoolchildren reminded me that kids were kids no matter what. After we spoke at the school assembly, Carol asked the children if they had any questions for us. A brave volunteer raised her hand and inquired, "Do you like cake?" And there it was — the beautiful innocence and oblivion that exists in the mind of every six year old. Though we'd talked about more serious topics and there was a clear war going on inside her neighborhood, all her little mind wondered at that moment was whether or not we liked cake. I was reminded of the innate purity born into every child and saddened to know that it was only a matter of time before this little girl would be corrupted by the world around her.

Remembering that the gang leaders and traffickers had once been something so innocent and pure broke my heart for them. They had simply been tainted by a corrupt system and were unable to find a way out. Though they tried to intimidate others with fear, I knew fear and manipulation actually ruled their own lives and had trapped them in a lifestyle that the deepest places in their hearts longed to escape.

Meanwhile, Liz and Aleeza had taken a bus to another area of Rio to sort out an issue with Liz's visa. They returned to the favela without a local escort and accidentally missed their bus stop on the way back. Because of this, they had to backtrack a bit to find the rest of the team. Jesse had lent them his phone, and the girls stopped at a bridge, overlooking the favela as they tried to make a call. During this process, they noticed some of our teammates who happened to be walking by and began to point at them.

Unbeknownst to Liz and Aleeza, their hand gestures had alarmed the gang members who guarded their territory very closely. The girls' phone had been mistaken for a camera, a highly forbidden object for outsiders in the favela. By the grace of God, Carol, our native Portuguese speaker, was part of the group passing by and intercepted threats being spoken by some of the gang members. The gangsters thought Liz and Aleeza had been taking pictures, a normally fatal blunder, and told Carol that they were going to shoot both Liz and Aleeza. Carol explained that the object mistaken for a camera was actually just a phone. She assured them that the girls were only trying to find the team, not photographing their territory. Liz and Aleeza saw Carol and approached her as the gangsters calmed down and gave them permission to pass, no bullets needed. Happy to have found the team, Liz and Aleeza were completely oblivious to what had just happened behind the scenes. They would never have dreamt that a simple hand gesture or a phone could have cost them their lives.

After a few days of intertwining our lives with this twisted system, many questions buzzed about my mind. I wished we could have magically stopped gang violence, drug trafficking, and the corruption of children in the snap of a finger. I felt overwhelmed by the darkness and hopelessness I'd seen in the favela. But then — a glimmer of hope. I heard that Tanya asked one of the YWAM leaders if it would be possible to pray for the head of Parada de Lucas' gang. The YWAM staffer made some phone calls and arranged a meeting for a few of my teammates to pray for the gang members. After their gathering, the gangbangers admitted that they had been planning on going to war that very night with another favela. However, because of receiving touching prayers, they said there was no way they could do such a thing. The gang leaders experienced the peace of the presence of God and could no longer wage war. My teammates left the gang members, each of them smiling and thanking the team for coming to their favela.

On our way out of Parada de Lucas, three people from a local Iris church joined up with our team. Before I'd even had a chance to wrap my brain around the past few days, they brought us to their ministry in the dumps of Rio. This trio visited garbage dumps every weekend to play with children, visit families, and often show films on a large projector. The three volunteers said that no one ever wanted to come participate in their ministry, and it was a dream come true to have thirty people willing to serve alongside them.

They escorted us to a dump about a half hour from the favela. Thirty minutes brought us to an entirely different world. Piles of garbage were surrounded by winding dirt roads and shacks where families lived. No Portuguese needed, I began kicking a soccer ball around with a little boy in the street, and others soon joined in. Moments later, one of the little boys started chasing me down the dusty street with a chicken as I screamed and he giggled behind me.

Later, my teammates and I made house visits with the volunteers guiding us. The children from this neighborhood excitedly followed us from house to house as we greeted different families and prayed for them. Along the way, I found a little boy who'd just suffered a minor scrape and stood in the street crying. I grabbed him and held him in my arms until his tears stopped. Whenever I tried to put him down, he lifted his feet and refused to touch the ground. The atmosphere reminded me so much of Africa — kids freely roaming the streets, playing soccer with half-deflated balls, jumping into the arms of strangers with trust and smiles. My heart was at home.

The sun began to set, and one of the girls who'd brought us to the dump, Stéphanie, said she would take us to her family's spare apartment to rest for a few days. I wondered what kind of family could afford an extra apartment and later found out Stéphanie was actually a famous Brazilian bikini model. She also happened to be the daughter of Bebeto, a legendary soccer player who had helped win the World Cup for the Brazilian team in 1994. I was quite impressed that a Brazilian celebrity chose to spend her free time in garbage dumps. As I spent more time with Stéphanie, I saw an inner beauty far more striking than her exterior. Cherishing her relationship with Jesus above her modeling career, she planned to soon travel to Mozambique to complete the same mission training school my teammates and I had attended.

We rested at Stéphanie's apartment for a few days and welcomed some old friends back to the team. Josiah and Astrid both made brief visits, and Natalie H. joined us for the remainder of South America. We also met up with two friends of Taylor L., Angela, and Taylor M. from Dallas. Peter and Bob, a couple of Texan fireballs, spent a few weeks in and out of Rio, joining us in the favela and hanging out with the team while at Stéphanie's. Peter and Bob had an amazing testimony of God leading them to Brazil and made a brief but powerful impact on our team.

Months before visiting us, Peter found out that our team would pass through Rio de Janeiro, a city on his mind and heart. He was considering joining our team in Rio and asked God for a prophetic sign to confirm whether or not he should fly to Brazil. The very next day, a Brazilian stranger showed up at Peter's church in Dallas. The Holy Spirit had told this Brazilian man to fly to Dallas and look for someone to preach at his church in São Paulo, Brazil. He had no plans in Dallas other than to obey what the Lord had told him.

The man saw Peter at his church and was drawn to him. Knowing Peter was the one God had chosen to preach in São Paulo, the Brazilian approached Peter and offered him some Havaiana flip-flops, a famous Brazilian brand. He informed Peter, "I think God told me that you are supposed to come with me to Brazil."

If that wasn't a clear confirmation, I'm not sure what is. Peter decided to travel to Brazil and began to pray about what God had in store for him. While still in Texas, he had a significant dream that he knew was from the Lord.

Peter was flying like a bird over a city in Brazil. The weather was foggy and dark. Peter saw himself arriving in the area where the false god of the city was located. His friend and co-pastor Bob was with him, and they saw lots of black stone. The two of them started praying by the false god, and some witchdoctors began to convulse as they prayed. When other people saw what was happening, they realized that a newer and higher power had come.

All the witchdoctors and those who worshipped false deities were struck with fear.

Peter woke up from this dream and knew that the city he'd just seen was Rio de Janeiro, Brazil. Shortly after, he called Bob and said, "Guess what? We're going to Brazil."

Months later, both Peter and Bob flew to Brazil and visited the pastor Peter had met in Dallas and preached at his church. From São Paulo, they bused to Rio de Janeiro and temporarily joined our team. During their time with us, several people decided to visit Rio's Christ the Redeemer statue, a famous Brazilian landmark and one of the New Seven Wonders of the World. The one hundred thirty-foot-tall statue of Jesus stood atop a large mountain in the center of Rio and boasted one of the best views of the city. People paid good money to take trains, vans, or cable cars to the top of the mountain to worship beneath the statue, catch a stunning view of Rio, and visit the debatably most iconic symbol in Brazil.

Peter and Bob decided to venture to the statue separately from the team and returned to us with an incredible testimony. Their day started off with blue skies and bright sunshine. They left early in the morning and had some struggles getting to the statue. In fact, it looked like they might not make it. However, the Lord had put this excursion intensely on their hearts, so they determined to make a way. They finally arrived at the statue and noticed that the foundation of the statue was black marble, just like the black stone Peter had seen in his dream. Underneath the statue, there was a Catholic church dedicated to Mary where people worshipped. Many Brazilians idolized Mary, the Jesus statue itself, and other idols. Most people liked the image of Jesus but had no personal relationship with him.

Peter and Bob started praying and worshipping near the statue. After just five minutes or so, large, dark clouds began to pollute the sky and pour rain — matching the dreary weather from Peter's dream. Peter felt that their "mission" was finished and suggested to Bob that they catch a train back to the bottom of the mountain.

As they waited in line, they heard a huge BANG! Suddenly, smoke was everywhere, and the cable cars were sparking. Peter and Bob had no idea what was happening. A man ran down from the statue and started talking to some friends who were standing near Peter and Bob in line. "You'll never believe what happened!" he cried. "No one will believe me!" In his hand, he held a large piece of marble, and he freaked out as he continued, "I am holding a part of the head of the Jesus statue!"

Peter and Bob asked what had just happened. The man informed them that he was standing at the base of the statue, and a bolt of lightning struck the head of the Jesus statue. He and those surrounding him ducked and heard rocks hitting the pavement all around them. The man finally looked up and saw that the ground was covered with little pieces of rock. He had seen lightning hit the head of Jesus with his very own eyes.

Peter excitedly asked the man, "Do you know why that just happened? That was an answer to prayer! We just prayed for God to tear down the false idols and spiritual strongholds in Rio!" Despite peoples' reverence for the statue, Christ the Redeemer wasn't Jesus at all. It was solely a false representation of God and an idol that exchanged peoples' chance for a real relationship with the Lord for a big piece of stone. With just a prayer, God struck the statue and demolished part of the head — a physical manifestation of God taking down the principality and the false symbol of Jesus. Peter's testimony was a reminder that no matter how much we did in the natural, it was the supernatural that really counted.

Thankful for our time with Peter and Bob, we parted ways in Rio and continued north as they returned to Texas. From Rio, we drove through Salvador, then onto our next stop — the beautiful city of Fortaleza, meaning "fortress" in Portuguese. Though the majority of Iris Global's bases were in Africa, a young couple was in the process of starting an Iris base in Fortaleza. Running alongside other Iris missionaries in South America was a rare opportunity and welcomed treat. The timing of our arrival was quite serendipitous as the couple had just been given a mansion that would become their home and mission base, and the keys were released to them two days after we arrived in Fortaleza.

After receiving the keys, we moved into the mansion, excited to help transform the building into an Iris base. Though the idea of staying in a mansion sounded like a dream, the reality wasn't quite so luxurious. The house was filthy and looked like it hadn't been cleaned in years. The front of the building was full of dead leaves and overgrown plants. Inside, termites had taken over the walls and dirty floorboards. The floors were caked with dirt, and cobwebs hung from the walls and windows. Since there was no furniture, I set up my sleeping mat near one of the many termite trails and hoped the insects would leave me alone while I slept.

Our time in Fortaleza entailed a mix of cleaning up the mansion and spending quality time worshipping and praying with the Iris Fortaleza team. We were privileged to visit their prayer house, located in the middle of a rough neighborhood but elevated enough to provide a stunning view of the city. The building now being used for prayer meetings had once belonged to a drug lord who used it as a lookout point for drug activity.

One afternoon, a few of us visited families in the favela surrounding the prayer house. We met a grandmother who was raising her recently deceased daughter's six children. The mother of the kids had come to Jesus just before her death, but their father was not a believer. He proved completely undependable and didn't contribute financially or emotionally to his children's lives. Therefore, the grandmother was carrying the burden of raising the children on her own. She looked tired and heavy-laden, so we attempted to share some encouraging words. We prayed for her and the children, something that used to make her fidgety and uncomfortable. But because of the Iris Fortaleza staff consistently showing her love, her heart was slowly becoming accustomed to receiving love and affirmation. When we prayed for the grandmother, she cried, her heart touched. This was breakthrough.

Another small group was asked to visit a YWAM school and speak. There were fifty to sixty students, and the team had no idea what they would share. A few began recounting testimonies and stories, and as they spoke, the presence of God fell in the room. Students started crying, falling over, and getting healed. Taylor M. announced that he'd received a word of knowledge that someone needed healing in his or her right shoulder. After calling people up for individual prayer, a woman approached Taylor and said she was scheduled to have surgery on her shoulder. When he'd called out the word of knowledge, her shoulder was totally healed. She said that she felt brand new and decided to cancel her scheduled operation.

Late Friday night, several of us went to the red light district of Fortaleza. Ministry to prostitutes was one of the focuses of the new Iris base, with intercession as a priority, followed by a commitment to spend one-on-one time with people in the street. The woman pioneering Iris Fortaleza explained that before doing anything, her team spent countless hours praying against the strongholds within the red light district. There was only so much one could physically do to stop prostitution. Putting an end to sex trafficking required a change in the hearts of men, deep healing from perversion, and an understanding of true identity. After regular prayers, the Iris Fortaleza team started visiting men and women on the streets, and the prostitutes complained that business had been slowly decreasing. Fewer men seemed interested in their services. Intercession was gradually changing hearts and shifting the spiritual atmosphere. Prayer was the key to complete freedom from prostitution.

As we walked the streets of the red light district, we stopped for men and women who looked like they needed some compassion. The first woman we met spoke in a voice so soft and coy that I could scarcely believe her job was seducing men for money. I found out that the timid young woman was an orphan and hated her life as a prostitute. She'd tried to leave the streets for a while but reluctantly returned to the red light district in order to pay for food.

We met several other women, as well as androgynous people whose genders were up for debate. Most were friendly and receptive to conversation, but they carried deep shame and had trouble accepting pure love from us. It seemed they didn't understand why anyone would want to offer them something without asking for anything in return. I was disgusted by the way customers had distorted the true meaning of love and how beauty had been perverted into such a twisted system of desperate moneymaking. Yet, in each conversation with the women on the streets, we saw hearts that were genuine. They loathed the system in which they were trapped and suffered shame they were never meant to suffer.

While on the streets, we met a woman sitting on the side of the road — not a prostitute, just a woman waiting for something. I'm not sure what. After chatting for a bit, we realized she was a Christian. Nicole asked the woman if she had any children, and she quietly responded, "No." Nicole asked if she wanted kids, and she sadly replied, "Yes, but I can't have children." Nicole asked if we could pray for God to heal her and open her womb. This struck a chord in her heart, and the woman began to cry as we prayed for her. With tears in her eyes, she told us God had brought us together. It seemed Fortaleza, the city that meant fortress, was full of people desperate for just that. Unfortunately, with the exception of this one woman, most seemed unaware of the God who'd promised to be the very fortress they were waiting for.

In between ministry time in Fortaleza, the team began to discuss our future plans, and the reality of rapidly diminishing time sank in. It was already October. We decided to plan a hiatus for the holidays, aiming to finish the South American continent before Thanksgiving and return to the Caribbean after Christmas. Though this birthed a new wave of ambition, it also created a bit of a time crunch. At first I thought it wouldn't be possible to cram so much traveling into such a short time period, but with the right combination of prayer and determination, you'd be amazed at how much ground you can cover.

We began our preparations for finishing the continent by saying farewell to our vehicles in Fortaleza. Four of the five original cars had faithfully carried us from the United States all the way to Brazil, perhaps one of the biggest miracles we'd experienced the whole trip. However, they were having more and more problems as time progressed, and the poor infrastructure of the roadways ahead would likely create major delays. We decided finishing via public transportation and getting rid of the cars sooner rather than later was the best option. We trashed our remaining pop-up and researched the best way to get rid of our vehicles. We found out it was illegal to sell the cars in Venezuela (our original plan), and unfortunately selling in Brazil was illegal as well. However, we learned that if we *donated* the cars in Brazil there were some loopholes we could jump through and legally leave them behind. And who better to donate to than our Iris brothers and sisters in Brazil who desperately needed vehicles?

We knew dealing with paperwork could take a long time and felt it was unnecessary to keep the whole team in Fortaleza for the process. Several of us had our hearts set on traveling to Manaus, a major jungle city in the Amazon. From there, we hoped to venture deeper into the jungle. The team decided to split up and meet in Manaus in a couple of weeks, gradually making our way to the city in small groups. The registered owners of the vehicles selflessly stayed behind in Fortaleza to sort out the necessary paperwork. Tanya also decided to stay in Fortaleza, wisely stationing herself there to await the birth of her second child. It was hard to believe her due date was already approaching. Tanya chose a "birthing team" to wait with her and assist with the delivery. Some others chose to stay behind as well, but the rest of us were released to move on. After the vehicle paperwork was finished, Tanya's baby was born, and those in the jungle returned, we'd all reunite in Manaus.

Though splitting up our team created difficult decisions for everyone, I heard the word "Manaus" loud and clear. I knew this was my last opportunity to get into the jungle, and I needed to hurry if I wanted to make it in and out before the rest of the team arrived in Manaus. Reluctantly, I said goodbye to some of my dearest friends and flew into the heart of the Amazon without them. The jungle was calling me.

I was joined by Taylor M., Natalie M., Elizabeth, Carol, Ted, Moose, and Ben. The eight of us knew we didn't have many days to travel to Manaus, get into the jungle, and arrive back in Manaus on time. Getting into the jungle was normally a complicated, expensive, and time-consuming endeavor. Trekking in with such limited time and money would require a miracle. However, our hearts had already begun to dream, so we prayed for a way to travel into the jungle from Manaus both quickly and cheaply. Neither goal seemed realistic, but we knew God would come through.

We spent a day researching and visiting different ports in Manaus, hoping for open doors. Sadly, we ended our quest feeling defeated. It seemed it would take at least three days on a boat and hundreds of dollars to get into the jungle — time and money we didn't have. But just a day later, the Lord sent us the answer to our prayers. Through unexpected contacts and four degrees of separation, we met a Brazilian named Paulo who lived in Manaus but regularly went into the jungle to minister to various tribes. Right away, this local Brazilian offered to boat us to a tribe he'd been working with for years. We ended up visiting an indigenous village on the Amazon River that required only a couple of hours of travel and about thirty dollars, including both boat fuel and food for a week. What looked impossible at first glance quickly unfolded into a perfect and smoothly executed plan.

We hopped on a boat with Paulo and glided through the waters of the Amazon, the hot sun browning our faces. After many curves of the river, we arrived in a beautiful village Paulo now considered his second home. Just three years prior, this tribe had been entirely "unreached." The villagers wore primitive clothes, if any at all, and had never heard the gospel. Santiago, the chief, and his partner Joanne were both alcoholics and had several children whom they treated poorly. Santiago regularly beat Joanne, and she finally left him as well as her children. She turned her back on her family and started to spend time with other men.

During this period, Paulo and two friends began to visit Santiago's village and share the love of Christ. At first, the tribe was very reserved and hesitant to open their hearts. Yet, after just one year of regular visits, Joanne received Jesus and began to change. Santiago saw her transformation and soon followed. He gave his life to Christ and desperately tried to stop drinking and smoking. However, his process of becoming free from addiction was not easy. Finally, feeling utterly defeated, Santiago went deep into the jungle, got down on his knees, and asked God to set him free. The Lord radically changed his heart, and his addictions were no longer a struggle. As Santiago embraced his newfound freedom, he became a loving father and husband. He decided to marry Joanne in an official ceremony and welcomed their fifth child, Samuel.

Though Santiago and Joanne had found lasting joy and healing, others in the village began to mock Santiago for becoming a Christian. Undeterred by their taunts, Santiago started to go to other villages and tell them the good news of Jesus. They wouldn't listen. Santiago grieved for their lives and cried out to God. Paulo and his friends continued to visit Santiago's tribe and started an organization to evangelize together. Santiago dreamt of translating the Bible into his tribe's mother tongue to help spread the gospel among his people. Gradually, despite a clash in beliefs, Santiago's community started to respect him and value his genuine heart.

At the time of our team's visit (now three years after Paulo's initial visits and two years after Joanne and Santiago's conversion), most people in Santiago's tribe still hadn't received Christ. However, their hearts were open, and they willingly accepted Christians in their village. My teammates and I felt blessed beyond belief to be able to experience the benefit of years of Paulo's work and dedication to this tribe. We were warmly welcomed by the entire community, as was a group of YWAM girls also visiting. The village children excitedly buzzed around us, asking us questions and cuddling into our laps.

We played with them for a while, then set up our hammocks and tents before attending an evening service with several families from the village. Afterwards, we attempted the art of sleeping in the jungle. I tossed and turned all night, constantly disrupted by squawking chickens and other unidentified animals. I tiredly emerged from my tent the next morning and chugged some coffee in the hopes of a functional day. Santiago invited us to go fishing with him, so Ted, Natalie, Elizabeth, and I tagged along. We headed to his canoe with several simple, wooden sticks from which line and hooks hung. Elizabeth squealed every time Santiago put worms on our hooks, which he found quite amusing. She shrieked in horror when a fish was finally caught and flopped around the bottom of the boat, causing Santiago to erupt into laughter.

After hours on the river, we didn't even have enough fish to feed our boatful, but we'd laughed enough to make the trip worthwhile. While "fishing," I noticed a large scar on Santiago's arm, and Natalie asked him the history behind it. He said a broken bottle had injured him years ago during a fight. It was hard to imagine this now gentle-spirited man acting out in such aggression. I knew God had drastically changed his heart, and that violent scar belonged to a man who no longer existed.

When we returned to the village, Santiago's children came running to greet him with huge smiles and hugs. It was evident that they absolutely adored him. He treated them with such gentle care and humility. I observed Joanne treating each of them with equally genuine care. It was a privilege to witness how God had transformed this family's life in such a short period of time.

Paulo offered to take us by boat across the river to visit another village for a couple of days before returning to Santiago's village. Our boat ride was followed by a sweaty hike with heavy packs strapped to our backs. We dropped off our belongings at the house of a local couple who graciously hosted us. After a brief break, we continued to hike through the jungle to visit houses and invite families to an evening church service. Along the way, we met an elderly lady in the middle of planting cassava (a starchy root) in a scorching, open field. Hunched over and exhausted from working, she complained of terrible pain in both her knees. We prayed for her healing, but she said the pain level was no different.

Late that afternoon, we trekked to a remote house where the evening's church service was held. Though we had just a brief time of sharing and praying, the man who hosted us was delivered from an addiction to alcohol and received the gift of tongues as an added bonus — not bad for a night in the jungle.

As we walked back to our base camp, we were warned to be careful of jaguars. I wondered how much of the warning was an attempt to rile up the foreigners, but when we passed by two local men who approached us with great concern, I realized this was not a joke. The men asked why we were hiking through the jungle at night and told us to be very cautious of the jaguars. I assumed they knew how to defend themselves, but we'd be dead in seconds if a wildcat crossed our path. Luckily, we arrived back at our tents free from any animal encounters.

The following morning, we hiked back to the sweltering field where the elderly lady had been planting cassava the day before. She was back to work in the heat, but today she greeted us with good news. Her knee pain was totally gone! Foolishly, I'd figured that her pain was unavoidable since she worked the fields every day. Yet, when she happily reported news of healing, I was reminded that we needed faith for both what didn't make sense and for what we didn't see. Sometimes, when we prayed for people, they weren't healed right away. At least, we didn't always *see* healing right away. But a lack of sight didn't necessarily mean healing hadn't taken place. I can't explain why, but sometimes what we declared in faith took a bit of time to catch up with reality. Though we'd seen nothing the day we prayed for the elderly woman, her body seemed good as new the next.

After receiving the good news, we spent the next couple of hours planting cassava with the woman. Every time I thought we'd planted all the roots, more mysteriously appeared in a large basket. Sweaty, tired, and overwhelmed, I barely made it through just one morning of farming. I wondered how this old woman survived this work each and every day.

Meanwhile, Ted, Moose, and Ben were with Paulo, his missionary friend Ana, and Baptista, a local they deemed "the Chuck Norris of the jungle." They were forced to carry huge, wooden boards through the jungle, up and down hills, in the scorching heat. Ana declared, "In this jungle, missionaries don't just come and preach. They come and work." Though the physical labor in the heat was hard on us, I liked what Ana said. Real faith required action to back it up.

Soon after, we hiked back to our boat and returned to Santiago's tribe for a few nights before returning to Manaus. Paulo asked us to participate in a conference at his church in Manaus during the upcoming weekend, and we agreed to leave the jungle early to do so. En route to Manaus, Paulo had to carefully maneuver our boat around the shallow patches of river that made it difficult to pass. The Amazon was desperate for rain, and the water level was extremely low. Paulo finally discovered an opening in the river that was deep, wide, and conducive to speed. Failing to pay attention to what was happening in front of him, he zoned out as he enjoyed the chance to drive his boat at top speed. I noticed another boat heading straight towards us, also going very quickly. I wrongly assumed Paulo saw this boat, but as they sped faster and faster and came closer and closer, I began to wonder. We were moments away from a head-on collision, and it was so obvious that I was now convinced Paulo saw the other boat and was driving like this in an attempt to be funny. I supposed that at just the right moment, Paulo would swerve away, and his friend driving the oncoming boat would laugh at his gutsy display of Amazonian audacity.

Suddenly, I realized this was not a joke and not at all intentional. Carol was lying down in the bow of the boat, her head inches from being crushed by the oncoming vessel. I screamed as I saw that we were actually about to collide, and Carol jumped up seconds before the two boats crashed together with a loud BANG! Our boat tipped to the side, and Carol's bag of valuables (including a new iPhone and camera) went flying into the Amazon River. Shrieking in horror, Carol jumped into the river hoping to save her bag. Without hesitation, Taylor jumped in behind her and began to swim through the murky water. After a few moments, we'd drifted so far that it was impossible to tell where the current had swept the bag and where it had sunk to the bottom. Defeated, injured, and frustrated, both Carol and Taylor got back into the boat where Paulo sheepishly drove us to shore.

We got out of the boat only to discover cuts and bruises that we hadn't noticed during the shock of the collision. My hip had a painful, purple mark at least seven inches long, and my knee was bloody. Carol was covered in bruises and had bad whiplash. Taylor was in pain as well. Both girls from YWAM in our boat were injured. One even had to go to the hospital for a leg wound. Luckily, Ben, Natalie, Moose, Ted, and Elizabeth had traveled in a different boat and arrived to shore unscathed.

The pain in my leg was tolerable, but I was furious with Paulo. He failed to apologize for the collision and wouldn't admit that he hadn't been paying attention at all while another boat was coming straight at us. He'd injured several people, destroyed someone else's boat, and lost Carol's valuables. Fortunately, no one had been severely injured, but if Carol hadn't jumped up when she did, she would have been. I saw how close her head was to hitting that other boat. We had been going so fast that the impact would have killed her or, at the very least, broken her neck. I shuttered at the thought of what we'd barely avoided.

Begrudgingly, I dragged myself to the conference that Paulo had asked us to attend. I was irritated that we'd left the jungle early for him, and he'd so carelessly transported us. Admittedly, I arrived at the conference with a less-than-pleasant attitude. We were given opportunities to preach and pray for those who attended, but all I wanted to do was sneer at Paulo until he offered some sort of apology.

Suddenly, I realized that I was embodying everything I regularly preached *against*. I knew unforgiveness and bitterness bred nothing but death, and I was called to bring life. Aware of my own hypocrisy, I snapped out of my bad attitude. Furthermore, I acknowledged that without Paulo, we would never have made it into the jungle on such a tight budget and with such little notice. He had made our jungle dreams come true, helping us at a moment's notice even though we were strangers. Paulo had been a part of making the impossible a reality for us, and I'd so quickly forgotten. I decided to forgive Paulo and be thankful for all he'd done for us instead.

As people came to the front to receive prayer, I walked around and laid hands on them. While moving from person to person, I touched a man's back and simply asked God to bless him — short and to the point. The man immediately grabbed Paulo and told him that the moment I'd touched him, he was healed from back pain. Excitedly, he asked Paulo to translate for me. I hadn't realized the man was in pain to start with, so hearing of his healing was an unexpected surprise. As Paulo shared the good news, my anger from earlier completely evaporated. In addition, God reminded me that His power to heal was not dependent on my attitude, my state of mind, or how I felt. Though my mindset and emotions were constantly shifting, my identity as a daughter of God did not change. Despite the bumps and bruises, my identity could never be taken from me. In a moment of sobering humility, I remembered that God's power couldn't be stopped by my feelings of irritation or my bad attitude. If He could only use perfect people, He wouldn't be able to use anybody. After many months of traveling through Brazil, I left with a new appreciation for the unchanging authority I carried as a child of God.

Chapter Seventeen

VENEZUELA: Praying for Seeds to Grow

During the conference in Manaus, still thinking the team would be arriving shortly, we received news that Tanya had not yet gone into labor. We decided to bump our team reunion date back and meet in Guyana (a small country bordering Brazil and Venezuela) instead of Manaus. This left us with a gap period of just under two weeks. The team at large had accepted the fact that we wouldn't have time to travel to both Venezuela and the Guianas (Guyana, Suriname, and French Guiana) if we wanted to make it home for the holidays. This meant that we would visit every country in South America except Venezuela, unless we somehow added this last country onto the Caribbean itinerary and traveled there after Christmas.

However, while brainstorming in Manaus, our small group wondered if a trip to Venezuela was actually out of the question. We had less than two weeks to potentially get in and out of Venezuela and arrive in Guyana to meet the team. Paulo offered us some Venezuelan contacts who were willing to help us last minute. With their assistance, we could feasibly complete a successful excursion to Venezuela.

While exploring our options, Ted and Carol decided to fly home early for the holidays. Ben, Moose, and Taylor found out that they needed to stay behind in Manaus to sort out passport issues. However, Elizabeth, Natalie, and I were determined to get to Venezuela.

In His divine goodness, God arranged things just right, and what had seemed like an impossible goal again became smooth and easy. Paulo connected us to his friend Raquelle who connected us to her friend Rosa who connected us to her friend Anamaria. After a few phone calls and two tiring bus rides, the three of us girls ended up at Anamaria's home in the city of Santa Elena, Venezuela. I could scarcely believe that just ten months ago, my teammates and I had arrived in Cartagena, Colombia and started the long journey down to the tip of South America. It seemed surreal that we'd circled the entire continent and had already arrived back at Venezuela, Colombia's neighbor to the east. After traveling through mountains and jungles, experiencing both icy winters and boiling summers, and most recently crossing the Amazon River, we had made it back to the top!

Anamaria, a fiery pastor of a local church, provided us with beds, constant food and coffee, and the entertainment of her children (two biological daughters and another young girl who lived at the house). Her seven-year-old daughter, Lupe, excitedly asked us where we were from as she threw in comments about her dream of going to Disneyland one day. I told her that I'd lived in California, just miles from Disneyland, and her face lit up in pure amazement. From then on, she introduced me to friends as "the one who lives near Mickey Mouse." When our new Venezuelan family found out that our palest team member, Elizabeth, was from South Africa, they confusedly asked her why she wasn't black. They constantly made remarks about her skin, and Lupe began to introduce Elizabeth as "the one who lives with tigers and elephants."

During our first night in their home, Anamaria sat with us and asked us to share our hearts for ministry. She assumed we were a typical short-term mission team who had pre-planned dramas for children's programs or cute skits to share with the church. Anamaria explained that she had a children's service scheduled for the upcoming weekend and asked what activities we normally did with kids. Slightly worried about what she'd think, we explained that our team wasn't exactly the most conventional group of missionaries. Our goal was to be led by the Holy Spirit, not to run programs that we could run entirely by our own strength. Our desire was to accomplish things that would be virtually impossible without the power of God. We told Anamaria that one of our main ministries was praying for the sick and seeing the power of God heal people. When we ran events for children, we expected the Holy Spirit to move just as powerfully as He did among the adults. The last time we'd run a children's program, we instructed the kids to ask God what He was saying, and they started drawing visions and prophetic dreams.

We weren't sure how Anamaria would react, afraid she might be disappointed that we didn't have everything planned or that we operated too "out of the box." But as we shared our hearts, a huge smile spread across her face, and she said our arrival was an answer to prayer. Her church had been contending for breakthrough in healing and seeing God's miracles, but most people had yet to experience such things firsthand. Anamaria wanted us to share with her congregation and pray for the breakthrough they'd been waiting for.

When we chatted that first night, everything appeared to click just right. We'd been brought to Santa Elena for a reason, and that reason seemed quite clear. We were eager to serve alongside Anamaria in any capacity, assuming we'd already figured out God's perfect little purpose for Venezuela. However, in keeping with the pattern of our journey, things didn't go quite as planned.

The next few days consisted of a bizarre series of events that revolved around Anamaria's demanding schedule. Our first morning, she knocked on our bedroom doors at 5 a.m. and told us to get up to pray. We groggily got out of bed to find Anamaria and a church member named Juanita passionately praying in the living room. After an hour or so, we drove to the church where we met other intercessors. I fully supported intercession, but I could hear the woman next to me repeating the same words over and over and over rather than praying something from her heart. She seemed afraid, as if she thought she needed to say the right words three hundred times or she hadn't prayed correctly. I sensed legalism and obligation, the stark opposite of the freedom to which God called His people.

The following morning, Anamaria's daughters banged on our doors bright and early for another startling wakeup and told us we had five minutes to get ready. Anamaria wanted us to go to the market to "evangelize." Unsure of what she was expecting, I reluctantly went to the market with Natalie, Elizabeth, and two of Anamaria's girls. I suspected that Anamaria wanted us to draw a crowd and start preaching as loudly as possible, but the thought of creating a spectacle and barking at passersby in Spanish horrified me. Instead, we decided to simply walk around the market, talk to people, and pray for them. However, the hearts of the people in Santa Elena were closed, and we were continually rejected. Anamaria showed up after about an hour of awkward attempts at prayer, and we told her that we'd neglected to accomplish anything significant. She explained that the people in her city were afraid of foreigners, and she had known all along that we wouldn't be well-received. It seemed that we'd been deliberately set up to fail.

Later in the week, we were out in the city with Juanita, the woman we'd met at our 5 a.m. prayer time. She received a call from Anamaria, who ordered her to drive us to the church right away to run the children's program. After our initial conversation about not having prepared dramas or specialized programs, we got the impression that Anamaria was not including us in her children's ministry and wanted us to focus on healing and sharing testimonies. Yet, without a second of warning, we were shoved in a car, dropped off at the church, and thrown in front of a group of kids. A bit befuddled by the demand to run a program out of thin air, we started asking the children to close their eyes and ask God what He was telling them. When they shared, their responses were, "I am a bad person," or "I need to be more obedient," or "I'm a mean sister." As I listened to the children, I noticed an alarming theme of fear and control.

Whenever we tried to talk to Anamaria or get information about the week's schedule, we were told she was busy. She expected us to do tasks for her at a moment's notice but blew us off when we had questions. I wanted to confront her about her attitude but felt it was not my place. Natalie and Elizabeth felt the same. We spent our days confused and frustrated.

After a few days, we received news that Taylor, Ben, and Moose got their passports sorted in Brazil and would make it to Venezuela after all. Juanita kindly offered to host the guys in her house. They arrived on Saturday, and the following morning, we attended Anamaria's church service together. We were shocked to see that her congregation was comprised of about only fifteen people. All of her meetings, all of the demanding orders, and all of her oh-so-busy schedule had given us the impression that Anamaria was the pastor of a megachurch. Yet, we realized that her congregation was just a tiny group of very fearful people. When Anamaria clapped, the congregation clapped. When she stood, they stood. When she knelt, they knelt.

Appalled by the way the congregation seemed to worship their pastor, I bowed my head and prayed that these people would have genuine encounters with the love of God and walk in true freedom. After worship, Anamaria called our team up front and gave us a chance to share. We talked about freedom, God's power instead of our own control, and identity. I hoped that truth would pierce Anamaria's heart and the hearts of her congregants. However, I wondered if our words would actually take root in their spirits or if they would merely be dismissed. I wondered what Anamaria really thought about us. I wondered why I had come to Venezuela at all. At first, I had thought it was to serve Anamaria. Yet, I soon realized God had not sent my team for the person seen in the front of the church but actually for a few of the least visible members.

Ben and I prayed for a quiet girl in the congregation who requested prayer for her family. While praying, Ben received a word of knowledge about wrist pain and asked if anyone in the girl's family had wrist pain. She extended her arm towards us and said that she did. We prayed for her wrist, and the pain left right away. Surprised, she went over and showed her friend. God heals His children, because it's His good pleasure. *That* is love.

Natalie, Elizabeth, and I spent time talking to the girl who lived at Anamaria's house (not her biological daughter) and realized her value was constantly being challenged. She was treated more like a servant than a daughter and needed to know that her worth didn't come from how many dishes she could wash but purely who she was as a daughter of God. So we spent time talking, laughing, and telling her she was beautiful (something I am not sure she'd heard many times before). She begged us to stay longer, and I realized maybe God had sent us just for her.

As the week progressed, we girls hung out at Juanita's house to spend some time with her as well as Taylor, Moose, and Ben. We realized it was God's perfect plan to get the boys to Santa Elena. If they hadn't made it, we wouldn't have had much of a connection with Juanita. Juanita was another person who was slightly under the radar but in serious need of being noticed. She worked for a tourism company that took people to beautiful waterfalls a couple of hours outside of the city, and she offered to take all six of us for free. We gladly accepted her kind offer. Juanita appeared discouraged when we left Santa Elena, but while at the waterfalls, her spirit seemed lighter. She had raised two sons who were now adults, and I think she felt a sense of family when she spent time with the boys on our team. She smiled as she watched Moose and Taylor playing in the waterfalls and told us girls that they seemed like two big kids. We laughed and agreed with her conclusion. I could tell that Juanita missed her own sons, and some piece of her heart came alive when she was with us. She told Natalie that she'd felt terribly sad lately, but when we came, she started to feel different.

Juanita opened up to us about how she'd been hurt within the church and was tired of being controlled. Part of her wanted to leave the church, but she also longed to see change there. She felt trapped and had no one to talk to. Her husband already had bitterness against the church, and she knew venting to him would only cause more. Within the church, she found herself unable to speak freely about the issues she observed. When she saw that we noticed the brokenness no one else wanted to admit, she opened up her heart to us. As we spoke with Juanita, encouraged her, hugged her as she cried, and prayed for her, I knew it was no mistake we'd come to Venezuela.

I wish I could say that by the time we left, everyone's problems were reconciled, and revival and change broke out in the church. Unfortunately, that didn't happen. When we said goodbye, there was still a lot that needed to be confronted and dealt with in that little church in Santa Elena, Venezuela. Despite the mess, we knew it'd been worth our travels just to be with Juanita and the girl who lived in Anamaria's house and some of those in the church who didn't normally get the time of day. At times throughout our journey, we witnessed people dramatically healed of physical ailments. At other times, we saw remarkable inner healing. Still, at other times, all we got to see were tiny seeds planted; and the best we could do was pray that they would grow into something beautiful.

During our last night in Venezuela, we received a message from Jesse and Tanya. I thought nothing could surprise me at this point, but their news shocked me. They had prayed in Fortaleza about changing plans and returning to America for the birth of their second child. Tanya asked for four different confirmations from the Lord and received all four. She and Jesse decided to fly back to the States for the delivery — and *not* return for the Caribbean. Someone else would lead the last leg; their time with the team was over.

We would still meet the rest of the team in Guyana, distressingly without Jesse and Tanya. The "birthing team" would meet us there without having been a part of the birth. The vehicle owners and others were ready to leave Fortaleza and would meet us in Guyana as well. Excited to see our teammates but taken aback by the loss of Jesse and Tanya, my small group said goodbye to Venezuela and journeyed towards the tiny trio of countries that would complete our South American adventure.

Chapter Eighteen

THE GUIANAS: South America Complete!

This was it — the final stretch of the continent. We would end our time in the Guianas, a group of barely-known countries on the northern coast of South America. Though considered one entity, the Guianas were actually comprised of three countries: Guyana, Suriname, and French Guiana. Technically considered part of the Caribbean, the Guianas exuded an Afro-Caribe vibe as well as cultural flavors from the countries that colonized them — England (Guyana), Holland (Suriname), and France (French Guiana).

My small group made our way to Guyana via a hellish route from Venezuela. Because there was no legal Venezuela-Guyana border crossing, we had to travel from Venezuela back to Brazil, then to Guyana — hitting a record three countries in one day. From the border of Guyana and Brazil, we made our way to the capital city of Georgetown, less than three hundred miles north but a nightmarishly long journey due to abysmal infrastructure.

Upon our arrival at the Guyana border, we were bombarded by minibus drivers who offered to transport us to Georgetown, claiming the best rates. Unaccustomed to bargaining in English, we happily negotiated prices in our native language after over a year of Spanish and Portuguese.

At around 2 p.m., our driver informed us that we would be in Georgetown by around ten or eleven o'clock that evening. After a couple of hours bumping along terrible dirt roads, our bus driver informed us that if we didn't reach a certain "checkpoint" by 6 p.m. we would have to rest somewhere for the night and continue traveling the following morning. Though the driver acted unsure as to whether we would reach the checkpoint or not, we later found out that it had never been a feasible option to cross and make it to Georgetown the same evening. Apparently, the lies of arriving by ten or eleven were not only absurd on such poor roads but also logistically impossible.

Just before 6 p.m., we were forced to pull over on the side of the road where we found a little hut, a food shack, and two local men who sat staring at us. I reluctantly set up my sleeping mat on the floor of the hut, already getting eaten alive by bugs. Throughout the next few hours, the hut filled with hammocks and several men from other buses that had also failed to reach the 6 p.m. checkpoint. We were instructed to sleep until 3 a.m., when we would get up and drive for a few more hours to arrive at the checkpoint by 6 a.m.

After a few hours of attempted sleep, we reloaded our minibuses and drove to the infamous checkpoint. Upon arrival, I realized why its closing would have presented problems for us. The "checkpoint" was actually a river that divided the road, and the only way to cross was by taking a crickity, old ferry that only made trips between 6 a.m. and 6 p.m. each day. The decrepit, small boat looked like it was about to fall apart, and watching several minibuses awkwardly drive on and off of it didn't inspire much confidence.

Nonetheless, we safely made it to the other side and continued our drive towards Georgetown. Besides frequently being stopped at intermittent passport checkpoints, our journey otherwise consisted of frighteningly fast driving. It was clear that our driver's priority was getting to Georgetown as quickly as possible; but as he recklessly maneuvered dangerous curves and unstable potholes, my priority quickly became arriving as *alive* as possible.

Meanwhile, dust from the roads poured into our vehicle and covered us from head to toe. We rotated between opening the windows in an attempt to not sweat to death and closing them to avoid choking on large clouds of dust. Almost twenty-four hours after leaving the border, we arrived in Georgetown with aching backs from the jarring ride, skin and hair covered in dirt, and luggage that had barely survived. My suitcase, which had been on its last legs for a while, realized its death along the way. When it was unloaded from atop the minibus, the inside frame was smashed in, holes had ripped in the sides of the bag, and my clothes and belongings inside were wet, muddy, and damaged.

Within days, the rest of the team arrived in Georgetown with similar horror stories. We laughed at the absurdity of our lives and excitedly caught up on our time apart. And sadly, we began our official debriefing of our time in South America. We spent time encouraging each person and sharing what good we saw in one another. As we spoke, I realized how much all of us had changed in the past fourteen months. We'd shared obstacles and victories together, and every moment (whether good or bad) had been well worth it. Though we'd worked with ministries throughout an entire continent, our most important mission had been the same in every country — our love for God and our love for one another.

We also spent some time processing the huge change that had just happened to our team. Losing our leaders so suddenly was a shocking change. Everyone supported the wise decision for their family, but we were still reeling from the fact that we'd never even said goodbye. As we discussed the future and how the Caribbean would pan out without Jesse and Tanya, it sounded like people were losing interest in going to the Caribbean altogether. The final leg of the journey was in danger of fizzling out.

My heart sank. Though most people probably think of the Caribbean as nothing more than a tourist destination, for years God had given me a vision to travel to the most impoverished islands. Many people used the Caribbean for vacation, for pleasure, for imports, for sex tourism, or for whatever else they desired. But my heart had been longing to go to the people who everyone else forgot. I yearned to visit the orphans, the widows, the prostitutes, the street children, and the families living in shacks within the islands — the people hidden from the view of those who used the Caribbean only for their own pleasure.

It broke my heart to watch such a quick loss of vision — and team members. Several of the girls decided to fly home after our reunion in Guyana instead of finishing the itinerary to Suriname and French Guiana. This meant only eleven of us would cross the finish line together at the end of South America even though we'd once been a team of over thirty people. Since the majority of my teammates were now unlikely returning for the Caribbean, I realized that this was a final goodbye for most of us. I hadn't been prepared to say goodbye to so many people this suddenly. And I certainly wasn't prepared to finish the journey without my full team, especially without Jesse and Tanya. It seemed like our team and vision was disappearing in the blink of an eye.

This didn't feel right. I didn't know what to do — so, I cried. Natalie M., a fiercely loyal friend, saw my tears and gave me her word that she would go to the Caribbean with me, even if it was just the two of us. We wouldn't give up. She later spoke in front of the whole team and announced, "Caitlin was crying over her vision for the islands. God gave her a heart for the Caribbean, and she should lead us. I'm following Caitlin's vision and going with her."

Person after person chimed in, each one agreeing that I should lead and make this happen. I couldn't believe it. When I had first joined the team, I felt like the weakest link in the entire group. Now, fourteen months later, my teammates were electing me to lead the last leg of our journey and complete our vision. Humbled and moved beyond words, I shared my vision for the islands and asked if anyone would actually come with me. Many hands went up. In moments, I'd gone from feeling like my dream had been stolen from me to feeling like I had been given an opportunity beyond my wildest dreams — the chance to lead my own dream the way I'd always envisioned it. *Incredible.*

On November 5, 2012, we began a series of tearful goodbyes when the first group flew home from Guyana. My teammates were far beyond friends; they were forever family. Unable to put my love into adequate words, I simply hugged them tightly, tears pouring out of my eyes. This was really goodbye.

The remaining eleven went on to finish the last two countries, Suriname and French Guiana. Though emotionally and physically exhausted by this point, we knew we had a mission to finish and vowed to move forward. We first traveled to

Paramaribo, the capital of Suriname, via minibus, ferry, and another minibus. Though Georgetown's English-speaking Caribbean flair seemed out of place in South America, Suriname's culture felt even more bizarre. Suriname exhibited an unusual clash of cultures including Dutch, Indian, Chinese, and Indonesian.

We found a small hostel in Paramaribo and met together to pray for God's vision for Suriname. Elizabeth had felt a special tug in her heart for the country and believed our time would be marked by random encounters that only God could set up for us.

On our first day, I went to the grocery store with Taylor M. who approached a stranger on crutches and offered to pray for his leg. The man shut down Taylor immediately. *Pure and cold rejection.* I wondered if all hearts in this country were so closed. A few hours later, we walked to a local church, just minutes from our hostel, to attend their evening service and to ask the pastor if we could serve his church. When we entered the church, there appeared to be only two congregants, but the pastor was too proud to step down from his stage to even acknowledge the presence of several clearly foreign visitors. We tried to speak to him, but we again felt harsh rejection and ended up leaving the church building.

Admittedly, my spirits were low. I was worn out to the core. I'd been suffering from a horrible ear infection that began in Brazil and was now causing pain all the way down to my jaw. I could barely hear when people spoke to me, and I was growing frustrated by the rejection from the Surinamese people. In addition, I was still trying to recover from the trauma of losing over half of our team before finishing the trip. My heart was heavy, and my motivation was severely lacking. I knew most of my teammates were already enjoying the luxury of proper beds, nice toilets, and pampering from their moms and dads. I reminded myself that the remaining eleven still had weeks ahead of us. I wanted to end in victory, not simply limp along at the end. But how could I do this?

After being rejected by the pastor, we decided to check out the city square and see if we could find some food or anything interesting going on. We noticed a large sign advertising a gospel concert and stopped under it for a moment. Two young Surinamese men approached us and explained that they ran a national Christian radio show for youth. We told them a bit about our journey, and they invited us to speak on their show in two days. We excitedly agreed, and my spirit began to come back alive as I saw God's faithfulness in bringing forth unexpected encounters.

The young men asked us if we'd like to see the radio station right then, so we followed them two blocks to the station where their friend was already in the middle of a broadcast. He introduced himself and invited us to sit and listen to the music he was playing. Suddenly, he told us to be silent. He was switching from music to talking, and we were live. Before I could even register that we were not, in fact, waiting for two more days before going on the air, a microphone was in my face, and I was on a live broadcast being aired throughout the entire nation. Flustered and slightly miffed that I just so happened to be the one sitting closest to the radio man, I gulped and coyly spoke into the microphone. "Hello Suriname…"

The broadcaster asked me several questions, and my mouth began to answer before I even had a moment to think. Afterwards, the man interviewed every member of my team, giving us each a very unexpected but special opportunity. At the end of the broadcast, Natalie M. was asked to pray for all of

Suriname. Our day of rejection had abruptly transformed into something amazing.

Feeling more hopeful, we headed to the hospital the next morning to pray for patients. We had such a great time talking and praying for people that we ended up returning the following day to pray some more. Some of the people whom we'd prayed for the first day seemed to be doing better physically and emotionally on the second day.

As we asked to pray for people, we noticed the large mixture of religions in Suriname including Christianity, Buddhism, Hindu, and Islam. Yet, no matter what religion people were, all of them told us that we were welcome to pray to Jesus. Despite my original impression of a cold and closed people, I started to feel an authentic warmth from the culture. I was fascinated by the way the different religious and cultural groups genuinely loved and respected each other and lived in peace and harmony.

Taylor M., Ben, and I prayed for a woman named Gloria who had lost all feeling in her leg out of nowhere. She said the doctors were unable to figure out the cause, and she was waiting for a diagnosis. Meanwhile, she struggled to walk on this leg and hoped the feeling would somehow return.

We laid hands on her leg and began to pray. As we spoke, her leg started to shake beneath our hands, and she excitedly reported that the feeling had come back. Gloria looked shocked. We asked her to try to walk, and she got out of bed and paced around the room. She smiled in awe. Ben declared, "Jesus just healed your leg." The other women in the room, Buddhist and Hindu, watched and clapped in celebration.

The unpredictable divine appointments continued when Ben walked to a nearby park to spend some time alone with the

Lord. A woman named Sandra approached him out of the blue and asked for help. She explained that her boyfriend had just broken up with her, and she was overwhelmed and heartbroken. She was afraid to face her children back home and was waiting in Paramaribo, unsure of what to do. Ben counseled her a bit and prayed for her as she began to cry. He asked if she'd be willing to meet him later at the park, and she agreed to return at five o'clock. Ben walked to our hostel and asked if any of the girls would like to come back with him to minister to her.

A few hours later, I accompanied Ben to the park and met Sandra. She seemed like an open woman, seeking love and wisdom, yet slightly uncomfortable in her own skin. As we talked, she slowly revealed pieces of her story to us, explaining that she had three children from three different men. Now, her most recent boyfriend had left her. She had no job and no way to provide for her kids. She felt lost.

Her eldest daughter, fourteen years old, repeatedly criticized Sandra for her poor choices and constantly declared that she would never be like her. Her other children were angry that their fathers were not around. Sandra kept saying, "I never wanted my life to be like this. I never planned this. I wanted one husband and father for my kids. I never wanted my life to go like this."

I realized that more importantly than forgiving the men who'd mistreated her or forgiving her children for their anger, Sandra needed to forgive herself. I prayed for Sandra and asked her to repeat these words: "I forgive myself. I am free from the words of my daughter. I am loved. I am free." After this, she seemed lighter. Sandra said she was ready to face her family now and more equipped to love her daughter. When Ben and I left Sandra, she was a smiling woman.

Days later, we continued on to our last country in South America, French Guiana. This final trek included another three-hour minibus ride to the border and a motorized canoe ride from one side of customs to the other. When we arrived on the French Guiana side of the border, we noticed a large sign that read "France." We found out that French Guiana was still a department of France, not a fully independent country. So technically, we were in France, South America, and the Caribbean all at once. What a way to end!

The drawback of being in "France" was French prices. We'd been warned that French Guiana was ridiculously expensive and decided to only stay for a few days to avoid going broke. Several people claimed we would need to spend at least forty euros a night just for a hostel, and we weren't sure how we'd swing these prices. We prayed that God would provide some type of miraculous accommodation, but we'd heard that affordable hotels didn't exist in the country. By the grace of God, an angel in a pickup truck appeared at the border and asked us if we needed a cheap place to stay. For no cost, just simply for the sake of being kind, he led us to a low-priced hotel near the border where we each paid around six U.S. dollars a night.

We'd heard that there were indigenous villages all along the river and decided to go for a visit. I told God I would be satisfied if He sent us even one person to touch with an encounter of love. Just *one* person would be enough.

A few of us bargained with a man on the river to take our group on his canoe to a nearby indigenous community. I had no idea if this would be awkward or awesome. We boated just fifteen minutes upriver and were dropped off for a couple of hours in a beautiful and quiet village. We cautiously entered the village and said hello to some people watching us, hoping they would receive our presence warmly. We asked someone if the chief was available in order to get his blessing to walk around the community and pray for people. We were immediately welcomed with open hearts and given permission to do as we pleased. While passing by a porch where a few people sat, we struck up a conversation with one of the women, who soon asked us to pray for her sick brother who was lying in a hammock just feet away from her.

We prayed for the man and the other women on the porch, and word of our visit quickly spread. Within minutes, other people from the community appeared at the porch to see what we were doing and lined up for prayer. I had asked God for just one person, but it seemed He had given us a whole village. For the next two hours, we talked and prayed with several of the villagers. One young man pointed to his ears, and it appeared that he couldn't hear or speak. While we prayed, he began to shake by the presence of God, and his face lit up with a brilliant smile. He still spoke no words but gave us the thumbs up signal, indicating that some type of healing had been received.

We then prayed for another woman with ear problems. From what I understood, her ears were clogged, and her hearing was affected. Still dealing with my own ear infection, I laid hands on the woman's ears, hoping both of us would get healed. Intriguingly, as I prayed for her, *my* ear opened. In addition, the woman began to lift her hands and praise God. She didn't explain what was happening, but based on her reaction, I assumed her ears were also healed. Oddly, when I took my hands off of her, my ear closed back up. (My ear ended up healing completely a few days later, but I found it interesting that my own ear opened and closed while praying for someone with the same condition). Afterwards, we were asked to visit another woman's house where we prayed for a few others until our boat came back to the village to pick us up. On our canoe ride home, we were amazed at how quickly and beautifully God had arranged this time for us.

Our team left French Guiana on November 14th and later received news that Tanya's baby, a little boy named Zion, was born that same day. Just as we were leaving the very last country of the continent and completing the vision for South America, new life came forth. It was a sweet reminder that every end meant a new beginning.

Unfortunately, we weren't able to fly home directly from French Guiana, which meant backtracking through Suriname and Guyana and flying from Georgetown. We stayed in Suriname for two nights en route and noticed a homeless man begging for spare change on the first evening. Breck stopped to talk with him for a few minutes, and a couple of people offered him coins and food. We walked back to our hostel, thinking very little of this encounter.

The following night, we passed by the same man and decided to talk to him some more. His name was Theo. He remembered Breck from the night before and thanked him for speaking to him instead of passing him by like everyone else. Theo explained that people normally ignored him or treated him like an animal, having no value for him because he lived on the streets. We spent time praying for Theo and simply chatting about his life and family. We quickly discerned that Theo was a far cry from the stereotypical addict on the streets panhandling to pay for drugs. His heart was genuine and pure, and the only thing he craved was love. I'll never forget his words. "You stopped for me. You talked to me. You treated me like a person. I feel better inside now." What had originally meant very little to us had meant the world to Theo. An encounter with love, no matter how big or small, changes people.

After a while, we headed back to our hostel, sobered by our interaction with Theo. I wondered if it was just a coincidence that this man's name literally meant "god." Holding back tears, it hit me — LOVE. This was what our journey was all about. We'd traveled for over fourteen months and through twenty-one different nations. We'd seen miracles, watched amazing prophecies realized, and rubbed shoulders with great leaders. But in the end, I realized every adventure, every snapshot taken in a foreign country, every skill learned, and even every healing miracle would have meant nothing without love. The greatest miracle possible is the simple love of the gospel, and that will never change. We can pray for healings, visit ministries around the whole world, and prophesy until our faces turn blue. But without simple, genuine love it's all worthless.

While reflecting on the journey, I contemplated the greatest lesson I'd learned along the way. After such an extensive trip, I hoped to fly home with something profound. Yet, the more I mulled over the past fourteen months, I realized this was and always would be the deepest thing I had to offer:

Love God. Love people.

That simple combination will never fail you.

"If I speak in the tongues of men or of angels, but do not have love, I am only a resounding gong or a clanging cymbal. If I have the gift of prophecy and can fathom all mysteries and all knowledge, and if I have a faith that can move mountains, but do not have love, I am nothing. If I give all I possess to the poor and give over my body to hardship that I may boast, but do not have love, I gain nothing.

Love never fails. But where there are prophecies, they will cease; where there are tongues, they will be stilled; where there is knowledge, it will pass away.

And now these three remain: faith, hope and love. But the greatest of these is love" (1 Corinthians 13:1-3, 8, 13).

Part Three: The Caribbean

Chapter Nineteen
Casting New Vision

It was now November 2012. Elizabeth and I were the last two on a plane out of South America, feeling as though we were slowly being tortured as we said goodbye to teammate after teammate. Not knowing who I would see in the Caribbean made it that much more painful. This could be the last time I got to hug some of my favorite people in the world.

I arrived in the States ready for a break but knowing God was not done with me. I asked my teammates to let me know whether or not they would join me for the Caribbean excursion by mid-December, giving me a few weeks to plan with some estimate of the team's size. Because the holidays provided a natural stopping point, the majority of the team decided to celebrate Christmas with family and then begin the next season of their lives. Though many had expressed interest in the Caribbean during our meeting in Guyana, only a handful chose to actually come. Even if it was only two of us, I felt a responsibility to complete the original vision for the trip. We'd told people all around the world that we were going to share the gospel in

Central America, South America, *and* the Caribbean. Somebody needed to fulfill our word and carry out the third and final segment of the Iris Latin America vision.

Throughout our time in Central and South America, I'd heard a wide variety of ideas about what our time in the Caribbean would look like. Back then, we'd envisioned nearly thirty of us traveling by boat, sailing from island to island, living a perfect adventure. Reality now looked like a very different picture.

I was okay with different. In fact, I kind of liked how things had drastically changed. Change birthed opportunity for new vision. The plan for the Caribbean was wide open. It was time to dream with God again.

Because there were over seven thousand islands in the Caribbean, I wasn't quite sure where to start. While looking on a map, I quickly realized it would take us years to visit all of the islands and knew I needed to prioritize.

I was focused on quality over quantity by visiting fewer islands but spending more time in each country. My heart was set on traveling to just a handful of the poorest islands and really getting "down and dirty." I wanted to minister in the prisons, in the shanty towns, and in the orphanages. Before separating from my teammates in Guyana, I had asked what others thought. A couple of people shared a similar vision — less countries with more time on each island. I suggested visiting Haiti, the Dominican Republic (also known as the DR), Jamaica, and maybe Cuba (knowing Cuba was extremely needy but doubting Americans would be allowed entry).

As I was discussing this idea with a few teammates, Taylor L. entered the room and overheard our conversation.

Interestingly, he announced that he'd recently had a dream that coincided precisely with what we were talking about.

Taylor could see a few islands from a bird's-eye view. The islands were large and located in the northern part of the Caribbean, close to the United States. Taylor was standing like a giant over the islands, able to see their topography perfectly, and he stepped easily from one island to another.

Immediately after he shared his dream, I looked at a map. Sure enough, there were a few large islands located in the northern part of the Caribbean, near the U.S. They included the four countries I had just suggested, as well as the island of Puerto Rico.

Later on, I asked a few friends to pray about how many countries should comprise the Caribbean leg of the trip. Though I had mentioned four specific nations, I repeatedly felt God telling me *five*. Several people confirmed this, also hearing five. As I continued to pray, I felt God was telling me to go to Puerto Rico — the fifth large landmass I'd seen earlier while looking at a map. Puerto Rico didn't seem to fit in with my vision of visiting the poorest countries of the Caribbean, so I was a bit unsure. I asked Jesse and Tanya to pray from afar, and they believed Puerto Rico was a definite "yes." I did a bit of research and found out that the Caribbean was divided into the Lesser Antilles and Greater Antilles. The Lesser Antilles consisted of a string of small islands stretching from southerly Aruba all the way north to the Virgin Islands. In the northern region of the Caribbean was the Greater Antilles, a group of larger islands comprised of Puerto Rico, Hispaniola (encompassing the Dominican Republic and Haiti), Cuba, and Jamaica.

This meant that if we just focused on the Greater Antilles, we would visit the four poorest countries in the Caribbean plus the U.S. territory of Puerto Rico. I still had many doubts that getting into Cuba was realistic, but I knew God was confirming these regions were the five He was speaking about. In January 2013, we would begin the last leg of the Iris Latin America trip by reconvening in Puerto Rico. From there, we would fly to the Dominican Republic, continue by bus to Haiti (these two countries are connected to form one large island), fly to Cuba (God willing), and finally fly to Jamaica. Jamaica would be our twenty-sixth and final country.

During my holiday break, I spent a significant chunk of time preparing for the Caribbean, doing hours of research, Skype calls, and emails. After very suddenly being designated our new team leader, I had mixed feelings. Such authority felt like both a huge privilege and a heap of unwanted pressure. Though leading gave me an opportunity to plan the Caribbean trip the way I'd always envisioned it, it also meant accepting the burden of anything that went awry.

By mid-December, I'd received news that only Natalie M. and Roberta would be joining me in Puerto Rico. Aleeza would meet us in the Dominican Republic and finish the remainder of the trip. This was shockingly less people than I'd hoped for. A team of just four women meant that the concept of "safety in numbers" no longer existed. We'd lost every man on the team, so we were left to fend for ourselves without our faithful protectors. In addition, smaller numbers demanded far more dedication from each of us. When we'd split into small groups within the big team, everyone had to step up and work ten times harder than normal. There was no space to hide and let someone else do the dirty work. We had to be on our toes at all times, ready to preach, clean, testify, counsel, whatever — because there was no one else to do it for us. This would now be our daily reality in the islands.

I felt the magnitude of this commitment as well as the weight of the spiritual preparation involved in leading such an unexpectedly modified team. I could no longer ride on the coattails of Jesse and Tanya's vision. I needed to get on my knees before the Lord and ask for the wisdom to lead. I also needed to pray for some testosterone to make its way down to the Caribbean.

As I wondered how things would pan out, God continually reminded me that this was a season to dream with Him as a daughter dreaming with her Father. My years of longing to minister in the islands were coming to fruition, and I needed to maintain a heart of gratitude, not a heart of worry. Serving in the Caribbean would not be a test of obedience but rather a test of belief. Would I dare to dream with God and trust Him to bless the desires of my heart?

After deciding that our first island would be Puerto Rico, I began to try to land contacts there. I was still a bit confused as to why we should spend any time in this affluent U.S. territory but knew God had added it to our itinerary for a reason. However, whenever I tried to connect with ministries in Puerto Rico, every door seemed to slam shut. I reminded myself not to become dismayed and focused on God's voice. Regardless of circumstances, I knew God had something significant for us in Puerto Rico. Natalie stood in faith with me and prayed for God to knock down whatever walls were keeping us from serving in Puerto Rico. She had a vision of a door that said "Puerto Rico" on it. *It appeared to be closed, but suddenly an invisible hand came from behind and opened it.*

Natalie also received a prophecy that we would encounter an influential man in Puerto Rico who would set us up for the rest of our time in the Caribbean. He would be a well-known man, and name-dropping would help establish us with vital connections. In addition, Natalie's friend saw a vision of a man traveling with us throughout the islands. We didn't know how or when, but we did believe God would open doors for us as well as bring us a male team member. We accepted the given prophecies in faith. I knew that doubtful situations did not change God's voice and that circumstances and feelings did not have the authority to challenge what was *true*. Though tempted to worry, I decided to press on despite how things appeared. Natalie, Roberta, and I took a leap of faith and booked our tickets to Puerto Rico before establishing a single contact on the island.

During the holiday break, I thanked God every day for His plans for the Caribbean team, for the people we would meet along the way, and for the doors He had promised to open in Puerto Rico. Time ticked away. I sent a million emails to ministries in Puerto Rico. I heard nothing in return…then more of nothing…and still nothing.

Just a week before our flights, I received an email from a pastor at Bethel Church in California. He'd mysteriously lost a message I'd sent him weeks prior and apologized profusely for getting back to me with such delay. He figured it was too late at this point but forwarded me the contact information of a pastor named Edwin in Puerto Rico nonetheless. I immediately emailed Edwin and told him about our team. Just fifteen minutes later, I received a response. After a couple of emails and a few phone calls, we had a ride from the airport, a free place to stay, and an amazing church to work with.

Before arriving in the Caribbean, God confirmed that He would prove faithful if we persevered even when we couldn't see what was happening. He was already testing our faith, and we were pressing onward in the hopes of great things to come. Though our Caribbean team was small, the ministry ahead was not. This last leg of our journey would be the completion of an epic vision — the final chapter of a beautiful story of faith, adventure, and God's love.

Chapter Twenty

PUERTO RICO: Fresh Flavor, New Favor

On January 10, 2013, I returned to my unpredictable missionary life as I said goodbye to my family, my comfortable bed, my hot shower, and my home turf. During my holiday break in the States, I'd already become accustomed to life back at home. I boarded the plane to Puerto Rico and faced that moment I dread every time I return to the mission field, that painful moment of tension between excitement for the adventure ahead and the fear of territory completely unknown. It's the ache of turning my back on my loved ones and everything familiar, while trying to be strong enough to run into my destiny. It's that moment where I am exactly where I am supposed to be, yet loss and fear try to tell me otherwise — and where pieces of myself are painfully squeezed out of me, making room for new cultures, new friends, and new missions.

Upon landing, the blast of warm air in the San Juan airport eased my spinning mind. The heat of the island made everything seem better. I excitedly reunited with Natalie M. and Roberta at the airport and found Pastor Edwin and his beautiful wife, Maggie, without any problems. Edwin and Maggie drove us to their home in the city of Arecibo where they lived with their daughter, Nahir, and son-in-law, David. They announced that we would be split up between their home and their friend's house. Roberta and I stayed with Edwin's family, who made us feel at home in every way. When Edwin had agreed to take us in so last minute, I assumed his family would be quite kind and welcoming, but their hospitality was even greater than what I'd hoped for. And when Maggie confessed her obsession with both cheese and chocolate, I knew we were a perfect match.

Meanwhile, Natalie was hosted by a wonderful woman named Barbie who regularly invited me and Roberta over. Barbie explained that when her husband built their home, he purposefully added extra rooms to accommodate guests. They wanted to provide a safe haven for missionaries and told us that their house was just as much ours as theirs. Barbie's daughter, Sally, agreed to accompany us around the island for the following ten days — taking us to home groups, prayer meetings, church services, homeless outreaches, and evangelism events on the beach and in the marketplace. Sally served as our island guide, outreach coordinator, and newest *amiga*. Full of love, generosity, solid faith, and lots of laughs, Sally became part of our Iris family almost instantly. God knew that I was missing many of my old teammates and that Sally was going through her own battle. Like sisters, we just understood each other and were able to encourage one another during this crucial time. Without a doubt, God had brought us together.

On our first Sunday morning in Puerto Rico, we visited Vida Abundant Church, a congregation pastored by good friends of Edwin and Maggie. They said that Natalie, Roberta, and I could each share a bit but requested that one person preach a full-on sermon. While traveling with twenty to thirty people, I occasionally shared testimonies with churches but always left the preaching to somebody else. We depended on a few regular speakers, and I was certainly not one of them. I didn't know if I could preach or not, because I'd never really tried.

But now, left without much of a choice, I was forced to step out of my comfort zone and do it. When we first arrived at Vida Abundant Church, I was really nervous, but the Holy Spirit gradually brought me peace. I opened my mouth, and the words flowed out effortlessly. My first sermon in Puerto Rico went much smoother than expected. After the service, one girl came up to me and said she was called to share the gospel in places far from home. When she saw me preaching, it confirmed that she could do it too, because I was young like her. I guess I wasn't the only girl God was calling out of her comfort zone.

Before leaving the church, Roberta, Natalie, and I spent an hour or two praying for each individual in the congregation. Unexpected prophetic words spilled from my tongue. People were crying and telling me I'd confirmed specific things in their lives, without me having a clue as to what I was saying. This was amazing.

After everyone else finally left the church, we prayed and prophesied over the pastor and his family. Touched by what the Holy Spirit was saying, they were moved to tears and hugged us with gratitude for our visit. The pastor and his wife insisted on taking us out to lunch and also blessed us each with very unexpected offerings. Amazed by their generosity, I humbly accepted a donation that covered my flight to Puerto Rico as well as half of my flight to the Dominican Republic. I was speechless.

In addition, the pastor of Vida Abundant connected us to a friend of his named Luis who led a church in the Dominican Republic. I had been in contact with someone from the DR for almost two months and had wasted countless hours exchanging emails, Skype calls, and messages in vain. I was desperately trying to nail down the contact and finalize our arrangements, knocking down the door with my own strength but getting nowhere. In the end, the man with whom I'd been communicating bailed on me. However, our new friend in Puerto Rico assured us that Pastor Luis would help us out. After a four-minute Skype conversation with Luis, we once again had a ride from the airport, a free place to stay, and ministry opportunities in the Dominican Republic. After months of communication and failing to plan anything productive, God provided everything we needed in just four minutes.

On Sunday evening, we met up with some local church members to assist with their homeless ministry. We distributed food and water to needy families and individuals around Arecibo. One of our stops was at Pousada de Amor, a place where homeless men and women were provided with food and beds during the week. However, during the weekends, the facility was locked. The local group from the church brought food on Saturdays and Sundays, giving meals to the homeless individuals before they slept outside in the parking lot. We approached each individual and prayed for them one by one. A young man named Julio told us that he was ten days clean from drugs. He prayed with us, renouncing his ties to drugs and breaking the chains of addiction off of his life. Julio's heart was touched, and he began to weep, filled with the hope that he could have a positive future. Natalie saw a vision of Julio speaking in a church, sharing his story with others. Though we only saw the first step of his restoration process, we believed God would complete His work and bring Julio into a beautiful destiny.

Afterwards, we drove to a large, dimly lit building with a dark field behind it. We were escorted down a long dirt path by one of the local guys who knew the exact crevices where certain homeless individuals were located. He led us into an abyss of darkness until we wound up in a dodgy corner where a couple appeared to be living or hiding — or both. The homeless man we encountered couldn't have been more than twenty-five, but he had already been sucked into a world of demons and drugs. Endless supplies of needles surrounded him, and he was so strung out that he couldn't put even one coherent sentence together. This man was a slave, heroin his master. A young woman stood close by but turned her back on us as we approached her. Smoking crack, she shut out the rest of the world and didn't acknowledge a single person who tried to say hello.

One of the women from the church began to weep as she watched the scene in front of us. Assuming she was disturbed by the severity of the couple's addiction, I admired her heart of compassion. But as Natalie talked to this woman, she found out why the situation was affecting her so deeply. The lady explained that she'd known the young man shooting up heroin since he was a little boy. Seeing him transform his life into a mess of drugs broke her heart.

And then, suddenly, I remembered. I remembered that the drug addicts we ministered to weren't always drug addicts. Once upon a time, they were precious babies in the arms of their mothers. Then they were little boys and little girls, kids who got excited when they learned how to tie their shoes and write the letters of the alphabet. Once upon a time, they were pure and innocent and clean. But then something — something grotesque — came into their lives and perverted all that was good. These little boys and little girls turned into men and women who lived in dark corners where they hid from the world and shot heroin into their veins. The disturbing reality of the situation in front of us was worth mourning. Unsure of what else to do, we prayed for God's presence to flood that place. The young man and woman were too far gone to understand any words we were saying, but we prayed that truth would penetrate their spirits. *Oh Lord, have mercy on these lost ones.*

The intensity mellowed a bit as our week went on, and God showed us rays of hope after showing us a glimpse of such darkness. During one youth meeting at Pastor Edwin's church, we shared testimonies with the young people, prophesied over some, and prayed for healing. One girl came with pain in her shoulder and back. It was a big problem for her, because she was a dancer and couldn't move normally with the pain. However, it's not a problem anymore, because God healed her during the meeting.

We also took some time to pray for those specifically called to the mission field. Natalie declared that she felt some people in the group were called to China, Indonesia, and Latin America. She wasn't sure who those words were for but announced them regardless. A young man stepped forward and said that he was called to China, some Arabic countries, and Russia. He explained that he knew a bit about China and the Arab world, but Russia was completely unknown territory for him. When he realized Natalie was from Russia (and speaking about China), he was intrigued. He also explained that the very shirt she was wearing confirmed that the Lord was speaking. His ministry was called Kingdom Come Ministries, and he'd had either a dream or a vision of a castle of many colors. Funnily enough, Natalie happened to be wearing a shirt with a castle on it and very colorful letters that read, "Let your kingdom come." *Lord*, I thought, *how very clever you are. You can use a Russian girl's T-shirt to confirm someone's calling.* God is just cool like that.

On Tuesday evening, God answered our prayer for a dose of team testosterone by bringing us our newest recruit, Alan. Though we hadn't even known of his existence just weeks prior, God had our Caribbean team planned out all along. The prophecy Natalie had received about a man traveling with us throughout all of the islands was realized when Aussie Alan joined our team. He had originally hoped to connect with us in South America but wasn't able. As soon as things lined up for him, he got in contact with Jesse who got in contact with me. Days later, Alan was on a flight to Puerto Rico. One of the most kind-hearted, humble, and generous people I'd ever met, Alan was a blessing to our team. He graciously put up with our girl talk, obsession with romantic comedies, and prayers about marriage. We loved to tease Alan about being caught in the middle of such conversations, but he took it all in stride and laughed his way through the next few months of being surrounded by women.

The morning after Alan arrived, he jumped straight into ministry with us. Sally drove Natalie, Roberta, Alan, and I to a rehab center for men — a great introduction to our strange life. The men who lived there were a mix of homeless, war veterans, and former drug addicts. We gathered the men and sat in a circle as many of them looked at us with skepticism. We explained that we were missionaries who had been traveling throughout Latin America since September 2011 and that we'd recently begun our travels around the Caribbean. Natalie shared some testimonies of how God had moved in rehab centers we'd visited in Colombia and Brazil. I shared the story of our friend Godfrey who had been set free from addiction in Belize. Alan and Roberta shared parts of their personal testimonies, and Roberta asked the men what their dreams were.

One by one, the men shared the deepest dreams of their hearts with us and with each other. One man dreamt of being a missionary. Another dreamt of having his own home. Yet another said he dreamt of preaching. Still others remained quiet and ashamed.

Discerning that poor spiritual decisions were creating such shame, we asked the men if any of them had made pacts with Satan. Several came forward, confessing vows they'd made with the devil, involvement in witchcraft, and demonic declarations from their pasts. We asked if anyone wanted to renounce those pacts and be set free by the blood of Jesus. Many did.

We offered to pray for each individual, and a man named Renaldo hesitantly approached me and Alan. He said that he'd done many bad things in his past, and terrible thoughts still haunted him. He listed some of his past crimes and then silently made a gesture indicating that he had shot people, too ashamed to speak the words aloud. I asked him if he'd forgiven himself, but it was clear he was not yet able to do so.

As Alan and I prayed for Renaldo, I saw two pictures. The first was a vision of his past. *He was hiding, about to do something destructive, but he was filled with fear.* The second picture was of his future. *He was dressed nicely, standing in front of a crowd with a microphone in his hands, speaking to children.* After we prayed, I asked Renaldo if anything in his childhood had caused him to be afraid. He paused for a moment, sadness filling his eyes. Slowly, he opened his mouth. "When I was young," he began, "My father did bad things to me. He beat me. He grabbed me. He did black magic. There were frightening things happening."

I wanted to tell him about the good I saw coming in his future, but he beat me to it. "You know, I had a dream that I was preaching in the future. But I just don't know if I could do that." I saw doubt written all over his face. Some part of him wanted to believe his dream, but more of him felt he was too much of a failure.

I told Renaldo that during prayer I'd seen a glimpse of the fear that ruled his past. I explained that the enemy was using fear to keep him from his destiny. I told Renaldo that he was created to be a protector and had a calling to protect children from feeling the same fear that he once did. I described my vision of him speaking to crowds, especially youth. I assured him that his dream would one day become reality and that his testimony would be a powerful example of how God could change someone's life. There was no reason to live in shame. The rougher a man's past, the more his story could show what a powerful transformation God was able to make.

As I confirmed Renaldo's dream rather than agreeing with the lie that he'd never be good enough, his eyes lit up. He looked like a child, eager and happy. His countenance shifted from shame to hope. He asked my permission to give me a hug, and I opened my arms to him. He embraced me, then went to each one of my teammates, declaring that he needed a hug from every person. When we said farewell, he was still smiling from ear to ear.

On Friday night, we were invited to speak at a service in the city of Camuy. The man from the church who'd offered to pick us up was an hour late, so we figured we were no longer wanted and would have a night off. Just before choosing which movie would take the place of a sermon, a man appeared at our door and apologized for his tardiness. I had really begun to warm up to the idea of sitting on a couch in my pajamas instead of preaching, but I reluctantly got in the man's car. A few hours later, I couldn't have imagined *not* getting into that car. That night was one I will never forget.

We arrived at the church where we were immediately escorted to the office of Tito, a large man who served as the main pastor. Unbeknownst to us, Tito was notoriously picky about who he let speak at his church and had a reputation for being hard to please. Completely oblivious of his prestige, we joked around with him, Natalie teasing him that his name meant "wild pork" in Russian. Tito erupted into laughter, his broad frame shaking in amusement. He asked us a few questions about ministry and explained that he'd translated for Iris' founder, Heidi Baker, in the past. He had great respect for Heidi and most likely had opened the doors to his church to us because we were a part of Iris Global.

After just a few minutes of informal questioning, Tito invited our group to the front of his large congregation and gave us full reign of the service. Though apparently an exceptionally rare occurrence, Tito let us do whatever we wanted after knowing us for five minutes. One by one, Roberta, Natalie, Alan, and I approached the stage, a captive audience eager to hear whatever we had to say. The congregation was so enthusiastic that almost every sentence was received by a "hallelujah" or "Gloria a Dios!" I could barely speak, because people kept screaming with such excitement. While feeding off the energy of the crowd, our hearts, minds, and spirits were opened in an unusual way.

Tito was already pleased while listening to the first three speakers, but as Alan shared the final testimony of the night, Tito soared beyond the moon. As Alan timidly approached the mic, he looked a bit unsure but hesitantly opened his mouth. He wasn't used to public speaking, which meant that he had no gimmicks, no processed sermons, no fakeness about him. Completely unassuming, he simply told a story. His genuine surprise at his own ability to tell a good story as well as peoples' positive reactions made the whole experience that much more endearing.

"Yeah, so my friend back in Australia had this little canary," he explained in his thick Aussie accent. "And his other friend took care of the bird while he was on vacation. And this bloke kept saying, 'That bird better not die while I'm responsible for it.'"

People already knew where this story was going and started to giggle in anticipation.

"Well, one day, that silly little bird fell off his perch and dropped dead."

Alan smirked and chuckled to himself. The congregation was laughing. Tito was grinning from ear to ear.

"So my friend walked away from the bird and was thinking he really didn't want to get in trouble for letting that bird die. But he was a Christian and knew that God raised people from the dead. So, he figured, why not raise a bird from the dead?"

People were on the edge of their seats, waiting to hear what happened to this little canary.

"So the guy said, 'Bird, be resurrected in Jesus' name!'"

Alan had a smug look on his face, everyone in the room ready to celebrate the potentially miraculous news.

"Well, a few minutes later, he walked back to the room with the bird cage in it, and the bird was sitting there, back on its perch, alive and well. This guy raised a bird from the dead."

The crowd went wild. Tito exploded with laughter, tears pouring from his eyes. Everyone was screaming, cheering, and laughing. Alan looked surprised that this simple story had generated such an intense reaction and humbly sat down, not realizing he had just become the star of the evening.

Pastor Tito walked to the pulpit and thanked us for speaking, still wiping tears of laughter from his eyes. Yet suddenly, he became very sober and started talking about visiting foreign places to spread the gospel. He admitted that when he traveled he was treated like a king.

"I stay in nice hotels. I eat good meals," he explained. "But these people here…"

He got emotional as he looked at our vagabond crew. "They sleep on floors, in tents, or wherever they can find. They don't care what sacrifices are required, and we need to bless them."

Not expecting this sudden shift in the service, I watched as Tito called up his congregation to collect an offering for us. He laid baskets on the stage and told people to come up and give generously. They lined up to get to the baskets. I couldn't believe it. One woman was so touched that we were willing to sleep on the floor that she approached us in tears. She looked around to see who was closest to her size, then took the jacket off of her back and handed it to Natalie. We hadn't told Tito about making sacrifices or being poor or having a tough life or anything of the sort. He just assumed things hadn't been easy and blessed us beyond words.

After the offering, Tito asked us to pray for the congregation. All four of us stood up front and began to announce words of knowledge and to prophesy over the church. Regrettably, I had *very* rarely stepped out in these giftings before being forced out of my comfort zone in the Caribbean. But that night, God showed me one little word, which turned into two, which turned into maybe a hundred. The Holy Spirit had never moved inside of me quite like this before. I started saying stuff into the microphone without realizing what I was doing. I saw a vision of a man painting and told him not to give up, because God wanted to use his art for His kingdom. Everyone in the congregation pointed to a man on the worship team behind me.

He later approached me and explained that my word confirmed a calling to the arts in Hollywood that he and his wife had been praying about for a long time.

As we shouted out words, the entire church rushed to the front in a request for individual prayer. Again, though I didn't normally receive many specific prophetic words for people, God supernaturally gave me an ability to lay hands on someone and receive knowledge about him or her. While I spoke the words aloud ("God says you have creative gifts" or "God wants to heal your depression" or "God is freeing you from guilt"), people were weeping, laughing, thanking God, and lifting up hands of praise. Simultaneously, my teammates were experiencing the same radical touch of the Lord's presence.

That night, there was a literal outpouring of the Holy Spirit. An unusually powerful presence exploded in that church building. People were getting healed of physical ailments, breaking free from depression, weeping with joy, and excitedly reporting how different prayers had confirmed very specific callings. We prayed until around 1:30 a.m. People waited in line for hours to hear what God wanted to tell them. I was taken aback that strangers would wait so long for *me* to pray for them. I wasn't a prophet or a pastor or a famous speaker. I was just Caitlin, a no-name missionary. Incredibly humbled, I spent the night simply partnering with God while I watched Him turn that church upside down.

At the end of the evening, Tito asked us to pray for him too and wept as he listened to the words God laid on our hearts for him. "Tonight was better than I could have ever dreamt of," he smiled, as he handed us a very full envelope. "This offering is for you. If you ever come back to Puerto Rico, you are welcome at this church. You don't even need to call ahead of time if you want to speak. Just show up."

We hugged him with gratitude and returned to our host families who were shocked when we relayed the events of the night. "Tito let you do whatever you wanted?" they gasped. "*Tito?* That's crazy!"

The more we conversed, the more we realized the opportunity we'd been given as a little group of nameless missionaries was seriously unheard of. And when we opened the envelope Tito had given us, we were even more shocked. There was one thousand dollars cash inside. That congregation, without knowing us, had put one thousand dollars into a basket for us. I was blown away.

I lay on my bed that evening, now probably close to 3 a.m., and cried out of sheer amazement. Not only had we been given an insanely generous offering, God had chosen to use our motley crew for such undeserved glory. A few hours prior, we hadn't even wanted to go to the service. We were picking out a movie and hoping our ride wouldn't show up! But God used us anyway. He revealed secrets to us and spoke through our lips. He used our ears to hear and our hands to heal. There was nothing at that church service that we could have accomplished on our own, yet we walked away being handed glory and blessing. Our night was unforgettable.

The following evening, we reconvened with the youth at Pastor Edwin's church to accompany them on a "treasure hunt." The youth were hungry to evangelize but unfamiliar with this method of spreading the gospel. We explained the process of praying, asking the Holy Spirit for signs and visions, waiting on His voice, and then going to find God's treasure.

We split into small groups, hit the town, and came back together at the conclusion of the evening to share our testimonies with one another. Everyone had encouraging stories to tell, but Natalie's group stood out the most. Her team was comprised of a girl around age seventeen, the youth pastor's wife, and David, the son-in-law of Pastor Edwin. It was the first time any of them had tried treasure hunting. Natalie asked the people in her group to close their eyes and ask the Holy Spirit for pictures. After a few moments, they opened their eyes, and each one reported that he or she had received nothing. Natalie said that they couldn't begin the treasure hunt until they had received something from the Lord. She'd seen visions already but wanted her group to hear God's voice as well. Reminding them that the same Holy Spirit spoke to all of us, she again told her group members to close their eyes and wait on the Lord. After a few more moments, they still said they'd received nothing. This went on for a while until the youth pastor's wife finally spoke up. She saw a vision of a hand with many bracelets. Natalie decided that the one sign would have to suffice for her three protégés and shared what she had seen with them — two people sitting down on a bench in a park, a homeless person, a chest problem, and the name Carlos.

Suddenly, the teenage girl spoke up. The mention of the word "homeless" triggered her to think about a program that helped the homeless called "Ama Como Él Ama" (Love As He Loves). The teenager sometimes helped out at this organization to distribute food to the homeless. Unsure of how this would fit into the treasure hunt, the group made a mental note of her comment and decided to begin the outreach.

All of our groups agreed to drive to a local park together, where we split off to pray for people. Natalie's group immediately noticed a lady and a man sitting on a bench. The woman had many bracelets up her arm. The group approached the couple and explained what they'd been doing and how God had shown them a picture of an arm with many bracelets. The woman on the bench started to cry and exclaimed, "God always sends His people to find me!" Suddenly, the woman recognized the teenage girl in the group. Apparently, her thoughts of Ama Como Él Ama were God-inspired. The teenager had met this woman while volunteering there in the past.

The group asked the woman if she was homeless, and although she currently was not, the man sitting next to her admitted that he was. Though he appeared healthy and sober, David received a word of knowledge about the man and asked him if he struggled with drugs. The man said that he did. He also brought up his brother (called Carlos, the name Natalie had received) and explained that he was going through a rough time as well. Carlos suffered from chest problems, as did the woman on the bench.

The group prayed for the couple, and both of them received Jesus. The group members exchanged contact information with the man and woman and invited them to their church in Arecibo. David, the teenage girl, and the youth pastor's wife couldn't believe what had just happened. They *did* hear from the Holy Spirit, and He used them powerfully in this divine moment.

The next day, Natalie, Roberta, Alan, and I were asked to preach at a different church; however, we heard reports that the couple did show up at Pastor Edwin's church in Arecibo. There, they gladly reunited with the youth from the treasure hunt. Meanwhile, we spent our Sunday at a church called Ciudad de Refugio where we were blown away by God's sovereign hand and His undeserved favor. We were welcomed with open arms into a tiny congregation with big hearts. Though I still barely considered myself a preacher, I had thoroughly prayed before speaking that morning and shared a message that I felt God put on my heart.

After the service, the pastor approached me and told me that I'd been prophetically preaching the entire morning. I didn't understand what she meant. She explained that without realizing it, I was confirming words for the church. And my teammates had done the same thing. They had addressed very specific issues significant for particular people in the congregation without knowing what they were saying. God is so amazing that He used us to answer peoples' prayers even when we were completely oblivious to the fact that we were doing that.

Before heading back to Arecibo, we received another extremely generous donation for our team. I'd never been handed so much unexpected money in my life. Everywhere we went, it seemed people wanted to financially bless us. But in all sincerity, our time with the different churches would have been enough of a blessing on its own. We repeatedly had the privilege of watching God touch peoples' hearts and getting to be a part of it. In every church, God gave us specific words for people, and many were moved to tears as they encountered the love of Christ. Countless people approached us to tell us that different things we'd said confirmed desires or promises in their hearts. Person after person told us how deeply encouraged and moved they were. I *knew* that God could have touched these people without us. He didn't need our help. But He chose to let us partner with Him, to be in on His secrets. He blew us away by revealing the tiniest of details to bring people hope.

The longer we stayed in Puerto Rico, the more I realized God had not just brought us there to serve others but to receive blessings ourselves. Though the heart of Iris Global was to go into the darkest places, God still had some pleasant surprises up His sleeve for His children. He undoubtedly brought us to Puerto Rico, meaning "Rich Port," and revealed unexpected riches that matched the island's name.

I found it ironic that Puerto Rico had originally caused some worry about finances. Before we had contacts on the island, I was concerned that we would have to pay for expensive lodging that would quickly kill our budgets. I feared using up most of our precious cash on our first island. Yet, through God's miraculous provision, we were not only provided with free, comfortable, and beautiful accommodation, but the churches where we served blessed us with lavish donations. Each member of our team left Puerto Rico in a better financial situation than when he or she had arrived.

In addition, starting our journey in Puerto Rico personally provided me a smooth transition coming from the States. Because the island was a U.S. territory, it contained much evidence of mainland U.S. culture yet maintained its own Latino flavor as well. It was nice to transition back to speaking Spanish in a place where most people were bilingual and could help remind me of the words I'd forgotten over Christmas break. I appreciated easing back into Latin American life with some familiar comforts from the continental U.S. As we traveled to the Dominican Republic, it felt a lot less like home. By the time we got to Haiti, we were in a different world. The gradual transition from place to place made the process a lot less jarring. God knew our itinerary before we did and was very intentional in caring for our hearts and needs.

Lastly, and most importantly, our time in Puerto Rico provided us with godly connections for our remaining time in the Caribbean. Though Puerto Rico itself didn't quite fit in with my vision to go to the poorest places, the pastors in Puerto Rico had the connections we needed to get into some of those places. I remembered Natalie's prophecy about meeting a man of influence in Puerto Rico who would help us have a smooth journey throughout the rest of the islands. Pastor Edwin was incredibly well-connected throughout the Caribbean, and working with his church opened up future doors for us. His friend had already connected us to Pastor Luis in the DR, and Edwin's brother, Manuel, offered to help connect us in Cuba. His contacts ended up unlocking incredible opportunities for us later in our journey.

Our time in Puerto Rico set us up very nicely for the islands to come. God had called us to the poorest islands in the Caribbean, but He wanted us to visit affluent Puerto Rico first in order to do so effectively. He showed me the futility of putting pressure upon myself to plan the itinerary. God had clearly designed our route from the start. We arrived on our first island desiring to bless others, but God showered *us* with blessings. Puerto Rico confirmed that God didn't just *allow* the dreams in my heart but blessed them beyond what I could imagine. I knew He was designing every step, and it was time to simply sit back, relax, and enjoy the favor of the Lord.

Chapter Twenty-One

THE DOMINICAN REPUBLIC: The Lost Get Found

Reluctant to say goodbye to our Puerto Rican family, we boarded a plane to the Dominican Republic with mixed emotions. I had fallen in love with Puerto Rico quickly and wanted to stay longer, but I was also excited for the adventures ahead in the DR. After a short flight, we landed in the capital city of Santo Domingo and were greeted by Pastor Luis and Julio, a friend from his church. While driving from the airport to the pastor's home, I could already sense a stronger Caribbean flavor than what we'd experienced in Puerto Rico. The main road from the airport into the city center hugged the coast, providing us with breathtaking views of sparkling, azure water. Palm trees hid people in their shade and swayed with the rhythm of the gentle ocean breeze.

On the way to Pastor Luis' house, we pulled over at a man's fruit stand where he treated each of us to a freshly cracked coconut. We gulped the sweet milk straight from the coconut, then scooped out the remaining fruit. This felt like the real Caribbean.

As we continued driving, the roads became a bit more industrial, and we could sense a shift from laid-back Caribbean life to a chaotic favela community. Luis' neighborhood was called La Canela, meaning "cinnamon" in Spanish. Just like the spice, this neighborhood was a flavorful little barrio, bustling with people, commotion, and noise. Whether dogs barking, stereos blaring, children playing, street vendors announcing their products, or motorbikes whizzing by, noise ruled La Canela at all hours. The neighborhood was comprised of a series of steep, up-and-down streets, weaving an intricate labyrinth of roads filled with colorful homes. The building where Pastor Luis lived was three stories high, and he, his wife Belkis, and their daughter Hedekel lived on the top floor.

Upon entering Pastor Luis' home, we were excitedly greeted by his beautiful and bubbly wife. Belkis had heard through the grapevine that Roberta loved a traditional Dominican food called *la bandera* which literally means "flag" in Spanish. Belkis had placed a bowl on the kitchen table covered in a cloth and declared that she'd prepared *la bandera* for us. She pulled the cloth away to reveal a literal *bandera* — a flag folded up in the bowl. She burst into laughter at our look of surprise, pleased by our reaction to her clever joke. Moments later, she whipped out the actual meal of *la bandera* and invited us to sit and enjoy. We shared an amazing spread of rice, savory meat, and sautéed vegetables.

While in Santo Domingo, we spent much time at Belkis' kitchen table, surrounded by good company and some of the best food of our entire Latin American journey. Meals were a time to enjoy the local culture, share our hearts with Pastor Luis and his family, and discuss spiritual revelation. Luis and Belkis explained that normally when visitors came to their neighborhood, they offered them a place apart from their house where they stayed on their own. They were careful about who they let sleep at their home. We were all surprised, because we were under quite the opposite impression. When we'd called Luis from Puerto Rico, he had offered us his home instantly, without asking a single question about us. But while in his house, Luis explained that the Holy Spirit had moved inside him during our brief Skype call, and he immediately knew he needed to receive us. Belkis, a prophetic woman, nodded in agreement, explaining that when she prayed for us, the Holy Spirit told her we came with pure hearts. Pastor Luis and Belkis said that they both knew our visit would be a blessing to them and that they wanted the blessing as close to them as possible, living inside their home. Belkis declared that God would use us to break spiritual strongholds during our time in Santo Domingo, and things would be broken off of us as well. We'd done nothing to deserve such high expectations or such a warm welcome. God had done it all, and we undeservedly reaped the benefits of His work.

Throughout the week, we learned more about the need to change the spiritual atmosphere in this neighborhood. Pastor Luis and Belkis told us about the history of the Dominican Republic, Santo Domingo, and La Canela in particular. A dictator had ravaged the country in the past, and their neighborhood was built on bloodshed and bones — some homes virtually erected atop cemeteries. Curses had been spoken over the land, and many people in La Canela still practiced witchcraft and regularly cursed the neighborhood.

Just as the team had prayed on the ancient Mayan ruins in Guatemala and in Machu Picchu in Peru, we felt we needed to break curses spoken over La Canela and declare God's blessing. During an evening church service, Pastor Luis explained more about the neighborhood's history and the bloodshed that marked La Canela. Our team then spoke about biblical accounts of land being cursed due to sin. We went on to explain that repentance for sin, even from generations past, brought forth restoration from the Lord. "If my people, who are called by my name, will humble themselves and pray and seek my face and turn from their wicked ways, then I will hear from heaven, and I will forgive their sin and will heal their land" (2 Chronicles 7:14).

We prayed as a church, repenting for the murder, the brutal history, and the witchcraft that dominated La Canela. We then declared God's ability to wash the land clean, to redeem La Canela from its violent history, and to bring forth a new generation of purity, righteousness, and godliness. We declared a blessing over the land, reading from Deuteronomy 33, where Moses blessed the tribes of Israel. "May the LORD bless his land with the precious dew from heaven above and with the deep waters that lie below; with the best the sun brings forth and the finest the moon can yield; with the choicest gifts of the ancient mountains and the fruitfulness of the everlasting hills; with the best gifts of the earth and its fullness and the favor of him who dwelt in the burning bush" (Deuteronomy 33:13-16). Witchcraft, sin, and violence had no power over the goodness of God and His ability to claim blessing in place of a curse.

Later that evening, we accompanied Pastor Luis and about twenty other congregants in a procession around the neighborhood. For forty days, the people in their church walked around La Canela every night from midnight until 2 a.m. During these two hours, they prayed for their neighborhood and anointed the land with oil. While joining them on their nightly march throughout the community, the issues of alcoholism, drug addiction, prostitution, and witchcraft were quite evident. At several specific corners, we stopped while an individual stepped forward to pray for God's power to reign in La Canela. Then Pastor Luis dumped oil on the ground, anointing the land to mark it as holy territory and believing this community would truly be transformed into a place of righteousness and blessing.

During our time in La Canela, God gave me a dream that seemed worth mentioning to Luis and my team. In my sleep, the Lord showed me how to take the prophetic declarations one step further.

My teammates and Pastor Luis' family went on the roof of their building to take communion together. As we took the bread and the wine, we exchanged the blood of Christ for salvation, freedom, and righteousness and declared these things over the city.

I knew this dream was from God and that I needed to mirror the events of the dream in real life. However, to be perfectly honest, initiating such action was a challenge for me. It was much easier for me to do practical work that produced tangible fruit than to spend time interceding or prophesying. Despite my personal preferences, I felt God was challenging me to be obedient to the dream He'd shown me and to believe in faith that following through would produce something significant in the spiritual realm. I told Pastor Luis and my teammates about my dream, and they accompanied me to the roof where we took communion and prayed for God to break down spiritual strongholds. I remembered that Belkis had told us from the start that we were going to break chains in the spiritual realm during our visit. Even though we didn't know what or how, I chose to believe something powerful was released.

While stationed in Santo Domingo, Natalie, Roberta, and I spent one of our afternoons picking up Aleeza from the airport with Pastor Luis. Excited to expand our Caribbean team a bit more, we gladly reunited with our faithful Aussie sister. Alan stayed behind and told Belkis he was going to take a little stroll around the neighborhood. Though intending to wander for just thirty minutes or so, he quickly became lost in the maze of La Canela and couldn't find his way back to the house. Unable to speak Spanish, he didn't know how to explain his situation or ask for directions. Not knowing quite what to do, Alan got in a taxi in the hopes that if the driver roamed the area, something would eventually look familiar. Yet, because he couldn't explain this thought process, the driver assumed it would be best to take a lost white guy to the closest bus station. This brought Alan to the opposite side of town. Now he was really lost.

Meanwhile, the four of us girls arrived back at the pastor's house where Belkis met us with concern. After greeting Aleeza, Belkis worriedly explained that Alan had gone on a walk and never returned. It was now dark, and Pastor Luis looked immediately panicked. I had no idea how dangerous this neighborhood was for a lone foreigner, but Luis said Alan's disappearance was a very grave situation. I was worried but felt helpless. The neighborhood kids caught wind of the situation, and a search began. Little boys roamed the streets yelling, "Alaaaaaaaaan!" while men from the church patrolled the area on their motorbikes. Hours passed, and no one had seen him. Midnight came and went, still no sign of Alan.

Pastor Luis said we needed to contact the police. My mind went from thinking Alan was lost to wondering if he'd been killed. I had no idea how we would ever find him. As a leader, what would I do if one of my teammates disappeared for good? *Oh God*, I prayed, *please keep him safe. Bring him back to us. Lord, bring him back to us unharmed.*

In the morning, Alan was still gone. Pastor Luis, a couple of local guys, Natalie, and I went to the police station. We talked to the police officers who explained that Alan had turned up at one of Santo Domingo's police stations late the night before. He'd spent the night there, slept safe and sound, and was already on his way back to Pastor Luis' house. Though confused about all that had happened, I was more relieved than anything. Alan was safe. No one had tried to harm him or rob him. God had totally protected him.

Ironically, in an odd series of events, Alan's disappearance turned into the best thing our team could have asked for. I assumed the situation had really stressed out Pastor Luis, Belkis, and everyone who'd been out on the streets looking for Alan all night. I knew people were exhausted, and I thought they would hate our team after the disturbance. But the complete opposite turned out to be true. So often, missionaries come into areas acting like they are faultless, flawless, holier-than-though beings. But when a community sees some vulnerability inside of you — when people are invited into your lives and can serve you as you simultaneously serve them — that's the kingdom of God. In La Canela, we didn't all speak the same language, but Alan's disappearance provided us, the church, and the community a reason to rally together. We were strangers who were given very serious motivation to act in unity.

The neighborhood children only attended school for a few hours a day and normally spent a lot of time feeling bored. Searching for Alan gave them a purpose, an opportunity to find someone and be a hero. This excited them. When Alan was found, they celebrated the victory as their own. And Alan, who'd just wanted to take a little walk, had turned from a stranger into a celebrity overnight. He was a neighborhood legend now. Every kid in La Canela knew Alan, and they flocked to him. Little boys with no fathers would come to the house every day just to sit with Alan. They spoke no English, Alan no Spanish. Yet somehow, they spent hours smiling and laughing, without any idea of what the other person was saying.

Everyone at the church knew Alan as well. A few people remembered the names of us girls, but no one forgot Alan. The congregants cheered him on to speak whenever we were at the church. They all adored him and loudly applauded every time he went up front. Pastor Luis fell in love with him and forced Alan to dance with him in front of the whole congregation, as everyone clapped with amusement. Alan's return to the community was like the story of the prodigal son wandering off and then coming home to his father. I'm sure his story will be used in sermons for years to come — the tale of the one who once was lost but now is found.

Once our team was safely and happily reunited, we hit the ground running. We asked Pastor Luis what kind of hands-on ministry was available in Santo Domingo, and we quickly filled our schedule with outreaches both inside and outside La Canela. Everywhere we went, young people from the church ministered alongside us. Pastor Luis had hoped to light a fire for missions within his church, and these little outreaches began to spark something. Several people from the church had been interested in evangelistic outreaches for a long time, but they'd never taken the initiative to organize them. We got the ball rolling for visits to a local prison, a leper colony, and even houses within the neighborhood. Once people saw how easy it was to jump in and how God worked so powerfully through these outreaches, they excitedly declared that they would continue the work after we left.

Pedro, a young pastor from Luis' church, accompanied us on every outreach, and the fire inside him transformed from a spark to a burning flame in just a few days. He had a natural gift for preaching and evangelism but wasn't yet operating to his full potential. The Lord had given him a vision to preach in every prison in the Dominican Republic, but he'd never been to a jail yet. He wanted to preach outside the church but had no platform to do so. Our time with Pedro opened up doors to poor and sick families within his neighborhood, as well as access to prisons and a leper colony. He loved the ministry we did together, and this was just the start for him. God is always faithful to complete the work He begins, and in the DR, He connected us to the right people to follow through with what we started. We knew we only had a few days to work in the city, but this sliver of time opened up Pedro's eyes to a whole new world. These transformational days undoubtedly stimulated long-term effects.

A couple of times, Pedro and others accompanied us to visit homes in the La Canela community and pray for people. One morning, Steven and David, two local boys, decided to join us and offered to pray as well. While walking through the maze of small homes that comprised La Canela, we encountered an older couple who asked for prayer for different health issues. The wife said she had pain in her back and knees, so we prayed for God to heal her. Afterwards, we asked if she could now do anything that she couldn't do before. She began to bend over and twist. Realizing that she hadn't been able to do those movements just moments prior, she excitedly praised God and celebrated her healing.

The woman was a Christian and wanted her husband to know Jesus as well. We asked how we could pray for him, and he explained that he had a heart condition in addition to diabetes. Earlier in the day, he had attempted walking from his bed to the front door but wasn't able. He'd become too dizzy and had to return to his bed. We prayed for God to heal him too and afterwards asked him to try to walk. This time, the man walked to the door and back without problems. His dizziness was gone.

The man sat back down and explained that he had not yet accepted Jesus into his life. But he was happy that God had chosen to heal him nonetheless. So were we. The man went on to explain that during that very week, God had begun to speak into his heart. God was inviting him into His love. Just one day prior to our visit, the man felt a real desire to go to church. He said he had been too sick to get there but declared that God had brought church to his house today. His eyes radiated with true joy. His body looked old, but his eyes were like those of a boy — excited, pure, and captivated by the love of His father. The man said he wanted to pray with us. Inside his little home, he accepted Jesus into his life. Because God had just touched his body, it appeared as if he would now be physically strong enough to get to a church building as he desired. But no matter what, I rejoiced that his heart was touched by God's love, and no sickness could ever take that away from him.

On Sunday morning, we went with several people from the church to minister in three prisons. We falsely assumed that our escorts had prearranged permission to visit, but when we got to the first prison, a juvenile center, we were denied entry. The jail officials told us we could not visit on Sundays. Next, we tried the women's prison. There, we were also denied entry. Our last hope was getting into the male prison. Pedro said that a pair of blue eyes would definitely work in our favor. Sure enough, after taking one glimpse at us, the guard immediately offered us access to the men's prison.

Once inside, we met up with an inmate who served as the chaplain of the prison's church. He'd just finished his morning service, but we asked if he could escort us to visit specific prisoners if he knew of anyone who really needed prayer. Instead, he offered us an opportunity to preach. He took us outside, handed us a megaphone, and told us to begin. Inmates had already begun to gather around us and glare at us with a mix of curiosity, perverse stares, and genuine interest. Overwhelmed by the stares, I handed the megaphone to Natalie who boldly jumped in. She started to preach in Spanish as many listened. Next, Pedro took the megaphone and preached with a rare eloquence and confidence. I was impressed. Afterwards, we prayed for many who had gathered around us. Some hearts seemed genuine; others seemed solely interested in interacting with women.

After a while, we were escorted to another area of the prison and were warned it would be far more aggressive. We passed through a long hallway where convicts roamed freely. The men leered at us — begging for our money and attention, touching us, and hassling us until we finally reached our destination. We found ourselves inside a tiny chapel, just a small room where several men were sitting in a circle. This time, we were given only a few minutes to preach, so Pedro shared a brief message before we prayed for the men one-on-one. Pedro reminded us of his vision to preach in every prison in the Dominican Republic, and this was day one. Our visit was the beginning of the fulfillment of his dream and had stimulated something inside of him. Full of fresh passion, Pedro declared that he would faithfully follow this dream in his heart and continue visiting prisons throughout the country after we left.

The following morning, Pedro and others accompanied us to a leper colony. I didn't know leper colonies even existed in the Western Hemisphere, but there was a small colony just outside of Santo Domingo. Upon arrival, we were greeted by a man in a wheelchair who had lost one of his legs and parts of his hands. He'd lived at the leper colony for years, working as the resident pastor. Though his appearance made it quite obvious that he had leprosy, I kept forgetting he was a patient whenever I heard him speak. He was full of joy, confidence, and the love of the Lord.

He invited us into a meeting room where most of the other residents had gathered. I looked around and noticed that many people were missing limbs and fingers. One man had only a partial nose, and one woman's eyes looked like they were falling out of her head. We greeted each resident, one by one, shaking their fingerless hands and kissing them on their cheeks. The discomfort I felt was a humbling reminder of my fleshly nature. I knew there was superficiality, vanity, and pride inside of me that still needed to die. My flesh needed to be crucified.

Yet, as our team was invited to share a quick word with the residents, I felt compelled to speak. I could feel God's heart for the people living in the leper colony. I knew He had chosen them to be His sons and daughters, and I was looking at God's family before me. I told the leper colony residents that we'd traveled all around the Western Hemisphere and felt privileged to meet God's children wherever we went — that in each place we were united with more brothers and sisters. I told them I was honored to meet more of God's family today, and I meant it. As I spoke about each one being called a child of God, I noticed a woman next to me moved to tears. I suppose that was not a message the lepers heard very often.

Even when we weren't *trying* to do ministry, ministry followed us around the Dominican Republic. One day, a group from Pastor Luis' church took us to Boca Chica, a famous beach in Santo Domingo. When a few of us explored the area to find a snack, we stumbled upon a fruit stand run by a group of Haitians who had moved to the DR to find work. They cracked open a couple of coconuts for us, and as we stood by their stand sipping the sweet milk, a Dominican man came by and started harassing one of the Haitian women. I'd noticed that Dominicans seemed to look down on Haitians, but this was the most blatant harassment so far.

Natalie fearlessly began to reprimand the Dominican man for bullying the Haitian woman, which only seemed to amuse him. He drove off snickering, the woman relieved to have him out of her sight. Despite the man's disrespect, the Haitian woman seemed touched that someone else had cared enough to stand up for her, something she was certainly not used to. Natalie asked if we could pray for each of the Haitians, and the two other women at the fruit stand stepped forward. Their faces transformed from fear and anger to smiles.

We asked the sole Haitian man at the fruit stand if we could pray for him as well. He responded with a reluctant "yes" but made it clear that he didn't believe in God and thought our prayers were futile. He explained that his whole family had been killed in the Haitian earthquake years prior, and he had been buried in the rubble himself for three days before being rescued. He wondered how his life could reek of such tragedy if God really existed. We told him if God had spared him and rescued him from the rubble, God must have a big plan for his life. The man smiled but looked skeptical. He went on to explain that he wasn't born into a Christian family. In fact, his family was highly involved in witchcraft. We told the man that his past didn't matter. When God gave new life, the past was washed away. The Haitian man nodded, indicating agreement; yet he simultaneously denied that he believed in God.

As we continued to chat, the man admitted that he had an encounter with God during the earthquake. While he was buried in the rubble, just before being found, he cried out, "Jesus, save me!" Though an unbeliever and a product of witchdoctors, the name of Jesus was what spilled from his lips in his hour of greatest need. He didn't know why he'd cried out for Jesus. The man said that after yelling Jesus' name, he saw a light shining in the rubble. The next thing he knew, dogs were sniffing through the debris, and he'd been found. He was rescued in that moment — the only one in his family to survive.

The Haitian man allowed us to pray for him, and I knew the wheels in his head were turning. Though he'd initially brushed off the possibility of God's existence, somewhere in his heart he knew God had encountered him in the rubble. He knew that Jesus' name had come out of his mouth and that bright light and rescue had followed his cry to the Lord. Pain was keeping him at a distance from God, but he could only deny what he'd experienced for so long. I hoped and prayed that the young man would allow God into his heart one day and would recognize God's divine hand in saving him. Even in the unknown, I was thankful that we got to meet him and hear his story. It was exciting to be included in what God was doing — to simply buy a coconut and hear about what God was up to.

Andy, one of the guys from the church, witnessed this whole encounter, and his jaw nearly dropped to the floor. He asked for a coconut, and this is what he got. Andy was so blown away by how God was moving in the midst of even the most mundane parts of life that he felt compelled to share the Haitian man's story with the entire church that following Sunday. By the end of our week with Andy, Pedro, and others, I knew members of the church were really starting to catch a fire for missions. We witnessed the start of a powerful evangelism team who would share the gospel around Santo Domingo for years to come. I left in full confidence that Pedro would revisit the houses within La Canela, the prison, and maybe even the leper colony. I knew God would do mighty things through his life and the lives of others within his church that would change their nation.

After a week in Santo Domingo, we prepared to move on to our next city in the Dominican Republic. We had originally planned to travel to Santiago, but after going in circles with our contacts there, we realized this was another closed door. Pastor Luis went to bat for us and made several calls to pastor friends around the country. We waited to see what opportunities came through. We needed to leave by Wednesday, and on Tuesday night we still had no idea where we were traveling. All we knew was that we were going to the bus station in the morning, and we would get on a bus to…somewhere. On Tuesday at midnight, about ten hours before our departure, our next destination was finally confirmed. A pastor from La Romana, a coastal city about two hours east of Santo Domingo, invited us to work with his church and stay with a family from his congregation. With no other options, we hopped on a bus to La Romana and hoped for the best.

We were picked up at the bus station and hosted by two of the most joyful people I'd ever met. Always-laughing Ramon welcomed us into his home, constantly calling us beautiful, giving us hugs, and sharing funny stories. His gorgeous wife, Lucy, showered us with hospitality as well — working tirelessly to prepare amazing meals and serving us with a smile. Once more, the kindness of strangers blew me away. I immediately felt at home and looked forward to hearing Ramon's infectious laughter each day.

One evening, while eating dinner, Ramon told my teammates and I that he'd seen us in a vision two weeks before we arrived. He had forgotten about the vision until that moment and suddenly realized he'd envisaged the whole scene before. He explained that he'd seen each one of us sitting around his table talking. We'd had no idea where we were going until just hours before our departure, but Ramon had seen us weeks ago. God had it planned all along.

We worked at Ramon and Lucy's church, attending prayer meetings and preaching, but the work outside the church walls is what really moved my heart. We connected with several women from the church who accompanied us to a senior home, a prison, an orphanage, and a Haitian community outside the city.

Visiting the senior citizen home was a priceless memory. As we entered the main gates, we were greeted by a sweet, blind woman. She brought us to a young girl, just twenty, who escorted us around the grounds. The girl was preparing to become a nun and explained that the senior home was managed by nuns. Despite the unflattering stereotypes, the women who worked there radiated with beauty. I wondered if the young girl ever mourned her decision to lead a life with no husband or children of her own, throwing away her opportunity for these things before she'd barely become a woman. Yet, her eyes were so full of joy. As she accompanied us to different wings of the center to pray for people, she giggled at the ornery old ladies and senile comments made by some of the men. Patience and grace spilled out of her with seemingly no effort.

We passed by another nun who was probably ninety years old. Weighing no more than eighty-five pounds, this tiny, frail lady greeted me with a hug so pure that it felt like God was embracing me through her. Natalie took one look at her beaming face and was moved to tears. "You know, sometimes we look down on nuns," she grieved. "We criticize them and make fun of them. But we have so much to learn from them. These people have already died to themselves. They are so full of joy, because they died to themselves a long time ago."

I realized that Natalie was right. These women didn't wait for selfish things and then get disappointed when they didn't happen. They laid aside all their selfish desires and lived only for Jesus. He was their one love, so they already had everything they wanted. It was beautiful.

Our heartwarming visits continued as we ventured to a local orphanage and a prison with a remarkable woman named Maria Teresa. She astonished me with her faith. Maria Teresa lived in a poor community and visited homes in her neighborhood almost every morning, sharing the gospel and praying for people. In addition, she regularly visited the orphanage and prison. She had almost nothing, but whenever she received something, she shared it with others. She waited for God to provide enough money for her to catch a bus to the prison and used those coins on bus fare instead of her own needs. She walked long distances to get to other places. She worked tirelessly, day after day, loving people with radical abandon yet receiving no glory. She was a faceless, nameless woman who would probably never receive due honor here on earth — a hero the world would never know.

I had already fallen in love with her genuine heart, but when I heard more of her story, I was in awe. Maria Teresa's father had been her closest companion, the man she adored. He was unjustly murdered, and three men were accused of the crime. Instead of resorting to anger or bitterness, Maria Teresa chose to love. God told her to go to the prison and pray for the men who had killed her father. She started visiting the men who had been accused to show them love. The three alleged killers all claimed innocence, but they were still awaiting trial, so there was no proof either way. Maria Teresa didn't care whether the men were guilty or innocent. She loved these men, and they loved her. Over time, she became a mama to them. They adored her and showered her with affection whenever she visited the prison. Maria Teresa was a walking story of forgiveness and God's redemption.

Normally, she went to the prison alone whenever she could save up enough bus fare to get there. This time, my teammates and I arranged for a vehicle and accompanied Maria Teresa. She was very glad to have company and thankful for transportation. We arrived at the prison and were told to leave all our belongings at a dodgy kiosk outside the jail. We waited in the scorching sun for about an hour and a half, our water bottles and sunglasses already confiscated. Finally, we were led into the jail where we underwent the most humiliating prison security inspection yet. We might as well have been prisoners ourselves. Each of us still reeling from the shock of that experience, we walked into the main meeting room where inmates were receiving visitors.

Immediately, we were greeted by smiling Angelio, one of the accused killers. He didn't look like he would hurt a fly. He was probably a few years younger than me, and I could see all he wanted was someone to hug. We sat down with him and chatted about his life. He said he used to live a godless life, doing drugs and getting into trouble. Open and honest about his past, he admitted he was far from perfect but declared that he had not killed Maria Teresa's father. He had been accused of committing the crime with two other men whom he claimed he'd never met prior to being thrown in prison with them.

Angelio wanted his freedom back but said that he was thankful he'd met Jesus in prison. He believed God had actually shown him mercy by bringing him to jail. All his friends from the streets had been killed. His life had been heading in the same direction, but God spared him. Now Angelio knew God, had cleaned up his life, and possessed hope in something greater. But the thought of *never* leaving prison was more than he could bear. He wanted to be free and start a clean life outside. He wanted to have friends he could trust. He wanted to see his mom.

We asked if we could pray for Angelio, and he knelt down in the middle of us, reaching out to hold Aleeza's and my hands. Tears poured down his cheeks as we prayed for him. Afterwards, he stood back up and said, "I didn't do it. I didn't do it." He looked like a child, scared and longing for comfort. Without knowing quite what to say, we sat with him and held his hands. Roberta sat with her arm around him, and he drank in her presence like a young child does with his mother. He broke my heart.

Visiting hours rapidly faded, and we had to say goodbye. Angelio left us with a smile, and I forced a smile back, knowing freedom was just steps away for me and maybe years away for him. I believed in his innocence but knew the corrupt system could easily find a way to prove otherwise. I wondered what Maria Teresa thought, but then I remembered that she didn't care. All she wanted was to love. And she did. She loved Angelio with all her heart. And he knew it.

Maria Teresa also accompanied us, with another group of people from the church, to a *batey* outside of La Romana. This was basically a poor farming community in the Dominican Republic inhabited mainly by Haitian immigrants. The people who lived in the bateys worked tirelessly to harvest sugarcane yet made close to nothing for their labor, while the rich batey owners sold the sugar and reaped the financial benefit of the farmers' hard work. Most of the owners lived in mansions in the city, turning a blind eye to the poverty that enslaved the people who brought their riches.

We met up with several people from the church and took a taxi to a batey just thirty minutes from La Romana. As soon as we were outside the city limits, it felt like a whole new world. Lush vegetation lined the streets, and sugarcane plants stood higher than grown men. We passed green fields filled with majestic acacia trees, a flashback to Africa. Everything we set our eyes on possessed natural beauty.

Finally, we turned off the main road and began to weave through fields of sugarcane. It felt like a maze until we suddenly emerged from the sugarcane and found ourselves in the middle of a cluster of homes — a dusty, small community that resembled Africa in every way. Curious children immediately surrounded us, and several adults came to greet us as well. Claudio, the chief of the batey, offered to escort us from house to house to pray for the sick. After prayer, we would do something with the kids.

The kids, however, were ready to have our attention *now*, so they accompanied us as we visited house after house with Claudio, laughing and curiously reaching for our hands. As we met the adults in the community, we discovered that many suffered from the same health problems. Loss of vision was one of the most common issues, and the reasons for blindness were shocking. Most of those unable to see had experienced some type of freak accident. Blindness had been the result of being thrown off of horses and other unusual head injuries. After listening to story after story of horrific events, I wondered what was going on here. It seemed like this whole community was living under some sort of twisted curse.

The saddest part of the situation was that no one wanted help from God. Hearts were closed. As we visited the sick and the downtrodden, we offered a message of hope, love, and healing. But almost everyone's response was the same. "I'll accept God next time you're here. Next time." No one wanted God today.

One of the blind men was also severely demonized, and Claudio took it upon himself to cast the demons out in front of all of us. As he started to rebuke blindness and sickness, the demons inside the blind man went crazy. The man grabbed a stick and began to try to beat Claudio, as Claudio continued to rebuke the demons. At the mention of Jesus' name, a battle began. Claudio was trying to hold the blind man down, screaming, "Out in the name of Jesus!" as the blind man went ballistic, swinging his stick at Claudio and trying to beat him up or kill him. As the brawl progressed, I couldn't discern what was the man's own doing and what was demonic influence. The children were all watching and began to shriek with laughter as the riotous scene unfolded. Finally, Claudio left the man, who was still angry and agitated. I was horrified. There was nothing funny about this.

Before we'd traveled to the batey, Ramon had warned us about the intensity of witchcraft among the Haitian communities. He said demonic activity was a normal part of Haitian culture, and the type of battle we'd watched between Claudio and the man was a typical event.

I was more than relieved when we got away from the chaos and organized a time to hang out with just the children. We sat them down and distributed treats we'd purchased in La Romana. After loading the kids up on candy and soda, they skipped home buzzed with sugar. They went on their merry way, not even slightly fazed by all the satanic commotion that was happening inside their community.

Though they'd been unbothered and even entertained by the demonic battle, I was not okay with what was happening. In fact, after just a few hours in the batey, I became physically ill. After returning to La Romana, I tried to rest but struggled. I wrestled all night with bad dreams and little sleep. In the morning, I got sick to my stomach several times and had no energy. By the evening, I had a full-blown fever and no physical strength.

Often when I was sick, I could pinpoint the source — being around a bunch of sick kids, eating something questionable, not taking enough time to rest, etc. But this time, I knew it was spiritual. I could feel it. I knew something significant was awaiting us in Haiti, and Satan was trying to scare me. He whispered lies into my ear. *"You can't even make it through one day in a Haitian community in the DR. You'll never make it through a whole month in Haiti. Look at my power. Look at what I can do to you."*

I knew the attack of the enemy was real, but I also knew the love of God was stronger. I rebuked the attack on my body. I rebuked witchcraft and curses that had been spoken over me in the batey. Slowly, I started to feel better. But then Natalie got sick. Then Alan. Then Aleeza. Natalie had a dream about worms crawling through her face and confirmed that this was a spiritual attack. We needed to pray and fight. We also needed to rest.

As our time in La Romana came to an end, we made taking a break a priority before traveling to Haiti. We'd heard about a nearby beach town called Punta Cana, allegedly one of the most beautiful places in the country. Ramon had a friend who worked for a travel agency and said he could get us reservations at a luxurious beach resort for a fraction of the normal price. The travel agent offered to arrange not only a cheap yet swanky hotel, but also airline tickets to Haiti. He claimed there were flights directly from Punta Cana to Haiti's capital. The plane tickets were the same cost as busing to Haiti, but we'd spend thirty minutes on a plane instead of fourteen hours on a bus. The choice seemed obvious. The travel agent said he would drive us from La Romana to Punta Cana, secure the plane tickets the following day, and deliver them directly to the resort in Punta Cana. If he couldn't get the tickets for some reason, he would return our money instead, and we'd have to leave a day earlier to catch the bus. Either way, we'd have everything sorted by that coming Saturday.

We headed to the resort with high hopes. Still a bit sick, I was desperate for this break, and the thought of a peaceful weekend on the beach seemed heavenly. However, upon arriving at the resort, I immediately felt uneasy. The staff was unhelpful and abrasive. Our room wasn't ready when we arrived, and we wasted precious time waiting for someone to assist us. Finally, we were offered a room that didn't even remotely match what we'd been guaranteed. The resort was comprised of countless "bloques," freestanding buildings with hotel rooms inside them. We were assigned to Bloque One, which was filled with young partyers who were constantly stumbling around our bloque drunk. They polluted the halls with noise until three in the morning and made it impossible to sleep.

We were moved to another bloque the following day, after being told to wait for a bag porter who never came. Our potential beach time disappeared as we waited in our hotel room for the promised staff member. Finally, we made a successful move, where the hotel staff waited until we forked over cash for an undeserved tip. Local vendors lined the pathways between bloques and grabbed and harassed us as we passed by. Trying to swallow my irritation, I finally made it to the beach where my eyes were assaulted by European tourists. Drunk men in uncomfortably small "bathing suits" tainted the beach with their immodesty. Scantily clad women flaunted their bodies every which way I turned. Material things suffocated me. When I looked around the resort, I saw nothing but empty people who put their joy in empty things. My spirit felt heavy.

Saturday afternoon came and went, and we realized that our trusty travel agent had failed to deliver our plane tickets or our money. After hours of failed attempts, we finally got him on the phone and found out he had never booked tickets and now claimed that he couldn't refund our money until Monday. I explained that we needed to be in Haiti on Monday, so he spun a web of words that made no sense, leaving me frustrated and confused. One of my friends was soon flying into Haiti to join us and was expecting me to be in the right country. If we weren't flying, we needed to bus back to Santo Domingo on Sunday and then bus from the capital to Haiti early Monday morning. If we waited for the travel agent, we would miss our bus and leave our newest teammate hanging. I sat in the lobby, made several phone calls, did research on bus tickets, and contacted the woman who would be receiving us in Haiti. Around midnight Saturday evening, I finally decided to give up until the following day. I felt far less rested than when I'd first arrived in Punta Cana and grimaced at the fact that I needed to be up in a few hours if I wanted to catch a bus back to Santo Domingo.

I was exhausted but decided to take a detour back to my hotel room to soak in a few extra moments of quiet before life got even crazier. The "scenic route" from the lobby to my bloque was a bit of a hike, but I wanted some time to enjoy the silence of the evening and the cool night air. I needed a moment of rest, even if it was just a brief one.

Though it was late, I didn't think twice about walking back to my room alone. I'd seen several security guards throughout the resort and trusted they'd keep me safe in such an upmarket hotel. As I strolled along, I tried to let go of the stress about getting to Haiti on time to meet my friend. I told my busy mind to relax, but as I walked I could sense that a man was following me. I subtly turned my head to get a glimpse of him and saw an outfit that looked like that of a security guard. Assuming a hotel employee was following me, I hoped he was staying close to keep me safe. Yet, as I continued walking, I felt more and more uneasy. We were approaching a dark and isolated area of the resort, and I knew no one else was around. I wasn't sure why, but I could tell the "security guard" was not following me to protect me. He was getting closer and closer, and I was growing increasingly uncomfortable.

About to pass by the beach (where anything could have happened and no one would have seen), I made an abrupt turn into one of the bloques. I hoped the man would keep walking past me, but he followed me into the building. Now I *knew* he was pursuing me with bad intentions. Feeling slightly panicked, I realized I had no way to escape him. With no other choice, I stopped and turned around to confront the man, unsure of what I would do or say. We were alone. No one could see that I needed help. I didn't know if he had a weapon or what he was preparing to do to me. As I turned to face him, the man was now right next to me. I caught a glimpse of him and gasped. He was touching himself inappropriately with one hand and beckoning me with the other. He mumbled something incoherent, but I could understand exactly what he was asking me for.

Wanting to scream but too scared to release a yell, I quietly breathed, "Please…no…."

The man didn't have time to respond before I ran from him as fast as I could. Heavy laptop in hand, I awkwardly ran to my bloque and hotel room, seeing no one along the way. I didn't know if the man was running behind me or if he was still standing in the hallway in a stupor of perversion. I just ran. After several flights of stairs, I finally got to my hotel room, out of breath and my heart beating out of my chest. Natalie, Roberta, and Aleeza asked what was going on. When I explained, Roberta immediately called the front desk to report what one of their hotel employees was up to. The hotel receptionist did absolutely nothing.

This was the final straw. I'd had enough. I'd come to Punta Cana already exhausted and hadn't rested the entire weekend. I was being attacked on every side. I felt sick, worn out, frustrated, and violated. I had no bus ticket, no plane ticket, and no way of knowing whether I'd make it to Haiti on time. In my very last attempt to get a moment of rest, I'd been targeted by one of the men who was supposed to be protecting me. In this battle, I was being struck mercilessly. What was happening to me?

I decided it was time to amp up the spiritual warfare. While praying, God showed me that I'd been on the defensive this whole time. I had been praying for protection against sickness and attack, hoping nothing bad would happen to me. But attack seemed to be following me. I realized it was time to pray on the *offensive*, to actively take a stand against the powers of darkness. I needed to strike the devil before he even had a chance to hit me first. My teammates needed to fight in the same way. Our weapons against Satan would be joy, praise, unity, and thanksgiving.

In the morning, the team decided to temporarily split up so some of us could meet my friend in Haiti and others could return to La Romana to get our money back from the travel agent. Within two days, we hoped everyone would be in Haiti together. Though we'd been forced to take a little detour, we wouldn't let frustration defeat us. In a way, it was good that the attacks against us were so blatant. It made us that much more aware of how we needed to fight.

Even in the midst of our disarray, God used the whole mess for His glory. Roberta and Alan graciously offered to return to La Romana to fight for our cash. They stayed at Ramon's house again and decided to visit Maria Teresa as well while they were back in the area. Aleeza had shared Maria Teresa's story with her mother, who felt so moved by her faith that she decided to send her an offering from Australia. However, Aleeza was unsure of how she could get that money directly into Maria Teresa's hands. When Roberta and Alan decided to return to La Romana, Aleeza asked them to deliver an offering to Maria Teresa personally. Meanwhile, Maria Teresa had been planning on heading outside of La Romana to get some supplies for her new business idea. However, God told her to wait one more day to leave La Romana. The day that she waited out of pure obedience, Roberta and Alan showed up in the city and handed her a generous offering. Our detour became somebody else's blessing.

In the meantime, Natalie, Aleeza, and I embarked on a three-bus journey to Haiti, totaling about fourteen hours of travel. First, we took two buses to backtrack to Santo Domingo and stayed there overnight. The next morning, we arrived at the bus station and prayed there were seats left on the early bus to Haiti. By the grace of God, everything went smoothly, and we transitioned from bus to bus without problems — allowing plenty of time to meet my friend.

The very instant that I got on the first bus, there was an unexpected shift in my spirit. Suddenly, I felt a strange burst of joy. I felt whole. I was laughing for no reason. So were my teammates. It made no sense, but everything seemed in its perfect place. The stress, frustration, and perversion from Punta Cana melted off of me. I looked around the bus and saw something that looked *real* for the first time in days. Authenticity refreshed me. I smiled as I pressed my head against the window of the bus and dozed off. Finally, on a crowded bus, rest had come.

In that moment, I realized that something strange had happened inside of me. Years ago, I would have felt this joy at the beach resort in Punta Cana. I would have been smiling like this while walking around the nice buildings and eating the good food. But I was different now. Even though Punta Cana looked pretty on the outside, its core felt so painfully fake. Emptiness, perversion, and superficiality had been choking me. I couldn't rest when everything inside of me wanted to run away. But on this bumpy local bus, I could breathe easy. Part of me was relieved, and part of me was disturbed that I felt happier on local transportation than at a beach resort. My sense of normal, good, and bad was all mixed up. I unintentionally discerned things I could have ignored in the past. My point of view had been flipped upside down, and nothing felt the way it used to. God was really shaking me up inside.

Chapter Twenty-Two

HAITI: A New Paradigm for Missions

Before traveling to Haiti, I had heard pretty much nothing but negative talk about this country. People called it a hopeless nation, a black hole that sucked up resources, a revolving door of missionaries, a country given to Satan, and a barren land. Rumor said Haiti was ugly, brown, and unfertile. I'd been told I would see a shift from green to brown the moment I crossed the Dominican Republic-Haiti border, a result of demonic curses. "No one knows quite what to do with Haiti," was the resounding opinion. "Don't waste your time."

Whenever I heard negative press about a country, everything inside of me wanted to prove people wrong. When people declared a hopeless nation, I wanted to declare hope. When people declared barrenness, I wanted to declare life. When people declared a curse, I wanted to declare a blessing.

The Lord had given me a vivid dream about Haiti way back in August 2012, and I had held it in my heart. Despite hearing how dreadfully ugly Haiti was, my dream revealed *gorgeous palm trees, sparkling water, and natural beauty.* I believed God saw Haiti like this, but I wondered what I would actually see when I got there.

Upon arriving in Haiti, I quickly realized that people saw what they wanted to see. Yes, it was true that parts of Haiti were incredibly polluted, poor, and destitute. But beyond the rubbish piles and the poverty, there was beauty so intense that it can't be put into words.

In Haiti, I saw green. I saw lush vegetation. I saw flourishing trees. I saw children laughing and faces smiling. I saw the same sparkling, clear water and palm trees I'd seen in my dream. Most importantly, I saw a nation bursting with endless potential and tenacious hope.

During our 2013 visit, we encountered a nation on the brink of change. Something significant was happening in Haiti's history — you could simply feel it in the air. It seemed like the people had hit a turning point, and the nation had already begun a historic upswing. There was still abundant need and appalling poverty, but Haiti was rapidly moving forward. The earthquake of 2010 was not the confirmation of God's hatred for this "ungodly nation." God loves Haiti. He loves His Haitian sons and daughters, and He has a plan of hope and prosperity for them.

Because of the unique nature of Haiti, our team's ministry time there unfolded quite differently than we'd imagined. Instead of witnessing healing miracles, overwhelming financial favor, or other demonstrations of the more in-your-face glory, we experienced God's glory through relationship. Most of our time was spent getting to know people on a much more intimate level than we could have ever done with our large team in South America. We opened our hearts to our new brothers and sisters, listened to their visions, and ministered to many individuals who were in the process of transforming Haiti.

To share this segment of the journey with us, God brought our team what felt like a personal gift to me — my dear friend Connie. Thankfully, my worries about arriving on time to meet Connie in Haiti's capital were dismissed as we snagged seats on the bus we'd hoped for and reached Port-au-Prince on the right day. I was elated to pick Connie up at the airport and see the face of an old friend. Connie had been one of my housemates during mission school in Mozambique and served as my source of entertainment, my deepest confidant, and my partner in crime. She had often caused me to start giggling in the middle of class and delighted in any opportunity to make me look like a troublemaker. She specialized in friendly mischief, spontaneous composition of ridiculous songs, and hysterical facial expressions. Connie's visit gave us a burst of joy, which was much-needed fuel at the end of a long journey. She joined us throughout our time in Haiti and flew back to the States just before the rest of us moved on to Cuba.

I enjoyed watching my teammates getting to experience Connie's infectious joy and immediately accepting her into our family of now six. Full of gratitude, I felt like God had chosen to privilege us six by letting us in on one of His greatest secrets. He was going to surprise the world with what He was doing in this little island nation. He was gradually pouring more and more fuel into the country, getting ready to throw a match down and explode Haiti with His glory. In Haiti, I felt like an undercover agent for God, secretly being handed fuel by my Father and shown which people to throw it on — knowing the explosion was coming really soon. God connected my team to pivotal leaders in Haiti's transformation, and I can't explain how humbled I was that He let my tiny team be a part of their lives and this upcoming burst of glory.

Our divine connections began before we even arrived in Haiti. A friend of my mother, June, had lived in Haiti years prior and connected me through Facebook to several of her friends living in Port-au-Prince. I started writing so many emails to strangers in Haiti that I was getting mixed up with who was who. But one man's emails really stood out to me, and I knew we needed to make meeting him a priority. His name was Pastor Bobby.

Bobby, originally from the U.S., was the head pastor of Quisqueya Chapel, one of the three English-speaking churches in all of Haiti. We attended his church on our first Sunday, and the moment he began to speak from the pulpit, I knew this man would shake the nation. He declared the very words that were on our hearts. He boldly proclaimed that Haiti was positioned perfectly for revival, because God loved to use the underdog to blow people away with His power and glory. God used the weak things of the world to shame the wise. (See 1 Corinthians 1:27.) Haiti had been declared the "poorest country in the Western Hemisphere," a disheartening identity. But Bobby declared that label of poverty was precisely why God would choose Haiti for a powerful movement of the Holy Spirit. He said that because of the devastating earthquake in 2010, the whole world was watching Haiti. This tiny country had attracted the hearts of people all over the globe, and people would see when God brought it from tragedy to victory. This was the first time I'd heard someone fearlessly declare that the negative words spoken over Haiti were lies and curses and that we needed to believe in something greater.

Early in our time in Haiti, Natalie had a dream and was unsure about the interpretation, but it all made sense as soon as she heard Bobby preach.

Our team was going somewhere together and encountered people in ornate robes. The robes were clearly expensive and looked beautiful with their deep purple and pink hues. These people wore fancy turbans as well. Politely they asked us, "Can you please leave our territory?"

As we walked away, submitting to their request, Natalie turned around and noticed one man looking at us. He was also dressed in a fine robe and turban, but he was different than the others. He was a middle-aged man with round glasses and gray hair. He sat continually looking at us.

Natalie used her arms to form the sign of the cross. She lifted her arms in a "T" to show the cross, then brought her arms forward to hug herself in an attempt to demonstrate the cross embracing us.

The man watching us smiled. Natalie knew "he got it." He understood what we understood. Our visit was for him.

During our first Sunday at Quisqueya Chapel, Natalie immediately knew the dream was about Bobby. Though Bobby was surrounded by people who looked nice and "did church," many seemed dry. Yet, he was starving for revival, craving a movement of the Holy Spirit, desperate for God to move in power in the country of Haiti.

However, his congregation was a bit hesitant. Though some people were open to whatever God was doing, many remained religious and prim and proper. They looked like "church people" — neatly dressed and knowing when to quietly sit and listen to the pastor and when to stand and sing the assigned hymns. I didn't want to judge the congregation, but I could see that several people didn't know the power, the joy, or the radical presence of the Holy Spirit. I believed many of these people truly loved God, but His wild passion was missing. Conversely, my teammates had *passion* written all over them for the world to see. No one said anything blatant to us, but we could sense that our presence was unwanted by some. When they noticed the freedom we carried, it was quite obvious that they politely preferred we leave their territory.

When we left the service, Natalie declared that Bobby was the man from her dream. His round glasses and gray hair matched what she'd seen, and she just knew that this man "got it." Though being directed by the untamed winds of the Holy Spirit caused some people to resist us, this was the very thing Bobby had been crying out for. He was the one we'd come for.

I approached Bobby at Quisqueya Chapel and explained that I was the girl who had been emailing him. Instantly, our hearts connected with Bobby's, and we knew we needed to spend more time together. He quickly adopted my team as his little "League of Nations" and invited us to stay at his home for a couple of nights. There, we shared ideas, food, and laughs with him and his beautiful wife. Bobby was hungering for more and more of God and was desperate to see Him move powerfully in his life, his family, his church, and his nation. He saw the same ticking time bomb that we did and believed God was getting ready to blow up Haiti with His glory.

Bobby knew God was on the move in a radical way in Haiti and wanted to involve us in what was happening. We spent hours praying with Bobby and for Bobby, anointing his whole church with oil, prophesying over his family, and breaking strongholds and curses over Haiti. In addition, Bobby scheduled numerous appointments for us to connect with various friends who wanted prayer, encouragement, or simple fellowship with like-minded people.

My favorite meeting took place at the home of South Korean Helen, one of the hidden fireballs in Bobby's congregation. We met her on a Sunday morning when Bobby brought her over to our group for prayer. Helen was facing many trials that had all piled up into one big mess. She had mistakenly been assumed as a woman of great wealth, and greed led to an attempted kidnapping. Though Helen didn't provide great detail, we found out that her colleague had caught wind of a plan conceived by several Haitian men that involved kidnapping Helen and holding her for ransom. Fortunately, Helen left her home in time to hide out for a while. She secretively stayed at a friend's house until threats subsided, but she felt unsafe returning to her old home and desperately needed a new place to live. Helen was in search of a new base for her ministry as well. In addition, she had been suffering from a relentless cough for months. Looking overwhelmed and broken, she approached us for prayer. We prayed that God would protect and provide.

Just two weeks later, we reunited with Helen in her brand new home. God had provided a new place to live that was beautiful, affordable, and fully furnished. Though monthly rent was a concept unheard of in Haiti, Helen needed this option, and the woman renting the house said it was no problem. Helen was also provided with a new house for her ministry base at the exact price she'd prayed for. Lastly, her persistent cough was healed. Helen looked radiant — healthy, happy, and in awe of God's speedy answers to prayer.

During our visit, Helen invited a colleague named Jasmine over to her house and asked us to pray for her. We asked Jasmine what she wanted prayer for. Poised and self-assured, she very matter-of-factly said that she was bipolar and would like to live a more normal life. We began to dig a little deeper. Eventually, Jasmine admitted that she had been abandoned by her mother and mistreated by her sister as a child.

Jasmine also divulged that she heard a voice who gave her instructions. The voice told her there was no God. It told her that if she kept smoking, she would go to hell. We asked her who she thought the voice was. She seemed unsure at first, then said she thought it was the devil. We asked Jasmine if she believed the voice when it spoke and if she really wanted to follow its instructions. She said she had no choice. She needed a guide for her life, and the voice was the only one guiding her. Jasmine said she couldn't hear the voice of God, so she was forced to follow this one.

Jasmine explained that she had begun to feel a "negative energy" in her childhood home in Jamaica. Her sister hated and cursed her, and whenever she wore her sister's clothes, she felt pain all over her body. When Jasmine told her mother about the pain, she immediately brought her to a psychiatric ward. Jasmine was diagnosed with bipolar disorder and put on medication. Her mother couldn't handle the situation and quickly sent Jasmine off to live with her father in Haiti.

Jasmine had been dismissed as mentally ill, but I told her that she was not crazy. I explained that we were all in a very real battle, and there were very real angels and demons around us. I told Jasmine that the negative energy and the voice speaking to her were called Satan. The positive energy was called the Holy Spirit. The negative energy, Satan, produced lies, death, condemnation, etc. The positive energy, the Holy Spirit, produced life, truth, freedom, peace, joy, etc.

We asked her if she wanted to hear the Holy Spirit instead of the voice. We asked her if she wanted to forgive her family and find freedom. We asked her if she wanted to stand in authority over the demonic guide that was controlling her life. She said "yes" on every account.

Natalie began by leading her in a prayer to forgive her family and renounce all pacts she'd made with Satan. Several of us prayed for her, and we asked her to repeat, "I am a daughter of God. Jesus Christ loves me. Satan has no power over me…"

As Jasmine repeated, she suddenly burst into tears and began to yell words from her heart. "I belong to God! Satan, I'm not your play toy anymore! I hate you!!!"

In that crucial moment, she shifted from being trapped to taking authority over what was happening in her life. I saw the deep pain from her battle and the true desire to defeat the enemy. We stopped fighting *for* her and began fighting *with* her as she spoke words of truth over her own life. This was breakthrough.

Finally, after much prayer, we all went outside, joined hands, and screamed "FREEDOM!" at the top of our lungs three times. Jasmine radiated with victory. She was no longer a prisoner. This woman was free.

* * * * *

Though we could have easily stayed in Port-au-Prince for the entire month, we decided to head outside the city for part of our Haitian adventure. We spent a few days in the region of Carrefour, just an hour outside of downtown Port-au-Prince. One of Natalie's friends connected us with a Haitian forerunner named Karly. An architect by trade but missionary by practice, Karly exhibited what a true servant of Christ was supposed to be. Karly spent his days visiting the tent cities and homes in Carrefour to bless families and pray for people. He was involved at a neighborhood orphanage and active with the youth in his church. Karly's home not only belonged to him, his wife, and their adorable son but also to the countless neighborhood children who flocked to their property. Every time we came to Karly's home, local kids were in the front of the house playing soccer, gathered in his living room watching a movie, or sitting on his porch waiting for a hug.

Karly often worked with visiting mission teams and led them throughout his village to be involved in his day-to-day ministry. Normally the teams stayed at "The Villa," a fancy establishment across the street from Karly's home. However, we were placed in a more modest house next door and invited to eat at Karly's house each night instead of The Villa. This turned out to be a huge blessing and an opportunity to transform from acquaintances into family. Each night, we enjoyed the delicious local food that Karly's wife cooked for us as well as the fellowship of new friends. As we joked around with Karly, he became like a big brother, and his four-year-old son became our team's new favorite person. The people who saw us interacting thought we'd been friends for a long time and were shocked to find out we'd just met.

Karly whipped us into shape by hiking us around his mountainous community and bringing us to various homes to pray for people. Many were sick and in pain. The need was great. At the top of Carrefour stood a tent city, a makeshift community formed of tarp tents after the earthquake. As we passed through, we were invited into some homes to pray. Whenever we prayed, the women put cloth on their heads, which was a sign of reverence for God while receiving prayer. If they didn't have a handkerchief handy, they all scrambled to find something before prayer started — even an old T-shirt — to place on their heads. Despite being told that *everybody* in Haiti believed in voodoo, my team was moved by the Haitian humility and reverence for the Lord.

We also visited a local orphanage with Karly, which immediately melted my heart. Most of the children living there were very young, around five or six years old. They eagerly surrounded us, ready to play. We organized a few rounds of "Duck, Duck, Goose" and then a game of musical chairs. The kids cheered with excitement and roared with laughter.

Aleeza spent her time holding a tiny baby, just a few months old, who was the most malnourished person I'd ever laid eyes on. I'd seen starving babies from places like Somalia on TV and in magazines, but I'd never seen a child so emaciated right in front of my eyes. Her legs were like fragile, skinny twigs with withered skin sagging off of them. She looked so delicate that I feared I'd break her if I touched her. Aleeza bravely picked this baby girl up and held her on her lap. She prayed for God to heal the little baby even though she looked lifeless. Her face was blank, and I knew if she hadn't been taken in by the orphanage, she would have died.

Three days later, we asked Karly to take us back to the orphanage for another visit. In just seventy-two hours, the tiny baby girl had transformed into a different person. She smiled when we picked her up. Her face had life in it. She showed emotion. I could scarcely believe my eyes. God was really healing this baby. Slowly but very surely, He was nursing her back to health.

The other children were happy to be reunited, and I spent most of my time chasing around a few of the little boys, tickling them as soon as I caught them, and swinging them in the air. I got tired much faster than the six year olds did and sat on the couch for a moment to rest. A quiet little boy approached me and crawled into my lap. He examined my ponytail and ran his fingers through my brown and blond hair, carefully rearranging where it fell on my shoulders. After he was pleased with his work, he cuddled into my chest, his arms wrapped around me.

I'd been having so much fun playing that I'd kind of forgotten these kids were orphans. Suddenly, I remembered why they were craving such love and attention. It was not normal for a little boy to be so starved for affection that he didn't care where it came from. That was never the way God intended the world to be. Though we were providing very temporary affection, I knew these kids needed so much more than we could provide in just a few hours.

This feeling of hopelessness was what many people let define Haiti, but this wasn't the end of the story. Though there were still lots of orphans at the time of our visit, God was raising up a generation of fathers for the fatherless. Karly was already serving as a spiritual father to many, and he was training countless young Haitians to follow his example.

In fact, Karly had been dreaming of organizing a youth conference for the young adults in his church and asked us to help him make it happen. He wanted to disciple the youth and begin a ripple effect of God's love. As these youth went deeper with God, they would become the revival Haiti needed. Karly invited several young adults to our team's accommodation (equipped with a large meeting room) for a three-day conference. My teammates and I taught on the father heart of God, our identity in Christ, and the authority we carried as God's children. The youth were open, eager to learn, and excited to pass on what they had learned to others. These future leaders were already creating a ripple effect.

Though Carrefour was great, we still wanted to explore further outside the city and began to pray for open doors. Through a friend of a friend of a friend, we connected with a German woman named Martina living in Gonaives, an area about three hours north of Port-au-Prince. Martina invited us to stay at the children's home where she lived, Mission de Vie. We'd found that most nonprofits in Haiti charged lots of money for visitors, some orphanages asking as much as ninety dollars per night to volunteer. When we inquired about the price of staying with her, Martina seemed confused as to why we would even offer money. Her orphanage was the first we'd encountered that didn't seem to depend on foreign teams for income. Though Martina was from Germany, she was the only foreigner living at Mission de Vie. She was married to a Haitian and gracefully and joyfully immersed in the culture.

Martina organized several meetings for us — praying for sponsorship program parents, orphanage staff, kids, and youth. At the staff meeting, we threw our original plan out the window and decided to simply wash the feet of all the staff members and pray for them one by one. One woman's stoic countenance cracked, and she began crying. As we prophesied over people, Connie was overwhelmed by a sense from God and told one of the women, "I feel like you are called to be a mother." This didn't seem like much of a stretch for a woman working at an orphanage, but the woman sneered. Connie was a bit taken aback by her reaction and wasn't sure what to think.

Natalie pried further to see why she'd reacted like that. Natalie asked the woman if there was anything she needed prayer for. Reluctantly, the woman offered, "I don't know why, but my husband and I can't have children. Before this meeting, I was crying out to God about this. I told God that if your mission team didn't say anything about me being a mother, I wouldn't listen to anything you told me." We were a bit stunned.

Shortly after, her husband heard the word Connie had received from the Lord, and he asked us to pray for both him and his wife. We went to their home later on and prayed for God to give them children. The woman's countenance had completely shifted from harsh and skeptical to soft and welcoming. She hugged us goodbye, blessing us and telling us to come back to Haiti soon.

At the end of our visit, Martina dropped us off at another mission in Gonaives called Much Ministries. We were greeted by an American couple known to locals as Papa Beaver and Mama

Kathy, the heart of Much Ministries. Beaver and Kathy traveled back and forth between Haiti and North America for ten years before making a permanent move to Haiti in 2011. They currently worked in an extremely impoverished community called Jubilee. Jubilee was comprised of a garbage dump, several shacks, muddy roads, sewage streams, and salt flats. You could choose to see the brown ugliness of it all, or you could choose to see the beauty. Papa Beaver and Mama Kathy chose to see the beauty.

Kathy's vision entailed taking things that others considered trash and making them into something beautiful. She started collecting trash from the rubbish dump in Jubilee and teaching the local women how to turn it into gorgeous jewelry. Years ago, she told the Haitian women of Jubilee that one day foreigners would be fighting over what they had. The Haitians laughed at Kathy. Not too long after, they began to sell the jewelry and stunning art that they'd rescued from the dumps and transformed into masterpieces. Foreigners started coming to visit the project, and some actually fought over who got what — all desperate to get their hands on what the Haitians had created. The local women who had once laughed at Kathy stopped in awe. Mama Kathy smiled. She'd seen the beauty in Jubilee all along.

Kathy named their line of jewelry and products "Second Story Goods." In regards to the materials she used to produce goods, she explained that being thrown in the trash was their first story. But Kathy and the local women rescued these materials from the dump and made them into something beautiful. Now they were on their second story. And this story was a good one.

Getting connected with people like Bobby, Helen, Martina, Karly, Beaver, and Kathy gave us a chance to witness many beautiful stories happening inside Haiti. However, opening up candid conversations with them also exposed some of the raw truth behind the ugly side of missions. These people had chosen to dedicate their lives to seeing a transformation in Haiti. They'd poured blood, sweat, and tears into the nation. Unfortunately, in the process, they'd seen foreigners coming in and out, often creating more harm than good. They'd seen people come with agendas who forced unhelpful ideas on the Haitians. And frighteningly, even more often, they'd seen people come to Haiti with *good* intentions who unknowingly created messes far worse than what they'd started with.

We spoke with a brilliant young man named Junior who was Haitian-born but grew up in the U.S. He was the founder of a brand called "The Gold of the Antilles," which employed Haitians to produce honey and other agricultural products. He believed agriculture was the avenue through which Haiti would escape the cycle of poverty. Junior shared wise words with us that I will never forget:

"People come to Haiti with visions of how to help the nation. Unfortunately, their visions usually don't involve Haitians. If you want to come from the outside, you *must* include the locals within your vision."

Lists of foreign-run orphanages, nonprofits, and churches began to run through my mind. I'd seen this in Haiti, Latin America, and Africa. People came to "help the poor locals," but they only employed other foreigners at their organizations. Or, if they did employ locals, it was for low-paying positions only. A foreigner was almost always the director. Imagine the effects this would have on the morale of the local staff.

I realized that some volunteer projects I'd been a part of personally may have created more harm than good. Though well-intentioned, I realized we could have really hurt or discouraged people. At the time, I'd had no idea.

Junior continued, "After the earthquake, foreigners came in to build homes in Haiti. Yes, people need homes, but they also need jobs. Groups should have come into Haiti and employed Haitian men to help them rebuild. Imagine being an able-bodied young man. Your house is ruined. You have no money. Now a bunch of junior high kids fly in from the States and erect a fancy building in front of your face in days. What does that do to your morale as a man? How do you think this makes these men feel? It's no wonder people start adopting a poverty mindset. They learn to expect handouts. They learn to expect foreigners to 'do it better.' This is not the way it should work."

I knew everything coming out of Junior's mouth was true. And I regretfully remembered that when I was a kid, I'd been on a team exactly like the junior high team he'd described. Everything we were taught in the States about helping — well, we needed to rethink it.

Junior went on to explain that many people harmed developing nations without ever even stepping foot on foreign soil, simply by sending products overseas. Many genuinely thought they were helping, but they weren't. People from the States, Canada, and Europe had been sending used clothes to places like Haiti for so long that the local production of clothing had virtually come to a stop in many of those places. No Haitians could keep up with the infiltration of foreign clothes. They couldn't produce anything as cheap as the secondhand clothes being sold in their country, which resulted in the local textile markets crashing.

The same thing happened to many farmers. Large American NGOs started sending rice into Haiti after the earthquake. They could produce in mass quantities in Miami and ship the rice to Haiti for a fraction of the price that the Haitian farmers needed to charge to make a profit. The Haitian farmers couldn't compete with the prices, so locals began buying from the States instead of their own people.

Unfortunately, America and other influential nations had played a large hand in destroying the Haitian economy. Our governments, our churches, and our individual citizens had attempted to "help" Haiti but ended up causing harm. As we spoke to people on the receiving end of the so-called aid, they told us stories of what foreigners had done to unknowingly destroy them. Sadly, this type of destruction was not unique to Haiti. It had also happened in many other developing nations around the globe and is still happening today.

Our time in Haiti was a true eye-opener for all of us. Speaking with people like Bobby and Junior really changed my paradigm for missions. I learned how crucial it was to be ever so careful when entering a foreign culture. Though we can dream to change the nations, we must include the local people within our visions. We can't do it without them — or at least we can't do it right.

Even though all this information tempted to discourage us, I still left Haiti full of hope. Many people had created more harm than good in Haiti, but there were still people like Bobby, Kathy, Beaver, Martina, Karly, Helen, and Junior who had brought positive change to Haiti. There were people who genuinely asked God for vision and executed their plans hand in hand with the local population. There were people who sincerely knew how to love their neighbors and lay down their lives for their brothers and sisters. People like this have changed and will continue to change the nation of Haiti.

I suppose the name of Kathy's "Second Story" products sums up the heart of Haiti best. Truly, we encountered a nation on its second story. The first story I heard about Haiti was poverty and strife. But its second story is one of transformation, prosperity, and hope.

Chapter Twenty-Three

CUBA: A Beautiful Prison

Though I'd always been a dreamer, certain ideas never really entered my realm of possibilities. While preparing for our trip in the very beginning, I knew I would travel to many places that others advised against, but Cuba never crossed my mind. It wasn't until I started planning for the Caribbean portion of the trip that I started thinking seriously about Cuba. I wondered if we could actually make our way to an island I'd always deemed inaccessible. My whole life I'd heard stories of "rebellious Cubans" who attempted boating or even swimming from Cuba to the United States and how such criminals deserved to be punished. I was pretty sure it was against the law to travel to Cuba directly from the States, and I'd heard about people getting in serious trouble for bringing Cuban goods into the U.S. All in all, it just sounded like traveling to Cuba meant playing with fire.

However, when I began to lay out the Caribbean itinerary, I knew my team was called to go to the poorest islands, which meant Cuba was a must. In addition, Cuba seemed to be part of what Taylor L. described when sharing his prophetic dream about the Caribbean — large islands in the northern part of the Caribbean, close to the United States. I knew God had specifically called us to *five* island nations and believed Cuba was one of them. I prayed that if we were truly meant to go, God would open up legal doors for us to gain access into the country.

During our time in Puerto Rico, God connected us to Pastor Manuel, the brother of our host, who assured us that it would be possible to get into Cuba. Not only did he have influential contacts on the island, he knew the ins and outs of acquiring visas, doing mission work within a communist system, and what things to watch out for during our time in Cuba. Entrusting us with fragile information, Manuel connected us to a couple of pastors who were willing to take a risk on us in order to further the gospel. Manuel also announced the good news that travel laws between the U.S. and Cuba had very recently changed. Legally, it was an ideal time to go to Cuba. Doors that once seemed impenetrable were now wide open.

Manuel explained that we had the option of getting a tourist visa or a religious visa. The tourist visa was just fifteen dollars, the religious visa one hundred dollars. With a religious visa, entry requirements were more stringent, but the visa allowed the freedom to preach. With a tourist visa, very little would be required for entry, but preaching or evangelizing would be out of the question.

We decided applying for a religious visa would be worth the extra money, but unfortunately, we soon found out that we needed six months to complete the application process. This meant we would have to go undercover as tourists, making our entry procedure much easier but our time in Cuba much riskier. We decided to apply for our visas from Haiti and went to the Cuban Embassy in Port-au-Prince. We were supposed to have our flights to and from Cuba reserved before applying for the visas but didn't want to spend hundreds of dollars on flights before we had visas in our hands. Stuck at a standstill, we went to the Cuban Embassy without proof of flights and prayed for favor.

At the Cuban Embassy, we were greeted by two flirtatious men, one of them the Cuban consul himself. Both men were too busy stroking our arms and gazing into our light eyes to notice that we were missing some of our required paperwork. These employees were all smiles, but they reeked of seduction and insincerity. As we sat waiting for the secretary to finish our paperwork, the attempt at brainwashing began. The men reeled off speeches about how perfect Cuba was — how the beaches were lovely, how the children were well taken care of, how the government provided for people so wonderfully, etc.

A large photo of the "Five Heroes" of Cuba was displayed behind us, and the consul asked us if we knew the story of the heroes. When we said "no," he rattled off a long story about five wonderful, valiant heroes from Cuba who went to the United States to uncover terrible terrorist activity. They only wanted to do good, and the U.S. government unjustly threw them in prison. Some of them received two life sentences, making it impossible to ever overturn the ruling. The consul himself handed me a book about the "Five Heroes," poorly written and full of English errors. It explained more about the history of these five men and why the U.S. government was so evil and cruel and unjust to them. (I later asked a Cuban pastor about the "Five Heroes," and he rolled his eyes as he explained that they were terrorists about whom he was sick of hearing.)

The consul then took us into a downstairs room in the embassy where propaganda related to the "Five Heroes" covered the wall. There was so much anti-American propaganda that I began to wonder if I would have problems in Cuba. "I'm from the United States," I explained to the consul. "Am I going to have issues in your country?" It didn't seem Cuba was particularly fond of my people.

"No, you're very welcome in Cuba," the consul crooned. "There are tons of Americans in Cuba. America doesn't like Cubans, but we *love* Americans." He flashed another fake smile, his greasy hair slicked back and shining. "You will love Cuba." He continued to smile and tell me how wonderful his country was, positioning himself directly in front of posters screaming with hatred.

After enduring uncomfortable conversation and attempted brainwashing, we were each presented with our tourist visas. "Enjoy your time in Cuba," the consul grinned as he escorted us to the front gate. We weren't even there yet, and I already knew it was going to be different than any place I'd ever seen before.

Just before we flew to Havana, Natalie had a noteworthy dream about being in Cuba and shared what she'd envisaged with us.

We locked up the doors to our house and headed out to find a place to eat. We were walking on an elevated road that allowed us to look down at a beautiful view of the ocean. At first glance, the scenery was stunning, but then Aleeza noticed there were pieces of wood floating in the ocean. It wasn't quite as clean as we'd originally thought. We noticed that the sky was changing, and someone explained that the weather changed three times a day in Cuba. Natalie turned to Roberta and asked, "We're in Cuba, right?"

Roberta responded, "Yes."

Natalie went on to ask, "We're in prison, right?"

Again Roberta replied, "Yes."

Natalie asked, "Then why is it so beautiful?"

In the morning, Natalie shared the dream with us, wondering how to interpret it. We'd heard many stories of Cuban Christians being thrown into literal prisons for their faith but hoped the dream was symbolic. We prayed intensely before getting on the plane, knowing our time in Cuba demanded a new level of trust in God's control.

Upon arrival, Cuba rapidly proved to be exactly what Natalie had dreamt — a beautiful prison. At first glance, Cuba was a beautiful country comprised of gorgeous beaches, stunning architecture, flourishing farmland, and perfect weather. But underneath the deceiving guise of beauty, the ugliness of communism, atheism, and control ran Cuba. People wanted to leave but couldn't get out. People wanted to share the gospel but were slammed with restrictions. People wanted to make money but were limited to pennies a month. They felt trapped. They felt suffocated. Truly, Cubans lived in a beautiful prison.

Our time in Cuba began by landing in Havana, where we passed through an exceptionally thorough airport inspection. First, we presented our passports and visas to a severe-looking customs official and looked into an iris scanner that examined our eyes to see if we were terrorists or illegal immigrants. After passing the first checkpoint, the airport official unlocked a door for me, which opened up to a second checkpoint. There, both my carry-on and I were scanned, and a woman ran a metal detector stick up and down the front and back of my body. Next, I stood in a line of nurses who interrogated me about my health and my plans in Cuba. The address I provided wasn't up to par, which caused a delay. Finally, one of the nurses let me through the final area of customs where I claimed my suitcase and presented my customs paper to the last official.

It was already past midnight, so we arranged for a hostel and planned to meet our pastoral contact in the morning. Before getting a cab, we exchanged some money, and I felt like I'd just been robbed. Most currencies lost a bit of value when exchanged, but the U.S. dollar was severely devalued in Cuba. National ATMs refused American credit cards, forcing U.S. residents to exchange their dollars and lose a large chunk of their cash. Other currencies, such as the euro, were exchanged at fair and reasonable rates. Immediately, I saw the manifestation of problems between the American and Cuban governments and its effect on my wallet.

Left without a choice, I took the pitiful amount of cash offered me for my dollars and got a taxi to our hostel. Unfortunately, the lovely accommodation that had been advertised online didn't exist. Instead, we were dropped off at a rundown apartment building where two young men were running a dodgy business that entailed putting up tourists in random peoples' spare apartment rooms. Though we'd been promised a dorm room that fit all five of us, we were told that room (which may or may not have actually existed) was full. The five of us were divided up. Alan was put in a crowded room with five strangers, Aleeza and Roberta in a strange man's apartment (who stayed the night there with them), and me and Natalie in an apartment full of men from India, England, and Chile. Natalie and I were instructed to take the bottom bunks and warned that our male roommates would soon be joining us. At this point, it was around 3 a.m., and I was too tired to argue. I crawled into my bunk and heard Peter, a sinister man from England, climb above me moments later. A drunken Chilean stumbled in around 4 a.m. and climbed up above Natalie's bed. I missed the days when a bad sleeping arrangement meant sleeping on the side of the road.

I wanted to check my email to see if the pastors I'd been communicating with had sent any pertinent information in regards to meeting up with them. When I asked about wifi (another promised perk of booking at this "hostel"), one of the men responded with a patronizing stare, a snicker, and "Ha, this is Cuba." Still unmindful of most day-to-day implications of the communist system, I hadn't even considered the possibility of a country without internet access. Even remote villages in Africa had internet. But the communist system did its best to cut its people off from the outside world. There was so much I hadn't thought about before. I began to learn quickly.

Luckily, there were payphones along the street, so we were able to call Pastor Bernardo in the morning, our first contact in Havana. He arranged for someone from his church to come pick us up at the hostel. We gladly packed our belongings and grabbed some food before leaving our dubious accommodation. We walked around the streets to try to find breakfast, and my communist learning experience continued. The large supermarkets and restaurants to which I was accustomed simply didn't exist in Cuba. In place of grocery stores, there were tiny rooms enclosed by bars where customers could peer through the windows and handpick each desired item. The selection was severely limited, and nothing was chosen outside of the control of the employees. I repeatedly tried to find a pack of mint gum and failed. Just acquiring the basics was a challenge, and anything even slightly extravagant was a lost cause. Finding a place to get breakfast was no simple task. We found a little restaurant decorated with deceiving pictures of hamburgers and other tasty items. Yet inside, we were presented with limited options — a piece of chicken, bread with ham, or bread with cheese. I ate a piece of chicken for just over a dollar. I later found out that my meal equated to one-eighth of a teacher's monthly salary in Havana.

After our meal, a jovial man with a huge, red car from the forties appeared outside our hostel. He drove us to Pastor Bernardo's house where we were greeted by his daughter. Before long, Bernardo and his wife arrived as well. I had been nervous about meeting Bernardo, because a lot of our previous email communication had been done through Google Translator. I could only write so much in Spanish and could only understand a percentage of Bernardo's responses, so I hoped we were actually on the same page. As soon as we met in person, I felt like I could relax. Our hearts immediately connected, and it just felt easy. We spent the rest of the afternoon and early evening learning about the Cuban government, the Cuban church, and our rough itinerary for the next few days.

Bernardo spoke frankly about the government but whispered even when we were in his home. He explained that Cubans often made a gesture as if they were stroking an imaginary beard to signal that they were speaking about Castro. Bernardo said, "Many people go to work and say, 'Oh, I love him so much [*simultaneously making the Castro symbol*]. I really love him [*beard stroke*]. But then they come home and speak the truth. They say, 'I hate that man [*beard stroke*]. I hate the things he does [*beard stroke*].'"

Bernardo was tired of the exhausting façade. Everyone was forced to pretend to love the government and comply with all kinds of unfair regulations. All people had certain limitations placed upon them, but it seemed the Christians suffered the most. The Christians who wanted to exalt God above the government were slowly gaining more freedom but still suffered for their faith. The government only chose to recognize certain churches, and the service hours in all churches (whether legal or illegal congregations) were regulated by the government. If services ran over the given timeframes, the pastors suffered whatever consequences the government deemed appropriate.

Bernardo said that spies were sent to investigate different congregations. He warned us never to speak about the government inside the church. If a spy were to hear any anti-government talk, Bernardo could be thrown into prison. He warned us that as foreigners, if we spoke against the government, we could also be thrown into prison or deported immediately and denied any future access into Cuba.

Pastor Bernardo's church was one of the many "daughter churches" of a much larger church. We would spend our first week working with several of the daughter churches, all unofficial congregations not registered with the government. During our second week, we would work with the legal "mother church." Bernardo explained that because we didn't have religious visas, it would be illegal to preach in any of these churches. However, the law allowed tourists to *greet* the church. While making sly facial expressions, Pastor Bernardo told us we could give the church a "greeting" that was five minutes long or two hours long. We could read in between the lines.

Before leaving the United States, my dad and I were talking about Cuba, still thinking entry was a likely impossibility. Knowing some of my teammates wouldn't hesitate to hop on a boat and hide all records of ever being in Cuba, he warned me, "Caitlin, don't do anything illegal."

"I won't," I assured him. "I'll be careful."

However, once in Cuba, I realized that if I was really going to do the work of the Lord in this nation, I was going to have to break the law. If I wanted to preach (ahem, I mean give a very long greeting), I would be taking a risk. But I couldn't come all this way and not share about Jesus. I just hoped that Natalie's prison dream was symbolic, not literal.

The Christians we met in Cuba were forced to break the law all of the time to spread their faith. Even our email communication prior to our arrival in Cuba had been illegal. After realizing wifi didn't really exist in Cuba, I asked Bernardo how he'd been coordinating with me via email. Turns out, he'd been secretly using the internet from a friend's business and could have been thrown in jail if the government found out what they'd been doing.

The government would also take issue if we stayed at the house of a church member. Bernardo arranged a hostel for us down the street from his home, apologizing that we couldn't stay with him but explaining the risk. This would be an interesting couple of weeks.

The following day, the man with the big, red car picked us up and dropped us off just outside Havana at the home of Pastor Jorge, a relative of Bernardo. Jorge began our day by bringing us to several sites around his village as well as various homes where he knew people wanted prayer. Everyone was lovely — friendly and hospitable — but many seemed quite discouraged. Jorge told us that he saw much sadness among his people. Many of his friends and congregants had family members who had managed to move to the U.S., but the relatives left behind were unable to visit. They desperately wanted to see their families but were told they could not. The American Embassy charged two hundred dollars for an application/interview to visit the States, and after interviews the Cubans were simply told "yes" or "no" without explanation. Those told "no" in regards to visiting the U.S. received no refund. People risked losing everything they'd saved to attempt to get out of Cuba, yet many didn't succeed. The results were disheartening.

After house visits, Jorge and his family served us an amazing meal that included their biggest delicacy — chicken. Though a staple food in the U.S., I learned that eating chicken was a luxury, and eating beef was almost unheard of. When I asked Jorge his favorite food, he answered, "I love chicken the most. But we can't afford to cook it very often. We are eating chicken today, but I don't know when I will eat it again."

I felt like I was eating money and humbly consumed the feast before me. It was one thing to accept a gift given out of abundance, but this family had given out of poverty. Jorge earned fourteen dollars per month, roughly the same amount an American would make in two hours if he was earning minimum wage.

Food was followed by an evening worship service. We walked across the street to Jorge's modest church building where our team gave the congregation a very long "greeting." Aleeza, Natalie, Roberta, Alan, and I each spoke for a few minutes about unity, each of our parts weaving together into one message. After the service, Pastor Jorge's son (who had translated for us) pulled me aside and told me that we'd really impacted his life. He said he was so encouraged by what we'd shared and how we interacted with one another. I felt like all we'd done was speak a few words and eat his family's precious chicken. Yet, our brief time together had impacted him in a way that only God could have ordained.

The next day, Bernardo arranged for us to visit a rural community with another friend of his named Pastor Estefan. I'd thought Jorge's neighborhood was poor, but this community was even more destitute. When I used the bathroom in Estefan's house, I noticed that in place of toilet paper, there were torn-up pieces of newspaper stacked on the toilet. His family was too poor to even afford toilet paper. Despite having close to nothing, Estefan and his wife fed us like kings and queens. I looked at the meal in front of my eyes — heaping portions of rice, beans, and pork. I fought back tears before I began eating, incredibly humbled by such generosity. What had we done to be treated so well? Would Estefan and his family have food for the rest of the week after feeding us so much? *Oh Jesus*, I thought, *how terribly spoiled I am.*

Serving alongside a man with such a generous and humble heart was a privilege. I felt like there was nothing we could do that would repay him for his kind offering. We ended up doing the usual — visiting homes and praying, organizing a youth service, and then preaching (I mean *greeting* the congregation) at an evening service. The highlight of our time was the youth meeting. As the community teenagers gathered, they asked us questions about our trip and how we'd been called to the mission field. They coyly giggled as we asked them about their own dreams and callings, and a few brave volunteers shared. As they spoke, I realized their dreams reached beyond the limitations the government put on them. They wanted to travel, explore, and spread the gospel. I was encouraged by their faith.

During our first weekend in Havana, we shared at Pastor Bernardo's church and attended a large worship event at *la finca*, meaning "the farm." Many churches from all over the Havana area, including Bernardo's, Jorge's, and Estefan's, gathered in a festival of hundreds out in the countryside. Jorge's son led worship as the Cubans sang along and danced with unmatched enthusiasm.

I will never forget the pure joy among the worshipping believers who had been persecuted for their faith. Pastors were regularly faced with the threat of imprisonment for preaching the gospel. Our team took a risk for two weeks, but afterwards we had the freedom to travel onward to countries where we could openly profess our faith. Until the fall of communism in Cuba, these believers would continue to live in persecution and risk. During the celebration, the people repeatedly cried out, "Cuba para Cristo! Cuba para Cristo!" (Cuba for Christ! Cuba for Christ!) Knowing what it meant for them to shout this phrase among the oppression, my heart was moved. It was far too easy to become complacent in my faith and take it for granted. But in Cuba, following Jesus was a choice and a battle every day. The people chose the hard road, the dangerous path. I was humbled to spend a moment among them, worshipping and shouting with them.

After an amazing week with Pastor Bernardo and his contacts, we moved to another area of Havana to work with their mother church. There, we coordinated with the vibrant worship leader, Hector, and the church's main pastor, Patricia. Behind closed doors in the main church, Patricia spoke openly about her frustrations with the government's control and the church's lack of freedom. She explained that her congregation wanted to do evangelistic outreaches but was constantly coming up against obstacles. For example, if they wanted to visit a prison, they had to apply for permission; yet it was very rare to be granted entry. Visiting a hospital to pray for people was out of the question, and street evangelism — just forget it.

However, Patricia was a fighter, and so was her church. She said Christians always found a way around the rules to spread the gospel. If one member of the church had a relative in prison, many congregants would tag along during visiting hours as "close friends and family" and then end up preaching inside the prison. Pastor Patricia said the Cuban Christians had learned to be very bold and would always find a way to accomplish their purposes. "The violent take the kingdom of heaven by force," Patricia stated (see Matthew 11:12). "You must be aggressive and bold to advance the kingdom in this country."

She talked about the issue of poverty in her nation as well, and I began to wonder what happened to children whose families could not provide for them. I remembered the consul back in the embassy in Haiti bragging about how wonderfully the government took care of its children. "Orphaned children are put in government homes and called 'Niños de la Patria,'" Patricia explained. (This roughly translates to "Children of the Nation.") "They are taught the things the government wants them to know."

It had taken less than thirty minutes for the men in the embassy to try to brainwash me and push propaganda on me. I could only imagine what these poor children went through. Cuba owned them.

"And if someone wants to start their own home for children in Cuba?" I asked, already knowing the answer.

"Impossible," declared Patricia. "They go to the government."

I felt like I was in some sort of sick movie, but this was really happening. Sadly, stuff like it (and far worse) is still happening all over the world every day.

In the evening, our education continued. We met with several of the cell group leaders from the church at our hostel, then split off for the night. Hector requested that each of us visit a different cell group with a different cell group leader. He sent Aleeza and Alan off with translators from the church and said that Natalie, Roberta, and I would be our own translators. Natalie and Roberta spoke fluently, but I wasn't quite at their skill level. I could mostly get by, but speaking alone at home groups was quite intimidating. I needed help.

Without a choice, we split up, and I followed my new friend Diego around the streets of Havana, walking for miles and visiting homes all over the city. As I walked down the streets with a man who had been a stranger just moments before, attempting conversation in Spanish, I had one of those "my life is so weird" moments. I prayed that the home groups would understand my awful accent as I kept walking, smiling, and traversing the streets of Havana with this man I'd just met.

Our first stop was a house full of young people. Probably between the ages of eleven and seventeen, the kids looked at me wide-eyed and curious. Diego introduced me and explained the journey I'd been on for the past eighteen months. When he explained that Cuba was our twenty-fifth country, I thought some of their jaws were going to hit the floor. I felt almost guilty as Diego spoke, realizing that traveling freely was a near impossibility for these kids.

Diego asked me to share what I had learned during the trip. *Where could I even begin?* I did my best to explain what God had been teaching me about sonship — about the importance of knowing our identity as sons and daughters of God and walking in the authority He had given us. I then asked the youth to share their dreams with me. One girl wanted to start a program to help the poor. One boy wanted to be a pastor. Some of the younger ones just wanted to play soccer forever. The oldest girl in the room looked at me, her eyes radiant, and said, "I want to do what you are doing so badly. Oh, that's my dream. This is so amazing. I want to travel and do what you do. I want a life like yours." She stopped talking, but her eyes kept dancing back and forth as she watched me, almost as if they were saying, *"Dreams really do come true."*

I thought about all the obstacles I'd faced in order to do what I was doing. Maybe my life *sounded* glamorous, but there were endless battles in this missionary lifestyle. I could only imagine how much harder it would be for a young girl from

Cuba. The chance her government would even let her outside of Cuba was slim. I saw the excitement in that young girl's eyes, and I prayed that God would grant her dream. I didn't know how that would ever be possible, but I knew God did impossible things. The kids and I gathered in a circle, and they prayed for me and I for them. "Let them dream with you, God," I prayed. "Make the impossible possible for these young ones."

Before long, Diego said it was time to move on, and we continued to visit house after house after house. One of the homes belonged to a kind woman who served as the neighborhood mama. She owned close to nothing but said everyone shared with everyone else. "If you need some soap, you go outside and yell, and someone will throw you some soap," she laughed. The inside of her house was so small that she had to keep a mattress leaned against the wall and place it on the floor every night after moving her one tiny table out of the way. "Four people live here," she explained. "When one of my friends moved in, she cried at first. It was so small. Can you believe four of us really fit here?"

It did seem unreal to squish that many bodies into such a crammed space. Yet, the woman of the house seemed genuinely happy. Diego and she laughed together as they discussed how ridiculous their living situations were. "I make eight dollars a month," the woman continued. "I'm a teacher, and that's what they pay me."

Diego added, "But the thing is, Cubans will give you everything they have. They can't afford anything, but they'll give you everything." He smiled, "We share whatever we have and take care of each other." He tugged on his shirt. "You know, we have clothes because people have come in and given us clothes. Without them, we really wouldn't even have clothes to wear."

"But how do you pay for other things?" I asked. I didn't understand. Sure, clothes could be donated, but what about food, schooling, appliances around the house, etc.?

Diego simply responded, "Glory to God. It's a miracle. God provides."

"But how?" I asked, wanting a more specific explanation.

"You can never understand," he smiled.

The woman nodded in agreement. "It's impossible for you to understand."

It's true. I still don't understand and probably never will.

After this conversation, the woman decided to join me and Diego to visit some more houses. We soon wound up a narrow staircase and ended up at the home of an elderly couple. The husband eagerly greeted me with some words in English; although his accent was so thick that I could understand him better when he spoke Spanish. He explained that his wife had been in bed all day with terrible pain in her stomach. He asked if I could pray for her and led me to her bedroom where I saw a beautiful, older woman lying in pain. Her eyes lit up at the sight of visitors. She declared, "I've been praying that God would send me an angel to come to my house and pray for me."

Diego's face lit up with amazement at God's timing and repeated what the woman had just said to make sure I really understood in Spanish.

"I'm not an angel," I said as I sat down beside her. "But I *can* pray for you."

I placed my hands on the woman and began to ask the Holy Spirit to overflow her heart. I asked for His joy, His peace, and His love to fill her to the brim. I commanded sickness out of her and love into her. After praying for several minutes, I opened my eyes and saw that the woman was weeping. The presence of God was so strong that we could feel His peace covering the entire room.

"How do you feel?" I asked, already knowing the answer.

"I feel the peace of God," she smiled.

"And your pain? Is it still there?" I inquired.

"No. I was in a lot of pain when you came, and now I don't have any."

We smiled at each other, knowing something divine had just happened in her little bedroom. It was already time to move on to another house, so I gave her a kiss on the cheek and said farewell.

On my way out, her husband asked me to pray for him, as he wasn't feeling well either. He also offered to pray for me in return. I gladly accepted. Afterwards, he said he wanted to give me a small present and handed me a book about prayer. Inside the front cover, he scribbled a scripture in Spanish — Psalm 32:8. It said, "I will guide you along the best pathway for your life" (NLT). Suddenly, I was reminded of my difficult time in Paramonga, Peru. In one of my weakest and most vulnerable moments of the entire journey, God had shown me that very same scripture three times. This word had given me the fuel to power through one of the darkest hours of the whole trip.

Earlier that day, I had been fasting and praying specifically about my future, asking God to give me peace about the many unknowns. I was physically tired from all the traveling, and my mind was full of questions about what to do and where to go when the journey soon came to an end. I had asked God to give me peace about my future, and once again, He gave me this psalm and reminded me that He had chosen the best pathway for my life. This time, that familiar word came through an old man from Cuba.

We continued visiting homes, probably totaling around eight or nine throughout the evening. People repeatedly met us with great joy (and lots of hugs and kisses) when they found out I'd come from the United States to visit them. Throughout the evening, Diego and his friends force-fed me way too much food, and though I begged them to stop, they simply chuckled and handed me more. By our very last home, I had to refuse the third cup of coffee offered to me, fearing I would actually vomit if I put anything else in my stomach. "Por favor, NO!" I begged Diego. He laughed and finally let me off the hook. After our last visit, he escorted me back to my hostel where I wobbled into bed, my stomach aching from being so full.

We spent the next few days working alongside Hector and attending different activities at his church including a "revival" service, missionary prayer meeting, and an overflowing Sunday morning service. Thousands of people attended the church every weekend despite the lack of space. Every crevice of the building was filled — overflow classrooms, hallways, areas just outside the church, etc.

While listening to Bernardo's and Patricia's frustrations with the government, I had initially thought we should pray against communism. But seeing a church too full to contain its own members, it was clear that the persecution of the church had resulted in overwhelming growth. Not only had the church grown in numbers, the dedication among believers was authentic and powerful. Unfortunately, Christians living in free countries sometimes took their religious liberties for granted and grew complacent in their faith. However, the Cuban Christians did not have the freedom to be lukewarm. Every believer had counted the cost of dedicating his or her life to the gospel and was willing to take the risks that came along with such a choice. Their faith was solid, firmly rooted, and genuine.

We spent one morning visiting elderly people from the church who wanted to attend services but were physically unable. Even among these house-ridden old men and women, I saw such deep faith that mine felt worthless. Despite their frail bodies, their spirits were incredibly strong. One feeble old man was undergoing chemotherapy for cancer and had lost feeling in his face. He was slowly experiencing improvements and believed in his complete healing. After we prayed, he insisted on escorting us to the door. We told him to just stay in bed, but for him, this was out of the question. Watching him struggle to get out of bed was painful, but I knew he would keep pushing until he got up. Finally, he was able to stand and hobbled to the door with a look of satisfaction on his face. "God is going to heal me," he declared. "He has already started. And when I am fully healed, I'm going to the church to share my testimony." I loved his raw faith. He was already planning to share his healing testimony before it had actually occurred. Discouragement was not an option for this man.

Cuba had challenged my faith more than any other place we'd visited thus far. However, just when I thought I couldn't be more humbled, my teammates and I were surprised with an evening that simply undid us. Pastor Jorge contacted Hector and asked if he could steal us back for a day. He had something planned for us in his village and said he would arrange to pick us up. We assumed he wanted us to preach a second time, so we arrived at his house ready to serve the church.

However, we quickly realized Jorge didn't want us to do anything except enjoy the company of his family, friends, and church members. The afternoon was simply a time of fellowship and friendship. We walked around the neighborhood with a couple of the girls, who showed us the city square and some of their favorite places. We talked to kids from the community and hung out with sweet old men who told us stories and teased each other. We sat with Jorge and his son and listened to what life was like over the past few decades in Cuba.

I learned that in 1991, when communism fell in Russia, the epidemic of poverty began to spread in Cuba. Prior to the nineties, people in Cuba hadn't been poor, because they received things from Russia. When Russia ceased to be under communist control, the relationship between Cuba and Russia changed, and Cuba no longer received what it needed. Instead of following Russia's lead, the Cuban government let its people become inflicted with extreme poverty and maintained a tight reign. In 1990-91, it was absolutely illegal to be a Christian. Jorge said that he and Pastor Bernardo had both been thrown in prison because of their faith. By 1992, there was more freedom to openly express one's faith. Wearing Christian clothes, displaying religious bumper stickers, and making other visible allegiances to Jesus were permitted.

Despite gaining these freedoms, Cubans remained extremely poor. Jorge said that before he had his own church, he and his wife used to bike twenty kilometers to attend services at the mother church. They would ride in the morning, go to the service, bike home, wash their clothes, let them dry, and then bike back for a night service! Poverty and persecution bred nothing but faith and increased determination. Their story was remarkable.

After this eye-opening conversation, Jorge gathered practically everyone from his church for a shared evening meal. They surprised us with a lavish feast. There was so much food in one room that I could barely believe my eyes. I immediately thought about what Jorge had told us about not having money and not knowing when he would get to eat chicken again. Yet, no one had hesitated to lavish their very best upon us.

We gratefully filled our bellies, then shared in a time of worship. Suddenly, we noticed that several people had snuck away into one of the bedrooms to do something. Moments later, they began parading into the family room and adorning us with gifts, as if the feast wasn't enough! Whatever the women had — hair ties, bracelets, earrings, makeup, and more — they handed it over to us. The kids drew us pictures and wrote out Bible verses in Spanish. One little girl had a real gold necklace, and she handed it to Aleeza, explaining that God had told her to give it away earlier that day. That was probably the only thing of value she owned; I couldn't believe it. Then, to bless us one step further, the church members asked if they could pray for us. They knelt down before us and laid their hands on our well-traveled feet.

In that moment, I was overwhelmed by the disgusting amount of selfishness inside of me. Yes, I was a missionary. Yes, I was a Christian. But in that moment, I felt like such a lie. I had been given so much more than I ever deserved and sadly took most of it for granted. I came from a country where persecution against Christians entailed teasing at worst. I had no idea what it felt like to bike twenty kilometers just to get to church or to go for months without eating chicken because it was too expensive or to be thrown in prison for professing my faith. People had asked me to preach in Cuba, but I was the one learning here — because I had no idea what this type of faith required. I caught a glimpse of Aleeza and saw that she was completely undone. She couldn't help but to weep, and I began to cry as well. I had never felt so humbled in all my life, receiving from those who had nothing but gave us everything. I too often clung tightly to the things I had, so afraid to lose. But these people weren't afraid. They would sincerely give the shirts off their backs for a brother or sister. They understood what it meant to sacrifice. They understood love. And God *is* love, which meant they probably understood Him a whole lot better than most of the world did.

Humbled, broken, and in awe, I received the prayers of my new Cuban family. Through teary eyes, I thanked them for their generosity and love. I don't know if or when I will return to Cuba and see them again, but I will not forget those people or their faith. I will never forget that beautiful prison.

Chapter Twenty-Four

JAMAICA: One Love

Cuba was amazing but so incredibly intense that by the time we reached Jamaica, I couldn't have been more grateful to be in our final country. Exhausted in every way, I looked forward to spending our last few weeks in a more laid-back atmosphere. Jamaica was slow-paced, beautiful, and just plain fun.

While booking our flights from Cuba to Jamaica, we encountered a slight ticket dilemma that rearranged our schedule a bit. Though originally planning to fly into Montego Bay and to later bus to Kingston, ticket options and prices forced us to fly into Kingston and bus to Montego Bay the following day. Initially, this seemed like a waste of time, as we now had to fly over a hundred miles *past* our desired destination, bus backwards to Montego Bay, and then return to Kingston ten days later. Aleeza insisted that this re-routing must be God's doing; however, I personally failed to see how any good could come from extra hours of unwanted travel. Nevertheless, we booked our out-of-the-way tickets and rolled with it.

Little did we know, Natalie would soon find out that she needed to pay a visit to the Russian Embassy in Kingston *before* arriving in Montego Bay. Though Russian-born, Natalie carried a German passport and no longer had Russian citizenship. After leaving Jamaica, she planned to fly to Russia to visit family, which required the acquisition of a Russian visa. The only place to apply for a visa in Jamaica was at the embassy in Kingston. Flying into Kingston first gave Natalie a chance to drop off her visa application at the embassy, proceed to Montego Bay, and allow the consul plenty of time to get her visa ready. If we had flown directly to Montego Bay as originally planned (and then traveled to Kingston over a week later), our final stay in Kingston would have been too short to allow the embassy sufficient time to process Natalie's paperwork before her flight. Though my human eyes had only seen an unwanted disturbance in our plans, God faithfully got us exactly where we needed to go.

After dropping off Natalie's application at the embassy, we hopped on a bus to the energetic beach city of Montego Bay. Though tired of traveling, I actually enjoyed the ride, admiring the vibrant landscape to my right and left. Jamaica proved to be a tasteful mix of natural beauty and gorgeous people — full of mountains, rivers, waterfalls, ocean views, trees, sleepy beach towns, and bustling cities.

Upon arriving in Montego Bay, we were greeted by a large Jamaican man named Shippie who drove us to Robin's Nest Children's Home, where we spent the next few days. This small orphanage was a bit off the beaten path and required zigzagging up bumpy mountain roads away from the city. The scenery around us resembled a remote rainforest until we finally arrived at an open oasis full of kids. The cheerful center sat atop a quiet peak with a brilliant view of the city. Thirty or so Jamaican boys and girls lived there as one family.

I was delighted to see the layout of the orphanage. It was comprised of well-constructed buildings, a modern playground, tiny patches of gardens with fresh vegetables, and even a swimming pool. This wasn't really an orphanage. It was a *home*.

We asked the best way to serve during our brief visit, and the staff put us to work at their homeschooling program. Most of the children attended a school closer to the urban center of Montego Bay; however, a handful of the boys were homeschooled at Robin's Nest. Because they were so far behind in school, their needs demanded extra attention. We enjoyed spending time with these boys, playing math and phonics games with them, reading books together, and getting a sneak peek at their school computer program. At moments, the kids feigned a "tough boy" attitude, but they could never keep it up for too long before feeling the uncontrollable need to smile or cuddle up to one of us.

After our visit, we said farewell to our new little friends and wound back down the mountain. We had bus tickets to Kingston for the following week, where organized contacts were awaiting our arrival. However, we had a few free days open to do whatever we wanted here on the other side of the island. Realizing we had not rested properly for about a month, we decided to take some time to simply rest and enjoy the natural beauty of Jamaica. We wanted to finish strong in Kingston and needed to refresh our bodies in order to do so.

A wide array of options inspired much debate about where to go, but our final decision was to hop on a bus to the laid-back beach town of Negril. We scored the last available beds at a small backpacker hostel, a crammed yet affordable alternative to the expensive hotels lining Negril's famous beaches. Simply thankful to get some sleep and be near the beach, I spent the next few days running by the water, swimming in the crystal clear

Caribbean Sea, and swinging in a hammock while talking with Jesus. I experienced both the sweet side and the brokenness of Jamaica. Despite its rough edges, I fell more in love with this place each day.

Jamaica truly was a mix of beautiful, charming, and tough — an awakening of every sense. Jamaica looked like elegant palm trees and brilliant, pink flowers. Jamaica sounded like reggae music and the colorful crooning of *Patwa* jargon. Jamaica felt like refreshing water and a cool breeze. Jamaica tasted like fresh coconut milk and spicy jerk chicken. But Jamaica, oh sweet Jamaica, smelled like the putrid stench of weed. Everywhere we went, the aroma of burning marijuana satiated the atmosphere — at the hostel, on the beach, in restaurants. It was inescapable. Even though the island looked like paradise at first glance, there existed deep levels of brokenness. The beaches, the delicious food, and the perfect weather were not enough to bring people true joy. They still felt a need to escape the reality of life through drugs and other temporary fixes. I was convinced that no matter how flawless people or places appeared along the journey, everyone's heart cried out for a savior.

The brokenness among Jamaica's men began to manifest in daily harassment. I disappointingly found it impossible to walk to the beach or city center without lots of unwanted attention. Over and over, I received the same three questions:

"Do you want to marry me?"

"Do you want to buy my jewelry?"

"Do you want to smoke some ganja?"

I began by politely declining all of these offers but slowly became more and more forceful with my responses. One day, a young boy aggressively followed me and repeatedly asked me to buy his cardboard-flavored chocolate, mercilessly harassing me and yelling, "Would it really kill you to spend one dollar?"

I told him that I didn't want his chocolate several times and finally retorted, "Would it kill *you* to listen?" My unexpected response silenced him as he looked at me slightly stunned.

Pestering vendors, awkward marriage proposals, and the exchange of drugs were some of the negative aspects of the island. However, in spite of these things, I didn't want to be anywhere else. I had dreamt of coming to Jamaica since I was a little girl, and this country held a special place in my heart. The Lord knew it was my dream to visit one day, and being in Jamaica was the physical manifestation of God's promise. While planning for the Caribbean leg of the journey, the Lord had told me to simply dream with Him. And here we were, in the final country of the trip, and I was standing on the island I'd dreamt of for almost two decades.

After our respite in Negril, we headed back to Kingston to fulfill our final ministry commitment. Through a complex chain of events, we connected with both a Bethel Church team and Kingston's own Christian Life Fellowship. Every spring, Northern California's Bethel Church (Iris Global's partner) sent teams all over the world for short-term mission trips. Because Iris' Heidi Baker had visited Bethel Church to officially commission the Iris Latin America team at the start of our journey, rejoining with Bethel now meant a lot to us. It seemed significant that we'd begun our trip with a blessing from Bethel, and now, nineteen months later, we'd come full circle and were ending with Bethel.

Upon arriving in Kingston, we were greeted by a few women from Christian Life Fellowship (CLF), the church that would be hosting both our Iris team and the Bethel team. Esther, a Jamaican ray of sunshine, organized the necessary arrangements for us, including host families for each of us to stay with. Alan stayed with one family, Roberta and Natalie with another, and Aleeza and I with a lovely woman named Betty.

Betty dropped us off at her house, then scurried off to collect the Bethel team at the airport. In the morning, our Iris team, the Bethel team, and the Jamaican pastors, elders, and their wives all met in one big room. As we shared our hearts and how the Lord had weaved all of us together into this intricate web of people, it was blatantly obvious that this was no coincidence. The more I heard about what had been going on behind the scenes, the more I stood in awe of what God was doing.

Unbeknownst to me, the Lord had been speaking intensely to both the Bethel team and the leadership at Christian Life Fellowship about our time together in Kingston. Julie, one of the Bethel team leaders, shared that the Lord had put the Caribbean on her heart for quite some time. She'd had a dream about being in Jamaica with her friend Nick, who she later asked to serve as one of her co-leaders. While Bethel Church was in the process of arranging over seventy short-term teams (that would be simultaneously sent to forty-eight different nations), Julie gathered a Jamaican team of twenty-two eager colaborers.

Bethel Church set aside forty-eight hours of back-to-back prayer times for each of the nations to which teams were traveling. Each country had one hour-long block dedicated to it, and Jamaica was assigned the final prayer hour. Just as Jamaica marked the completion of the around-the-clock prayer time, Jamaica was our team's finale as well.

Meanwhile, the Jamaican pastors and their wives from Christian Life Fellowship were hungering for a radical move of the Holy Spirit. Several of the Jamaicans had a desire to connect with Bethel Church, others with Iris Global, still others with both. A woman from the church had had either a dream or vision about a bunch of white people being on the stage at CLF but didn't know what it meant. The pastors knew exactly what it meant. The woman had seen our reunion long before it happened. We looked around at each other's pale complexions and laughed as we acknowledged that her vision was about to be fulfilled.

As people at Bethel and CLF were praying and growing in expectancy, my teammates and I were busy hopping from island to island, completely unaware of any of this backstory. Our connection to the group started with a simple email I sent to a friend of my parents. They knew a man named Leo who currently lived in Kingston but had formerly attended their church in the States. Leo and his wife had visited a friend's house in Kingston for Christmas dinner where they connected with Pastor Bruce from Christian Life Fellowship. Though Bruce and his wife normally spent the holiday with a different relative, God had changed things during Christmas 2012. Because of this rearrangement, Leo and Bruce began talking, and Leo asked if Bruce had any interest in hosting a mission team at his church. Shortly after, Bruce emailed me and explained that a Bethel team was also interested in visiting his church and wanted to do a healing conference sometime in April 2013. He asked if I'd be interested in partnering with Bethel.

From there, I contacted Bethel's Julie, and we decided to serve together if the timing worked out. I had decided early on to visit both Montego Bay and Kingston but felt our team was meant to serve in Montego Bay first. When I asked Julie for her team's dates in Kingston, they coincided exactly with the dates our team wanted to be there. This sounded like God to me.

To make things even crazier, when we met the Bethel team in Kingston, Natalie immediately recognized two of the women. I caught a glimpse of them and could barely believe my eyes. When Bethel had launched their mission teams the previous spring, we'd connected with one of their teams in Peru. We had worked with these ladies exactly one year ago in Lima. It was hard to believe a whole year had passed since then. These women were on their second annual Bethel mission trip, and we were on our nineteenth month of travel.

"You're still traveling?" one of them exclaimed. "I can't believe it!"

"We can't believe it either," I laughed. "Jamaica is our last country though — number twenty-six. We were supposed to travel for less than a year, but things didn't turn out quite as planned."

That was an understatement. However, I was thankful for the change in plans. Though God had taken me on a journey far longer and more chaotic than what I'd expected when I left the States, it had been well worth it. I asked the Lord to give us an exciting end to our journey, and He certainly did. The expectation among Bethel and CLF was great, and my own excitement began to grow as we continued to share all God had been doing behind the scenes for many months without realizing it. CLF had never imagined that Bethel, Iris, and their church would all be working together one day. It seemed a powerful and passionate trio, and we knew God was going to do great things when we came together and simply believed.

We began our time in Kingston with a healing conference at Christian Life Fellowship. People from the church and community poured into the CLF sanctuary, where we gathered for three days to invite the Holy Spirit and see what He did. The Bethel team took the reins in leading teaching sessions, and every session was followed by a time of prayer that our Iris team participated in. Throughout the three days, we prayed for hundreds of people to be healed physically, emotionally, and spiritually. From the first night to the last day, God touched and freed many people. I'd longed to experience an outpouring of miracles in Jamaica, and the Holy Spirit broke loose in CLF. People were getting healed left and right. A leg grew out, a woman with Lupus was healed of all pain, eyes were healed, backs were restored, etc. I tried to record as many testimonies as possible, but they were endless — a good problem to have!

As people were healed of various ailments, they marched to the front of the church to share their healings. One man in the congregation had a friend who was stuck at home with a sick daughter but wanted to be at the conference. The man listened to other people share testimonies and started texting them to his house-ridden friend. While she read the stories of healing on her phone, the Holy Spirit invaded her home and touched her daughter; the fever left her body.

Natalie received a word of knowledge that someone in the congregation was allergic to water. She saw a picture of itchy, irritated skin from the allergy. As she shared the word aloud, I wondered if it was even possible to be allergic to water and where she'd gotten this idea from. Sure enough, the following day, a man from the congregation grabbed the microphone to share his odd healing testimony with the church.

"I was allergic to water," he declared. "Whenever I showered or got sweaty, my skin would feel itchy for twenty to thirty minutes afterwards."

I looked at my teammates in disbelief. This was really happening.

The man went on, "But I've been dancing around the church, getting sweaty, and I am not itchy! I've been healed!"

On the first night of the conference, I prayed for a young man who had problems with heart palpitations and shortness of breath. On my way home that night, I happened to bump into the young man in the parking lot. He approached me and exclaimed, "I'm so glad to see you! I need to tell you something! I've been running around and around, and I'm not short of breath!" He was grinning from ear to ear. This was good news.

Another young Jamaican man named Matthew, who helped serve as a chauffeur for our team, shared an amazing testimony with us. Matthew explained that just getting to the conference was a miracle in and of itself. Though born in Kingston, Matthew had been studying in Montego Bay (several hours away), as well as spending time in the Cayman Islands where his family lived. He was scheduled to start an internship back in Montego Bay after visiting the Cayman Islands, but he ended up taking a little detour to Kingston. He needed to help with wedding preparations in the city, and his internship was pushed back two weeks. He knew the Lord had brought him to Kingston for this specific time, and he had come to the conference with high expectations.

Matthew had been in a snowboarding accident five years prior while attending boarding school in the States. He had three herniated disks, which were extremely painful. After the accident, Matthew had to throw away his dream of becoming a professional soccer player and dealt with depression as he couldn't do the physical things he used to do. He had spent a long time rehabilitating his back and doing physiotherapy. Doctors warned him that if he didn't keep the muscles around his back strong, he would be at risk for paralysis later in life. However, Matthew no longer has to fear such a thing, because during the conference God completely healed and restored his back. All pain left; all disks were restored. Matthew, age twenty-one, was suddenly able to bend over and do things he couldn't do since age sixteen.

My favorite healing testimony, hands down, belongs to Betty, who hosted Aleeza and me. Betty had worn glasses for over a decade but wasn't even thinking about her eyes at the conference. In fact, when Betty stood up for prayer, she asked God to heal her back pain. As people prayed for her back, she received a surprise she hadn't asked for. Her eyesight was unexpectedly restored. She was so shocked she could see without glasses that she completely forgot about her back. Realizing that her vision was the same whether her glasses were on or off, Betty started telling everyone around her what had just happened. She shared the good news with me and Aleeza as we got into her car to drive home — the first time she'd driven without glasses in years. "We're your guinea pigs!" we joked. "Betty, you better really be healed if you're going to drive right now!"

Betty, Aleeza, and I laughed the whole ride home. Every time we stopped behind another car, Betty read the license plate numbers aloud and asked me to confirm the accuracy. With every correct answer, we erupted into more giggles. Betty was so dumbfounded that her joy and laughter were contagious. God just loved to surprise His children.

During the conference, we dedicated some time to bringing this joy out into the streets. We gathered in small groups and walked to Papine Square, a popular Rastafarian hangout spot down the street from CLF. One group had prayed before hitting the streets and received the name "Norman" from the Holy Spirit as well as the words "shack" and "upstairs room." One of the women in the group knew without a doubt that they were meant to find Norman and confidently began to yell, "Normaaaaan!" as she walked through the streets.

Suddenly the Holy Spirit whispered into her heart, *"Norman is in the hardware store."*

Without hesitation, she walked into the nearby hardware store, went to the counter, and asked, "Can you get Norman for me?"

The person at the counter replied, "Sure, he's out back." Moments later, Norman came out to greet the woman and her group. They shared what God had showed them previously, believing the shack represented a feeling of nothingness that Norman was currently experiencing and that the upstairs room was part of a two-story house that represented coming blessings. Touched, Norman explained that he was a Christian without a church home and allowed the group to pray for him. He was happy to meet brothers and sisters from Christian Life Fellowship and said he would like to join their congregation.

Though I'd known God was going to do great things in Kingston, the magnitude of testimonies springing forth from this city exceeded my expectations. I was awestruck by God's creative hand in the many miracles, healings, and divine appointments. However, the best miracle I experienced in Jamaica was a personal gift of God's redemption that moved my heart and sealed my trust in Him. While we were at the conference, I looked around at the twenty-two members of the Bethel team as well as the four people I'd been traveling with throughout the Caribbean. Being in such a large group reminded me of the way things used to be when we were traveling throughout Central and South America. It brought a sense of nostalgia and a bittersweet mix of sadness for the absence of my former teammates and gratefulness for the new friends God had brought into my life. I wasn't sure how it was possible to feel such intense joy and such deep sorrow at the same time.

On the second evening of the conference, one of the Jamaican worship leaders came running up to me yelling, "Caitlin! Caitlin! I need to speak to you after the service." I wondered what was so urgent. I'd prayed for so many people that I'd forgotten who was who and figured she might have had a testimony to share with me later on.

After the service, she pulled me aside. "My name is Toki," she announced. "I don't know why, but God put a burning desire in my heart to pray for you. I don't know what it is, but I just have to pray for you."

Before she said anything more, tears began to pour out of my eyes. I had been traveling for nineteen months, and it had been an emotional journey of extreme highs and extreme lows. As it all came to a finish, my mind raced with a million thoughts. I didn't know where I was going when the trip was over or where I'd end up. I was constantly being asked to preach with wisdom and power, yet I often felt lost and overwhelmed myself.

Although ashamed to admit it, I confessed to Toki that being at a healing conference was almost unbearable for me. "I have had excruciating back pain for five years," I explained. "I travel the world praying for people and seeing people healed. I want to celebrate with them, but it is so hard to watch others get healed while I am in so much pain myself." Confessing one of my deepest inner struggles, I went on, "I almost had to leave one of the conference sessions the other day, because I was in so much pain. But how could I walk out of a teaching about healing because of pain? It just doesn't make sense."

I knew no one could see the daily agony inside my body, because everything looked fine from an outside glance. They couldn't see how hard the past five years had been — especially the past nineteen months of sleeping on floors, bumping along jarring dirt roads, being squished onto backs of pickup trucks, and doing other activities that were rough on my back. God broke Toki's heart for me, and she saw what no one else did.

We talked for a long time, and she prayed for me and prophesied over me. Without a clue as to how prophetic she was, Toki began to hear downloads of information about my life and my family. I was amazed by every word, blown away by every detail that God had cared to notice and share with this woman. As Toki prayed for me, I felt healing and freedom. And when she prayed for my back, I actually started to feel better. For the first time in years, I could remember what it felt like to not be in constant pain. For the first time in years, I had hope for my own healing, not just the healing of other people.

God was already redeeming some of the pain I'd experienced throughout the trip by bringing me Toki. But His powerful restoration only got better. After the conference, the Bethel team split into two groups — one heading off to the countryside, the other stationed in Kingston. After many changes of plans, our Iris team was asked to stay in Kingston with the city team. One morning, the leader of the city team, Nick, invited us to visit Bethel's accommodation to pray for us. We were driven up to the beautiful mountain home where the Bethel team was staying. The view was breathtaking, overlooking the city and the ocean.

Nick said his teammates wanted to wash our feet and pray for us. As they prayed for God to bless us for the sacrifices we'd made, so much was going through my head. Tears began to flow from my eyes remembering the past nineteen months of my life — remembering the pain of being separated from friends and family during crucial moments, the devastation of being robbed of my most valuable possession, the discouragement of illness, the frustration of endless car breakdowns, the nights sleeping on the side of the road, the moments of paralyzing fear, and the reality of just being plain exhausted. People often asked to hear about the glory, the healing testimonies, and the stories of adventure. However, most didn't acknowledge the pain and sacrifice that came alongside those stories. As the Bethel team prayed for us, grief I'd buried in my heart came to the surface. Our trip had been amazing, but it hadn't been easy. And someone noticed. Someone cared. Someone took the time to stop and bless us.

As the five of us — Alan, Roberta, Aleeza, Natalie, and myself — sat there receiving the blessing of having our feet washed, I couldn't help but to think about the many people who *weren't* sitting there with us. I couldn't help but to remember the beautiful faces of my teammates, my *family*, who had gone home after the completion of South America and not returned for the Caribbean. I couldn't help but to mourn the loss of their presence and to wonder how different things would have been if they had traveled the islands with us. Everything inside of me so deeply wished they were sitting beside me getting *their* feet washed in Jamaica too.

I remembered that Natalie had told me many months ago (long before we separated in South America) that the Holy Spirit gave her the number "seventeen" and told her seventeen people would finish the trip in the Caribbean. While traveling with just five people, I figured that had simply been a mistake. However, in Kingston, I felt the Holy Spirit prompting me to count the number of people on the Bethel team standing beside us. I asked Nick how many people from his team remained in Kingston, and he said that after many rearrangements, they were a team of twelve. The twelve Bethel members plus our Iris five formed a final team of seventeen. We had become one unit, and just as Natalie had heard many months prior, we finished in Kingston with seventeen people.

As we began to talk about how honored we felt by our Bethel brothers and sisters, I was again reminded of God's sovereign hand — how God truly was in control, how God didn't make mistakes, and how God redeemed even when we did make mistakes. I will never know God's original plan for the Caribbean, but in my heart I believe that God did choose seventeen people from the initial Iris team to finish in the islands. Because of a wide variety of factors, this plan did not unfold quite the way we'd always imagined. However, despite unexpected changes and circumstances, God is sovereign. He said seventeen would finish, and He does not lie. Through a divine web of connections, God sent us twelve brothers and sisters from our partner ministry to complete the journey in Kingston with a number that had been chosen from the beginning. Though our hearts grieved the absence of our Iris family, God redeemed and restored our story in such an unexpected yet beautiful way. We knew that the location and timing of our trip's finish was no coincidence. This was God's sovereign plan.

God confirmed in many ways that this was the right time to end our journey. Way back in Mexico, I'd been given a word by one of my teammates that God would take me into full bloom during the trip. At that time, I felt scared, insecure, and much closer to withering than blooming. While the Bethel team prayed for us, one of the girls told me that she felt God was saying I had come into full bloom during the trip. This time, I felt like it was true. I was still far from perfect, still lost or frustrated half the time, but I knew I'd blossomed into an entirely new person. And I knew God was telling me it was time to start a new season where I would bloom somewhere else. Our Iris Latin America journey had finally come to an end.

I wanted God to give me an exciting ending to our story. Well, He gave me a final chapter far better than anything I could have created myself. Not only did we see healing miracles in Jamaica, we saw God's divine hand wrap up our entire journey into a holy moment of redemption. We saw God's blessing, His honor, His grace, and His complete control of everything.

During our final days, God reminded me of the real reason we'd started our journey in the first place. While visiting a hospital near the church, we encountered an elderly man who looked a bit confused and had trouble hearing us as we spoke. "We're here to pray for people," we explained. "Can we pray for you about anything?"

The old man looked at us with sad eyes and declared, "I have no one — no one. I'm seventy-five years old, and I have no one. I'm nothing."

We sat beside him, spoke to him, and eventually prayed for him. Tears began to squeeze out of his eyes.

"Thank you, thank you," he declared. "Thank you for blessing me."

Overcome with emotion, the tears continued as the melancholy man finally had someone visiting him. I wondered when the last time he'd had a friend was. My heart nearly broke in half.

Sitting with the man, putting our hands on his lonely shoulder, and praying for him was better than any physical miracle I could have ever asked for. In Mozambique, God taught me who I was — His daughter. My identity came from intimacy with the heart of the Father. From my identity came authority, and that authority of the Holy Spirit is what brought forth the amazing testimonies throughout the trip — cancer healed, the lame walking, deaf ears opened, and blind eyes healed. *But* we are not meant to seek after signs and wonders. Instead, signs and wonders should be the natural result of a heart that is pursuing love. There is nothing better than love, because there is nothing better than God, and God *is* love.

The words "one love" from Bob Marley's famous reggae song have become an unofficial slogan of Jamaica, and I can't think of any better way to sum up the story of Iris Latin America.

> "One love, one heart
> Let's get together and feel all right
> As it was in the beginning (One love)
> So shall it be in the end (One heart)
> Alright, 'Give thanks and praise to the Lord and I will feel all right.'"[2]

In Jamaica, the phrase "one love" refers to a universal love for all people. No matter what your color, gender, beliefs, or ethnicity, you shall remain under the covering of "one love" for every person. After visiting God's children in the largest cities of Latin America, in indigenous tribes in the jungle, on the streets of red light districts, inside prisons, in orphanages, on farms in remote villages, and everywhere in between, we saw the true "One Love" moving and breathing upon all of them. We saw God's love for all His children — from the fairest ones to the darkest ones. We saw God's love for the jungle chief, the prostitute, the prisoner, the orphan, the mayor, the rich man, and the poor man. We saw no bounds on God's love. He simply moved and loved everywhere we went. He loved everyone.

Jesus said the two greatest commandments were to simply love God and love people. (See Matthew 22:36-40.) Often, we overcomplicate the gospel, but the pure concept of love is really what it's all about. Despite the abundant physical healings we witnessed, the financial miracles we encountered, and the great stories of God's glory we experienced, none of it can really compare to the greatest miracle of all — the love of Christ. The most mind-blowing phenomenon we can ever experience is that God, who created the entire universe and who knows every tiny detail, chose to die for us so that we may live. The most amazing discovery is that our Heavenly Father chose you and me to be adopted into His beautiful and holy family. The most astounding gift is that I mess up all the time, but God still loves me. The most stunning revelation is that I am just a normal girl, but when God moves in me, we can change the world together. You don't need to travel to twenty-six countries to experience God's miracles. You don't even have to leave your home. All you need to do is love God and love the people around you. That's the true gospel. That's the true Jesus. And that's the best ending to our story — one love.

Epilogue

Twenty-six countries. Nineteen months. Countless flat tires, car breakdowns, personal freak-outs, sleepless nights, and moments of roaring laughter. And then, in a blink of an eye, our journey was really over.

When I joined the Iris Latin America team in September 2011, I had no idea what I was getting myself into. My planned eleven months on the road quickly turned into nineteen, and I'd be lying if I said the journey wasn't far more than I'd bargained for. I was stretched in ways I never dreamt possible; sometimes the process was so painful I thought I would burst.

I think it's safe to say that my teammates would agree. None would claim that this trip came without challenges. Honestly, there were many tough moments *not* recorded in this book — times when we prayed for people who *didn't* get healed, instances when we couldn't agree on decisions no matter how long we talked them over, moments when we all felt like giving up. We would be deceiving you if we said no one ever got cranky, tired, or frustrated. Sometimes we whined about stupid things or cried out of sheer exhaustion or snuck away to secret places in an attempt to hide from the world.

As I've shared testimonies of miracles and healings, far too many people have responded, "I could never do what your team did." But *we* weren't the ones doing it in the first place. I can't heal anyone on my own, nor can anyone I know. It is the Holy Spirit moving through us that heals. The purpose of sharing our story is not so that readers can put me and my teammates on a pedestal. If that's all I've accomplished throughout this book, then I have failed you. We are not heroes; we are not superhuman. We are ordinary people with extraordinary dreams. And we've simply said "yes" to the extraordinary God who fulfills them.

When God invites us into His story, I believe it's our responsibility to share it with others. I want the world to know what God is up to, because He's up to amazing stuff! I want the world to know that God still heals cancer, opens deaf ears, causes the lame to walk, grows out limbs, opens blind eyes, heals backs, and sets people free. I want people to know that anybody — *anybody* — can be a part of these testimonies. God delights in letting us be a part of His story. And yes, certain chapters will come at a very real cost. However, the things sacrificed will never compare to the things gained. Nothing this world has to offer can compete with the pure, unconditional love of Jesus Christ. My God is amazing.

Once upon a time, a little girl who belonged to a mighty king found out that his promises were real. After dreaming impossible dreams with the king, the girl watched them become possible before her eyes.

As the little girl walked towards her happily ever after, the presence of the king lived inside of her, whispering into her heart, **"Believe and be love."**

So she believed, and she loved. Remarkable people believed and loved with her. And as the king's words came true, they all had a beautiful story to tell.

Endnotes

[1] McMillan, John Mark. "How He Loves." *The Song Inside the Sounds of Breaking Down.* Integrity Media, 2005. CD.

[2] Bob Marley and The Wailers. "One Love/People Get Ready." By Bob Marley and Curtis Mayfield. *Exodus.* Island/Tuff Gong, 1977. Vinyl.

If you enjoyed *Believe and Be Love* and would like to see photographs from the journey, you would love **What Glory Awakens** by **T.K. Lindsey**.

Caitlin Ann's teammate, T.K. Lindsey, is an incredibly talented photographer who captured the beauty of Latin America through film. Artistically mixing photographs, personal blogs, prophetic poems, statistics, and quotes from the journey, Lindsey has produced a creative masterpiece. Please support his work and ministry by purchasing a copy of *What Glory Awakens* (available for purchase in 2014).

AND

If you'd like to read more about Caitlin Ann's adventures or donate to her ministry, please visit her blog:

http://furiouslove.blogspot.com

Thanks for reading!